WITHDRAWN
UTSA LIBRARIES

RENEWALS 458-4574
DATE DUE

ETHICS AND EMPOWERMENT

Ethics and Empowerment

Edited by
John J. Quinn
and
Peter W. F. Davies

Ichor Business Books
An Imprint of
Purdue University Press
West Lafayette, Indiana

First Ichor Business Book edition, 1999.

Selection and editorial matter copyright © 1999 by the estate of John J. Quinn and Peter W. F. Davies
Introduction copyright © 1999 by Peter W. F. Davies
Other chapters (in order) copyright © 1999 by the estate of John J. Quinn; Frederick B. Bird; John Kaler; Julia M. Christensen Hughes; Keith Pheby; Peter W. F. Davies and Anne Mills; Julia M. Christensen Hughes; Ian McLoughlin, Richard Badham and Paul Couchman; Edna Ojeifo and Diana Winstanley; Barbara Goodwin; Christopher Moon and Celia Stanworth; Johnston Birchall; Richard C. Warren; Paul Joyce and Adrian Woods; Peter Jones

All rights reserved.

Published under license from Macmillan Press Ltd, Houndmills, Basingstoke, Hampshire, RG21 6XS

This edition available only in the United States and Canada.

03 02 01 00 99   5 4 3 2 1

Library of Congress Cataloging-in-Publication Data applied for.
Ethics and empowerment / edited by John J. Quinn and Peter W.F. Davies. — 1st Ichor Business Book ed.
    p. cm.
   A collection of 15 papers, half of which are revised versions of ones presented at a conference organized by COPE (the Centre for Organisational and Professional Ethics at Brunel University) and held in September 1996 in London.
   Includes bibliographical references and index.
   ISBN 1-55753-173-0 (cloth : alk. paper)
   1. Employee empowerment Congresses.   2. Social responsibility of business Congresses.   3. Professional ethics Congresses.   I. Quinn, John J., 1948–1997.   II. Davies, Peter W. F., 1956–   .
HD50.5.E85   1999
658.4'08—DC21   99-28642
                                                    CIP

Printed in Great Britain

Library
University of Texas
at San Antonio

Dedicated to the memory of
John Quinn
who died shortly before this book was completed

Contents

Acknowledgements	ix
Notes on the Contributors	xi
Introduction Peter W.F. Davies and John J. Quinn	1
1 Is Empowerment Ethical? Why Ask the Question? John J. Quinn	23

Part I   Ethics and Empowerment: Power, Control and Autonomy

2 Empowerment and Justice Frederick B. Bird	41
3 Does Empowerment Empower? John Kaler	90
4 Organisational Empowerment: A Historical Perspective and Conceptual Framework Julia M. Christensen Hughes	115
5 Ethico-power and the City Keith Pheby	147
6 Ethics, Empowerment and Ownership Peter W.F. Davies and Anne Mills	170

Part II   Theory, and the Experience of Empowerment Strategies

7 Beyond Rhetoric: A Typology of Empowerment Strategies Found Within One Organisation Julia M. Christensen Hughes	197
8 Empowerment and Teams: Ethics and the Implementation of Socio-technical Systems Ian McLoughlin, Richard Badham and Paul Couchman	235

9	Negotiated Reality: The Meaning of Empowerment *Edna Ojeifo and Diana Winstanley*	271
10	Empowerment in a Government Agency *Barbara Goodwin*	300
11	Ethics and Empowerment: Managerial Discourse and the Case of Teleworking *Christopher Moon and Celia Stanworth*	326

Part III   Business and Society: The New Empowerment Responsibility

12	Empowering Consumers through Co-operatives *Johnston Birchall*	347
13	Empowerment in a Community of Purpose *Richard C. Warren*	369
14	The Social Responsibility of Businesses: To Empower Employees by Listening and Responding *Paul Joyce and Adrian Woods*	393
15	Ethical Guidelines for an Empowered Organisation *Peter Jones*	412

Name Index	427
Subject Index	433

Acknowledgements

I would first like to acknowledge the contribution made by John Quinn. He was the driving force behind COPE (the Centre for Organisational and Professional Ethics), and originally organised the *Ethics and Empowerment* conference in September, 1996. He had completed much of the editorial work on this book before his sudden and tragic death in the summer of 1997.

Due to other commitments, I could not really get to grips with picking up the pieces of this work until January 1998, and have been greatly helped in many ways by Keith Dickson at the Division of Management Studies, Brunel University. I would also like to acknowledge the patience of all the contributors who have had in some circumstances to update their work, give me repeat information, answer pernickity details about references, and have also had to wait a year longer than expected to see publication of their work.

Finally, I would like to thank Stephen Rutt, Publishing Director at Macmillan's Business Press, for his sticking with this project.

Peter W.F. Davies

The publishers are grateful for permission to reproduce Table 4.1, reprinted with permission of Academy of Management, PO Box 3020, Briar Cliff Manor, NY 10510–8020. (*The Empowerment Process: Integrating Theory and Practice* (Table), J. Conger and R. Kanungo, *Academy of Management Review* 1988, Vol. 13, No. 3. Reproduced by permission of the publisher via Copyright Clearance Center Inc.)

Notes on the Contributors

Richard Badham is Professor in the BHP Institute for Steel Processing and Products, and head of the research programme on Managing Innovation and Change Across Cultures (MICAC) at Wollongong University, Australia. His most recent book, co-authored with David Buchanan, is *Winning the Turf War: The Micro-Politics of Organisational Change* (1998).

Johnston Birchall lectures in Public Policy at Brunel University. His main interest is in 'Third Sector' businesses such as co-operatives and mutuals, and in user-control of public services. His books include *Building Communities: The Co-operative Way* (1988), *The People's Business* (1994), *The International Co-operative Movement* (1997), and *Decentralising Public Service Management* (with Christopher Pollitt, 1998). He edits the *Journal of Co-operative Studies*.

Frederick Bird is a Professor of Comparative Ethics at Concordia University in Montreal, Canada, where he teaches in the Departments of both Religion and Management. He is author of *The Muted Conscience: Moral Silence and the Practice of Ethics in Business*, and (with J. Gandz) *Good Management: Business Ethics In Action*; as well as 'Moral Universals as Cultural Realities' in *Ethical Universals in International Business* (edited by N. Brady).

Paul Couchman is Senior Research Fellow at the Centre for the Management of Integrated Technological and Organisational Change in the Department of Management at Wollongong University, Australia.

Julia M. Christensen Hughes is an Associate Professor in the School of Hotel and Food Administration at the University of Guelph, Ontario, Canada. Her research interests include workforce diversity, empowerment and organisational change. Julia is currently serving a three-year term as Director of Teaching Support Services at the university where she is exploring principles of empowerment as they relate to a variety of educational issues, including student learning processes and faculty development.

Peter W.F. Davies was until recently Senior Lecturer in Strategic Management and Business Ethics at the Business School of Buckinghamshire

Chilterns University College. He was a founder member of COPE (the Centre for Organisational and Professional Ethics) with colleagues at Brunel University. Formerly a mining and production engineer, and with a PhD in the philosophy of technology he is now a freelance academic-writer, and Visiting Professor at Buckinghamshire Chilterns University College. He is a Fellow of the Royal Society, and edited *Current Issues in Business Ethics* (1997).

Barbara Goodwin has been Professor of Politics at the University of East Anglia, Norwich, since 1996 and was formerly Professor of Political Philosophy at Brunel University and a founder member of COPE. Her publications include *Using Political Ideas* (4th edn, 1997), *Justice by Lottery* (1993), and two books on utopianism and political theory. Her current research focuses on ethics in large organisations.

Peter Jones is a consultant working with individual managers and teams, in the areas of change management and organisational development. A particular interest is in helping organisations move from traditional models to high-performance teams. Clients range across most business sectors, including pharmaceuticals, financial services and professional services in both the public and private spheres. He previously worked in high-technology US and UK companies as an HR and IT director.

Paul Joyce is Professor and Director of the Management Research Centre at the University of North London, having previously worked in the insurance and engineering industries. This research centre specialises in the management of innovation, and in recent years Professor Joyce has carried out research on strategic planning, business networks, and the role of entrepreneurship in business innovation. He co-authored (with Adrian Woods) *Essential Strategic Management: From Modernism to Pragmatism* (1996) and has recently completed a new book on strategic management.

John Kaler is a Senior Lecturer in the University of Plymouth Business School, teaching business ethics, cultural issues in business and jurisprudence. He is a graduate of the Universities of Sussex and London, and co-author of *An Introduction to Business Ethics* (1993) and *Essentials of Business Ethics* (1996).

Ian McLoughlin is Professor of Management at the University of Newcastle upon Tyne. He is co-author of *The Process of Technological*

Change (1988), *Technological Change at Work* (1994) and *Enterprise without Unions* (1994). He is also co-editor of *Innovation, Organisations and Technology* (1997), and author of *Creative Technological Change: Shaping Technology and Organisation* (1998).

Anne Mills is Senior Lecturer in Human Resource Management and Organisational Change at the Business School of Buckinghamshire Chilterns University College. Her main research interests include organisational transformation in Central and Eastern Europe, HRM, and Business Ethics. She is developing research in the area of business ethics in Central and Eastern Europe.

Chris Moon is Senior Lecturer at the Anglia Business School, Danbury, Essex. He is also Programme Director of the Postgraduate Diploma in Human Resource Management, and for the MA in Organisational Ethics. He has taught business ethics on various MBA programmes, published widely in the ethics area, and is currently the UK secretary of the European Business Ethics Network.

Edna Ojeifo studied at Imperial College Management School, and now works as a consultant with Visual Thinking, specialising in brand development and brand management.

Keith Pheby has taught and researched in organisational ethics in America, Great Britain and Japan. He is particularly interested in the relationship between ethics and power, and the possibility of designing corporate and urban structures capable of sustaining ethical cultures. He is Head of Innovation and Research for Cohrum Ltd, which designs computer-gaming simulations to aid organisations in this process. His recent publications include 'The Psychological Contract: Enacting Ethic-Power' in Davies, P.W.F. (ed.), *Current Issues in Business Ethics* (1997).

John J. Quinn was Lecturer in Decision Theory, Strategic Management and Business Ethics in the Department of Management Studies at Brunel University. He was a founder member of COPE, and organised the Ethics and Empowerment conference which was the catalyst for this book. His research interests centred on business ethics in small businesses, and issues of strategic control. He authored (with M.J. Goold) *Strategic Control: Milestones for Long-Term Performance* (1993).

Celia Stanworth is Senior Lecturer in Human Resources and Industrial Relations at the Business School, University of Greenwich. She also researches at Westminster University Business School. Her research interests are the future of work and non-standard working patterns, and she has published widely in the area of teleworking.

Richard C. Warren is Principal Lecturer in the Department of Business Studies at the Manchester Metropolitan University. He holds degrees from the polytechnics of Wolverhampton and Plymouth, and the University of Manchester. He was a merchant seaman for five years before working in the Commercial Department of the shipowners A.P. Moller. His research interests are business ethics and industrial relations, and he has published articles in a variety of journals, most recently in *Business Ethics: A European Review*.

Diana Winstanley is a Lecturer in Human Resource Management at Imperial College Management School, and has written three books and over 30 articles on management, including her most recent one (with Jean Woodall), *Management Development: Strategy and Practice* (1998).

Adrian Woods is Dean of the Faculty of Social Sciences at Brunel University. Previous to this he was Head of the Department of Management Studies also at Brunel University. His research interests are mainly centred around small firms, including work on strategy, training and growth. He was co-author with Paul Joyce of *Essential Strategic Management: From Modernism to Pragmatism* (1996).

Introduction
Peter W.F. Davies and John J. Quinn

RATIONALE

The rationale for a book on Ethics and Empowerment goes way beyond merely taking two popular 1990s management buzzwords and sticking them together to create an interesting topic. And it also goes way beyond providing a written forum for ideas first presented at an Ethics and Empowerment conference organised by COPE (the Centre for Organisational and Professional Ethics at Brunel University and Buckinghamshire Chilterns University College) held in September, 1996.

The chief rationale is that there is a longer-term questioning of the role of business in society, centering around some key questions. For example: to what extent should businesses provide 'meaning' in jobs and careers? How do you encourage creativity (an oft-named ultimate source of competitive advantage) without an organisation falling apart? (that is, how do you reconcile control mechanisms with innovatively creative expression?). Is a minimal degree of empowerment a basic human right and a matter of justice, of ethics? What levels, degrees and types of empowerment should organisational members have? Why do so many 'empowerment programmes' appear to fail? How do you define genuine empowerment? Can empowerment really work in a capitalist shareholder-driven society? Will stakeholderism provide the best macro-structure for genuinely ethical empowerment to work?

These and other such questions are addressed in this book. A longer-term re-evaluation of the public's overall ethical expectations of the role of business in wider global society has coincided with the individual's changing expectations for a more meaningful, more empowered, and less controlled, working life. Given this, *Ethics and Empowerment* provides an ideal focus for the current interest in Business, Ethics and Society. But 'current' by no means implies a short-term relevance for this volume. The 'current' issues surrounding ethics and empowerment, as explored in this book, reveal ideas and concerns that have run throughout the whole of the twentieth century in management circles, but which are now being articulated in a slightly different language. It will therefore be a key text to have on your shelves for many years to come.

STRUCTURE AND LAYOUT

About half the contributions in this volume were originally presented as papers at the COPE conference on Ethics and Empowerment held in London in September 1996. These were substantially revised in the light of comments and discussion at the conference before being submitted. Then, along with the other contributions submitted directly, they were all put through the normal process of an edited text.

There are 15 chapters in all. After John Quinn's opening chapter, the book is split into three sections. Part I, Chapters 2–6, are those which examine ethics and empowerment through focusing on issues of power, control and autonomy. They develop ideas about the 'power' in em*power*ment, propose differing perspectives as to how to look at power and control, and question under what context the exercise of power in em*power*ment can be ethical, and respect individual autonomy. In Part II, Chapters 7–11 combine theories of empowerment with the actual experiences of empowerment programmes and strategies in organisations. They generally have a large case-study content as a means of both testing and developing theories and ideas as to what ethical empowerment might be, in particular focusing on the organisational context. In Part III, Chapters 12–15 look at ethics and empowerment from the wider debate about business, society and social responsibility. Co-operative and communitarian ideas are developed, along with the more commonly known idea of stakeholderism. As businesses become more 'socially responsible', a natural outcome will be a more ethical, and empowered, working world.

Each of the 15 chapters are summarised following, and mainly stand alone in terms of being readable in any order, though there is *some* cross-referencing between the chapters, as well as in the next section itself.

SUMMARY OF CHAPTERS

Chapter 1 John Quinn in the opening chapter 'Is Empowerment Ethical? Why Ask the Question? sets out to cut through the hype, confusion and rhetoric found in both those supporting and critiquing empowerment, and to offer an alternative model for ethical empowerment. He identifies two underlying aspects which suggest why it is necessary to ask the question 'is empowerment ethical'? in the first place. First, the word 'empowerment' is conceptually interpreted in two different basic ways, either as *'taking* power' (for example in the feminist literature and movement), or as *'granting* power' (which dominates the management literature and practice). Second, definitional imprecision of the term empowerment has grown in proportion to its popularity, thereby confusing the ethical implications (see Bird, Chapter 2, and Christensen Hughes, Chapter 4, who attempt to rectify this).

Quinn then notes two ways to argue that empowerment is an ethical endeavour. The first draws on Mary Parker Follett who roots (the notion of, not the word) empowerment in business's duty to serve society – a rule-utilitarian approach requiring maximisation of workers' talents. The second is rooted in building high-trust organisations, desirable in itself as enhancing mutually beneficial reciprocal relationships in the workplace, but motives and outcomes may not be in line with each other; exploitative management motives may lead to unintended 'good' empowerment, and vice-versa.

Empowerment has been critiqued from a number of angles, and Quinn makes an interesting exploration of the validity of two of them – lean production, and total quality management (TQM). Lean production by nature is a 'tightly-coupled system' where the actions of one worker can soon halt production; loyalty, learning, commitment and trust therefore *have* to be engendered on the shopfloor, often 'disempowering' middle managers (who resist it, and/or get 'delayered'). The counter-argument is that genuine empowerment requires *'loosely-*coupled systems'; tight systems (like the army) means you act *as if* an order had been given, and then only within narrow parameters. Moreover, the risks and stress of coping with production fluctuations are now transferred onto the employee. From a TQM angle, some argue that quality standardisation necessarily means greater control, however it is dressed up; loosening controls in one area only leads to tightening them in another. A little power is reallocated, the hierarchy remains intact, and capital has now enlisted the worker's intellectual capacity as well. However, employee development is required for TQM to work, and this supports it as an ethical endeavour.

Quinn argues that there are many reasons to suggest that neither the practice nor the principles of empowerment are based on ethical reasoning. So should it be rejected? Not so; the real question concerns a matter of degree. Given a capitalist framework, the key question is: to what extent can empowerment contribute to a more, rather than a less, ethical way of managing? Quinn makes the important point that certain preconditions for greater ethicality in empowerment are necessary. He suggests three: a developing organisational culture of empowerment, a change in systems and practices commensurate with higher trust, and training and personal development of employees. Evidence would seem to suggest on this last point that middle and senior management should also be included (Argyris, 1991).

Quinn suggests that it is as much a question of ideologies as of evidence. There has to be another way between the ideological viewpoints of John Dewey (organisational life as an edifying forum of teamwork and sharing), and Michael Foucault (organisational life as controlled violence). That 'other' way Quinn identifies as being rooted in both distributive and procedural justice – an idea explored further in the next chapter by Bird, and later on by Davies and Mills (Chapter 6).

Part I Ethics and empowerment: power, control and autonomy

Chapter 2 Frederick Bird, in his chapter 'Justice and Empowerment', sets out to provide a conceptual framework for understanding the application of power in organisations. He argues that such a framework is needed if we are to understand and assess how a particular organisational change empowers (or disempowers) workers. His framework contains three dimensions: form (that is, what does one have power over), degree (the extent of power, from scant to total) and agency (the unit that has power: individual, team, trade union, and so on). He then illustrates the application of this framework through the use of four case studies.

Bird stresses that the forms of power are not necessarily interdependent. An organisational change that empowers workers in one form need not empower workers in other forms and may, indeed, disempower workers in some other form. Thus, for example, in a case study of a workers' co-operative Bird noted that although the workers had enhanced governance powers in that they were involved in overall organisational policy making there was no difference in the way the work of the co-operative was managed compared with similar firms that were not co-operatives. So governance empowerment does not imply task empowerment, and experienced it as positive leading to greater job satisfaction. More commonly, workers experienced task empowerment within a team-based structure. They also, as a by-product rather than planned output, experienced personal empowerment through training and personal development. In no case was there any significant adjudicatory or contractual empowerment. These are the areas that have traditionally concerned trade unions in the Anglo-American culture and we have noted above how empowerment programmes have proceeded contemporaneously with measures to limit the power of trade unions.

Having developed this conceptual framework and presented empirical evidence to demonstrate the multi-dimensional nature of empowerment, Bird proceeds to the normative question: what powers should workers have within their organisations? He answers this question from the perspective of workers' (and employers') rights and responsibilities. He starts by rejecting the notion of labour as simply a commodity to be bought and sold according to market conditions. Instead, he argues that workers along with other stakeholders constitute the organisation and as such have rights within, but also responsibilities towards, the organisation. He moves on to discuss these rights and responsibilities within the conceptual framework employed elsewhere in his chapter, emphasising that there are no absolute standards and that the notion of fair, or just, empowerment has to be understood within the context of a situation.

It might be argued that many critiques of empowerment have fallen short or been misdirected because they have adopted too narrow a notion of power. In particular, perhaps, in focusing on task empowerment they may have been oblivious to other forms of empowerment. Bird's framework allows us to take a broader view of empowerment and to recognise the potential for trade-offs between different forms of empowerment.

Chapter 3 John Kaler in 'Does Empowerment Empower?' explores the apparent paradox that worker empowerment need not necessarily increase the power of workers. Building on the Hobbesian distinction between original powers and instrumental powers, Kaler distinguishes between personal power and positional power. Personal power we are born with or acquire and exercise as individuals, if sometimes in a social context. Positional power we acquire and exercise through acting within a certain social role. Furthermore, he argues, organisational power is archetypically positional power. Kaler then goes on to develop this notion of (organisational) positional power through consideration of the powers of command, accountability and responsibility.

The powers of command and accountability are, for Kaler, two sides of the same coin. If A has the power of command over B, then B is accountable to A for carrying out those commands. Thus power and accountability are seen as mirror positional powers within organisations. Responsibility, conversely, is the lot of the commanded, it is what the commanded is to be answerable for and possibly blamed for: a kind of self-accountability. According to Kaler these responsibilities of subordination are equally, if not more keenly, felt and stressful as the responsibilities of command, and typically these responsibilities of subordination are increased by empowerment programmes. He justifies this claim by reference to two key drivers in the move towards empowerment: the quality movement and the delayering of organisations. In the former, the responsibility for quality is moved as far from the centre as possible to employees at the coal face; in the latter, as layers of junior and middle managers are removed workers are forced to take on their managerial responsibilities, if often exercised through self-managing teams. (Kaler does not explicitly discuss the possibility of technological substitution of these management layers though he does mention the electronic surveillance of 'empowered' workers in the Alliance and Leicester Building Society.) But how does this change in responsibility affect the distribution of power within organisations? Although, the empowered employee is now more in command, in the sense that there are more areas of her activity over which she has discretion and does not have to respond to commands, the extent of her accountability has either not changed or increased. There is no lessening of the power of those over her to call her to account. This then is Kaler's explanation for the empowerment paradox: empowerment may result in or from changes in some elements of the positional power within organisations but will also result in the increased responsibility and hence accountability of employees.

Chapter 4 Julia Christensen Hughes in her first of two contributions, entitled 'Organizational Empowerment: A Historical Perspective and Conceptual Framework', approaches empowerment with two key issues in mind. The first is that work has historically had (and still does have) a large degree of meaningless for many people which expresses itself in a fundamental tension between free-will and the need for organizational control. How is empowerment to be put into in practice in such a context? Second, she notes (like Bird, Chapter 2) that there is a lack of clarity concerning what empowerment means to differing people, both academically and to those who are trying to make 'it' work. She tackles these points by giving a historical overview in the first half of the chapter, charting the struggle for empowerment in the workplace. In the second half she reviews definitional aspects of empowerment, focusing on the basic notion of power, powerlessness and control. She then goes on to propose five distinct types of empowerment which people may adopt (thereby thwarting empowerment initiatives), and examines them from the aspects of objectives, processes and implementation barriers.

From the factory system (late 1700s to early 1800s) to the era of scientific management (mid-1800s to early 1900s), Christensen Hughes sets empowerment in the context of critiques of capitalism, alienation, control, deskilling, and rise of trades unionism; the measures of control become less overt as time progresses. With the systems age (up to the mid-1900s), it is noted that the challenge of the human relations movement never really shifted entrenched power-relations in the workplace. Likewise, although calls for fundamental change in the 1970s and 1980s resulted in ideas like QWL and industrial democracy, such initiatives seemed yet again to fail to make any fundamental changes. What then of the 1990s? Christensen Hughes suggests that empowerment has lost credibility due to its being aligned with downsizing, and so on. With greater contracting-out, it is full-circle back to the 1700s with similar 'capitalist' worries about monitoring and control re-emerging, only this time technology is providing more insidious forms of control. The still unresolved tensions between capital and labour provide the rationale to next examine multiple meanings of empowerment.

In reviewing the definitional literature, Christensen Hughes concludes that there does exist the possibility of subordinates pursuing meaningful goals within organisational contexts, but possibly not during times of radical organisational change, thereby frustrating motivational empowerment strategies. She then draws on this literature to propose five paradigmic perspectives on empowerment: Rationalist–Functionalist (as power-sharing strategy), Pluralist (as a mechanism for enhancing self-efficacy), Interpretive (as social construction), Radical (as a mechanism for radical social change), and Post-modern (as an illusive ideal involving the liberation of society and the self). With capitalistic goals and values, and materialist philosophy still intact, it seems that the radical and post-modern perspectives provide a genuine route forward for empowerment. This entails re-evaluating the purpose of our selves (and hence our business institutions) – something reflected in the contributions by Warren (Chapter 13), and Davies and Mills (Chapter 6).

Chapter 5 Keith Pheby in his chapter 'Ethico-Power and the City' considers empowerment from how 'integrated diversity' can be achieved. This requires an examination of the notions of boundary, identity, enclosure, place and division. Japanese city and civic life (influenced by spending 18 months recently at Kyoto Business School in Japan) is used as a vehicle for inquiring how empowerment can be enhanced in more general organisational life, asking what type of 'spaces' can yield community which can ethically sustain us. In relation to this he introduces his own notion of *Ethico-power*, underpinned by an autopoietic view of organisational dynamics.

Pheby wonders about the nature of an ethics that enables a vending machine full of alcoholic drinks in a suburb of Kyoto to remain unvandalised. What is the self-understanding of the ethical self, and how is it anchored in a huge organisational metropolis – cities which are more usually pictured as places of social fragmentation and alienated youth? This leads him to a discussion of the political striation of space where Cartesian influence in the West has led to the subordination of the material body to the 'knowing' mind, in which the former is then 'subjected to a host of regulatory disciplines' – issues of power and control which Pheby enlightens the reader through the work of Foucault. Foucaultian 'disciplines' lead to docility and subtle enclosure by institutions (education, corporate life, and so on), in which the self becomes the principle of his/her own subjugation. Pheby though does not accept this negative view of power as the whole story, hence the neologism *Ethico-power* for which he retrieves (rescues) 'responsibility' from its eighteenth and nineteenth century utilitarian and deontological roots as the 'imposition of moral command', and replaces it as 'a mode of "responding" which flows directly out of the respect for difference'. Drawing on the Greek idea of virtue, the self-disciplined subject does not need universal laws.

Returning again to civic life in the metropolis, Pheby notes Angotti's idea that *neighbourhood power* can offset the inequalities brought about by centralised governance. Translating this to organisational life, and drawing on the concept of autopoiesis (organisations as self-referencing systems of communication with a high degree of autonomy and circularity), we have the basis whereby diversity is respected and integrated; where empowerment can genuinely take place. To enact one's own environment however (to be empowered) the (employing) organisation has to have attained a certain degree of self referentiality; but even though autonomy is contextualised within a dynamic process, ethical empowered selves can still be formed. The classical view would have us believe that we (humans) are wholly contextualised in that we are atomised individuals inhabiting a world of meaning not of our own making; Pheby insists that individuals *are* discrete systems, but yet can exist even though inevitably linked to other systems.

So, how is social cohesion to be maintained given such respect for diversity? Pheby admits that trust, transparency, respect for difference and power-sharing are key mechanisms, and also admits that such systems 'are immensely fragile and difficult to sustain'. Creating our own virtual villages and social units though is unlikely to be overly encouraged by those in power, and made still more difficult by centralised capitalistic structures, but the possibility is still there (see Birchall, Chapter 12, and Davies and Mills, Chapter 6).

Chapter 6 The chapter by Peter Davies and Anne Mills, 'Ethics, Empowerment and Ownership', begins by distinguishing pseudo-empowerment from genuine empowerment. The former, they argue, is based on a view of labour as a means to a business end whilst the latter can only result from treating employees as ends in themselves. Furthermore, they argue that worker co-ownership is necessary condition for genuine empowerment which cannot be achieved within a capitalist firm.

The authors identify two perspectives that lead to pseudo-empowerment. The first, which they term the pragmatic approach, considers empowerment to be just one more management tool for enhancing competitive advantage. It is introduced in response to market and organisational requirements and employees could be disempowered as readily as they are empowered if conditions were seen to demand it. The second perspective is rooted in labour process theory. This regards empowerment, in line with other management strategies, as a means of enhancing the control of capitalists, represented by their agents (managers), over the workers. This perspective stresses the increased responsibility placed on workers by empowerment rather than the increased discretion they may enjoy. The authors hesitate in commiting themselves to this labour process theory, suggesting instead that the pragmatic approach contains the potential for increased control and may result in increased control as an unintended outcome.

When considering genuine empowerment the authors develop the argument that empowerment should be something that is permanent and just and is the property of the employee as of right rather than something that is in the gift of management. From there they develop the argument that empowerment should not be judged in a consequentialist fashion in terms of its contribution to the success of the business, but rather non-consequentially in terms of justice and the rights of workers as members of organisations. But this requires a fundamental change in the status of employees from hired hands to partners which, in turn, requires a change in the cultural and legal status of firms from capitalist-owned to employee-owned.

The authors proceed to exemplify the operation of empowerment through shared ownership by a case study of the Scott Bader group, in which the shares are held in trust for the employees. The case study shows how employees are indeed genuinely involved in the policy-making of the company in a way that is quite different from most other businesses. In that respect, the employees can be said to be governance empowered and adjudicatory empowered (Bird, this volume). What is not discussed by the authors is the extent to which employees of Scott Bader are task empowered. Although the employees share a sense of pride of ownership, it is unclear whether the rights associated with this shared ownership manifest themselves in the form of empowerment over job design, work pacing, and so forth.

Part II   Theory and the experience of empowerment strategies

Chapter 7   This second contribution by Julia Christensen Hughes entitled 'Beyond Rhetoric: A Typology of Empowerment Strategies Found within One Organization' reports on a largely ethnographic study within an organization (the Canadian subsidiary of a US-based quick-serve restaurant chain) whose official line identified empowerment as a policy and practice to which it was strongly committed. Christensen Hughes finds, however, that first, within the company there is not one understanding of empowerment but several existing contemporaneously; second, whichever understanding of the term is taken managerial practice did not conform with the empowerment rhetoric for much of the time and third, there can exist a deep contradiction in attempting to implement empowerment in an organisation that is characterised by a short-term profit mentality and a strong commitment to tight, numbers-based controls.

Christensen Hughes suggests a classification of empowerment strategies based on the management focus implicitly (and sometimes explicitly) embodied within the empowerment activities. Four typological categories are suggested: customer service; cost/productivity; quality/process and employee. In the organization studied, customer service was the initial justification for, and focus of, an empowerment programme supported by corporate communication and training. Staff were given enhanced discretion in their dealings with customers resulting in increased customer and employee satisfaction. However, it did not result in increased returns, making it difficult for managers to make the short-term financial targets they were set. It also resulted in management resistance based on a loss of control over operational routines and consistency of service standards.

The next focus of empowerment was cost/productivity. Although this was framed in terms of job enlargement and enrichment it was widely perceived by employees as a way of giving them more responsibility – taking on the administrative roles of managers – without more rewards and without adequate training. The cost/productivity focus of the new approach to empowerment was reinforced by a series of new controls that actually reduced the employees' discretion and the customer service they could provide. For example, the authority to respond to customer complaints was taken away from the people serving the customer and located higher up the branch managerial hierarchy. The change in empowerment focus led to widespread cynicism not only among employees but also among all levels of management, whose comments in the absence of employees became increasingly dismissive whilst having to persist in publicly expressing the view that empowerment worked.

In parallel with these discredited experiences of empowerment, she found that there continued to exist within the organization, especially among central support staff, a belief in the normative value of empowerment. This also took two forms. The first is that empowerment should focus on quality/process, that is, employees should be empowered to improve quality management processes in all the organization's activities. Second, empowerment should truly focus on employees (unlike the deceit of the cost/productivity focus) to develop employee commitment to the organization's aims and culture. Neither of these approaches – which are arguably the focuses that are dominant in some other empowered organizations – managed to overcome the control focus in this organization. This does, perhaps, raise the question as to whether the fundamental fault of the management of this organization was not the way they implemented empowerment – though the chapter highlights a number of unethical aspects of this implementation – but the decision in the first place to introduce empowerment into an organization whose culture and practices were the antithesis of empowerment.

Chapter 8 Ian McLoughlin, Richard Badham and Paul Couchman, in their chapter 'Empowerment and Teams: Ethics and the Implementation of Socio-technical Systems', consider the ethical issues involved in the process of introducing organisational change and, in particular, in the role of change agent within such a process. Their discussion is based around case studies of the introduction of team-based cellular manufacturing into three plants in Australia.

The authors' starting point is Mumford's (1996) view of socio-technical systems design as an ethical alternative to downsizing, business process re-engineering, and so forth in meeting the competitive needs of business whilst improving employee conditions. Mumford argues that there are five implicit elements to the employment contract: the knowledge contract; the psychological contract; the efficiency contract; the task contract; and the values contract. The change agent, then, needs to be aware of these contracts and the interdependencies between them. Where there are conflicts between the contracts the change agent should act as a facilitator and mediator to evolve a middle way, bearing in mind always the ethical touchstone of socio-technical systems which is that workers are ends in themselves not merely means to a corporate goal. The authors argue that this represents a somewhat idealised view of organisational possibilities and that the reality that faces change agents, as exemplified by their three case studies, is a messy and political one rather than a situation of rationality and honesty. They show, by considering each of the five elements of the employment contract, how attempts to empower workers through team-based working can be deliberately and accidentally thwarted by other players pursing different agendas.

This leads the authors to consider how the change agent ought to react when what is seen as an ethically-correct change such as employee empowerment is being impeded or corrupted by others in the organisation with differing objectives. This is a particularly acute problem for an external change agent, such as an academic involved in an action research project, who has, at best, a temporary stake in the organisation. Does the change agent have an ethical duty to pursue the change in the interests of the employees? Does the change agent have the ethical right to proceed this way? The authors answer 'yes' to these questions, arguing that as organisational change through socio-technical systems design is a political process, then the change agent cannot stand outside this process and still be effective. In a sense this brings us back to our first distinction between self-empowerment and external empowerment: are the change agents right to assume powers for themselves or should they restrict themselves to the powers explicitly granted to them by the commissioning agent?

Chapter 9 Edna Ojeifo and Diana Winstanley in their chapter 'Negotiated Reality: The Meaning of Empowerment' provide a case study of the empowerment programme implemented in the UK by 'Technon' (pseudonym for a large multi-national company). They argue that the literature on empowerment can be classified within four perspectives defined by two dimensions: an *individual–organisation* dimension and a *prescriptive (goal focus)–interpretive* (meaning focus) dimension. In their study the authors are interested in the meaning of empowerment for the individual employee, and they identify three interrelated groups of situational factors that help provide an understanding of this sense of meaning: context, expectancy and experience.

Empowerment programmes can not be isolated from other events occurring in organisations and the perception of empowerment will be conditioned by the *context* within which it is implemented. The authors found that in 'Technon', as in so many other instances, the empowerment programme was contemporaneous with corporate downsizing and was an organisational ploy to increase productivity: to do more (or at least the same) with less. They also noted that although empowerment is not a cost-free or resource-free option the organisation did not provide this required support. Furthermore, they found the organisation did not undertake the thoroughgoing systems changes – especially in providing access to information – required to make empowerment fully real for the employees. These aspects of the context of empowerment, then, influence how it is interpreted by employees. This interpretation is also found by the authors to be influenced by the employees' *expectancy* of empowerment. Although within the company there was a good understanding amongst employees of the aims of and reasons for the empowerment programme, individual employees had positive or negative expectations of the programme leading them to interpret their experiences differently. A general view was a lack of employee confidence in management's ability or willingness to deliver real empowerment and fully to move to the necessary high trust culture. The third group of factors influencing the employees' interpretation of empowerment was their *experience* with the empowerment programme itself. This reinforced the findings regarding context and expectancy. The employees experienced a managerial reluctance to let what were seen as the natural consequences and requirements of empowerment unfold. Inadequate resources were committed in terms of training and career development so that employees felt they lacked the knowledge and skills fully to realise empowerment. Perhaps most crucially, the organisation did not provide access to the information employees believed they needed if they were to make empowered decisions.

Using information gleaned from the company's annual Employee Motivation Satisfaction Survey, the authors found that, overall, a majority of employees did feel themselves to have been empowered by the company's programme, in the sense that they had greater discretion in decision-making and that this had led to an increase in job satisfaction. However, the authors' research makes clear that empowerment has multiple meanings to the parties involved, and this appreciation of the value of empowerment means neither that the employees necessarily experienced the programme as intended by management, nor that their experience of empowerment could not be enhanced *if* the organisation and its managers were willing to engage in more radical change consistent with their rhetoric.

Chapter 10   Barbara Goodwin's contribution, 'Empowerment in a Government Agency', is based on a case study of a public sector organisation in Britain responsible for the distribution of welfare benefits. The 1979–97 Conservative government placed great stress on making the public sector 'business like'. One result of this policy was the adoption by public sector managers of the discourse of business management, including the idea of empowerment. Goodwin questions whether there are characteristics of the public sector that make inappropriate or unworkable the principle or the practice of empowerment as understood within the private sector.

Goodwin finds that within this government, agency-empowerment is understood more in terms of cascading responsibility down to lower levels of the organisation rather than in terms of enhancing the degree of discretion allowed to members of staff. This contrasts with the traditional hierarchical practices within civil service departments where responsibility was passed up to higher management levels. She notes, however, that this increased responsibility has been accompanied by externally imposed targets (set by government) but that the factors determining whether these targets can be achieved or not lie largely outside the control of the responsible staff member. There are clear motivational problems (Hill, 1995; Goold and Quinn, 1993) and ethical problems – at a minimum it appears to contrast with the Golden Rule of treating others as one would wish to be treated – associated with setting unachievable targets. Goodwin goes on to show how it can also result in unethical behaviour such as deliberately misrepresenting statistics or handling easy cases in preference to complex cases as the former contribute to target attainment although the benefit claimants in the latter might be in greater need.

An important question raised by Goodwin is whether there are circumstances where it would be unethical to empower (that is, increase the discretion of) employees. In the case of the agency studies there are clear rules setting out the benefit to be paid to clients according to their circumstances. This can raise serious moral dilemmas who find themselves having to provide benefit to those they judge are working the system whilst being unable to help others they judge to be in greater need.

She notes that this may not differ in kind from the situation facing, say, a car assembly worker who has no discretion over how he fixes a panel but the decision for the car worker is not such an intensely ethical one as that faced by the agency employee who is dealing with the poorest in society.

Goodwin raises the question of whether agency staff members should have discretion in the application of these government-established rules: whether moral judgement should be allowed to prevail over the 'objective' application of rules. Even at the most senior levels, agency employees have little or no discretion over what is delivered to the claimant although they may have discretion over the internal activities of the agency are managed: they can have process empowerment but not product empowerment. Goodwin, then, questions whether it is an unethical deceit to suggest to such employees performing rule-bound tasks that they are empowered, particularly when they have to achieve targets without breaking these rules.

Chapter 11 Christopher Moon and Celia Stanworth in their chapter 'Ethics and Empowerment: Managerial Discourse and the Case of Teleworking' question the assumption that empowerment is generally ethical suggesting that the nature and context of the task influence the form and extent of empowerment. Their work is based on a study of how teleworkers experience empowerment.

The term teleworker has come to refer to two different sets of workers. The first is defined in terms of a task and relates to staff who spend most of their working time on the telephone dealing with actual or potential customers or members of other groups with which the organisation has regular dealings. The second is defined by the location of employees away from the organisation's premises – and often at home – who communicate with the organisation by telephone. It is the latter group of workers which Moon and Stanworth's chapter addresses, though clearly these two sets of workers intersect as there is a large and growing number of workers who fall into both categories.

The authors note that much of the literature on the second form of teleworking deals with professional employees with specialist expertise engaged in high value-added activities and possessing strong labour market power who are seen as achieving empowerment, self-actualisation and personal growth through flexible arrangements that allow them to optimise both domestic (bringing up the children in a rural setting) and employment (working for a large multinational) arrangements. They may be seen as the pioneers of the virtual organisation and indeed the virtual society. But, it is argued, the experience of many home/teleworkers, particularly those in the intersect of the two categories described above or engaged in routine data entry such as inputing survey data, is quite different. Although they may benefit from some aspects of living remotely from the office, technological means are used to ensure they remain subject to surveillance. Empowerment of such workers with less specialised skills and a weaker labour market position is tightly circumscribed; the promise of increased discretion and consequent flexibility does not match the performance. Employees remain controlled not liberated by the changed organisation of work.

Although disillusioned by the practice of empowerment, the authors do not regard the empowerment programme as forever defeated. They suggest, however, that for empowerment to become valid for most teleworkers, and indeed for most employees in traditional work settings, its ethical character must be made explicit both deontologically, in articulating the rights and responsibilities of both employer and employed in an empowerment programme (agreeing with Davies and Mills, Chapter 6), and teleologically in identifying the costs and benefits to both parties. Their conclusion argues that this requires a shift away from evaluating business performance simply in monetary terms and implies that, in turn, this requires a move to a stakeholder rather than a shareholder or managerial model of the firm.

Part III   Business and society: the new empowerment responsibility

Chapter 12   Johnston Birchall in his chapter 'Empowering Consumers through Co-operatives' charts the development of the British consumer co-operative movement from its roots in the early to mid-nineteenth century. As we have seen above (Christensen Hughes, Chapter 7), the rise of the empowered consumer demanding high quality in both product and service is often given as one explanation of the need for employee empowerment. However, although there are consumer pressure groups (such as the Consumers Association, user groups for particular software packages, the Gas Consumers Council, and so on), in the main consumers in making purchases do so in a highly individualistic and disorganised fashion. As such, their influence over the behaviour of suppliers is fragmented, indirect and weak. In the mid-nineteenth century, working class poverty and the power asymmetry between consumers and producers led to widespread adulteration of foods and the supply of shoddy clothing and shoes. This led to several attempts to establish consumer co-operation as a means of consumer protection and an expression of political principle, culminating in the founding of the co-operative movement as it exists today. Fundamental to this notion of consumer co-operation was the elimination of profit by the return to purchasers (members) of any surplus made by the co-operative. Birchall shows how the co-operatives grew and then reinforced their position by backward integration, first into wholesaling and then into production, followed by the introduction of its own newspaper and eventually its own political party.

Birchall raises a number of issues in the history of consumer co-operation that have resonance in today's debate on empowerment. The first issue is the relationship between consumer empowerment and worker empowerment. In the literature on contemporary management, the latter is seen as entailing the former but Birchall shows that in the co-operative movement the interests of workers and consumers were more often opposed, both theoretically and in practice. This left consumer co-operatives in an ambiguous position on the left in British politics, particularly among Marxists wedded to the notion of the sovereignty of labour. Goodwin (this volume) shows how today increasing expectations among users of government agencies, reinforced by government-inspired User Charters, can lead to worker antagonism.

The second issue raised by Birchall is that of maintaining the interest and commitment of consumers to their co-operative. Over time, membership of co-operatives has declined as has participation in their democratic processes. The Co-op has become just another High Street shop. Arguably, empowerment too will become just another way of doing the job, another form of words used by managers. This leads to the third point raised by Birchall, that being a co-operative needs to be perceived as being something different if it is to attract customers and involve members. Co-operative shops, as a result of member pressure, adopted a clear ethical stance in refusing to sell goods from apartheid South Africa and the Co-operative Bank has a very clear ethical trading policy. Consumer empowerment here has made a difference. Similarly for employee empowerment to be real it must be seen as making a difference in a moral sense, not as management by stress but as providing genuinely enhanced work.

Chapter 13 Richard Warren's 'Empowerment in a Community of Purpose' raises the question of whether it is sufficient to conceptualise organisations and the employment relationship simply in economic terms. He rejects approaches that would see the firm as a nexus of contracts arguing that, more than ever, the firm must be seen as a social institution, and in particular one that should provide the basis for the moral development of its members. Warren thus rejects the utilitarian neo-classical economic interpretations of empowerment that would characterise it simply as reaction to competitive pressure in which both workers and managers gain from more effective responses to customer needs. He also, however, rejects the critical views of Foucaultians and neo-Marxists who criticise empowerment as being necessarily another and more advanced form of managerial control and exploitation. He goes on to reject the relativistic ethics underpinning these schools arguing instead for an ethics based on historically stable virtues.

Warren grounds his analysis in the belief that ethically to evaluate a management practice such as empowerment requires an analysis of the purpose and practice of individual businesses and the actors within them, not abstract concepts such as business or managers, and dismisses the descriptive generalisations to which such abstraction leads. Furthermore, he argues that actors in business, including managers, ought to adopt a stakeholder approach rather than focusing entirely on shareholder value, aiming at contributing to a broader social good than increasing individual wealth (important though that is). That is, businesses should become communities of purpose acknowledging their wider social role.

This position is a consequence of Warren's advocacy of businesses as intermediate associations in the sense used by Durkheim. Warren argues that with the decline of the family and local communities, people engage in more temporary and less socially embedded affiliations. This leads to the weakening of the sources of moral teaching leading in turn to a threat to the preservation of social order. Under such conditions an individual's employing organisation increasingly becomes one of the more permanent frames of reference for the individual for moral as well as other judgements. Thus, whereas Fukuyama (1995) argues that the existence of intermediate associations provides the basis upon which large business organisations can grow, Warren argues that these business organisations are themselves intermediate organisations, alongside schools, churches and so forth, and should recognise their moral influence and use it for social good: that is, they should become communities of purpose.

It is within the context of a business as a community of purpose that Warren sees the possibility of ethical empowerment. Empowerment is ethical insofar as it contributes to practice, in MacIntyre's sense, serving the common good through the development of internal goods. Such empowerment is not designed nor practiced simply to achieve greater control, nor is it simply a variation on the employment contract. Ethical empowerment, for Warren, is an element of a virtuous organisation in which its members are valued holistically for their intrinsic worth, personal needs are important, and relationships are superogatory rather than contractual. Through such empowerment organisational members not only enhance their practice but become better citizens.

Chapter 14 The theme of the position of the firm in society is continued in the chapter by Paul Joyce and Adrian Woods, 'The Social Responsibility of Businesses: To Empower Employees by Listening and Responding'. They initially make their case arguing that 'listening and responding' to employees is not only a socially responsible thing to do, but also ties in directly with current management thinking in terms of enabling employees to have more discretion in the workplace – part of a wider reformation of liberalising industry and commerce. The rest of their chapter is then based on a 1995 survey of 659 business establishments in central London, the majority of which were owner-managed small firms. They identify a sub-set of firms that characterise themselves as socially responsible and investigate how that social responsibility is made manifest. As a result they conclude that the socially responsible firm is best understood as the firm that reconciles its need for satisfactory profit with a contribution to a broader social good that can be either internal to the firm, represented by concern for employee well-being, or external to the firm, that is, concern for the wider community in which the firm is located, including their customers, this contribution being not simply profit-oriented. In coming to this conclusion Joyce and Woods explicitly reject the ethics of Friedman's argument that the socially responsible business is the one that concentrates on profit maximisation and eschews explicit social goals, relying on government regulation to provide business with a moral framework. They take a more catholic view of the objectives of the firm, arguing that there is no moral imperative on firms to adopt any particular objective so it is quite permissible for different firms to have different objectives. In this sense Joyce and Woods reject the disempowerment of owner-managers implicit in Friedman's argument, freeing them to exercise choice over the objectives they wish to pursue.

Amongst the firms that saw themselves as socially responsible, Joyce and Woods found many that expressed a commitment to the idea that employee well-being was an important business objective. Furthermore, a number of firms stressed the importance of employees' views for business decision-making. Joyce and Woods argue that where listening to employees is underpinned by a high trust relationship the firm might be seen as having a 'partnership-oriented culture', that we might well term 'empowerment'. Furthermore, they identify a positive correlation between firms that listen to their employees and firms that listen to their customers, reinforcing the idea that empowerment is best seen as something that emerges from, or is a characteristic of, a sympathetic culture rather than a management tool to be employed in an instrumental way. This leads the authors to see such organisations as engaging in alternative 'ethically pluralist' forms of corporate governance with empowered employees as an important component of this ethical plurality. They might be seen, then, as challenging both the conflict resolution and the benevolent autocratic management practices associated with the traditional manager–managed dichotomous model of the firm, replacing it with one based on negotiation among trusting 'partners'.

Chapter 15 Peter Jones, in the final chapter, 'Ethical Guidelines for an Empowered Organisation', continues the theme of the wider social responsibility of business from the point of view of a business person and management consultant. He locates the beginning of a move in Britain towards an advocacy of empowerment and other changes in the nature of the implicit employment contract partly within a political reaction against the dominant philosophy of the 1980s and early 1990s, and partly within developments associated with changes in the business environment. That philosophy he sees as one that equated competitiveness with cost-cutting which in turn was equated with downsizing, this view being supported by a raft of government measures designed to facilitate the shedding of labour by lessening statutory employment protections. According to Jones, the reaction within the political debate saw the stakeholder concept gaining greater currency. Within businesses the reaction was a result of a growing realisation that first, business growth at some stage had to be based on building rather than cutting and second, for the flatter structures organisations have adopted to work then the needs of the people working within those structures have to be addressed. Such thinking also ties in with actually getting the promised and elusive benefits of large investments in IT technology; the 'hardware' fails to deliver desired results because the 'soft' side (people) is neglected. Hard-line 'command and control' management systems *have* to give way the more established the stakeholder view of business and society becomes.

Jones sees the emergence of new employment structures and modes of working as being the re-affirmation of an ethical role for businesses that had been lost from sight over the preceding decades. He argues, like Follett 70 years earlier, that a business has a responsibility to serve society not just its shareholders and that part of the way of serving society is through respect for and the development of its employees. Furthermore, he argues like Warren (this volume) that the workplace is an important forum for the development of personal ethics and that managers, through their organising of work and through example, have a responsibility to take this seriously. The idea of responsibilities and rights between a business and its stakeholders is argued by Jones to be essential to the notion of an ethical business. Specifically he suggests a charter of responsibilities and rights for the employee in an ethical business, these generating a reciprocal set of rights and responsibilities for managers. From the practice of these responsibilities and rights in industry, an internally-generated empowerment would emerge. Such a process is essential because otherwise business will merely default back to the minimum legal standards laid down by government.

FINAL WORD

The 15 chapters of this volume give the reader a wide-ranging introduction to the themes of Ethics and Empowerment, two words which are set to stay central for a long time in management. Highly interesting case-study material is set alongside a number of theoretical frameworks, all of which will add much value these two buzzwords. The *loose* ways in which they are often used in the management literature has also been the subject of scrutiny in this book, and so it will not only help the reader clarify their own thoughts, but also provide useful ideas for classroom study.

I am not sure if the final shape and detailed content of this book is as my friend and colleague John Quinn originally intended, but I am sure he would have endorsed all the chapters as making important contributions to the vital Business Ethics debate.

References

Argyris, C. (1991) 'Teaching Smart People How to Learn', *Harvard Business Review*, vol. 69(3), May/June, pp. 99–109.
Fukuyama, F. (1995) *Trust: The Social Virtue and the Creation of Prosperity* (London: Hamilton Press).

Goold, M.J and Quinn, J.J. (1993) *Strategic Control: Milestones for Long-Term Performance* (London: Pitman).

Hill, S. (1995) 'From Quality Circles to Total Quality Management', in A. Wilkinson and H. Willmott (eds), *Making Quality Critical: New Perspectives on Organisational Change* (London: Routledge), pp. 33–53.

Mumford, E. (1996) *Systems Design: Ethical Tools for Ethical Design* (London: Macmillan).

1 Is Empowerment Ethical? Why Ask the Question?
John J. Quinn

> For we are trying to think out the form of organization whereby authority may go with three things: knowledge, experience and the skill to apply that knowledge and experience.
>
> *Mary Parker Follett, quoted in Graham (1995)*

INTRODUCTION

Empowerment is desirable, is it not? Almost by definition, the idea that people may have greater power over some aspects of their own lives seems to be a good thing. And in the majority of areas where the term is used – for example, feminism, consumerism and urban planning – this is generally the position taken. Even where the activity involved might be socially or otherwise undesirable, empowerment might be seen as positive if misdirected. Thus we are told of the 18th Street Gang in Los Angeles '[Gang members] taught kids who came from other countries how to survive...18th Street empowered a lot of kids [telling them] "This is how you do it in America"' (*Observer*, 24 November 1996). In the emergent debate on communitarianism, empowerment would appear to be a necessary prerequisite if individuals are to take more responsibility for shaping their own lives and the lives of those around them.

Why then has the reaction to empowerment in the workplace been so equivocal? Why, in a business context, are we driven to ask the question, 'Is empowerment ethical?'.

Perhaps it is that the word empowerment is itself equivocal. On the one hand empowerment suggests the *assertion or taking of power* by the individual or group. It represents the victory of autonomy and freedom over repression and coercion. On the other hand, however, empowerment suggests the *tolerance, granting or imposition of power* to the individual or group by some external agent. In accepting such empowerment the empowered might be seen as recognising and acquiescing to the power of those above. These two perspectives on empowerment, it can be argued, raise quite different ethical questions.

Where the term empowerment has been discussed outside of the workplace, it is generally the first perspective – self-empowerment – that has been taken, though often in tandem to some extent with the second. Thus the first moves towards the empowerment of women in western society were taken by feminist activists' asserting of their rights to equality of representation, treatment and opportunity and this was later formalised and reinforced by suffrage and equal rights legislation. Even now, however, it is far from being custom and practice in many parts of society. Similar comments might be made about the empowerment of ethnic minorities, homosexuals, and the disabled, though arguably the empowerment of this last group is still some distance behind that of the others as empowering them has more significant resource implications.

Within the context of modern organisational and management studies, it is the alternative perspective on empowerment that is pervasive; that is, empowerment as the management practice of allowing to workers, or indeed imposing on workers, more problem-solving discretion. Indeed, to the extent that the rhetoric of empowerment has developed, at least in Britain, in parallel with the legislatively supported and encouraged decline of trade unionism, it might be argued that this managerial version of empowerment has grown at the expense of the alternative version of worker empowerment as achieved through the exercise of collective industrial power.

The location of empowerment within the management literature is imprecise and indeed there are several different dimensions to the notion of empowerment. Bird (this volume) distinguishes five forms of empowerment (personal, task, contractual, adjudicatory and governance), and six degrees (scant, marginal, consultative, co-determinate, effective and total). The management literature on empowerment has dealt primarily with task empowerment, with a secondary focus on personal and governance empowerment. Furthermore, as with so many of the terms that might loosely be seen to make up modern management, the discussion of empowerment has rapidly diffused through several strands of the literature including, for example, operations management, human resource management and strategic management. Again like so many of these terms, as empowerment has become popularised through the work of gurus and other management consultants it has gained greater currency whilst at the same time becoming less precise in its meaning. This imprecision and at times confusion in both the object and context of empowerment is important as different interpretations of the concept of empowerment and different practices may have associated with them different ethical implications.

In what follows we will consider what it is in the practice of empowerment within organisations that causes it often to be opposed by the supposedly empowered (and considered unethical by many), whilst at the same time both questioning these criticisms and offering an alternative model for ethical empowerment.

EMPOWERMENT AS AN ETHICAL ENDEAVOUR

Everyone is empowered to some extent at work. People are not automata and in even the most Tayloresque situations workers will exercise some element of decision-making and choice. To this extent the question is not whether employees should be empowered or not, but rather the extent to which the employee's decision-making authority should be constrained or expanded. This is not, of course, a new debate but it is being argued in a new language and, as we will see, with new reasons.

Although one might not want to claim that Follett, writing in the 1920s, was really arguing within an empowerment discourse that had not then emerged, the opening quotation makes clear that the ideas inherent in the notion of empowerment are not new. As Graham's edited collection of Follett's work shows, the distribution and exercise of power within organizations is a recurring feature in Follett's writing in which she rejects command and control models and the exercise of management by 'power over' approaches arguing instead for 'power with', recognising the contribution that all can contribute to the success of an organization.

Follett's justification for this position is an explicitly ethical one, but unlike most modern writers on the subject she did not see it as primarily an issue of the ethics of employer–employee relations *per se*. She believed that business had a duty to serve society in the best way it could; she further believed that this could only be realised if the full potential of each individual within the business organization were developed and applied (again Follett could here be seen to be presaging the customer-driven view of business organisations though she would not have been so crude as to identify the good of society with the materialistic desires of consumers). Thus, in characterising as win–win this trilateral relationship – management, employee and customer (society) – Follett anticipated much of the contemporary management discourse, including empowerment.

This argument of Follett is largely rule utilitarian in character. Society's benefits are maximised when employees are empowered to contribute their full talents to the operations of the firm. As such her argument is similar to, but different from, much of the recent justification for empowerment that takes the line that empowerment is right (ethical) because it produces the best business results and what is good for business is good for society. That is, business is seen as an ethical undertaking and a management practice such as empowerment is itself ethical in so far as it contributes to business success (Friedman, 1970; Sternberg, 1994).

A somewhat different ethical justification for empowerment is that its practice necessitates ethically desirable changes in the workplace, and implies high discretion on the part of the employee. Fox (1974) sees the level of discretion as the characteristic discriminator between high and low trust relationships at work. This does, however, raise the question as to what extent does the introduction and practice of empowerment in organisations indicate that these organisations are actually beginning to put more trust in their employees. If empowerment is simply a reaction to market conditions and the perceived need for greater flexibility in the face of more empowered and discriminating customers, then we can only conclude that additional discretion in decision-making is being granted only reluctantly and does not in fact reflect any real change in the degree of trust of managers in their employees.[1] This would support the argument expressed by critical theorists that empowerment can at best be seen as a transitory and unstable development that can be withdrawn by management as readily as it can be conferred.

However, even in the absence of high trust relationships it is still possible to argue that empowerment is ethical in so far as it requires changes in organisational practice that benefit the empowered employees. If empowerment is to work as planned, employees do gain more discretionary decision-making powers that do lead to more job satisfaction; employers are required to provide employees with the opportunities for training necessary for the development and exercise of their newly required powers; this does lead to employee self-development and the opening up of new opportunities; it does lead to more accomplished workers enhancing organisational and national competitiveness. Furthermore, in contrast to the need for employees in traditional organisational structures to effect received decisions employees in empowered organisations are given voice leading to a diversity of valid responses and the possible breakdown of culturally defined limits on the acceptable. Thus, although the motives of the empowering agent may be exploitative and unethical, there can be unintended (and for the employer possibly unwanted) conditions and outcomes that are beneficial both to the empowered employees and to society.

THE ETHICAL CRITIQUE OF EMPOWERMENT

Much, though by no means all, of the ethical critique of empowerment has related to the practice rather than the principle of empowerment and, in particular, to elements of modern management practice, often imported (in modified forms) from Japan. In what follows we will briefly consider two such related elements – lean production and total quality management (TQM). Empowerment is a *sine qua non* of these management approaches but it is far from clear that they can be, or are, implemented in an ethical fashion.

Empowerment as the requirement on workers to take more responsibility for decision-making is seen as central to the notion of lean production as developed in the Japanese automobile industry and later taken up by western manufacturers (Womack, Jones and Roos, 1990). Whether by multi-skilling (widening the skills base of the worker), the removal of buffer stocks (producing the need for rapid decision-making) or giving workers authority for what were previously management decisions (allowing operatives to stop the line in the event of a production or quality problem), the scope for decision-making allowed to and expected of production line employees was increased as plants moved towards lean production.

The ethics of this approach to empowerment is not uncontentious. Womack *et al.* themselves are not unaware of criticisms of the system noting, though disagreeing, that, 'Critics argue that [lean production] makes *Modern Times* look like a picnic. In Charlie Chaplin's widget factory at least the workers didn't have to think about what they were doing and try and improve it' (Womack *et al.*, 1990, p. 101).

Protagonists for lean production, however, also argue that the practice of lean production is ethical because the power relationship implicit in effective lean production is reciprocal rather than unidirectional (top-down) leading to a mitigation of the undesirable effects of management practices associated with traditional production methods. Thus Womack *et al.* argue that lean production is *fragile* as in the absence of buffer stocks the system is tightly coupled. A halt in production at one stage in the process through, for example, industrial action or the recalcitrant actions of demotivated employees, can rapidly bring the whole process to a stop. In this way management introducing lean production exposes itself to a high degree of risk in the event of workers not complying with the rules of the system. To guard against this, management has to pay extra attention to motivating and maintaining the loyalty and commitment of its workforce (Oliver and Wilkinson,

1992). So, for example, lifetime employment is necessary to align worker and management interests thus alleviating this risk. Developing this line of thought, it might indeed be argued that empowerment gives employees a tool to criticise (and control) management. Empowerment entails training workers and making additional organisational information available to them, providing the conditions for greater worker control of the enterprise through the bottom-up development of worker participation and worker democracy (Smith, 1994). Furthermore, the shift in knowledge-based power within the organisation resulting from empowerment has been interpreted as the disempowerment of junior and middle management, and in many cases the removal of these management layers (Wilkinson et al., 1992).

Other commentators on lean production have been less sanguine. McCardle et al. (1995) point out the need for organisations to be loosely coupled if empowerment is to be genuine. In tightly coupled, or fragile, systems employees are given power but the characteristics of the system mean that their discretion in deciding when and how to exercise that power is severely constrained. Thus the dominant production mode in motor manufacturing remains the production line and such complex, tightly coupled systems require 'instant' responses if they are not to go out of control. In a sense, therefore, empowerment for workers in tightly coupled systems means being asked to act *as if an order had been given* rather than taking the time to reflect upon the course of action that would be most appropriate in the circumstances. This is the direct opposite of the notions of creativity, flexibility and individual responsibility implicit in other understandings of empowerment. The idea of the empowered worker acting as if an order had been given brings to mind the analogy of military training. Soldiers in a modern army are trained instantly to obey orders from their officers. Obedience and discipline are highly-rated characteristics of the fighting man or woman. But it is also expected of the soldier, and built into their training, that in active battlefield conditions s/he will act autonomously and exercise individual discretion as the circumstances so warrant. The intensive training is designed to ensure that the behaviour displayed by the soldier under unanticipated conditions is that that would have been ordered by an officer had one been present.

Parker and Slaughter (1995) claim that lean production is indeed a misnomer, deliberately chosen to mislead through its positive connotations. After all, they argue, if something is not lean it is obese or wasteful, terms that have clear negative associations. These authors argue that rather than lean production a better term for this approach would be *management by stress*. Variations in the system's performance are absorbed not by the build-up of buffer stocks but by variations in the pace of the employees' work. This in turn can have great physical, social and psychological costs for the worker though with relatively little cost to the employer. In this way, the empowerment that occurs within lean production can be seen as shifting the risks and costs associated with fluctuations in production rates from the employer onto the employee.

Empowerment is not, of course, restricted in its application to lean production systems, although it does largely appear to be associated with the concept of 'doing more with less'. Perhaps more commonly and more broadly, empowerment is associated with the increased emphasis on quality. Juran and Gryna (1993) include a discussion of empowerment in a chapter entitled Developing a Quality Culture. For them empowerment is defined as workers at lower levels of the organisation being encouraged to take decisions for which they have been trained, plus the provision of support rather than criticism when mistakes are made. Such empowerment, they argue, is part of the necessary cultural changes required for quality management to work. Likewise, for Oakland (1989) empowerment, understood to mean the active involvement of all employees in decisions about quality, is a necessary condition for the effective implementation of total quality management. Furthermore, given that the drive towards total quality management is itself, at least in part, seen as a response to a more discriminating and better informed customer, employee empowerment can be seen as a necessary concomitant of customer empowerment.

To the extent that empowerment as part of total quality management concerns itself with employee development it can be viewed, as we have seen, as an ethical endeavour. But, although the driving force for total quality management is external – the search for competitive advantage in the era of the more discriminating and empowered customer – its implementation focuses on internal processes that can be seen as components of the organisational control system, though Kerfoot and Knights (1995) argue that where management control is enhanced through empowerment this is an *un*intended outcome of the process, rather than the seeking for increased control *per se*. However, Legge (1995) presents the argument that whilst the total quality management literature is often presented using the rhetoric of empowerment, the reality is one of subjugation: increased quality requires greater standardisation entailing greater control, whether unintended or not. These control elements of total quality management dominate the empowerment elements and, indeed, provide the limits within which empowerment may be exercised. From this perspective, therefore, the ethics of empowerment needs to be located as a subset of the ethics of control. Hill (1995) makes the point that empowered employees must have authority to change situations for which they are made responsible. In many instances where quality circles had been introduced into UK companies, the circles were limited to advice rather than having powers of decision-making and implementation. The decision-making power still resided in line managers who often were not members of the circle and were not committed to the particular quality circle or the very idea of quality circles. Indeed, in many cases such quality circles were seen as a threat to the middle managers for whom frustrating the work of the circle became a sensible personal strategy. But as we noted with lean production, the granting of authority carries with it the risk of a loss of control, particularly when the action follows immediately on the empowered decision as may be the case, for example, in the service sector where an employee is in direct contact with a customer. This can lead to the apparent paradox of employee empowerment and the loosening of controls in some aspects of the work process being accompanied by a tightening of management controls in other areas (Christensen Hughes, Chapter 7 this volume). It can also be seen as one of the reasons for the growing use of codes of conduct, codes of ethics, and so forth (Webley, 1995) as organisations put new boundaries on, and provide new guidelines for, the practice of the discretion available to empowered employees. In this case, empowerment might be seen as at best a minor reallocation of power within organizations without any change in its hierarchical distribution and at worst simply a relabelling of existing responsibilities. Furthermore, the use of controls and codes to limit empowerment may be regarded as symptomatic of persisting low trust and Theory Y attitudes inimical to genuine empowerment.

Figuring prominently in the empowerment literature is the concept of employee commitment, another word that has positive ethical connotations. There is, however, a degree of ambiguity in the use of this term. The argument vacillates between commitment as a precondition for empowerment, in the sense that only the committed employee can be expected to exercise empowerment in the interests of the organisation, and commitment as an outcome of empowerment. Implicit in this latter argument is the idea that empowerment is seen as desirable and rewarding by the employee. To some, of course, this may be an example of false consciousness as empowerment is viewed as another management tool to get more out of employees. Thus both Sayer (1986) and Tomaney (1990) argue that empowerment, that is, allowing to or imposing on workers the power and responsibility to solve problems, can best be seen as the owners of capital finding new ways of exploiting labour, in this case through the increased intellectual commitment of workers.

Cappelli (1995) suggests a still more sinister explanation for the spread of empowerment in the United States. In that country certain elements of employment protection legislation, including, for example, the right to enhanced payment rates for overtime and eligibility for trade union representation, apply to employees (non-exempt) but not to managers (exempt), where manager was understood to involve supervising others. A court ruling extended the category of exempt from managers to those who were *largely not supervised*, that is, employees with a great deal of discretion and autonomy in their actions. Thus firms that redesign or redefine work to empower their workers can at the same time reduce the protection available to them under the law. Parallels might be drawn with the UK experience of firms changing the status of workers from employees to franchisees or self-employed workers on contract as, for example, those who carry out daily door-to-door milk deliveries.

MAKING EMPOWERMENT ETHICAL

We can accept that few organisations – particularly business organisations – pursue empowerment for its own sake. The justification for introducing empowerment is not that it is the right thing to do, where right is understood in an ethical sense, but rather that it is the right thing to do in a business sense (rejecting the notion that the latter implies the former). As such, empowerment is generally a subsidiary objective, subject to a higher goal such as improving quality, lean production or organisational delayering. Furthermore, the rhetoric would generally have it that this higher goal is itself subordinate to the ultimate goal of satisfying customer needs. Also, we can see from the foregoing that there are many reasons for viewing empowerment as practised in the workplace as unethical. In many instances empowerment is seen as one more tool for management to use to increase pressure on workers to deliver greater productivity and reduce costs. Furthermore, it is devious in so far as it deceives employees into collaborating in their own exploitation (Burawoy, 1979).[2] And where empowerment *may* provide some benefits to employees – in tightly coupled systems – this benefit is seen to be one of increased power within a confrontational situation. This view is rooted in an ideology that sees all employment relations as zero-sum games with empowerment awarding management gains at the expense of worker losses. Thus, this suggests that neither the principle nor the practice of empowerment is based in ethical reasoning.

But whilst accepting empowerment is a tool of management practice, it is inadequate to reject it as unethical simply on those grounds. The issues are whether within the capitalist system there are more or less ethical ways of managing, and whether empowerment falls into the more or the less ethical category. This assumes a reformist rather than radical ethical position with regard to the employment relationship; that is, it assumes that the lot of employees in capitalist organisations can be incrementally improved and asks whether empowerment can contribute to such improvement. This position might indeed be rejected on the grounds that empowerment is just a more successful, and hence more pernicious and unethical, tool for exploiting labour in so far as it more effectively deceives labour into controlling itself and redirecting its energies – both physical and intellectual – in the interests of capital. In this sense empowerment might be seen as the final building block in the capitalist panopticon for the observation and control of labour.

The counter argument to this criticism is that empowerment is the most ethical form of managing within a capitalist enterprise because through it the individual employee does in practice gain more discretion over his or her actions and consequently, in most cases, gets more job satisfaction and develops more fully as a person. This discretion is not, of course, absolute and remains limited both by acts of management *fiat* and by the fact that all employees are working within a system that requires consideration of constraints both internal (for example, the need to integrate one's work with that of others) and external (for example, delivery times). Indeed in some circumstances there may be strong ethical arguments for not extending discretionary decision making powers. Examples might include situations concerning health and safety or situations where discretion might lead to the possibility of patronage and corruption (Goodwin, this volume).

However, not rejecting empowerment outright as essentially and necessarily unethical does not require one to accept that empowerment is ethical *per se*. Rather, one can accept the possibility of ethical empowerment and then the question becomes not whether empowerment is ethical or unethical but rather which management practices represent ethical or unethical forms of empowerment. We have already seen how lean production, whilst being couched in the language of empowerment, might be better seen a management by stress. Christensen Hughes (this volume, Chapter 7) shows how empowerment programmes can be corrupted by managers who are not committed to the principle of empowerment and instead believe that 'empowerment', like a bonus scheme or an advertising campaign, can be simply switched on or off depending on the state of the company's business. Furthermore, for empowerment to work there has to be a change in the access to information within organisations with need-to-know decisions being made by the empowered employees rather than by managers. Such developments in IT systems may be resisted. We cannot, therefore, make *a priori* judgements on the ethics of empowerment, rather each case has its own situational characteristics and it is an empirical question whether the practice is ethical or unethical.

Ethical empowerment, then, does not just happen, nor is there an ethical empowerment template that can simply be imposed on an organisation with inappropriate and unaccepting systems and culture. However, three mutually reinforcing developments appear to be necessary conditions for ethical empowerment to become real within an organisation.

- First, there needs to be the development of a culture of empowerment: that is, a high-trust culture where employees are confident that they can exercise genuine discretion, that they have the power to act on their judgements and they will not be penalised for making occasional mistakes when they employ their enhanced decision-making responsibilities. Sako (1992) distinguishes three kinds of trust: competence trust, contractual trust and goodwill trust. All three seem to be necessary characteristics of the employer–employee relationship in the ethically empowered organisation. The employer needs to trust that the employee is competent to exercise the discretion granted to him/her; to trust that the employee will not exploit his/her increased discretion in a way that violates the formal or informal employment contract; and to trust that the employee will act in the best interests of the organisation. The employee, in turn, needs to trust the employer to be willing and able to manage an organisation with relatively autonomous decision makers; to trust the employer not to exploit empowerment as a tool for severing contracts, cutting staffing, and so forth; and to trust the employer to treat the employee as a stakeholder in the organisation with a common interest in the organisation and to trust that the employer will not simply withdraw empowerment in the light of short-term performance shortcomings.

- Second, there is a consequent need for organisations to change their systems and established practices so that they are consonant with empowerment. Information and control systems in the pre-empowered organisation will generally be more suitable for relatively low trust, low discretion, command and control methods of operation that are practically, symbolically and ethically inappropriate to the empowered organisation.
- Third, there is the need for the organisation to provide employees with the tools to become empowered. That is, employees have to go through a process of personal development and be provided with training and additional information if they are to be capable of exercising the additional discretionary decision making responsibilities implied by empowerment. This reinforces the need for a high-trust culture as the organisation has to accept the risks associated with the organisational power shifts consequent on the personal development of its employees.

Such ethical empowerment has the potential for being believed in by employees and not being regarded, as so often (for example, Watson, 1994), as simply the latest management fad, the 'flavour of the month'. It also creates the possibility of radical change in the power relationships in organisations which may, at least in part, account for the antagonism towards empowerment from conservative managers, employees and employee representatives, alike.

If it is to be believed in by employees, empowerment cannot simply be imposed by management *diktat*. Rather it has to be introduced through a process of discussion and negotiation establishing the norms of reciprocity and trust. It is suggested here that these discussions should take place within the framework of a 'good conversation' as described by Bird (1990, 1996) and Quinn (1996). That is, the discussions should be vocal, reciprocating, issues-oriented, rational, imaginative and honest. A discussion with these characteristics should ensure that employees feel fully involved in the development and implementation of empowerment and reassured as to its character and its impact.

A CONCLUSION

When the arguments and counter-arguments have been elaborated, the ethics of empowerment is seen to be as much a question of ideologies as of evidence.

Weaver (1997) identifies two organisational ideologies that fit well the alternative views on the ethics of empowerment. One such ideology, which Weaver sees as rooted in the work of the pragmatist philosopher John Dewey, is that organisations are (or at least have the potential to be) edifying forums in which people can develop a collectivist ethic reflected in team work and sharing. The other ideology, for Weaver rooted in the work of Foucault, is that of organisations as controlled violence. From the first perspective, empowerment represents the stage of employees achieving the level of self-expression as the makers of decisions on how best a job can be done rather than simply implementing a set of instructions. From, the second perspective empowerment is, depending on one's preferred metaphor, one more brick in the wall, or one more tool of subservience and self-control.

It has been argued here that neither of these perspectives necessarily captures the reality of empowerment for employees. Undoubtedly for some, programmes that are labelled empowerment have little to do with giving greater discretion to a trusted workforce and have everything to do with cutting employee numbers and/or increasing managerial control. On the other hand, it may be the case that there are examples of empowered workers managing to shake off the shackles of systematised operations to gain full discretion in the organising of their work – though such examples, particularly in large firms, are hard to come by in the literature. It appears however that in most employment situations empowerment is a game of give-and-take, at the same time both liberating the employee whilst burdening him or her with increased responsibilities. The ethics of the situation is then an issue of both distributive (what is the result of the empowerment of employees) and procedural (how is empowerment implemented) justice.

Notes

1. This raises the question, not addressed here, as to whether we can distinguish between trust as a psychological state and a relationship characterised by trust-like behaviour but in which trust is absent.
2. Keller and Dansereau (1995) make a similar argument though they view the result more positively. Their case is that empowerment is best understood as a characteristic of the subordinate–supervisor dyadic relationship, and that the supervisor who is perceived as empowering by the subordinate increases the self-worth of the subordinate and his/her perceived degree of control. This is then reciprocated by the subordinate acting in a way that will benefit the supervisor; that is, the subordinate becomes self-controlling.

References

Babson, S. (ed.) (1995) *Lean Work: Empowerment and Exploitation in the Global Auto Industry* (Detroit: Wayne State University Press).
Bird, F. (1996) *The Muted Conscience: Moral Silence and the Practice of Ethics in Business* (Stamford, Conn: Quorum Books).
Bird, F. (1990) 'The Role of "Good Conversation" in Business Ethics', in *Proceedings of the First Annual James A. Walters Colloquium on Ethics in Practice* (The Wallace E. Carroll School of Management, Boston College, Chestnut Hill, MA).
Burawoy, M. (1979) *Manufacturing Consent: Changes in the Labour Process under Monopoly Capitalism* (Chicago: University of Chicago Press).
Capelli, P. (1995), 'Rethinking Employment', *British Journal of Industrial Relations*, vol. 33(4), pp. 563–602.
Fox, A. (1974) *Beyond Contact: Work, Power and Trust Relations* (London: Faber & Faber).
Friedman, M. (1970) 'The Social Responsibility of Business is to Increase its Profits', *The New York Times Magazine*, p. 13 ff.
Graham, P. (1995) *Mary Parker Follett – Prophet of Management* (Boston, MA: Harvard Business School Press).
Hill, S. (1995) 'From Quality Circles to Total Quality Management', in A. Wilkinson and H. Willmott, *op. cit.*, pp. 33–53.
Juran, J.M. and Gryna, F.M. (1993) *Quality Planning and Analysis*, 3rd edn (New York: McGraw Hill).
Keller, T. and Dansereau, F. (1995) 'Leadership and Empowerment: A Social Exchange Perspective', *Human Relations*, vol. 48(2), pp. 127–46.
Kerfoot, D. and Knights, D. (1995) 'Empowering the "Quality Worker": The Seduction and Contradiction of the Total Quality Phenomenon', in A. Wilkinson and H. Willmott, *op. cit.*, pp. 219–39.
Legge, K. (1995) *Human Resource Management: Rhetorics and Realities* (London: Macmillan Press).
McCardle, L., Rowlinson, M., Proctor, S., Hussard, J. and Forrester, P. (1995) 'Total Quality Management and Participation: Employee Empowerment or the Enhancement of Exploitation?' in A. Wilkinson and H. Willmott, *op. cit.*, pp. 156–72.
Oakland, J.S. (1989) *Total Quality in Management* (Oxford: Butterworth-Heinemann).
Oliver, N. and Wilkinson, B. (1992) *The Japanisation of British Industry: New Developments in the 1990s*, 2nd edn (Oxford: Blackwell).
Parker, M. and Slaughter, J. (1995) 'Unions and Management by Stress', in S. Babson, *op. cit.*, pp. 41–53.
Quinn, J. (1996) 'The Role of "Good Conversation" in Strategic Control', *Journal of Management Studies*, vol. 33(3), pp. 381–94.
Sako, M. (1992) *Prices, Quality and Trust: Inter-firm Relations in Britain and Japan* (Cambridge: Cambridge University Press).
Sayer, A. (1986) 'New Developments in Manufacturing: The Just-in-time System', *Capital and Class*, vol. 30, pp. 43–72.
Smith, T. (1994) 'Flexible Production and the Capital Wage/Labour Relation in Manufacturing', *Capital and Class*, vol. 53, pp. 39–63.

Sternberg, E. (1994) *Just Business: Business Ethics in Action* (London: Little, Brown & Co.).
Tomaney, J. (1990) 'The Reality of Workplace Flexibility', *Capital and Class*, vol. 40, pp. 29–60.
Watson, T.J. (1994) *In Search of Management: Culture, Choice and Control in Managerial Work* (London: Routledge).
Weaver, W.G. (1997) 'Dewey or Foucault? Organisationa and Administration as Edification and as Violence', *Organization*, vol. 4(1), pp. 31–48.
Webley, S. (1995) *Use of Codes of Conduct in UK Based Organisations* (London: Institute of Business Ethics).
Wilkinson, A. and Willmott, H. (eds) (1995) *Making Quality Critical: New Perspectives on Organisational Change* (London: Routledge).
Wilkinson, A., Marchington, M., Goodman, J. and Ackers, P. (1992) 'Total Quality Management and Employee Involvement', *Human Resource Management Journal*, vol. 2(4), pp. 1–20.
Womack, J.P., Jones, D.T. and Roos, D. (1990) *The Machine That Changed the World* (New York: Macmillan).

Part I
Ethics and Empowerment: Power, Control and Autonomy

2 Empowerment and Justice
Frederick B. Bird

INTRODUCTION: FORMULATING THE QUESTION

How much say should those who work for organisations have in the organisations for which they work? How much influence should they be able to exercise over the pace and patterns of their own work, over the development of their own careers, over the direction of their organisations? Should businesses be operated like democracies? Should workers be treated like partners? These questions have been raised time and again since the beginnings of industrialisation. They are being raised again and now by the current interest in programmes that promise, among other things, to empower workers. Corporations are being counselled today to empower their workers and democratise their organisations because such changes are deemed to be both just and fair as well as good for business (Kanter, 1983, chapter 6; Lawler, 1986; Foy, 1994; Ackoff, 1994).[1]

We are concerned in this essay on the relationship between efforts to enlarge the power of organisational members and justice. Our concern can be phrased a number of ways. We can inquire, for example, about the ways in which programmes designed to 'empower' workers actually extend power, discretion and influence to workers. What kinds of powers do workers gain: do they gain power at the board level? or in their capacity to determine wages and benefits? Are workers being extended too little or too much power? Are the arrangements of organisational power fair and fitting? We can inquire as well about the extent to which programmes designed to 'empower' workers address, avoid or evade issues raised about the justice of organisations. For instance, do these programmes allow employees genuine due process rights to have their claims heard and/or adjudicated fairly? Do these programmes provide fair procedures to allow employees to participate in their own evaluations (Culbert and McDonough, 1980)? As a result of these programmes do employees receive fairer distributions of organisational rewards or greater say in how tasks, risks and rewards will be allocated? In this essay we will especially address the question of justice by analysing the impact of diverse kinds of empowerment programmes on the overall relationship of workers with their organisations.

We can best evaluate the justice and effectiveness of current 'empowerment' programmes by viewing them as one of a number of different kinds of efforts designed to enlarge the influence and say of workers within the firms in which they work. Although the term 'empowerment' has only gained currency in recent years, the ideas that workers should exercise greater power and that workplaces ought to be more democratic have been championed by advocates and reformers since the beginnings of industrialisation. For most of the past century and a half, these concerns were primarily voiced by workers themselves and organisations of workers. For example, beginning in the nineteenth century various producer co-operatives were established in which the workers were at the same time the shareholder/owners. Employees worked for plants whose policies they helped to establish through annual shareholder meetings and boards they directly elected. Employees at these plants exercised much greater power than ordinary employees at plants where they were just employees (E. Greenberg, 1982). In recent years a number of plants have been bought out or taken over by employee groups who have assumed greater responsibilities for organisational management (Gunn, 1984, chapters 3, 4, 5). Still, there have never been very many producer co-operatives. The trade union movement championed a different and much more widely supported approach to empowerment and workplace democracy. Unions have argued that employees ought to be able bargain collectively for certain rights and prerogatives that affected especially the condition, pace and rewards of their employment. Correspondingly, the power that workers held was not held individually or as work units but as members of bargaining units. Although workers often voted for their own representatives and leaders, firms were not really structured democratically. Rather firms established contractual relations with employee groups as they did with other suppliers and customers. For many years, the trade union model provided the dominant image of what was involved in 'empowering' workers. As a result of legislative initiatives, in Europe this model of empowerment was extended by stipulations that allowed and required representatives of employee groups to sit on the governing boards and executive councils of corporate organisations. A 1951 law in Germany required that half the board seats be filled by employee representatives, and this system of co-determination has been followed in various ways in other European countries (Cotton, 1993, chapter 6).

Over the years, the status of workers within firms has been enhanced as well by a number of incremental changes which offered more rights, discretion and opportunities to individual employees as well as to work units. In many areas original at-will contracts have been modified and limited by notions about seniority, tenure, fair warnings and wrongful dismissal (Werhane, 1984; Glendon, 1981, chapter 4). As a result of legislative changes and collective bargaining, workers have gained expanded rights to safe and healthy working conditions, workmen's compensation, larger and more secure and transferable pension provisions, unemployment insurance, freedom from harassment and discrimination, and minimum wages. As working members of corporate organisations, they have gained what Selznick refers to as 'constitutive rights' (Selznick, 1969).

In recent years champions of empowerment and workplace democracy have arisen especially from among several different managerial groups. A number of people have addressed these issues indirectly by raising concerns about the justice of organisations (Sheppard, Lewicki and Minton, 1992). They have argued that businesses are much more likely to experience disruptions, shrinkage and lower productivity if workers feel they are being treated unfairly. Moreover, these observers add that workers' sense of whether they are being treated fairly is more decisively influenced by whether the procedures used are deemed to be just than by actual outcomes. If workers feel they can voice their concerns to people who seriously listen and consider their positions, they are likely to feel justly treated even when they often do not receive exactly what they initially hoped for. Citing this data, observers have advocated that firms ought to provide employees with greater say in processes directly bearing upon their work and adjudications of their claims (J. Greenberg, 1996; Ewing, 1989). Although these advocates of organisational justice have not directly championed worker empowerment, they have argued for increase involvement of workers in deliberations bearing upon the character, evaluation and rewards of their work.

Over the past several decades both worker empowerment and some forms of workplace democracy have been championed as integral elements of schemes designed to re-organise corporate organisations to make them both better places to work and more competitive. Although these schemes bear quite different names and originated from different places and philosophies, they share both a common concern to enhance the quality of organisational workmanship and a common assumption that the fitting social organisation of work was as important for productivity as the fitting use of technological resources. Quality of Work Life (QWL) programmes, like total quality management (TQM) and continuous quality improvement (CQI), have all assumed that corporations would perform better if work units had greater power to determine their tasks and how they ought to be done, and workers were more directly involved in these deliberations (Cotton, 1993, chapters 3, 7, 8). Job enrichment programmes and quality circles have been introduced for similar reasons (Lawler, 1986, chapters 4, 6, 7, 8). Used in connection with these kinds of programmes, the term 'empowerment' identifies a range of management strategies to increase organisational effectiveness through greater worker participation (see Kaler, 1996; Christensen Hughes, 1996; Goodwin, 1996).

Finally, a number of businesses have sought to extend greater power to workers by developing some form of profit-sharing schemes that allowed employees to buy or earn shares as a contractual right of their employment. Employee stock-ownership programmes assume several forms but all remunerate workers in part through earnings or shares they gain ownership of by virtue of their employment. As a result, individual workers gain marginal influence as shareholders and opportunities for additional compensation beyond their wages and salaries. Hundreds of companies have now developed some form of employee stock-ownership plan (Blasi, 1988; Lawler, 1986, chapter 9).

As this brief historical survey indicates, the terms 'empowerment' and 'workplace democracy' have been and can be used to identify a wide variety of conditions. There has not been, nor is there now any recognised consensus on what these terms mean. To be sure, these terms have been used generally to describe organisational arrangements which augment the influence and discretion of workers and increase their participation in some forms of organisational decision-making. There is, however, no acknowledged agreement either with respect to the specific types of powers which ought to be enhanced and/or with regard to whether this enhancement ought to be extended to individual workers, work units, worker organisations, or employees as a group.

Given this diversity of practice and opinion, we can then re-phrase our basic question: namely, what forms of the 'empowerment' of workers seem to be fair as well as fitting both for the workers themselves and for the organisations for which they work?

We assume that systems of empowerment or workplace democracy are just only if they are fair and fitting both for workers and for the organisations which hire them. However, having made this assumption we still need to determine what forms and degrees of power we have in mind and whether these powers are exercised by individuals, work units or workforces. The point of this essay is to raise and address this question regarding the fair and fitting allocation of powers to workers. Although we are raising a question that is clearly theoretical, we will address this question not abstractly but practically. We will review a number of cases and reflect on what we can learn from these examples. In the end, we will examine and defend a number of practical guidelines which emerge from this analysis. However, before we can undertake these case studies, we need to establish several points of reference for distinguishing between different forms and degrees of power which workers may exercise.

TYPES, DEGREES AND AGENTS OF POWER

Types of power

The powers exercised by workers and/or extended to them by various kinds of empowerment programmes may assume at least five different forms, which we name as: personal powers, task powers, contractual powers, adjudicatory powers, and governance powers. With respect to each of these forms of power, workers may also assume varying degrees of influence. Since the increased power which empowerment programmes are designed to augment may vary in both form and degree, the term 'empowerment' may be used with a considerably wide range of meanings. Unless we are clear about the types and degrees of power we have in mind, the term 'empowerment' is likely to be used carelessly and rhetorically without clear and specific references.

By power we identify the capacity to bring about desired results even in the face of possible resistance (Weber, 1978, p. 53). This capacity may arise and grow as a result of a number of factors including access to wealth, the possession of valued technical know-how, the support of others, the exercise or threatened exercise of force, the ability to persuade, as well as many other factors (Bird and Gandz, 1990, chapter 7; Pfeffer and Salancik, 1978). Often power is characterised in relation to these sources (see Lukes, 1974). In this chapter we are instead interested in describing forms of power in relation to how this capacity is exercised or utilised by people who work for organisations. By 'forms of power' we identify distinguishably different practical uses of this capacity within organisations, regardless of the source. We use the phrase 'degrees of power' to discuss comparatively the extent of power possessed by any person or group compared to that possessed by others. It is important always to discuss degrees of power comparatively in relation to specific actors rather than abstractly. There are no absolute measures of power. Rather, whenever we are referring to greater or lesser power, we are either explicitly or implicitly making relative comparisons or invoking standards by which these comparisons might be made. We will discuss this issue regarding measures of power further on in this section. In the meantime we can observe that one of the problems with the popular use of the term 'empowerment' is that it is typically used vaguely to describe an indeterminant increase in the degree of some not clearly specified form of power.

Personal powers

By personal powers we identify personal capacities which individuals can exercise as a result of either skills they have developed or opportunities provided for them. These especially include capacities to manage one's own life and to further one's own career (Simon, 1990). Personal powers identify in particular a person's ability to develop and use his or her intelligence, wit, strength, character and charm to augment their lives (Spinoza, 1930, part III; Hobbes, 1968, Book I, chapter 10). Employees often feel personally empowered, for example, as they are able to acquire and perfect a number of skills which make them both more marketable and useful to their organisations. These may be technical skills, computer skills, linguistic competencies, interpersonal abilities, and so forth. They also feel empowered by their abilities to act in ways that increase their opportunities to advance their careers by promotions, transfers and other means. The need for greater personal power has been championed by those critics who have been especially concerned at the ways the organisation of work often leaves low and medium-skilled employees with little or no opportunities to improve upon their circumstances. They express dismay for those who work in dead-end jobs and have little time or no means to take training programmes to upgrade their skills.

Task powers

These powers identify the abilities and opportunities directly to influence and shape the character, scope, conditions and pace of work. How much discretion is actually extended either to individual workers or work units to manage these kinds of responsibilities? To what degree can these units assume responsibilities for dividing up tasks, delegating jobs and determining the conditions and pace of work? To what degree can they rotate through jobs, enlarge and enrich assignments, and take on ancillary tasks like purchasing, auditing and quality assurance often handled by outside staff positions? A number of people have advocated increased task powers for workers as an antidote for the ways job assignments often reduce work to boring, routine and mindless tasks. Overly-simplified tasks have the effect of deskilling workers. Overall the consequence leads to what Braverman describes as 'the degradation of work' (Braverman, 1974). In response to these conditions, a number of critics have begun developing job enlargement and enrichment programmes as well as opportunities to rotate through several different kinds of assignments, thus adding greater variety and challenge to their work (Cotton, 1993, chapter 7; Lawler, 1986, chapter 6). Often in practice the critical element in task powers is the degree to which workers are authorised to make decisions regarding the performance of their work without having to seek approval from superiors.

Contractual powers

These powers point to the capacity of workers to determine the basic conditions that affect the status of their employment. Fundamentally, contractual powers identify the abilities to establish contractual relations free from coercive or manipulative forces. These include the capacities to have some say in establishing the terms of contract, to freely choose to accept or not to accept these terms, to bargain for changes in these terms, to evaluate how well these terms are being honoured, and to make complaints and have these complaints seriously heard if people feel these terms are not being honoured. Contractual powers include most importantly the ability to determine rates and forms of compensations, including wages and other benefits, lengths of contracts, as well as conditions for their renewal. Contractual powers incorporate as well the abilities to affect how people are evaluated and rewarded on the basis of these contractual understandings. To what degree are workers either individually, as work units or as professional or trade unions groups able to voice their concerns, bargain, and/or enter into deliberations which determine these matters? Contractual powers have especially been the focus of trade union negotiations.

Adjudicatory powers

These are related to but slightly different from contractual powers. Or, rather, they represent a specific contractual power, namely the capacity to raise complaints and to defend oneself against complaints made by others. These powers may assume several forms, including the discretion to resolve conflicts and complaints by those involved, the capacity to receive fair hearings, and the ability to review questionable

48   Empowerment and Justice

judgements through some form of due process or natural justice (Ewing, 1989). Although many businesses with unionised workforces often have developed standardised grievance procedures to handle these kinds of issues, most other plants have institutionalised few such adjudicatory processes (Saunders and Leck, 1992).

Governance powers

These powers describe the abilities to govern organisations either directly or through identifiable representatives. Broadly stated, these are the powers to establish policies, to develop organisational strategies, to set budgets, to apportion resources among units and functions within organisations, and to appoint administrators to direct organisations. These powers are clearly exercised by boards of directors. They are also exercised by any groups or individuals who can measurably influence how boards act, whether these be major shareholders, major creditors, executives, or specific organised constituencies. These powers are exercised also in less overt forms by any individuals, groups or units who in measurable ways are able to influence policies, strategies, budgets, apportionments and appointments. Sometimes divisions or units are delegated these powers within specified parameters (Ackoff, 1994). To the degree that work units actually exercise budgetary, policy and apportioning powers, they are in practice helping to govern those sectors of their organisations over which they have been delegated jurisdiction. To the extent the corporations treat different units as value or profit centres, they necessarily extend to them some of these powers (Halal, 1993). Still, while units and divisions are often extended some of these powers, their discretion often remains fairly tightly circumscribed by budgetary constraints and fiscal controls (Ackermam, 1975). Ownership often provides a basis for exercising governance powers even though extensive power over budgets, policies and strategies may be exerted by parties which possess no formal ownership claims.

Those who formally exercise governance power thereby hold positions of organisational authority. They occupy positions which possess the acknowledged prerogative to make decisions within specified guidelines which are binding over others within their jurisdiction. We can re-state this point by saying they possess the legitimate power to authorise certain kinds of organisational policies.

These then represent five quite different forms of power which employees may exercise. Empowerment programs may in varying degrees augment the power of workers in one or more of these forms.

Degrees of power

Although people readily talk of having, getting, exercising and losing power, they are often notoriously vague about the degrees or extent of power they have in mind. Unlike wealth and energy, for which some agreed-upon objective measures exist, there is little consensus about the appropriate increments by which to gauge power. However, without some sense of measure, discussions about increasing or decreasing degrees of power are likely to become very impressionistic. In the paragraphs that follow we propose a rough scheme for approximately calibrating different degrees of power.

Power can only be measured in relation to the realisation of particular objectives or sets of objectives. For example, we can estimate degrees of power both broadly with respect to the governance of an organisation or more specifically with respect to the capacity to gain higher wages for employees. It is too narrow to argue, as Dahl has, that power can only be gauged in relation to specific decisions (Dahl, 1961). After all, power is sometimes most influentially asserted so that certain policies and practices never find their way on the agendas of deliberative bodies: they are tacitly accepted as legitimate without discussion or debate. Even here power is gauged by the capacity to preserve without overt opposition specific policies and practices. While power in these kinds of cases is often unobtrusive (Lukes, 1974; Hardy, 1985), its strength is still measured by the capacity to realise identifiable objectives. We can obviously measure degrees of power wielded over time by different but regularly interacting parties, such as corporate managers and trade unions or small, independent suppliers and the large corporations who buy most of their products. In each case we must gauge degrees of power not globally but in relation to objectives or sets of objectives because of the difference in character of these objectives. For example, it is very difficult to make meaningful comparisons between degrees of personal, task, contractual, adjudicatory and governance power. To be sure, there are often ways in which the ability to exercise significant degrees of one kind of power, such as governance power, in turn can influence the ability to exercise other forms of power, such as contractual power. However, these transfers of power from one form to another are not automatic and cannot be assumed. Personal power may not occasion or augment contractual power. Task power may have little impact on personal or governance power. Still, in certain settings, being able to exercise one form of power can make it easier to exercise another. Because this is possible but not automatically the case, we need to examine structures and conditions which can both facilitate and limit these kinds of transfers.

We have defined power as the capacity to realise valued objectives even in the face of possible resistance. The inability to attain valued objectives may occur both because it is impossible to meet, limit, neutralise or overcome whoever or whatever may oppose our efforts or because we are unable in the first place to mobilise in enough strength the resources we expect to draw upon for this effort. Sometimes people are able to work at realising their objectives without having to meet and overcome any resistance. The oft-cited distinction between 'power to' and 'power over' is related in large part to the presence of some form of resistance. Some observers use these terms to distinguish between two different kinds of power, the first being more consensual and the second being more authoritarian (Ackoff, 1994). However, this interpretation is too limited. Fundamentally 'power to' refers to the capacity to realise objectives whether resistance must be confronted and managed or not. 'Power over' refers to the capacity to limit and overcome resistance. Resistance can assume quite varied forms. It may occur in the form of groups who are organised to oppose the objectives which a party seeks to realise. It may assume the form of people who do not wish to co-operate and have to be forced, persuaded, cajoled, bribed, honestly rewarded and/or tricked into doing so. Resistance may also manifest itself as ignorance which has to be overcome, timidity which must be risen above, and wishy-washy divided states of mind which must be integrated. In all these instances people possess 'power to' realise their objectives not only on the basis of the resources they are able to bring to bear, but also of their 'power over' factors that resist this realisation. 'Power over' refers to the capacity to limit, overcome and/or neutralise factors which resist the fulfilment of their objectives. Such power need not assume authoritarian traits. The 'power to' realise objectives can be diminished not only by resistance in one or more of several forms but also by the attenuation of the resources which parties draw upon to assert power. For example, power may be reduced by the decrease in personal energy, by a falling off of moral support and/or by legal and social changes that alter the access to sources of power.

The amount of power which may be exercised in relation to particular objectives is not necessarily fixed and limited. This statement is valid for any of the forms of power we have been describing. As they develop their skills, augment their resources and cultivate their connections, workers can often exercise more personal, task, contractual and governance powers without at the same time appreciably reducing the powers of any other party. Often, as workers gain task powers through self-managing teams, management at the same time enhance their effective capacity to realise their objectives measured by higher levels of quality in the goods and services produced as well as higher levels of productivity (Cotton, 1993, chapter 8). In many settings, to be sure, there are contests over who will be able to exercise how much power. Often, as one party gains influence, others lose it. These kind of exchanges in which the total power available seems to be fixed are not typical. They arise usually when parties become especially combative and when parties are vying for the authority to exercise specific controls. As we will observe in the cases discussed further on in this chapter, with several noticeable exceptions, empowering workers does not necessarily occasion the disempowerment of any other parties.

For heuristic purposes, we will identify six different degrees of power, which we name as follows:

1. scant power,
2. marginal power,
3. consultative power,
4. co-determinate power,
5. effective power, and
6. total power.

We will describe the differences of each degree briefly and in ways that are applicable for all of the five forms of power which we have been discussing.

People possess *scant power* when they are able to exert no appreciable influence on realising their objectives. Whether this situation arises because of their own lack of skills, knowhow, connections or wealth or because others control and dominate them, they are effectively powerless with respects to objectives they seek. Unable to affect improvements in their work conditions, in their contractual relations, or even in their own careers as organisational members, they feel they are in a position either to submit to circumstances they do not like or to leave (Hirschmann, 1970). This discretionary ability to quit, however, is rarely experienced as a positive power. It is not a means of gaining the objectives one sought as a member of the organisation, it is simply the capacity to seek to realise these objectives elsewhere.

People possess *marginal power* to the degree they can exercise some modest but not really decisive influence in realising their objectives. Marginal power typically assumes the form of the ability to voice one's concerns and to receive an attentive hearing from others involved. It is the power of electorates to vote. Those who possess marginal power can neither determine nor necessarily shape outcomes or the choice of agendas on which they vote. Others who exercise effective power may take their interests and their voiced concerns into account. But these interests and concerns may also be ignored. Still, those who possess marginal power have the capacity to adjust and modify their circumstances in modest ways. They often work to make the best of conditions which they did not choose but they cannot appreciably alter. Marginal power allows them to act in little but significant ways to redefine given circumstances in their own lights rather than passively submitting to the definitions imposed by others.

Those who possess *consultative power* are able in significant measure to attain or shape their valued objectives. They exercise enough influence, skill, economic resources, and/or support from others that they can either partially realise their goals or at least affect in part how these outcomes turn out. Within organisational or political settings, those with consultative power are able to insist their interests and views be incorporated in whatever actions are taken. They are able to exercise what Galbraith described as 'countervailing power' and what others have referred as veto powers (Galbraith, 1954; Banfield, 1961, chapter 11). Recognised trade unions exercise consultative power with respect to corporate organisations as do faculty associations within universities. Consultative power is the kind of influence exercised by well-recognised and protected minorities.

Co-determinate power is greater. It is the kind of influence exercised by minority governments or partners. Those with co-determinate power can often significantly shape outcomes. They can realise much of what they set out to achieve. They are, however, limited in what they can accomplish. Because of their own lack of greater resources, skills and connections, because of the resistance they face and/or because of comparably greater influence exercised by others, they usually succeed in realising some objectives by compromising others. Or they modify their objectives recognising this resistance and/or opposition. Co-determinate power still remains comparably weighty and influential. In many organisational settings in which multiple interests are at play, co-determinative power is often as influential and as capable as any party or person can hope to be. Trade unions in North America rarely exercise this much power with regard to governance, although they do sometimes with respect to contractual powers. In Europe, trade unions are often represented in equal numbers on boards and as a consequence often exercise something close to co-determinate degrees of governance power.

Effective power is like majority power: it represents the capacity to determine outcomes even when others oppose these objectives. It represents the ability to pursue one's career successfully in the face of opposition from friends, family or competitors. It represents the ability to determine the character and pace of tasks even though others push for alternatives. Because they possess sufficient resources, competencies, votes and connections, and/or because others can exert less effective power, such people can establish policies and determine courses of action even when others oppose them. However, effective power is not unlimited power. Those who possess effective power must take account of others who oppose them or resist their projects, and who correspondingly exercise some degrees of marginal, consultative or co-determinate power. Often, in order to reduce resistance and thereby augment their capacity to realise their goals, those with effective power offer compromises and consolations to gain the neutrality, if not tacit support, of those who oppose or resist them. In fact if they do not do so, they may lose the effectiveness of their power over time. This is because in constantly having to face and overcome opposition and resistance they must correspondingly divert resources from their ultimate objectives to these efforts, leaving, as a consequence, fewer resources to direct toward their goals.

When people possess *total power*, they are able to realise their objectives without having to take account of any form of effective opposition or resistance. They can dictate terms with respect to the objectives they seek. They can act autocratically like dictators, at least with regard to the objectives over which they exercise this influence; they are able to dominate what takes place.

This model of six degrees of power provides a standardised reference for roughly measuring degrees of power in the realisation of specific objectives. When we are attempting to gauge the power possessed by particular persons, parties or groups, then we must add two other considerations: namely, over what duration are they exercising power and what is the scope of the objectives over which they possess or do not possess power?

The ability to exercise power in whatever degrees may be persistent or episodic. With regard to a specific objective or set of objectives, individuals or groups may regularly exercise approximately the same amount of power, or their ability to exert power may be irregular and erratic. The ability to influence others, to realise goals or to overcome opposition often increases and then recedes. Obviously, those interested in empowering workers seek to augment specific forms of employee power on a sustained, regular basis.

Often the range of objectives over which we can wield significant degrees of power is limited and small. In contrast, what distinguishes a totalitarian government or authority is its ability on a sustained basis to exercise autocratic power over a very wide range of activities. Its power is not only autocratic – in the sense that it can get its way with little or no appreciable opposition – but also that it is able to do so with regard to such a wide range of human concerns. Totalitarian regimes leave few zones of indifference in which individuals might exercise personal or task powers.

People may possess different degrees of quite different forms of power on a sustained or irregular basis. Empowerment programmes refer to organisational policies or activities designed to augment on a sustained basis the degrees of powers which workers exercise with respect to one of several typical objectives. As we critically examine empowerment programmes, we need to ask not only what forms of power workers are gaining, but also how much increase in degrees of power is involved. We also need to ask a third type of question: namely, to workers identified with what status is this power being extended?

Agents of power

If workers are to be empowered, then it makes a considerable difference if power is to be exercised by individuals, small work groups, labour or professional organisations acting as representatives of workers, large departments, or the workforce as a whole and/or its chosen representatives. Who precisely are expected to be the agents of power? Power may be exercised by workers in a number of different guises. Policies that strengthen the influence of workers in so far as they act collectively through their unions may decrease the influence they are able to exercise as specific individuals. The critical issue turns on which particular constituencies workers are viewed as being members of. Are they viewed as being individual employees of the organisation, as members of work unit teams, as colleagues within departments, as constituents of professional or trade associations, or as individual shareholder/employees? Workers may recognise themselves as being at once members of several different kinds of constituencies: an employee, a colleague, a member of a work unit, and a trade unionist. Furthermore, s/he is likely to exercise both different forms and degrees of power insofar as s/he acts in relation to one or another of these roles or statuses.

It is important to make these observations, even though they may seem comparatively obvious, because empowerment programmes differ decisively in terms of the constituencies towards which they are directed. The workforce as a whole, as employee-owners, are the objects of empowerment in producer co-operatives. Quality management programmes extend power both to workers as members of work units, and to individual employees as students in various training programmes. The programme management policies of University Hospital (to be described later) extended power to newly formed medical care units as collegially-managed departments. These several different empowerment programmes thus differ not only by focusing on different forms of power, but also on different assortments of constituencies.

CASES

In the paragraphs below I examine several cases for illustrative purposes. With the exception of the first example, these cases are based upon our own field research.

Producer cooperatives in the plywood industry

A number of plants in the plywood industry in North America have been organised as producer co-operatives, and in 1982 a dozen plants in Washington, Oregon and British Columbia represented about 10 per cent of the industry. Each employs from about 150 to 300 workers. These producer co-operatives were established with several guiding principles. The owners are all workers who own shares or share units, and each owner-worker has one vote in two semi-annual meetings, which legally govern these plants. These meetings establish or confirm basic policies and business decisions and elect from their midst boards of directors, who in turn meet bi-weekly. Owner-workers are kept well-informed regarding the activities of their boards and frequently and actively discuss board decisions and developments. All workers receive the same hourly pay no matter what their skill level or status. They also receive dividends as recommended by the board and ratified by the semi-annual membership meetings. Each producer co-operative hires a number of non-member employees who are usually assigned to a number of specified tasks, including managerial jobs, office work, ancillary off-site operations, and contract technical work. Frequently new hires remain non-shareholders during a probationary people and until they can raise enough money to buy a share, which often costs over $10000 (Greenberg, 1982; Gunn, 1984, chapter 4).

Worker-owners genuinely like working for these co-ops. They like the pay, the guaranteed work and working conditions. They possess a strong sense of collective responsibility, and compared to plywood workers at non co-op sites they are more willing to cooperate on projects at work. They develop good communications with their supervisors, and overall they feel they work for businesses which they own.

Still, the shopfloor organisation of work is just like that in non-co-op plants. Work units are not collegial, self-managing groups. The pace and character of work is the same as at non-co-op sites; although the rate of accidents is slightly higher. The attitude towards supervisors is not appreciably different. Workers do not demonstrate noticeable camaraderie either at work or off site, and working at these plants is associated with no philosophical or ideological commitment (Greenberg, 1982).

The worker-owners are empowered, quite strongly, in several ways. In these small to medium-sized businesses they exercise effective governance power. They own and they establish the basic guidelines for the companies for which they work, both directly through semi-annual membership meetings and indirectly through the board which they elect. As worker-owners they possess a significant measure of contractual power. Once they have passed through their probationary periods, as worker owners they are in position to effect pay and dividend levels. However, they have little impact on how their work is evaluated. There are few incentives to engage in such performance appraisals since all workers receive the same pay rates and possess equal votes. These plants are radically egalitarian in this sense: all owner-workers are of equal status; no one enjoys more seniority and there are no higher positions for which people might compete; everyone's vote is equal. In other organisations hierarchical work arrangements are often unfair and rigid. They often *de facto* dis-empower, especially newer and less-skilled workers whose opportunities for advancement are blocked and/or whose current compensations are disproportionately small compared to those higher up. In contrast, these producer cooperatives neither block the chances of these workers to move to other positions nor undercompensate them.

These plywood cooperatives do not, however, extend to workers any greater personal, task, or adjudicatory power. In a fundamental sense, the governance power they exercise is as owners of shares rather than as workers. Non-shareholding employees continue to work for these cooperatives, and many of the supervisors are hired on this basis. No attempts have been made to democratise the work processes. Commenting on these characteristics, one observer described these co-operatives as 'egalitarian (for owner-members) capitalist partnerships' rather than worker self-managing enterprises (Gunn, 1984, p. 129).

A greenfield site

In the late 1970s company J decided to construct a new manufacturing plant near Chester, a small mid-western town which was mid-way between and about an hour and a half drive from the state capital and from the state's largest city. Company J decided to install at this site the latest, most advanced technology. The plant was to operate around the clock. Correspondingly, the eventual workforce was to be composed disproportionately of highly-skilled engineers, technicians, managers and accountants with few low-skilled and unskilled positions in maintenance, warehousing and site-services. At the outset, management determined that in so far as possible work on site was to be conducted through self-managing teams. Hence, with only a dozen managers and engineers thus far on its pay-roll and before any other employees were hired, the company hired a consultant named Roger Davies to help them design and establish the social organisation of their workforce.

Recognising that most of the workers at the plant were likely to be middle-class employees, Davies felt that the social organisation of the company ought to resemble something more like a middle-class home than a construction site. He sought to design working arrangements that elicited strong, active commitment from the workers, and several principles guided working arrangements at this site.

- First, most of the work was done by self-managing teams. Team members exercised many of the responsibilities normally assumed by supervisors and staff. They took responsibility for scheduling work and vacations, managed budgets allocated for their units, and negotiated with outsider contractors and suppliers. At night and on weekends they made their own decisions regarding operations. Teams often took great pride in their own accomplishments, and one team boasted about how they saved $6000 by negotiating with a local supplier rather than working through the company's central purchasing offices. A number of teams pointed to innovations they had introduced which had increased both the efficiency and productivity of the plant. Within a few years of its opening, the plant was far outproducing several competitor plants which were built even later using practically the same technology. In most cases these teams were guided by managers who served as nominal supervisors but acted more like coaches or facilitators. Over time these managers gained in their ability to delegate and not attempt to solve problems by themselves as they arose. In several cases this position was rotated among team members.

- Second, tasks were rotated among team members, and over time as teams discovered that their members were not all equally qualified to undertake all tasks assigned to them, the system of rotation was modified to allow people to rotate through those tasks for which they were both most qualified and most interested. As a result of these two principles, the range of tasks which workers performed was much broader and more diverse at this plant site than at other sites which company J operated.
- Third, the plant operated on the principle that 'if you see a problem, then it is yours'. This phrase was cited repeatedly like a motto or slogan and implied several things. People cited it to argue that workers did not have to ask permission from others in order to do any number of things which they judged to be in their own and in the company's best interests. They could and should take the initiative themselves, making on-the-spot decisions about the quality of products and discarding what they judged to be not up to standard. They could, in an often-cited example, decide to take time off if they were not feeling well or if there was a family crisis. As one senior manager noted: workers were to be treated as adults capable of acting independently and responsibly. At the same time, this slogan was invoked as a way of saying that every person was accountable for how well the plant worked. 'If you see ice on the road and there is no sand spread over it', one manager observed, 'then you are responsible either for getting the sand or finding someone else to do it and finding out why sand had not yet been spread over the ice'. One might expect that this slogan would lead a number of workers to become selectively blind so that they would not have to assume responsibility for problems they felt belonged to others. However, the consequences were the opposite. Employees were praised for seeing problems, managing them by themselves insofar as they could, or calling attention to them and seeking help from others when they could not.
- Four, the plant used a battery of psychological tests to screen potential employees. The original consultant, Davies, who devised or

selected these tests, argued that they served as a means of identifying people who were genuinely capable of working in teams; people capable of assuming independent responsibility, of 'standing on their own two feet', in Davies' words. They were also designed to identify people capable of caring about their co-workers and working collaboratively.

- Five, everyone hired at the Chester plant was initially required to participate in a six-day training programme (which was later reduced to three days a number of years later), especially designed to help people develop their communications skills. The focus was on learning how to handle interpersonal interactions well. The programme helped people learn how to listen to others better, how to raise problems more directly, and how to address and resolve conflicts. Workers at the Chester plant frequently joked about this emphasis on conflict resolution. Still, as a consequence of this training programme, workers became used to confronting each other directly but diplomatically when their performances were less than expected. Co-workers were confronted about sloppy dress, poor quality in their written reports, scheduling problems and the like.

After a decade the level of worker satisfaction at the Chester plant was extremely high, much higher than at any other site operated by company J. The plant had undergone two additional expansions bringing its total workforce to over 700 employees. There had been very little turnover and few requests for transfer in spite of the fact that the plant was located near neither of the two major cities in the state. One potential problem never really surfaced: this was the issue of how to reward workers for high achievements. One typical way of rewarding achievers is to offer them opportunities for advancement or promotion, but in flat organisations for which people continue to like to work these are few opportunities for advancement. At Chester the plant hierarchy remained remarkably flat, and since few managers left these were few opportunities to promote highly achieving workers. In such situations companies often offer other rewards, but this plant had few alternative rewards to extend. For example, there were no stock-option plans to allow workers to benefit from the overall growth of the business during these years of expansion. To be sure, salaries grew faster than inflation but provided little extra benefits. Fortunately, this potential dilemma never really arose at Chester for two reasons: one, the plant expanded twice thus creating new managerial positions which were filled by highly-achieving insiders; and two, company J acquired other sites to which they transferred successful managers from Chester, thus freeing managerial positions at Chester to which other, highly-achieving workers could advance.

Of the several different forms of power, the programmes at Chester especially allowed workers, within limits, to exercise greater task power. Through their work units they were able to shape the pace, character and scheduling of tasks to which their units were assigned. They also gained access to greater personal power in two ways. Through the training programmes, and their subsequent implementation in their work units, many developed their communication skills and the ability to adapt to changing circumstances. They were able to draw upon these competencies both to put themselves forward for advancements and to qualify for these promotions. Because they were able to exercise these social skills well, employees collaborated together in ways that had a professional aura that stood these workers well in their own efforts to advance their careers. Workers also gained personal power as patterns of job rotations and alteration both exposed them to a wider range of tasks but also allowed them to develop competency in performing these jobs. The slogan that workers ought to assume responsibility for problems they saw reinforced the sense that employees both could and were expected to develop their abilities to address issues and solve problems or to call upon or direct others to do so. In these several ways, work arrangements at Chester allowed employees to cultivate greater repertoires of competencies, as well as the firm confidence that they could indeed develop these skills better than they would have been able working at other sites. Given real opportunities for advancement within the company as a whole, efforts to cultivate these skills seemed sensible and worthwhile.

Arrangements at Chester extended workers' limited contractual power. Through their units they were able to exercise some influence on how performances were evaluated and which workers were put forward for promotions. They enjoyed practically no governance powers but modest adjudicatory powers. Over the years, workers at Chester developed genuine competency in informal conflict resolutions. As a result, it was fairly easy to raise complaints and get them considered by members of collegial units, and conflicts were often resolved quickly and simply. In some cases, though, conflicts required more time. Respondents described one case where a team met for over 13 hours as they worked through complaints about one member who had been performing below expectations.

Workers at Chester were almost unanimously enthusiastic about their work arrangements. The task and personal powers they exercised enabled them to work not only with the sense that they could effect noteworthy accomplishments both for the organisation and on their own behalf, but also that they could and should exercise reasonable discretion both about how they worked and how they pursued their own careers. We heard only a couple of muted critical questions. One concerned the powers of departments to contract for external supplies and services: we heard a number of stories voiced by those directly involved about how the decentralising of purchasing decisions had effected economies for the company. Decentralising also permitted departments to foster ongoing relationships with specially favoured contractors and suppliers. Almost everyone involved recognized the dangers involved in these practices but felt that most people acted responsibly. They noted as well that abuses under decentralised purchasing policies were likely to be limited just because they were bound to be smaller than when connected with corporate-wide purchasing. Still, respondents named several questionable decisions in which quality or price were thought to be compromised. However, they also assumed that these kinds of problems were integral to the overall working arrangements at Chester, which they warmly applauded.

The other critical comment concerned the lack of minorities in the workforce at Chester. Compared to other sites within company J, Chester hired fewer visible minorities and experienced difficulty in retaining the ones they did hire. This fact concerned the people in human resources at Chester, who felt that cultural differences between minorities and other workers was central to this problem, either because minority workers had difficulty adjusting to the working milieu or because this milieu in turn was not tolerant enough of alternative senses of time and work. In at least two ways this problem was not incidental or accidental at Chester. The organisation of work was based on the assumption that workers could co-operate best if they shared common values. Applicants were tested to see if they possessed attitudes and value commitments likely to render them good colleagues, and the training programmes were further designed to introduce and reinforce common values. With such a strong emphasis on value congruence, it is not surprising that minorities who might not fully share these values would less frequently be hired and would be more prone to leave if they felt their own values were not fully appreciated and respected.

Quality management in the 1990s

By the time the 1990s began, company J had grown measurably, largely through a number of acquisitions. As a result it possessed manufacturing plants in a number of different states as well as in several Canadian provinces, with approximately 5000 employees. A new chief executive officer, who had previously managed a competitor company in the same industry, had recently assumed command. Within a short period he initiated a number of programmes and policies, including more active pursuit of international markets as well as much greater involvement in developing international sites. Some of these policies promised, along with a number of other objectives, to increase the empowerment of workers, and in one way or another were all quality management programmes.

Company J overtly embraced a number of ideas associated with quality management. These included greater attention to customer satisfaction, a leadership style that emphasised working with people rather than commanding them, as well as what they referred to as employee empowerment. By the latter phrase they signified that they permitted and expected employees to take on more responsibilities including some tasks previously undertaken by staff. At the same time the company introduced an overlapping programme called 'Organisational Effectiveness'. OE involved an emphasis on discovering simpler more effective business processes, a set of training programmes dedicated to improving communication skills among managers and workers, as well as a mandate to explore ways of enlarging and enriching work assignment by sharing and rotating tasks. These several initiatives were launched at the same time as a policy calling for all managers to review their responsibilities and to develop plans to manage their work by establishing realisable, practical objectives. As a result of these several developments, company J was abuzz with voiced concerns about continuously improving the quality of workmanship, finding ways to simplify business processes, working to develop shared leadership, and empowering workers. It was clear that the company wanted to find better, more effective and more efficient ways of realising their objectives and utilising their resources, and that finding fitting ways of extending greater power to employees was viewed as integral to this process.

These several overlapping initiatives were associated with three developments: organisational changes involving both the flattening of hierarchies and the creation of self-managing teams, the development of a range of training programmes, and the active, shared search for more effective ways of doing their business.

Organisational changes involved restructuring to reduce the managerial levels between the top and the bottom of the organisation, and the transformation of most lower level work units to operate more like self-managing teams. Both of these changes involved eliminating a number of lower level managerial positions but not usually those of immediate supervisors. Work units were expected to collaborate together like colleagues, to rotate tasks among themselves, and to assume several managerial or staff assignments. Each unit was expected to assign among its members four co-ordinating responsibilities: for quality assurance, safety and health, training, and administrative management. The latter especially included scheduling and negotiating with other internal or external suppliers or contractors. While in many instances existing units were reorganised along these lines, in some cases largely isolated positions were grouped together to form collegial units. In one case, several secretaries and receptionists working on different floors were grouped together in ways that allowed them more easily to substitute for each other and to alternate selected tasks. At the same time, additional responsibilities were added so that the receptionist, for example, also became responsible for scheduling the use of fleet vehicles and for arranging teleconferencing. As a result of these changes, employees assumed responsibility for a wider range of tasks, worked with others more like colleagues, and exercised a limited number of staff and administrative duties. As team members directly became the local spokespersons for health, safety and quality concerns, the overt interest in and ownership by employees about these matters markedly increased. Likewise, because the responsibility for scheduling became their own, members of units often became more co-operative in addressing these issues in mutually beneficial ways.

At the same time company J launched a number of different training programmes. A few lasted only a couple of hours; several took place over two or three days. The facilitators' training programme lasted 18 days. Some were brief workshops designed mainly to acquaint employees with these several programmes and to gain their support. The director of OE was continually running what he described as awareness workshops. One training programme was targeted to cultivate facilitation skills for supervisors and employees who would subsequently assume responsibility for helping to build and organise teams out of existing or newly-formed work units. Other workshops focused on developing better communication and conflict-resolution skills. These workshops, which taught employees how to give and receive feedback, how to assert claims and deal with conflicts, and how to run meetings, were given throughout the company at all of its more than a dozen manufacturing sites. Courses were also offered on more specific topics such as 'shared leadership', 'career planning', and 'increasing human effectiveness'.

One administrative assistant talked about how she had especially benefitted from the latter course. It helped her, she said, in learning how to set identifiable goals and to work to realise them. It had encouraged her 'to stretch' and 'to take risks'. She felt that she had not only benefitted from this course at work, but had found ways to use what she learned to improve her interactions with her teenage children.

At the same time as these organisational changes were being introduced and the training programmes were being initiated, company J made a concerted effort to encourage its managers and other employees to think about how they could do their work better. They were called upon both to analyse what was going on – to look at 'what is' – and to imagine more effective ways of performing what had to be done – to think about the 'to be'. There was talk of simplifying business processes, of new alignments, and of contracting with external suppliers tasks best performed by others. This emphasis on organisational self-analysis and re-imagining was connected with efforts to foster what was referred to as 'self management by objectives'. Each part of the business was to establish clear objectives after first analysing their strengths, weaknesses, opportunities and threats. What is impressive about these efforts at organisational re-thinking was the degree to which the company urged its workforce in general to get involved in the process collegially both through their work units and between superiors and subordinates. They used the phrase 'development dialogue' to refer to the efforts especially designed to foster the communications between levels of the organisation.

These several different programmes and policies produced a number of benefits viewed broadly from the perspective of employee empowerment and enhanced corporate performance. Employees generally liked arrangements that rendered their jobs more varied and challenging. Workers generally enjoyed working more collaboratively. They were more willing to trade off tasks and to cover for each other. Many workers felt that they had individually benefitted from learning better communication skills. Much more work was now being performed by semi-self-managing, collegially organised work units. Through these units, workers enjoyed at least marginally greater say about the pace, organisation and condition of work. Almost all employees saw these programmes as efforts by the company to improve their competitiveness in an increasingly competitive industry. Workers at the acquired plants' sites felt especially apprehensive. They worried that the company might sell off poorly performing divisions or plants, and they were willing to do whatever they could to help make their plants perform more effectively.

They welcomed these several initiatives as clear signs that the company was genuinely interested in their sites. As an indirect but important by-product of these initiatives, employee trust levels increased especially at these acquired sites. An official at one of these sites found that there was a strong positive correlation between increases in employee trust levels and decreases in reports of mistakes, accidents and incidents. When trust in the corporation increased, employees worked more carefully and incidents reports fell off. When employees had feared their sites would be sold off and when the corporation was laying off workers, the trust level lowered and incidents rates went up. Interestingly, as the corporation introduced these quality management initiatives, incident reports decreased measurably.

However, these quality management initiatives were not as wholeheartedly applauded as the early initiatives had been at Chester. The newly restructured work units worked effectively as self-managing, collegial units to the degree that the lower-level manager/supervisors were able to shift from their former roles to their new ones as facilitator-coach-administrators. Many found this shift very difficult to accomplish. Their difficulties were of several kinds. They had to learn how to delegate a number of their previous tasks to unit members who were acting as coordinators. In some cases, the supervisors had to spend considerable additional time in helping others learn how to perform new tasks with competence. They were also responsible for helping unit members to work together more collegially, less competitively and less impersonally. These were large undertakings, especially when units members were either slow to learn, resistant, individually abrasive or individually excessively ambitious. The supervisors were still held responsible for their units' performances because they were the representatives of these units with whom senior managers usually communicated.

At the same time, these supervisors still served as the major formal conduits of information and expectations from the upper management. Because a number of policies and programmes were being introduced at about the same time, the supervisors were expected to introduce and support these initiatives in their units. They were called to champion not only the several different quality management policies, but also the corporation's commitments to employment equity and workplace diversity, improved customers services, larger environmental concerns, the new company policy on harassment, as well as the recently adopted corporate code of ethics. The company expected a lot more from their supervisors. As a consequence many supervisors felt that their work loads had increased even though certain, limited tasks were now to be exercised by the rotating co-ordinators. They gained no increase in status or pay; rather many felt that their status was diminished as the difference between them and the members of their units declined. If power is, as we have argued, the capacity to realise chosen objectives, then many of these supervisors initially experienced a decline in power. They had less leeway to command or order others so that their units could meet the goals set by the corporation. They had been asked to advocate and/or facilitate the realisation of even more objectives. Correspondingly, in many cases they sensed that they were not performing as well as expected.

The corporate director of quality management viewed the supervisors like bottlenecks because they seemed to block or slow down what otherwise would be natural, reciprocal interactions between senior management and the first-line work units, both of whom he judged to be very vocal in their commitment to these initiatives. This metaphor was probably more apt in other ways as the director himself recognised. A significant volume of organisational innovation was being introduced and guided by the people holding these positions. They were acting like the narrow neck of an hour-glass through which many different activities were being launched. These supervisors were being asked to foster a number of corporate initiatives at the same time as they were being expected to learn new roles and yet held accountable for the performance of their work units.

The introduction of quality management was associated with several other ambiguities. As these programmes and policies were introduced, company J was also both laying off a number of employees and increasing hours of work. As managerial positions were eliminated, they reduced their workforce; but at the same time they increased by two the number of hours worked per week. In the minds of many workers, quality management correspondingly was associated with cost-cutting efforts and heavier work loads. A company-wide employee survey detected other concerns. Employees felt that the new collegial arrangements had the effect of extending too much tolerance for poor performers, and they also felt these arrangements meant that more time was being spent in organisational politics. Politics here referred to the time spent debating policies and actions and championing the interests of particular units. The survey also indicated that employees felt that not enough efforts were being devoted to helping employees develop their own careers. Overall, quality management programmes were viewed as top-down management initiatives. One executive characterised quality management initiatives as efforts by senior mangers to push democracy down into the workforce.

Quality management programmes modestly increased workers' task powers although less markedly than earlier at Chester. They extended only trace degrees of adjudicatory and contractual powers and no governance power. Compared to the earlier experiences at Chester, workers made few comments about personal powers they gained. To be sure, occasional employees had benefitted from the courses they took, but the sense of opportunity and the experience of personal accountability and responsibility were markedly less. These programmes were, after all, connected with downsizing not expansion. At the acquired sites they were regarded with apprehension as management initiatives from the acquiring company's headquarters. Furthermore, these policies were replacing former ways of doing business which were familiar, and to which many workers and managers remained loyal. They were viewed as packaged programmes with delegated authority; the discretionary mandate and responsibility associated with the slogan about solving the problem you see was not present. Because supervisors often felt overwhelmed by the new sets of tasks and conditions they were expected to master, they often seemed to lean on the groups they guided rather than facilitating and energising them. Feeling burdened themselves, they passed along jobs, duties, expectations and new roles to learn rather than challenges and opportunities. Rather than fostering collegiality, they often seemed to pass along just new ways of sorting jobs and assignments.

Programme management at University Hospital

University Hospital adopted quite a different approach to empowering its workforce. It had instituted Continuous Quality Improvement programmes in a number of work units among staff support services, hospital administration and in selected wards. These projects allowed workers in targeted units greater latitude in structuring their tasks, fostered more collegiality among them, and for the most part improved the quality of specific products or services. These projects will not, however, be the focus our considerations in this chapter. Rather, we will examine the way the hospital restructured the organisation of its clinics in keeping with a model they referred to as Programme Management (PM). Programme management called for clinics, departments and specialities to be grouped together in a limited number of medical care units (MCUs), each of which were given considerable budgetary and programmatic discretion. Programme management called for physicians, surgeons, nurses and technical staff to work collaboratively together within these units, providing multidisciplinary coordinated medical care. The units were to be grouped in relation to certain types of treatment such as neurology, cardiac services, intensive care, emergency care, oncology and so forth, based upon commonalities of the patients being served. The MCUs were to be co-directed both by a nurse responsible for the administrative services, and a physician responsible for the clinical services. A number of other hospitals had already introduced programme management with what they judged to be commendable results, and University Hospital was just beginning to institute its version of PM at the time we conducted our research. Although as a consequence we cannot fully evaluate the results of this restructuring, we can still analyse the way it seemed to alter and affect the relative power of those who worked at the hospital.

University Hospital is a university-based, tertiary care hospital located in a large city. It has an excellent public reputation based on well-publicised instances of remarkable treatments. It serves as a major site for training medical students, and many of the medical faculty at the university are connected with the hospital as supervisors of students, as clinicians themselves, and as researchers. An extensive amount of research is carried on in conjunction with the hospital, which, among its structures, houses an active well-funded research centre. Over the past dozen years the hospital has expanded quickly and currently suffers from a lack of space. Although many patients with less difficult problems are expected to go to secondary care hospitals or local clinics for treatment, they often show up at University Hospital because it is near or because they are seeking out what they regard to be the best treatment available. Correspondingly, many of the medical and nursing staff feel besieged by mounting requests for their care.

Like other hospitals, and similar to universities, school systems, accounting firms and social work agencies, University Hospital is what Mintzberg refers to as a Professional Bureaucracy (Mintzberg, 1979, chapter 19). It shares a number of features with these other organisations that are worth commenting on. A large part of the workforce was constituted by highly-trained professional physicians, nurses and technicians, professionals who had developed standardised skills and ways of working through long years of training and professional socialisation. It was expected that they could work on their own with considerable discretion and without close supervision because of this careful, supervised training and because of the professional ethics they were expected to internalise in the process. Because of this discretion, individual professionals often can decide to offer more thorough or thinner services to their clients depending on their time, abilities and interests. They are also in a position in varying degrees to ignore or evade the needs of the organisations for which they work (Mintzberg, 1979, p. 374). Much of the work of these professionals is done with clients rather than with machines or even co-workers. Although hiring decisions are often formally made by department heads, eventual colleagues often play a role in interviewing and commenting on applicants for unfilled positions.

Professional bureaucracies are usually loosely structured and co-ordinated organisations, and many of the decisions about types of services to be offered are made on a decentralised basis by the professional themselves. Basic budgetary decision are, nonetheless, usually made by the central administrative offices. If particular departments, centres and specialities want to expand, then they usually have to put their requests as persuasively as they can to central administrators or administrative councils. Still, entrepreneurial individuals and areas may work to build up particular specialties or departments and may succeed from time to time in attracting external funding.

Although some were unique, many of the concerns voiced by the professional staff at University Hospital were typical for professional bureaucracies. To a degree, nurses felt they were under-appreciated. They provided most of the ongoing, direct care for patients and often had an excellent, immediate sense of what they needed. However, treatment decisions were usually made by physicians. Physicians in turn felt they were overworked and often overmanaged by the hospital administration. They complained that they were not adequately represented on the executive council of the hospital, and had to serve on too many committees that took too much of their time. They felt they were being constantly pushed along by a endless line of patient requests, which it was their duty to serve, and that they had little control over their budgets. In their minds, they thought that the corporate, businesslike way the hospital was organised at the centre conflicted with and limited their professional discretion and responsibilities. The hospital administrators in turn felt they had only modest ability to guide, limit and direct what happened at the hospital. Many of the decisions affecting work at the hospital and the allocation of their resources were made on a piecemeal basis: individual physicians made treatment decisions; university departments added or reduced faculty, who also served as clinicians; clinician-researchers attracted or failed to attract external funds; entrepreneurially-motivated physicians expanded or reduced in size particular ambulatory clinics; special funding appeals secured or failed to secure expensive equipment; and the provincial government variously changed its funding formulae and priorities. From the perspective of administration, a constant and extremely varied stream of requests were being made on their financial resources. Could more funds be allocated so that department X could hire a very prestigious clinician-researcher? Could more beds be opened up for chronic care patients? Could extra moneys be found to offer extra compensation for nurses in this or that clinic? How was the need for more social workers to be met?

In their different ways, nurses, physicians and administrators felt they had less power than they needed to provide the kind of excellent health care they assumed the hospital was committed to providing. Their work loads were becoming excessive, and the uncompensated time they were expected to spend was incrementally increasing. In response to these and several other concerns University Hospital decided to institute Programme Management.

Programme management restructured the clinical practices at the hospital into 15 medical care units. The MCUs were given broad discretionary budgetary powers to hire or contract for the time of nurses and physicians. They could determine how much to spend on equipment, supplies, medicines, laboratory and radiological services, and other support services. They were expected to identify and establish priorities for the component services and forms of treatment they offered, and were given power to co-ordinate activities and to cultivate closer working relations between the medical and nursing staffs. The MCUs were to act as large, collegial units of 40 or more professionals, support staff and personnel.

Through the MCUs the professional staff gained specific powers. Although it is too early to evaluate the full outcome of these innovations, several consequences are worthy of note. The nursing staff clearly gained status. The importance of their role in providing good medical care was underlined both by appointing a nurse as the administrative co-director of each MCU and by making nurses answerable to the joint physician–nursing team managing each unit rather than to a separate nursing hierarchy. Nurses were to be treated as colleagues within the MCUs. Furthermore, to reinforce the integral role of the nursing staff in providing good medical services, the hospital eliminated the position of Vice-President for Nursing and appointed the person who had held this position to be hospital director of Programme Management. Correspondingly, the Vice-President Medicine position was eliminated and replaced by a position with the title Vice-President of Clinical and

Strategic Services. A number of budgetary powers were also decentralized to MCUs. They were expected to manage ward costs, outpatient programmes and outreach budgets, and to act as multidisciplinary, self-organising units. At the same time the discretion of a number of smaller clinic specialities and offices were reduced. Decisions which they had made on their own about types and extent of care had to be cleared through the MCUs' governing councils, which had power to establish priorities among these services. Programme management had the effect of rendering many of these units more collegially accountable.

These changes had no measurable impact on the personal and adjudicatory powers of the professional staff. They did not affect the degree to which individuals could pursue their careers, and they did not really alter the basic substance of contractual powers. Still, they modified the setting in which contractual decisions were first deliberated and then made. To a greater degree these decisions were to be made collegially rather than administratively. Tasks powers were not dramatically changed, and working conditions were not altered. The set of jobs that had to be done continued to be what it had been before. Physicians, nurses and technicians continued to perform their work with professional discretion. However, to a degree the ways they approached decisions with regard to the pace and character of their work seems to have changed. Although the traditional hierarchies among medical staff continued unaltered, the restructuring of clinical services gave increased weight to the judgements of nurses, who were now treated somewhat more collegially. In modest ways physicians had greater say in terms of the importance assigned to various tasks, if for no other reason because of the budgetary powers delegated to the MCUs. MCUs were both permitted but also required to establish priorities for themselves. These changes were connected with increased governance powers over budgets and policies which professional staff gained through their medical care units. The medical staff did not gain more representation on the hospital executive council. A measure of governance power was extended not to individuals nor to physicians or nurses as a whole but to these professionals as colleagues within a number of semi-self-governing working units.

The hospital senior management hoped that as a result of these changes the professional staff would use their discretionary powers to attend more closely to the good of the hospital and the excellent medical care it sought to provide. They hoped that these changes would encourage the professional staff to act less as simply self-interested entrepreneurs and more as collaborating colleagues. The hospital management also hoped that these changes would, in the words of the former Vice-President of Medicine, be able to elicit or inspire from the professional staff 'greater commitment, passion, and imagination for the hospital and the care it offered'. To the degree that these altered work arrangements have elicited greater enthusiasm and commitment from the professional staff, then it appears they have also occasioned several beneficial by-products. Greater commitment meant that more work was done well: fewer people were seeking free rides. More time, energy and imagination were available, and with greater psychic and moral resources at hand the professional staff within these units felt they had greater leeway in discharging their responsibilities. They felt marginally less like assembly-line workers continuously dominated by externally originating demands upon their time, energy, compassion and know-how. They also saw how attending to the good of their units as whole in turn benefitted them.

OBSERVATIONS

Workers can augment their power within corporate organisations in many different ways, and the cases discussed above present a spectrum of varied examples. We can make several observations when these cases are reviewed from the perspective of the workers themselves:

1. Increases in one form of power do not necessarily occasion or produce increases in other forms of power. For example, the ability to exercise effective governance power at the corporate organisational level, as exemplified by the plywood producer co-operatives, does not necessarily lead to the ability to exercise much task power at the level of work units, or personal power in relation to careers. Similarly the ability to exercise additional task and governance powers at the department level, as exemplified by University Hospital, does not necessarily translate into greater abilities to exercise other forms of influence personally or organisationally. The considerable task powers exercised by work teams at Chester had little impact on their scant capacity to exercise governance powers. Unless expressively called for, increases in one form of power may have little impact on other forms of power.
2. Aside from the instance of the producer co-operatives, in all of these examples workers moderately increased their task powers. In no case were workers able to radically redesign the jobs that had to

be done. In a number of instances workers were given a wider range of tasks to perform in keeping with basic assumptions that inform job enrichment programmes. In several ways they were able to affect the pace and pattern of work, and in modest ways they were able to exercise greater discretion over how they actually performed their work. They were often encouraged, if not directly called, to take initiatives. This attitude was well-represented by the slogan at Chester that if workers saw a problem, then they ought to take the necessary steps to fix it. The increase in task powers occasioned a noteworthy response, and in varying degrees workers gained a sense of ownership over the jobs they performed. They were no longer just undertaking work which fundamentally belonged to someone else. Because they had the capacity to shape how these tasks were done, they correspondingly developed more of a sense of their own craftsmanship over work which they regarded as their own.

At the same time in all these cases, their work became more collegial. They were as a result both more accountable to their co-workers but also more supported by them. The discretion they exercised over the character and condition of their work, they possessed as members of working groups. Thus, their sense of autonomy was enhanced by becoming more interdependent with, rather than independent from, their co-workers. The experience of the receptionists at one of company J's sites well illustrates this experience. At the same time as they were given greater latitude over how they did their work, they were expected to co-ordinate their work more closely with their co-workers. As a result, workers often felt more rather than less accountable for the quality of their work.

3. In many instances workers also increased their own personal powers, although only in a few instances was this outcome directly aimed at. Company J had launched courses to help employees develop certain communicative skills, and in many cases workers gained increased personal powers as a by-product of these developments. Whenever they were able to learn new useable skills, and whenever they were given opportunities to pursue their own careers, many workers responded. Although they may well have shunned courses on interpersonal skills before they began their employment at company J, employees learned to recognise the utility of these classes. They saw how these skills enabled them to work together more effectively and, perhaps more personally important, how these skills enabled them to represent their own interests more persuasively.

4. In none of these cases did workers significantly increase their adjudicatory powers. Little or no attention was paid to issues related to the rights and prerogatives of workers with respect the handling disputes, complaints and grievances. Several observers have argued that one of the basic powers which workers ought to be able to exercise is a minimal level of adjudicatory power so that they can defend themselves against what they judge to be unfair complaints, they can grieve about what they consider to be unfair treatment, and they can appeal what they regard as unfair assignments (Ewing, 1989; Gunn, 1984). The trade union movement has long campaigned to augment and protect these powers for the members of their associations. In contrast, in none of these cases were any efforts made to address these concerns. While discussing hundreds of different examples of contemporary efforts to increase worker involvement, neither Cotton, Kanter nor Lawlor make any mention of attempts to enhance, strengthen or reinforce these kinds of adjudicatory powers (Cotton, 1993; Kanter, 1983; Lawler, 1986). It is as if the discussion of workers' power has not yet been extended to include concern about this form of power.

   Indirectly, workers at Chester were able to exercise marginal degrees of adjudicatory power largely because the plant had institutionalised conflict-resolution procedures within work units. Workers were thereby able to raise complaints, to voice concerns, and to resolve internal disputes through informal hearings with co-workers. Formal due-process procedures had not, however, been established.

5. Only in modest ways did any of these empowerment programmes extend or strengthen the contractual powers of workers. Programme management did allow medical care units some discretion on hiring decisions, but still in no way affected the basic contractual stipulations that informed the working relations of physicians, nurses and technical staff. PM had no impact on how performances were evaluated and rewarded. The quality management programmes at company J assigned to working units the responsibility of evaluating the performance of their members, and democratising performance appraisals often meant that workers had more opportunity to discuss these assessments as part of give-and-take discussions. It also meant they had reduced opportunities to appeal them if they felt these evaluations were unfair. Aside from these small examples, empowerment programmes in these cases did not measurably affect contractual powers. This absence is noteworthy, partly because

traditionally the trade union movement has been especially committed to strengthening and protecting the contractual powers of employees. Trade unions have treated many quality management programmes with considerable suspicion. In a number of instances they have actively opposed management efforts to introduce quality of work-life (QWL) programmes because they feared that management hoped to use these initiatives to reduce trade union influence (Rinehart, 1978). In fact many QWL projects failed as a result of this opposition. Where these projects have succeeded, however, they did so often because unions co-sponsored them. Interestingly, in the latter instances the major contribution of QWL programmes has been to improve the character of labour–management negotiations. In these cases, although QWL programmes did extend greater task powers to employees in their semi-self-managing work units, their most significant outcome has been to strengthen and reinforce the contractual powers of workers by making their relations with management less adversarial (Cotton, 1993, chapter 3).

Contractual powers are fundamental. They represent the capacity of workers to influence the status and basic character of their relationship with the organisations for which they work. By means of these powers workers are able to identify, assert and protect their rights. Because both governments and trade associations have played a major role in working to set forth and protect contractual rights, management has often taken little initiative in these areas. They have frequently regarded both governmental and trade unions initiatives to extend contractual powers to workers as intrusive actions likely to reduce or eliminate their own discretion.

To a degree governments have seen fit to define and protect these powers. Moreover, as a result of government actions, the contractual powers of workers have greatly expanded during the twentieth century. As a consequence of legislation and court judgements, workers today are able to exercise a number of contractual powers they did not earlier possess. For example, in most settings they are protected from arbitrary dismissal. They are guaranteed minimum wages. If they are injured on the job, they will be duly compensated for medical care and lost time. Through public social insurance schemes, they are assured minimal pension benefits, and these are usually supplemented by additional pension programmes connected directly with their place of work. If they feel they have been slighted or discriminated against because of their gender, minority status or handicap, they can appeal for redress. If they think that their employers have not honoured their contractual obligations, they can sue.

Trade and professional associations have especially championed these powers and managers have often, therefore, only extended these powers as a means of outbidding the unions. Unions themselves have frequently pushed for greater contractual powers for workers but have done so in ways that augment and reinforce the power of their associations as the official agents of the workers. As a result of actions taken by trade and professional associations, many workers today enjoy higher wages, more job security, greater rights to negotiate the clauses of their own job contracts, and more opportunities to grieve or complain when they feel these stipulations are not respected. Workers exercise these rights both as individuals and as members of trade and professional associations.

6. In these cases workers at several sites increased their governance powers. The situation at the producer co-operatives is clearest. Worker-owners there governed their own plants through annual meetings and elected boards, but this governance power did not translate into any significantly greater task, personal or contractual powers. Workers for company J exercised practically no governance power. Professional workers at University Hospital exercised modest amounts of governance powers through newly-constructed medical care units; they were able in minimal ways to govern their departments and alter or establish guiding organisational policies.

7. Contemporary empowerment programmes, such as the ones we have examined at company J and at University Hospital, primarily have been developed as management initiatives in order to realise a range of management objectives. Directly, these programmes have sought to increase the involvement of workers in their organisations, to enhance collaborative efforts among them, and to extend their discretion with respect to specified tasks. Correspondingly, they have established quality circles and focus groups, enlarged and enriched job assignments, surveyed workers' views, developed self-managing teams, and authorised workers or teams to make a greater range of decisions on their own. Management groups have introduced these initiatives as part of their larger concern to increase the effectiveness of their organisations. For the most part these kinds of initiatives have not been undertaken because management groups primarily thought it was fair and fitting for workers to exercise greater degrees of power.

In particular ways, which we have examined, a number of these programmes have modestly added to the power of some workers. Their task and personal powers have been augmented by programmes which have extended to them enhanced discretion, by established self-managing teams and added venues for voicing concerns. In a few instances workers have exercised greater governance powers at least with respect to their work units. These extensions, however, have been made possible not primarily because management groups were moved by a sense of what they judged to be fair and fitting – that is, a sense of justice – but because greater worker involvement and empowerment has seemed to promise increased organisational commitment by these workers and overall improvements in organisational performance. For the most part, as management groups have introduced initiatives like these, they have not considered, nor were they attempting to provide, practical answers to the question of how much power was it appropriate, feasible and right for workers to exercise. Rather, they were concerned to increase organisational effectiveness. Greater say and involvement by workers was seen as integral to the process.

8. The initiation and implementation of contemporary empowerment programmes, such as those we have examined, are frequently limited and undermined by a number of factors which render them less effective both for workers and their organisations. Often programmes are introduced along with a variety of other management initiatives which in practice take precedence over them. In particular, because these programmes are often instituted in hope of improving overall organisation performance, those implementing them are often constrained over short periods of time to meet targets, comply with plans, and observe guidelines established by the larger quality improvement, re-engineering or organisational effectiveness efforts. Quality management programmes at company J were introduced along with initiatives aimed at downsizing, delayering, re-engineering, and providing more effective leadership. In the process, however, empowerment programmes are shortchanged: they receive minimal resources, attention and commitment compared to other initiatives. Moreover, they are often both overtly opposed and surreptitiously resisted by those who either continue to operate according to the former structures of authority or benefit from them (Kanter, 1983, chapter 9).

Too often these initiatives flag because those initiating them are not able to find ways of effectively increasing the practical power of the supervisors who are called upon to facilitate and implement empowerment programmes. Often these supervisors are called upon to share administrative and policy-making powers with those below them while not receiving for themselves adequate delegation of authority from their superiors (Matejko and Rubenwitz, 1980). Because these problems are so pervasive, Foy set aside two chapters in her book on empowerment cautioning managers not to 'disempower the middle' and not to 'castrate supervisors' (Foy, 1995, chapters 10, 11). This problem is only effectively addressed to the degree that supervisors themselves gain in authority or power as a result of these initiatives. They may do so in several ways: their powers may be enhanced as a result of training programmes that help them to increase their competencies at facilitation and their interpersonal communicative skills; or they may gain power, as supervisors at University hospital did, by gaining greater discretion over budgets, policies of their units, and human resource management. Alternatively, they may gain through increased influence and recognition among their superiors. Without some reasonable enhancement in their resources, authority and/or status, supervisors are likely to feel overlyextended and thereby disempowered by these initiatives.

Overall, the workers in these reviewed cases increased certain but not other powers. We have commented briefly on how they viewed these developments, and have noted the quite different approaches to worker empowerment. With these cases in mind as points of reference, we would now like to address the question we asked at the outset: namely, what forms and degrees of power is it fair and fitting for workers to exercise?

JUSTICE AND EMPOWERMENT

Over time, a number of often opposing views have been held about the extent of power which workers ought to be able to exercise. The advocates of workplace democracy argued that workers ought either to govern or be represented in sizeable numbers on the governing bodies of their organisations. By virtue of the fact that their labours add significant value to the resources which business organisations turn into marketable products and services, these advocates insist that workers must be well-represented in policy-setting councils. They also have championed ways of organising work that allow employees through self-directed teams to supervise and direct their own tasks. In opposition, many representatives of management have maintained that a fully-fledged model of workplace democracy would be unworkable in practice and also unfair to investors, debt-holders, and other constituents who would, as a result, not have their interests well-asserted and defended.

How much power, and in what forms, ought workers to exercise? We argue that it is just and good, both for workers themselves and their organisation, for workers to exercise several forms of power in fair and fitting degrees. What this means we will shortly explain.

Empowerment programmes extend power in some forms to workers. Is the power which 'empowered' workers exercise fitting and fair? How do these contemporary shifts in power alter the overall arrangements of power within organisations? It is argued that these 'empowerment' programmes are both welcomed by workers and good for businesses. But are they just? To what degree, if any, do they address the on-going debates about the extent of power which managers, investors and workers ought to exercise? To what degree do they address and overcome workers' complaints, in so far as they are legitimate, about their lack of power? Because these diverse programmes in several ways treat workers with greater dignity and allow them more discretion and responsibility, they seem to be both appreciated and appropriate. But are they extending to workers more symbolic rather than real power? Or, are they allowing for modest increases in certain forms of powers, while indirectly limiting other forms (Gruber and Trickett, 1987)? These programmes have in different and modest ways increased productivity and worker satisfaction. But have they occasioned allocations of power within organisations that are more fair and just?

To address these questions, we need to arrive at standards for identifying the just allocation of power, and these should be both practical and ethically defensible. We can identify these standards in turn by examining fully the character of involvement of workers in the organisations for which they labour. Workers do more than contract to sell their ability to perform specified tasks over allotted time in return for designated compensations. Their involvement with these organisation is far richer and more multi-dimensional. Business organisations do not just hire workers: they are also constituted by them. Workers help to bring into being the organisations for whom they labour. Without the ongoing actions of their workers, managers and others, organisations would cease to exist as social realities. As social realities, organisations are continuously being re-constituted by the fact that their constituents perform the tasks expected of them. Furthermore, workers are rights-bearing members of these organisations, and they possess a kind of civic status within the polities of their firms (Selznick, 1969). Correspondingly, they can make legitimate claims on their organisations to be treated fairly as defined by law and agreed-upon customs. Additionally, workers live out a goodly part of their lives in the organisations for which they labour. In measurable yet quite variable ways, they either grow as persons or do not, cultivate friendships or do not, advance or do not advance their careers, depending on the social and work environments in which they perform their tasks. Business does not just contract for the employment of workers' labour. They also implicitly contract for a significant segments of their lives.

For their part, business organisations seek more from workers than the performance of specified tasks; they want them to perform their tasks with commitment. That is, they want employees to perform their work with the aim of realising organisational objectives and in keeping with organisational standards without needing continuous surveillance. They expect workers to work effectively and industriously (Westley and Bird, 1996), to interact in specified ways, to show deference and respect where appropriate, to be prompt and to be in regular attendance (Mowday et al., 1982). They expect workers to avoid what some observers refer to as anti-role behaviours: that is, behaviours in which people take advantage of their organisations by fudging the rules, appropriating supplies, over-charging expenses, and/or working carelessly (Parks and Kidder, 1994). Moreover, they expect workers to act courteously, to extend themselves from time to time on behalf of co-workers, to represent their organisations well in dealings with others (Graham, 1991; Organ, 1988, Van Dyne et al., 1994). In a word, most business organisations expect their workers to behave civilly.[2]

Given this complex, multidimensional relationship between workers and the organisations for which they labour, what powers is it both fair and fitting for them to exercise? What degrees and form of power should workers justly possess? These questions are best addressed not globally and generally, but in relation to each of the five forms of power we have discussed.

1. Workers ought to be able to exercise significant measures of personal power, from consultative to effective degrees, depending on the extent to which they have developed their own skills. They ought to have opportunities to learn and cultivate their competencies at the same time as they labour. They may, to be sure, learn in diverse ways: from the experiences with which their jobs confront them,

from new or alternative tasks which they take up from time to time, from their interactions with co-workers, customers, contractors and the like, as well as from designated classes, seminars and training programmes. Some employees take advantage of these opportunities more than others. They grow on the job much more markedly than do others. Generally, better educated, more entrepreneurial workers are likely to utilise these occasions for self-development. From the perspective of the organisations, however, we can argue that they bear the responsibility for making a range of these opportunities available. They can do so in multiple ways, as we have just indicated, through job enrichment programmes, job rotation schemes, promotion opportunities, training programmes, and allowance for time off. Characteristically, the personal powers which workers are able to exercise are limited not only by lack of genuine opportunities, which organisations ought to extend, but also by their own individual resistance to learning and growth. While organisations bear no responsibility for the latter, they ought to do what they can, given the character of the work they do, to make opportunities for personal growth possible. Although they have often not directly aimed at extending personal powers, empowerment programmes have frequently served to augment these powers as a by-product of their other concerns. Kanter observes that organisations that foster career opportunities tend to be innovative as well (Kanter, 1983, p. 102).

2. To the degree that they are willing to develop the necessary competencies and are also willing to assume corresponding amounts of accountability, workers ought to be extended appreciable degrees of task powers. Generally, employees labour more effectively when they feel they are able to exercise discretion in terms of the timing and character of their tasks. They work better generally to the degree they can bring a sense of craftsmanship to their efforts. They work more competently and industriously when their efforts are not too closely supervised, and they feel these efforts are genuinely valued (Glisson and Durrick, 1988). They work most effectively when they are performing tasks with discretion, visibility, and a sense that their work makes a difference (Kanter, 1977, chapter 7). Typically, professionals are granted far more discretion by organisations than other workers, in large part because they can be trusted to work well. This trust is in turn based on the fact that professionals are both extensively socialised into how they should act by long years of training and apprenticeship, and held accountable for good conduct

by their professional associations. The autonomy which professionals enjoy is in part correlated with collegial patterns of accountability. Interestingly, the same correlation exists with respect to self-managed work teams. Individual workers are able to exercise much greater power in determining how they perform their tasks because their work units in turn hold them accountable and collectively establish relevant guidelines. Current empowerment programmes have served in a variety of ways to expand the task powers of workers. As a result, employees affected by these programmes have greater say over the way they perform their jobs, their job satisfaction has increased, and they work more effectively (Cotton, 1993).

3. It is somewhat more difficult to spell out the degrees of contractual power which workers ought to be able to exercise. Skill levels and labour market forces make a difference. Those workers who possess highly developed skills which are also in great demand are generally able to exercise much greater contractual powers than unskilled labourers for whom the demand is minimal. By virtue of the bargaining power of their trade and professional associations, many union members and professionals enjoy much greater contractual powers than workers not represented by any labour organisation. These variations exist. For the present we will not endeavour to judge whether these factors cause some workers to possess more or less contractual power than seems fitting and fair. Rather, we will attempt to identify certain features and degrees of contractual power which all workers ought to possess. We need to note first that governments have already spelled out a number of these. As we have already observed, by means of legislative enactments and judicial reviews, employees of business organisations today have been extended a number of basic contractual rights and powers. These include the protection against wrongful dismissal, the right to apply for unemployment benefits, minimum wage guarantees, the right to claim public pension benefits, protection against discrimination on the basis of minority status or gender, guarantees for workmen's compensation in the case of injury, and allowance for pregnancy leaves. This list is significant. One hundred and fifty years ago, few workers enjoyed any of these powers (Selznick, 1969). It is worth adding, nonetheless, that these powers exist in principle but not always in practice. Particular employers may ignore these provisions, evade them from time to time, and interpret them in ways that reduce their impact. One of the reasons it is important to extend at

least consultative degrees of adjudicatory powers to workers is so that they can effectively appeal to have these provisions enforced.

We would like to examine other contractual powers that workers ought to be able to exercise in addition to those guaranteed by governments. No matter what their status or skill level, whether they are salaried, waged or piece workers, employees ought to be able to negotiate or renegotiate their contractual status fairly. Correspondingly, they ought to be able to participate actively, either in person or through chosen representatives, in their own contractual negotiations. This means that at least minimally they should be fully informed regarding the terms and evaluation of their work. It also means that their voiced concerns regarding both these terms and evaluations ought to be seriously considered by their employers. If they are to be able to participate actively in these negotiations then the communications between them and their employers must be open and reciprocal. They ought to possess the power/right to be able to hear all relevant information bearing on the contractual terms of their work and be able as well both to speak up and receive a considered hearing of their corresponding concerns. Without these powers they cannot enter fully into contractual negotiations, no matter what terms they may be negotiating.

We can spell out more fully what open and reciprocal communication ought to be like. To begin with, for both parties communications ought to be forthright and not deceptive. Parties should neither intentionally lie nor withhold information which others would consider vital to their interests as negotiators (Bok, 1978, 1983; Bird, 1996). To be sure, because negotiations take place over time and utilise some measure of bluff, bargaining and delay, parties are not expected initially to be more forthcoming than those with whom they are negotiating. However, they are expected to bargain in good faith and, therefore, they are expected to disclose relevant information in a timely matter to match and encourage the disclosures of their negotiating opposites (Carson *et al.*, 1982). Additionally, both parties ought to be responsive and attentive to what the other says. Minimally, this requires both parties to be accessible so that others can address and bargain with them. Many workers feel that interactions regarding their contracts are like bypassing monologues; they find it hard to get the focused attention of their employers. Furthermore, if they are lucky enough to get their employers' attention, they feel the latter are often not really very attentive. Neither party ought to ignore the communications of the other or be evasive in their responses. Both parties ought to be able to expect that what they say will be seriously considered (Shapiro, 1993), which means that they can expect intelligible responses in which the others comment thoughtfully on the initial communications. These conditions which make for open and reciprocal communications correspond broadly with several of the basic stipulations constitutive of what contemporary observers refer to as procedural justice within organisations. These call for clear, consistent interactions in which parties are able to represent their own positions, and the others remain accessible and responsive (Tyler, 1987; Sheppard, Lewicki and Minton, 1992; Cropanzano, 1993).

Minimally, the power to negotiate actively, which is basic to all other contractual powers, requires that workers be fully and honestly informed, able to voice their own concerns, and able to receive a serious hearing. Correlatively, workers ought to be able to participate fully in the evaluations of their own work. Frequently performance-appraisal exercises are one-way, mechanical and/or superficial. They ought as well to be not only open and reciprocal but also substantive. They ought to serve as occasions when workers and their employers can thoughtfully review not merely the performance of employees but also the overall character of their relationship. For their part, workers ought to be able to comment on the degrees to which employers adequately supply conditions that enable them in turn to perform their tasks as expected. Each party ought to be able to comment on the evaluations and requests of the other (see Culbert and McDonough, 1980).

In relation to the terms used in this essay, we are arguing that workers ought to be able to exercise, individually or through their representatives, sufficient power to negotiate so that they can expect employers attentively to consult and consider their views. We can add that it is not only fair and fitting for employers to extend workers this degree of contractual power: it is also in their best interests. To the degree that workers feel that their views have been seriously considered, they are much more likely to regard as just the eventual terms offered by their employers, and they are correspondingly much more likely to cooperate with them. For example, when they feel that they have been able to voice their concerns and employers have seriously considered their views, workers are much more likely to accept without overt objections downsizing and pay-reduction decisions. For instance, in response to pay reductions, the response of workers in two plants were quite different. At the plant where workers felt they could not speak up, the rates for quitting and for shrinkage were more than twice as large as at the plant where they felt they could (Greenberg, 1996). Other studies indicate, more generally, that workers are much more likely to accept as fair corporate decisions about salary schedules if they felt they have been involved in the process (Folger and Konovsky, 1989).

Empowerment programmes have thus far only indirectly operated to increase or defend contractual powers of workers.

4. Workers in themselves ought to be able to exercise marginal to consultative degrees of adjudicatory power. If they are going to be able to protect themselves against wrongful dismissals, arbitrary and unfair appraisals, and changes in the terms of their work that seem unfairly to reduce their opportunities, they need to be able to appeal these actions to third parties within their organisations. Likewise, to be able to protect themselves against unhealthy working conditions, discrimination and harassment and to have opportunities to appeal against decisions that they think unfairly deny them promotions, transfers or training experiences, they must possess the power to make and have their complaints heard. Adjudicatory powers are basic. Although they have been the focus of those concerned about procedural justice (Tyler, 1990; Lind and Tyler, 1988), organisational due processes (Ewing, 1989) and the practices of natural justice in organisations (Freedman, 1993), empowerment programmes have seldom attempted to articulate, augment or defend them.

5. Workers, by themselves or through their representatives, ought to be able to exercise marginal degrees of governance power. The question of how much power workers ought to be able to exercise with regard to the overall governance of enterprises has been widely debated. We will not enter into this debate here, but note in passing that various constituent groups ought to be able to represent their interests in how organisations are governed in degrees proportionate to their contributions to, and their legitimate claims on or against, their organisations. Boards bear the responsibility for representing all these interests for the good of the organisation as a whole. It makes sense, correspondingly, to argue that workers ought to be represented on boards and that boards ought to represent the concerns of workers along with other constituent groups.

It is a mistake, we think, to discuss governance powers exclusively in relation to how organisations are governed as a whole. In certain forms, governance powers have been exercised by divisions, departments, and even teams. Citing the traditional Catholic doctrine of subsidiarity, Ackoff has recently argued for delegating certain governance powers to smaller units within organisations, arguing that these units can often exercise these powers more effectively (Ackoff, 1995). Within broad parameters established by the organisation as a whole, he asserts that many companies would be better off delegating significant amounts of budgeting powers, policy determinations and executive hiring decisions to these smaller units (see Halal, 1993). Programme management at University hospital fits this model even though these changes were introduced without any explicit reference to this philosophy. What is interesting about this model for the purpose of this essay is that the devolution of selected governance powers to smaller units also allows for some forms of worker involvement in governing. Interestingly, this model, as illustrated by experiences at University hospital, allows workers to participate in governing, in setting budgets and policies, not so much as abstract representatives of workers but on the basis of the work they do and the skills they exercise. With the exception both of the case of producer cooperatives in North America and the example of co-determination in Europe, empowerment programmes have not emphasised the importance of governance powers. The principle of subsidiarity allows for a way of reconsidering the appropriate division of governance powers and the ways and degrees these powers can and ought be extended to workers.

Notes

1. The research on which this paper is based was made possible by a grant from the Social Science and Humanities Research Council in Canada. The research itself has been undertaken cooperatively by Manuel Velasquez of Santa Clara University and Frederick Bird of Concordia University.
2. I have developed the ideas found in these two paragraphs in the Sproule Lectures, given at McGill University in 1996. In these lectures, which bore the title 'The Civic Mandate', I developed these ideas at greater length and extended them as well to other stakeholder groups.

References

Ackerman, R. (1975) *The Social Challenge to Business* (Cambridge: Harvard University Press).

Ackoff, R.L. (1994) *The Democratic Corporation: A Radical Prescription for Re-creating Corporate America and Rediscovering Success* (New York: Oxford University Press).
Banfield, E. (1961) *Political Influence* (The Free Press of Glencoe).
Bird, F.B. (1996) *The Muted Conscience: Moral Silence and the Practice of Ethics in Business* (Westpoint, Conn.: Quorum Books).
Bird, F.B. and Gandz, J. (1990) *Good Management: Business Ethics in Practice* (Scarborough, Ontario: Prentice Hall).
Blasi, J.R. (1988) *Employee Ownership: Revolution or Ripoff?* (Cambridge, Massachusetts: Ballinger).
Bok, S. (1978) *Lying: Moral Choice in Public and Private Life* (New York: Vintage Books).
Bok, S. (1983) *Secrets: On the Ethics of Concealment and Revelation* (New York: Vintage Books).
Braverman, H. (1974) *Labor and Monopoly Capitalism: The Degradation of Work in the Twentieth Century* (New York: Monthly Review Press).
Carson, T.L., Wokutch, R.E. and Murrmann, K.F. (1982) 'Bluffing in Labor Negotiations: Legal and Ethical Issues', *Journal of Business Ethics*, vol. 1, no. 1, pp. 13–22.
Christensen Hughes, J.M. (1996) 'Beyond Rhetoric: A Typology of Empowerment Strategies found within one Organisation', paper presented to the Centre for Organisational and Professional Ethics conference on 'Ethics and Empowerment', London, 13 September.
Cotton, J.L. (1993) *Employee Involvement: Methods for Improving Performance and Work Attitudes* (Newbury Park: Sage).
Cropanzano, R. (ed.) (1993) *Justice in the Workplace: Approaching Fairness in Human Resource Management* (Hillsdale, New Jersey: Lawrence Erlbaum Associates).
Culbert, S.A. and McDonough, J.J. (1980) *The Invisible War: Interests at Work* (New York: John Wiley).
Dahl, R.A. (1961) *Who Governs? Democracy and Power in an American City* (New Haven: Yale University Press).
Ewing, D.W. (1989) *Justice on the Job: Resolving Grievances in the Non-Union Workplace* (Boston: Harvard Business School Press).
Folger, R. and Konovsky, P. (1989) 'The Effects of Procedural and Distributive Justice on Reactions to Pay Raise Decision', *Academy of Management Journal*, pp. 115–30.
Foy, N. (1994) *Empowering People At Work* (Brookfield, Vermont: Gower).
Freedman, B. (1993) *Rules of Natural Justice* (Montreal: Concordia University) (Handbook for Members of University Tribunals and Administrative Decision-Making Bodies).
Goodwin, B. (1996) 'Ethics and Empowerment in a Government Agency', paper presented to the Centre for Organisational and Professional Ethics conference on 'Ethics and Empowerment', London, 13 September.
Galbraith, J.K. (1954) *American Capitalism: The Concept of Countervailing Power* (Boston: Houghton Mifflin).
Glendon, M.A. (1981) *The New Family and the New Property* (Toronto: Butterworths).

Glisson, C. and Durrick, M. (1988) 'Predictions of Job Satisfaction and Organizational Commitment in Human Service Organizations', *Administrative Sciences Quarterly*, vol. 37. pp. 161–81.
Graham, J.W. (1991) 'An Essay on Organizational Citizenship Behavior', *Employee Rights and Responsibilities Journal*, vol. 4, no. 4, pp. 249–70.
Greenberg, E.S. (1982) *Workplace Democracy: The Political Effects of Participation* (Ithaca, New York: Cornell University Press).
Greenberg, J. (1996) *The Quest for Justice on the Job: Essays and Experiments* (Thousand Oaks: Sage Publications).
Gruber, J.M. and Trickett, E.J. (1987) 'Can We Empower Others? The Paradox of Empowerment in the Governing of an Alternative Public School', *American Journal of Community Psychology*, vol. 15(3), pp. 353–71.
Gunn, C.E. (1984) *Workers' Self-Management in the United States* (Ithaca, New York: Cornell University Press).
Halal, W.E. (1993) *Bringing the Power of Free Enterprise Inside Your Organization* (New York: Wiley).
Hardy, C. (1985) 'The Nature of Unobtrusive Power', *Journal of Management Studies*, vol. 22(4) (July), pp. 384–99.
Hirschman, A.O. (1970) *Exit, Voice, and Loyalty: Responses to Decline in Firms, Organization and States* (Cambridge, Mass.: Harvard University Press).
Hobbes, T. (1651, 1968) *Leviathan* (New York: Penguin Books).
Kaler, J. (1996) 'Does Empowerment Empower?', paper presented to the Centre for Organisational and Professional Ethics conference on 'Ethics and Empowerment', London, 13 September.
Kanter, R.M. (1978) *Men and Women of the Corporation* (New York: Basic Books).
Kanter, R.M. (1983) *The Change Masters: Innovation for Productivity in the American Corporation* (New York: Simon-Schuster).
Lawler, E.E., III (1986) *High-Involvement Management* (San Francisco: Jossey-Bass).
Lind, E.A. and Tyler, T.R. (1988) *The Social Psychology of Procedural Justice* (New York: Plenum Press).
Lukes, S. (1974) *Power: A Radical View* (London: Macmillan).
Matejko, A. and Rubenwitz, S. (1980) 'The Sociotechnics of Working Life: Experience from Sweden', *Europa: A Journal of Interdisciplinary Studies*, vol. 3, no. 2, pp. 115–84.
Mintzberg, H. (1979) *The Structuring of Organizations: A Synthesis of Research* (Englewood Cliffs, New Jersey: Prentice-Hall).
Mowday, R., Parker, W. and Steers, R. (1982) *Employee–Organizational Linkages: The Psychology of Commitment, Absenteeism, and Turnover* (New York: Academic Press).
Organ, D.W. (1988) *Organizational Citizenship Behavior: The Good Soldier Syndrome* (Lexington, Massachusetts: Lexington Books).
Parks, J.M. and Kidder, D. (1994) '"Till Death Do Us Part..." Changing Work Relations in the 1990s', in C.L. Cooper and D.M. Rousseau (eds), *Trends in Organizational Behavior*, vol. I (London: Wiley), pp. 111–36.
Pfeffer, J. and Salancik, G.R. (1978) *The External Control of the Organization* (New York: Harper & Row).

Rinehart, J.W. (1978) 'Work Humanization and the Labor Process', unpublished essay, University of Western Ontario.
Saunders, D. and Leck, J. D. (1993) 'Formal Upward Communication Procedures: Organizational and Employee Perspectives', *Canadian Journal of Administrative Studies*, vol. 10(3), pp. 255–68.
Selznick, P. (1969) *Law, Society, and Industrial Justice* (New York: Russell Sage).
Selznick, P. (1992) *The Moral Commonwealth: Social Theory and the Promise of Community* (Berkeley: University of California Press).
Shapiro, D.L. (1993) 'Reconciling Theoretical Differences among Procedural Justice Researchers by Re-evaluating What it Means to Have One's Own Views "Considered": Implications for Third Party Managers', in R. Cropanzano (ed.), *Justice in the Workplace* (Hillsdale, New Jersey: Lawrence Erlbaum), chapter 3.
Sheppard, B.H., Lewicki, R.J. and Minton, J.W. (1992) *Organizational Justice: The Search for Fairness in the Workplace* (New York: Lexington Books).
Simon, B.L. (1992) 'Rethinking Empowerment', *Journal of Progressive Human Services*, vol. 1(1), pp. 27–39.
Spinoza (1930) *Selections*, ed. J. Wild (New York: Charles Scribner's Sons).
Tyler, T.R. (1987) 'Procedural Justice Research', *Social Justice Research*, vol. 1, no.1. pp. 41–65.
Tyler, T.R. (1990) *Why People Obey the Law* (New Haven: Yale University Press).
Van Dyne, L., Graham, J.W. and Dienesch, R.M. (1994) 'Organizational Citizenship Behavior: Construct Redefinition, Measurement, and Validation', *Academy of Management Journal*, vol. 37, pp. 765–802.
Weber, M. (1978) *Economy and Society* (Berkeley: University of California Press).
Werhane, P. (1985) *Persons, Rights, and Corporations* (Englewood Cliffs: Prentice-Hall).
Westley, F. and Bird, F. (1996) 'The Social Psychology of Organizational Commitment', unpublished essay.

3 Does Empowerment Empower?
John Kaler

INTRODUCTION

With 'empowerment' we have an example of a well-established though little used word which has been taken up and given new currency by writers on management. Exactly what it means within that context is difficult to say. As with other management buzz-words, the concept associated with it has become a commodity: something sold to management practitioners via bullet-pointed paperbacks telling them 'how to do it'. As with any other commodity, these buzz-word concepts have to be constantly re-packaged to keep demand buoyant. Usually this takes the form of intensification. Thus, 'quality' becomes *total* quality', and 'customer *satisfaction*' becomes 'customer *delight*'. (The first books on 'absolute total quality' and 'customer ecstasy' cannot be far off.) The ultimate intensifier is to append 'beyond' to the buzz-word, resulting in, for example, *Beyond Total Quality Management* (Bound, 1994; McHugh *et al.*, 1993). Alternatively, the re-packaging takes the form of qualificatory disclaimers and we are told what, contrary to popular misconceptions, the thing is not. (We are told, for example, that 'participative management' is not 'organisational democracy' (Plunkett and Fournier, 1991, p. 18). Such can be the scale and contradictoriness of the disclaimers that we might sometimes be left wondering what exactly the thing is, or even whether it has been qualified out of existence. (The notion of a degenerating problem shift springs to some minds (Lakatos, 1970)) This, it could be suggested, is the fate of empowerment. For we can be told that contrary to what might seem like a reasonable expectation, 'empowerment is not about increasing the power of employees' (Randolph, 1995, p. 30). This confounds reasonable expectations, because how then can we make sense of the fact that as a term of managerial art, empowerment is virtually synonymous with '*employee* empowerment'? (So much so that the former is little more than an abbreviation for the latter.) For surely if any set of people are empowered, be they employees or whatever, then, by definition, their power *is* increased? How could it be otherwise given the very meaning of the words 'empowered' and 'empowerment'?

What will be argued here is that it does make significant if highly qualified sense to talk of empowerment not increasing the power of employees, but that it requires a good deal of explication of the nature of organisational power before that sense can be made clear. Hence, despite its apparently self-contradictory nature, the question 'Does empowerment empower?' is not one which we can rule out *a priori*. Note though, that it is a question which is only being asked of empowerment as a term of managerial art. This is not just because this is the context which is of concern here (although that is reason enough), but also because it is the only one in which there is any sort of case to answer. Outside the managerial context, the question of whether empowerment empowers probably is a contradiction in terms. It certainly is for empowerment in that generalised, everyday sense from which the specialised managerial use derives. It is also, though less obviously, the case for empowerment in a third specifically democratic sense, against which the managerial usage is both compared and contrasted (Kinlaw, 1995, pp. 13–16). In fact, as we shall see, it is in the *contrast* with democratic empowerment that it becomes possible to talk of empowerment not increasing the power of employees in the case of the managerial variety. So although the question of whether or not empowerment empowers is only being asked of the managerial variety, it follows that an answer requires an explication of the democratic variety as well. Moreover, to properly understand both these specialised usages, the undifferentiated everyday usage from which they both derive must also be analysed.

EMPOWERMENT IN GENERAL

As an everyday lexical item, the word 'empowerment' is no more than the sum of its semantically significantly parts. To '*em*power' is simply to bring about the possession of power. In so far as the word has much currency, it is used to denote a situation in which that bringing about is effected through legal or at least vaguely official means. For example, police officers not only 'proceed in a westerly direction', they are also 'empowered by law'. Less usually, 'empower' is used of situations in which the possession of power is brought about by any means at all, be it official or unofficial, mental or physical, natural, supernatural, or whatever. Thus, in its usual and more restricted usage, 'empower' is mostly a somewhat fancy synonym for 'authorize'; while in its less usual and broader usage it is mostly a decidedly fancy synonym for 'enable'. In either case, the noun form 'empower*ment*' can be used for both the event of bringing about the possession of power or else the resulting condition of possessing that power; in other words, for both the process and its outcome.

This much is straightforward enough and makes clear the necessary connection with increasing the power of the empowered that, unsurprisingly, holds good for 'empowerment' in this its fundamental and everyday sense. What difficulties there are arise not from 'empowerment' as such, but rather the root word for which it is merely the addition of a prefix and suffix, namely 'power' – an endlessly discussed concept, especially in sociological literature but also, by extension, in writings on organisational theory.[1] Fortunately, these are not discussions which need be gone into here. It can be readily accepted that power takes many different forms. Distinctions between them need be recognised only as far as this contributes to an understanding of 'empowerment' as a term of managerial art: the sense ultimately at issue here. (I shall not, for example, bother to distinguish between 'power' and 'influence'.)

DEMOCRATIC EMPOWERMENT

The democratic conception of empowerment is clearly very close to the everyday. What makes it 'democratic' is that it is all about transferring powers of decision-making from the governing to the governed. It is therefore about democracy in something more than just the basic sense of 'government by consent': that is, having governments accountable to the people they govern (usually through periodic elections). Indeed, the underlying assumption of democratic empowerment is that accountability alone is not enough. People, it is said, have to 'take control of their own lives' to make society 'truly democratic'. Rather than leaving decision-making to politicians or (worse) 'faceless bureaucrats', citizens in a truly democratic society should do it themselves or, at least, participate in the decision-making process. The problem, it is said, with mere accountability, is that is compatible with a situation in which decision-making is wholly under the control of those in governing positions. The people can ultimately pass judgement on that decision-making but are otherwise uninvolved. They can therefore end up having to live with decisions that are not to their liking. More generally (and here democratic empowerment links up with the ideal of 'direct' as opposed to 'representative' democracy), people have been rendered passive in areas where they have both a right and duty to be active. The solution to both problems is therefore to transcend mere accountability and transfer as much decision-making as possible from those who are accountable to those to whom they are accountable; that is, from the governing to the governed. In this, democratic empowerment is clearly at one with our undifferentiated everyday use of the word empowerment. Both entail an increase in power for those being empowered, with democratic empowerment merely marking out the particular case of power increasing through an enlargement of people's decision-making capacities. (Clearly, the more people can take charge of the decisions affecting their lives then in that respect, the more power they have.) It is unsurprising, therefore that the whole concept of democratic empowerment can be effectively summed up in that ubiquitous slogan of the 1960s and 1970s: 'power to the people'. This was a period when the concept of democratic empowerment was very much to the fore, with talk of 'black power', 'worker's power', and even (God help us) 'student power', as well as of 'national liberation movements', 'women's liberation', 'gay liberation', and so on. It is doubtful that the word 'empowerment' ever had much currency in these discourses (at least in published works). However, as a common element in all of them is a call for a greater share of power for what is seen as the dispossessed or marginalized, one can say that the idea is very much present.

EXTENSIONS OF DEMOCRATIC EMPOWERMENT

It is probably true to say that it is only when taken up by management theorists in relatively recent years that the word 'empowerment' has had much circulation beyond its somewhat restricted everyday use. There is also perhaps proof of the growing ideological dominance of such theorizing in the fact that, following upon its use by writers on management, the word then starts to be used in contexts where the democratic variety, or at least something close to it, is the kind of empowerment at issue. We find this quasi-democratic usage in relation to such public and personal services as education, health and welfare provision, psychotherapy, urban regeneration, and the like.[2] The people being empowered are the students, claimants, patients, council tenants, and so on. What is supposed to happen is that instead of being the passive recipients of the decisions of officials and professionals, these people now make some decisions for themselves or (more probably) participate in the decision making process along with the officials and professionals. Consequently, such empowerment involves a transfer of power from those in a relatively privileged position in terms of authority or expertise to those who are relatively disadvantaged in either respect. This is clearly analogous to the situation of democratic empowerment even where the relationship involved is far removed from anything like the governing-to-governed one of democratic empowerment proper. Perhaps most crucially, the similarity extends to the fact that, as with democratic empowerment proper, the transfer of power also takes place within a context where despite the power disparity between them, the relatively privileged are in some way accountable to the relatively disadvantaged. This is not, of course, in the way that (democratic) governments are accountable to an electorate, but certainly in the way that officials are accountable to citizens, or professionals to their clients: that is, as people who are there to serve the interests of students, claimants, patients, council tenants, and so on.[3]

Finally, having hinted at proof of ideological dominance in what looks to be the popularisation of the word 'empowerment' through writings on management, modesty in the face of this reflected glory demands acknowledgement of the fact that this dominance is much less to do with the intellectual force of such writings than the brute political reading of a growing marketisation of societies, leading to more and more institutions either becoming businesses or being run 'like businesses'.

MANAGERIAL EMPOWERMENT

On the face of it, managerial empowerment is close to the democratic sort. Whatever USP (unique selling point) writers on the subject might bring to their accounts, they all seem to agree that what defines empowerment in an organisational or business context is that it is to be understood in contradistinction to what is invariably spoken of as 'traditional command and control management'.[4] Under this contrary system as little power as possible is given to all those in relatively subordinate positions and to shop-floor workers in particular. Everything is as far as possible subordinated to commands issuing from the top, with gradually diminishing degrees of discretion for all those beneath until those at the very bottom are left with as little as possible. With its opposite, the 'empowered organisation', things are of course reversed. As much power as possible is given to all those in relatively subordinate positions and to shop-floor workers in particular. Commands from the top are kept to a strategic minimum and there is as much discretion as possible at every descending level and especially the very bottom. As with the description of the command and control model, this represents an ideal to which organisations can merely aspire, but in broad outline at least the picture is clear enough and it appears to be one in which, as with democratic empowerment, power is being transferred from the top to the bottom. We even find a self-conscious echoing of a specifically 1960s and 1970s notion of democratic empowerment in talk of the empowered organisation as 'the liberated organisation'[5] – an elaboration which not only adds a touch of radical chic to an otherwise staid managerial doctrine but also gives an even greater appearance of paradox to any assertion that empowerment within organisations is not about increasing the power of employees.

Before attempting to unravel that seeming paradox, two very particular defining features must be added to the very general characterisation of managerial empowerment that has just been given. The first is the previously noted feature that it is very specifically a matter of *employees* being empowered. The second is that it is strictly a matter of *managers* doing that empowering. In other words, organisational empowerment of the kind at issue here is only to do with employees being empowered by managers.

This is obviously not true of empowerment in general or even of all empowerment within an organisational context; one might talk, for example, of an 'empowered' board of directors (Lorsch, 1995). However, it is true of empowerment as it generally features in management literature. Here the empowerment is of employees by managers because of the defining contrast with the command and control model. This entails that it is the empowerment of employees which is being spoken of because it is these same people's lack of power under that opposing system which is providing the comparison. Likewise, because the contrast is with two opposing models of *management*, it follows that empowerment has to be something within the gift of management for discussion to take the form it does: that is, a debate about which of the two approaches to adopt. Obviously, were empowerment not in the gift of managers there would be nothing to debate.

This is not to deny that pressures of various kinds can be at issue in determining whether or not managers should adopt a policy of empowerment. Still less it is to deny that empowerment could be a policy imposed on managers (by legislation or the threat of industrial action, for instance). But it is to say that this would not then be empowerment in the sense discussed in literature on management theory. That, whatever the pressures influencing the decision, must in the last analysis be a management decision in order to be the policy issue it is presumed to be in that literature – and therefore here.

This point is also worth making to clear up confusion regarding the apparently sage contention that managers cannot 'give' empowerment, employees have to 'take it'.[6] If this means that employees have to be empowered for empowerment to take place, then of course it is true by definition. If it means that empowerment cannot be imposed on employees but must be willingly accepted by them, then as a question of the successful implementation of a policy of empowerment it might be true to some greater or lesser extent. But if what is being denied is that empowerment is something within the gift of managers, then it is clearly not the sort of empowerment at issue in management literature and therefore here. That sort of empowerment must first be given by managers *before* employees can take it. Otherwise it is not the policy issue it is being presumed to be.

Having required this form of empowerment to be something done to employees by managers, it must of course be allowed that there is not necessarily any sharp distinction between the two roles. Managers can also be employees; and in the case of public companies, invariably are. Moreover, as something which cascades down the organisation, empowerment is something which will apply to managers along with shop-floor workers. None the less, empowerment within a business or organisational context is usually taken to be something which happens to employees who, whether or not they are also managers, occupy a relatively subordinate position – even if in some cases their subordination is only to those occupying the topmost management position. Also, the ultimate subjects of the empowerment process has to be those at or near the bottom of the organisational pyramid (there is nowhere else for it to go). No only that, but because they are the *most* commanded and controlled under the old system, the people at the bottom are nearly always the dominant focus of the process and are, of course, the people most equatable with 'employees'. So while some qualification must be allowed, it is usually justifiable to speak of empowerment as something done to 'employees' by 'managers'. For this reason also, and despite its somewhat misleading connotations, I have chosen to speak of 'managerial empowerment' rather than an alternative such as 'organisational empowerment' which, although it would serve to mark a distinction from other forms of empowerment, would not convey that notion of empowerment as an instrument of managerial policy which concerns me.

TWO DIFFERENT FORMS OF POWER

There is a distinction made by Hobbes between two different forms of power which, when suitably modified, can play a crucial part in understanding the way that empowerment of this managerial variety need not involve increasing the power of employees. Hobbes speaks of the distinction as being between 'original' (or 'natural') powers and 'instrumental' powers. He seems to see the difference as being between powers belonging to those 'Faculties of Body, or Mind' which we are born with – such as 'extraordinary Strength, Forme, Prudence, Arts, Eloquence, Liberality, Nobility' – and those capacities we subsequently acquire by the exercise of original powers or by force of circumstances – such as 'Riches, Reputation, Friends and the secret working of God which men call Good Luck' (Hobbes, 1968, p. 150).

As it stands, this is obviously a very fundamental division between different forms of power, perhaps offering a framework within which other and less fundamental forms might be placed.[7] I propose, however, to derive from it a related and equally fundamental division which although perhaps not as categorical as Hobbes's (it may well allow overlaps), will serve our very particular purpose better. It is a distinction between those powers which, whether genetic or acquired, belong to us as lone individuals as against those which we possess through occupying a social role of some kind. So, for example, it is one thing to be born with intelligence or acquire an education, quite another to be a judge, general, private soldier, prisoner, manager, shop-floor worker, or own the company, possess mineral rights, have an aristocratic title, and so on. I shall speak of the first as 'personal' powers, the latter as 'positional'. Note that as with Hobbes, I am only concerned with power as an attribute of individual human beings. So when I speak of 'positional power', this is not to be confused with the power of a particular set of social arrangements to influence events. Rather, it is a reference to power that is possessed by an individual human being in a positional as opposed to a personal *way*.

Note also that while, as I stated, the personal way might be genetic or acquired, the positional way is, of course, strictly acquired. This is so even if, as might be the case with such things as the ownership of property or the possession of a title, acquisition is at the moment of birth. The point is that ownership of property and the like are not anything we carry around with us as physical or mental characteristics. In that sense, they are not 'personal'. Rather they are attributes rooted in social relationships. We possess them because of a position we occupy in relation to other people. That position gives us the power in question. Essentially, therefore, positional power is exercised through other people. It is the way they behave in virtue of our occupancy of that position which constitutes the power in question, either because it forces them to do what we say, inclines them to defer to our wishes, or whatever. Almost needless to say, positional power can far exceed the personal sort in scale and scope. For example, large, loud, cunning and well versed in the operation of financial transactions though he undoubtedly was, Robert Maxwell could not have done what he did had he not been in charge of Mirror Group Newspapers and the Maxwell Communications Corporation. The point about positional power is that it can enlarge our merely personal power by putting the power of others at our disposal. As Hobbes puts it with reference to 'the Power of a Common-wealth' as an example of instrumental power, 'The Greatest of humane Powers, is that which is compounded of the powers of most men, united... in one person... that has the use of all their Powers depending on his will' (Hobbes, 1968, p. 150).

POWER IN ORGANISATIONS

What gave Robert Maxwell his positional power was his role within a group of interlocking organisations, and it is in terms of *organisational* position that we can most sharply mark out an otherwise sometimes hazy distinction between personal and positional power. One can, for example, have all the strength and cunning imaginable yet exercise very little power if excluded from positions of influence within organisations. Conversely, one can be significantly lacking in the qualities which make for a forceful personality yet exercise a good deal of power because of occupying just such a position (think of Maxwell's sons for instance).

Organisations do more than just make the distinction clear, of course; they also very largely account for the disparity in scope and scale between the two forms of power. In any relatively advanced society, power is very largely exercised through formally structured organisations of some kind – be they voluntary associations, business companies, government ministries, or whatever. Consequently, it is the fact of operating through these dominant instruments of power which, more than anything else, accounts for the potentially greater scale and scope of positional as opposed to personal power. Things might be different in smaller, less complex societies, of course. Their relative absence of formally structured organisations allows more of a role for a purely personal form of power – being bigger than anyone else, for example. However, in a complex, industrial society such as ours, power is both largely positional and also largely organisational. (Perhaps the only significant exception to this rule is in relation to fame or social prestige, where there can be power which is positional in the sense of being dependent on social relationships, yet not also organisational in the sense of being dependent on a role within a formally constituted body of some kind: the situation of the divorced Princess Diana, for instance.)

The fact that power as exercised through organisations is not only the paradigm of positional power but also its chief vehicle of expression, does not mean that the two are identical: that positional and organisational power are one. Power within organisations can also be personal. It can stem, for example, from expertise or force of character rather than place within the organisational hierarchy. What we can say, though, is that in the ordinary run of events, power in organisations is very much more about the positional variety than the personal. For example, although there might be some exceptions, the forceful junior manager will nearly always have less influence on the organisation than a very much senior manager however lacking in forcefulness.

What we can also say is that positional power is very much more integral to the notion of an organisation than its purely personal counterpart. Beyond some vaguely defined limit, the exercise of personal power within organisations is a disruption of what is supposed to be the case. It is an exceeding of authority: a going beyond what place in the organisational hierarchy supposes. The point is that while personal power is clearly a factor within organisations, it is not a purely organisational form of power. The same qualities of intelligence and so on which constitute personal power can also function outside an organisational context. This is not the case with any sort of role within a formally constituted hierarchy; by definition, it can only exist within an organisational context. (The fact of such a hierarchy is integral to being 'an organisation'.) And, of course, hierarchical role is not only an exclusively organisational form of power, but also a paradigmatically positional form as well. In fact, in terms of the sort of exclusively organisational power constituted by hierarchical role, we can virtually define 'an organisation' as nothing more than a vehicle for the exercise of positional power through hierarchical role: positional being the kind of power which, as the previous section noted, is exercised through *other* people.

COMMANDING AND HOLDING TO ACCOUNT

There are two very different ways of exercising positional power within an organisation: one way based on command, the other on accountability.[8] In a certain respect, the two ways are the very opposite of each other.

For command, the dividing line is between those who issue instructions and those who receive them. For accountability, it is between those who are answerable and those to whom they are answerable. So whereas with command, positional power is about a *downward* movement through the organisational hierarchy, with accountability it is all about an *upward* movement. From a command perspective, someone's positional power within an organisation depends on the number of hierarchical levels that are either directly or through intermediaries, following that person's instructions. For accountability, it depends on the number of levels that are either directly or through intermediaries, ultimately answerable to that person.

The hierarchical levels themselves are, of course, exactly the same ones in each case. Though they differ in direction, command and accountability will very obviously mirror each other. What goes for one will, directional factors aside, go for the other. The reason for this is, of course, because accountability within organisations is also about following commands. It is concerned with if, and how well, instructions of one sort or another have been carried out. In terms of organisational structures, what we are accountable for is what we have been commanded to do. Consequently, though accountability and command do mirror each other, it is very much a case of the former reflecting the latter. In other words, given that it is all about being answerable for carrying out instructions, it follows that the system of accountability within an organisation will be a response to its system of command. What is required by way of command determines what needs to be required by way of accountability. So, for example, where instructions are detailed and frequent, so is the sort of supervision demanded. Conversely, where they are loose and infrequent, couched in terms of aims and objectives for instance, then the appropriate sort of supervision will be equally loose and infrequent – perhaps demanding no more than that the aims and objectives are met in some more or less permissible fashion.

We can summarise by saying that the matching systems of command and accountability will together amount to nothing less than the basic management structure of the organisation. Who commands whom and who is accountable to whom constitutes its hierarchical divisions. And as the examples just given illustrate, the style of management – tight, loose, or whatever – is fundamentally constituted by the manner in which command, and therefore accountability, are structured. Put even more generally, command and accountability make up the system of positional power within organisations and this, in its turn, constitutes their fundamental management structure; which, given the earlier definition of an organisation as 'a vehicle for the exercise of positional power', is only to be expected.

POWER AND RESPONSIBILITY

To be at the receiving end of managerial commands is to be 'held responsible' for carrying them out and, moreover, for carrying them out effectively. This is a very particular sort of responsibility. It is not, at least not in the first instance, about eligibility for praise and reward. If that follows, it will follow subsequently and as a consequence of carrying out what was required in some particularly effective way. Being 'held responsible' on the other hand, is all about being answerable for things going wrong. It is about liability for blame and punishment if what was required was not carried out or not carried out effectively. As such, it is very much bound up with accountability, for what accountability is all about is being answerable for things going wrong. What a system of accountability is supposed to do within an organisation, is to provide a means by which people are answerable for failures and shortcoming in relation to what they are being held responsible for. In its turn, what they are responsible for depends on the commands issued to them; commands which, as we saw in the previous section, determine what they are accountable for. Thus, the function of responsibility within a management structure is as a kind of intermediary between command and accountability: a specification of what, as a consequence of commands, people within the organisation are accountable for.

These rather obvious points are worth making to remind ourselves of the very different situation of people within organisations when they issue rather than receive commands. Here the really dramatic contrast is between the people at the very top of the organisation and those at the very bottom. Those at the top issue but do not receive commands – there is no one to issue them; those at the bottom receive but do not issue commands – there is no one to receive them; while those in the middle will, to varying degrees, alternate between issuing and receiving. (It is these differing relationships to commands which *place* people at the top, the bottom, and the middle.)

The fact of issuing but not receiving commands means that whatever responsibilities those at the top might have, and whatever their accountability (to boards of directors or whatever), neither those responsibilities nor that accountability will take the form peculiar to those beneath them in the organisational hierarchy. Neither of them will be the sort of responsibility and accountability which follows from receiving commands; the sort where, as we have seen, the responsibility is for carrying out commands, and the accountability is for any failures or shortcoming in that carrying out.

This exclusion is important because there is a tendency to think of responsibility only in terms of the issuing of commands and not also their receiving. We speak of the 'responsibilities of command', of the 'burdens of office', and of 'power bringing responsibilities'. In so doing, we choose to measure what we refer to as the 'burden of responsibility' as simply a matter of the scale of our responsibilities. It is what we are responsible for in terms of the organisational area which counts: a section as opposed to the whole plant, a big company as opposed to a small one, a part of the job as opposed to the whole thing, and so on. By this measure, it is clear that the further up the organisational hierarchy a person is the greater his or her burden of responsibility.

So it is, but this should not blind us to the fact that there is the other kind of responsibility which comes from being at the receiving end of commands. What I would argue is that this other kind of responsibility carries a burden which can make up for in intensity what it lacks in scale. This is because in being a responsibility for carrying out commands, it is both more direct and specific than anything thrown up by responsibilities of scale. It is one thing to bear responsibility for the overall performance of a part or even the whole of an organisation, quite another and potentially just as stressful a thing to be responsible for meeting the requirements of an immediate superior. The latter inevitably involves a degree of subordination to a specific individual which the former does not. It is also a form of responsibility in which the further down the hierarchy it goes, the more and more linked it becomes to the performance of specific tasks and hence the more subject to monitoring it becomes. In contrast, the further up the hierarchy they feature the less specific and day-to-day responsibilities of scale become. Also, it could be suggested, the less dependent any final reckoning is on individual performance rather than a collective contribution or even the exigencies of circumstance – the behaviour of competitors, market trends, and so on. It is no wonder then that, contrary to what was once a popular notion, stress is now seen as no less a feature of the shop-floor than the executive office.[9] In the latter case, the pressure stem from those much-recognised 'responsibilities of command'; in the former, from those less-recognised responsibilities relating to being at the receiving end of commands: what might, in contrast, be called 'responsibilities of subordination'.

For all but those at the very top and bottom of organisations (the non-receivers and non-issuers of commands respectively), the two forms of responsibility and their attendant stresses will be combined because of their alternation between receiving and issuing commands. What we can say though is that the further down the organisational structure people are, the more responsibilities of command decrease and those of subordination increase; while the further up they are, the more responsibilities of command increase and those of subordination decrease – which in the last analysis might well make the burdens of responsibility more or less equal at all levels. Certainly, while those at or near the top face a final reckoning for their overall stewardship which those at or near the bottom do not, it is also probably true that on a day-to-day basis it is more blessed to give than receive when what is handed over are commands – if only because it is a good deal more comfortable to be answered to than answerable towards.

EMPOWERMENT IN CONTEXT

Empowerment is often presented as a form of, or extension of, employee participation.[10] To some extent this is obviously correct. In being about employees taking over some management functions, empowerment obviously does overlap with some forms of employee participation. In particular, it resembles earlier moves to 'job enrichment' or 'job enlargement' – trends distinguished as concerned with the 'quality of working life'. What it is not so obviously linked to is participation in the perhaps core sense of shared decision-making.[11] That is, a situation in which management shares its power of decision-making with employees (as in, for example, the German system of co-determination). If empowerment did involve this form of participation, then would be overlapping with what we have distinguished as 'democratic empowerment' and, as such, would entail increased power for employees. It follows then, that determining whether or not empowerment necessarily produces such an increase requires determining whether or not it necessarily involves participation in the sense of shared decision-making.

Problematic also is the link which is very often made between empowerment and that perhaps dominant theme in present-day management, the attainment of 'quality', total or otherwise, in the production of goods and services (basically, a situation of 'zero defects' and an overall responsiveness to the needs of customers). What makes the linkage problematic is that it rests on the claim that for quality to be attainable, staff must be empowered; that they must, as the jargon has it, 'take ownership' of quality for its goals to be met.[12] Whether this claim is true is not an issue to be settled here. An alternative and earlier view would be to stress management control systems as the solution to problems of quality.[13] What does seem undeniable though, is that empowerment as a doctrine has evolved within the context of the drive for quality; not just chronologically, as another phenomenon for the 1980s, but conceptually as well. We see this in the fact that empowerment is very often, perhaps more often than not, embedded within quality programmes: seen as an element within that approach rather than a policy in its own right. (An example in the next section will illustrate this.)

Altogether less problematic is the association which undeniably holds between empowerment and another 1980s phenomenon, namely 'delayering'.[14] Given that elimination of whole levels of middle and line management which constitutes delayering, there would seem to be little option *but* to adopt a policy of employee empowerment; for if there are fewer managers to manage them, particularly at a supervisory level, then clearly workers are just going to have to manage themselves rather more. Moreover, how are they going to do this except by being organized into 'self-directed work teams': that is, groups of worker which, as far as possible manage themselves? Thus, delayering would appear to necessitate not only empowerment in general but also the very particular form of those self-directed work teams which, as examples will illustrate, it invariably takes.

Whether driven by the 'push' of quality, the 'pull' of delayering, or simply justified as an approach in its own right, empowerment is invariably presented as something which will release the 'full potential' of staff.[15] Freed from management command and control they will acquire the initiative and commitment which will enable them to achieve quality, cope with delayering, or to generally just perform better. In short, empowerment is seen as a way of maximising the productive capacity of staff: making them more efficient and effective through an enhanced ability to work efficiently and effectively. This links empowerment to staff development and training (again, something examples will illustrate). It involves development in that it is about enhancing the abilities of staff, and about training in so far as this is necessary for achieving that enhancement.

EMPOWERMENT IN PRACTICE

Empowerment takes many forms depending on the nature of the organisation and the judgement of the managers implementing the policy.[16] For McDonalds in the UK it has meant agonising about whether staff should use standardised greetings to customers or be free, 'within guidelines', to improvise. (British customers were put off by that very American quality of eager conformity which the standardised greetings manifested.) For the publishers HarperCollins, empowerment has meant *compulsory* community work for staff (doing gardening for pensioners, and so on) in order, it is said, to instil the team spirit necessary for commercial success. For the restaurant chain Harvester, part of the Forte group (now owned by Granada), empowerment has meant the organising of restaurant staff into self-directed teams, and a consequent loss of a whole bottom layer of management (assistant branch managers). Each team has a series of 'accountabilities' – things they are responsible for – which they divide between them. Teams have no leaders, but include at least one 'team expert': someone who knows what the 'accountabilities' involve. Initially appointed, 'experts' are now elected by the team members. As well as the more obvious duties of restaurant staff, 'accountabilities' include things such as monitoring sales figures and even recruitment. Training and some personnel issues are handled by a 'coach', leaving the branch manager to concentrate on marketing rather than, as in the past, overseeing the day-to-day running of the restaurant.

When linked to computer operations, empowerment can be combined with a great deal of very detailed monitoring. At the accounts headquarters of the Alliance and Leicester Building Society, empowerment has meant giving staff dealing with telephoned inquiries discretion to award refunds to complaining customers. However, all calls to the line are recorded, and the speed, frequency and length of responses electronically monitored. As a notice posted upon the department accurately puts it:

> Empowerment defines freedom to take action to achieve objectives within a predetermined framework and a set of values. It implies change, trust, and more informal decision making but not lack of control.

With the Rover group (now owned by BMW) we see all of the linkages noted in the previous section. Here empowerment has to be seen in the context of Rover's switch to Japanese-style quality production methods from around 1988 onwards (based on their association with Honda), combined with their participative 'New Deal' for staff agreed in 1992.

There has been delayering through a reduction in the hierarchical levels within the various business units from twelve to six (the aim is five). Responsibility has shifted to production teams coordinated by a team leader who has no disciplinary function, is elected at some plants (for example Longbridge), and appointed at others (for example Land Rover). As a consequence, the responsibilities of the diminished band of line managers has switched from a 'task orientation' (getting the job done) to a 'people orientation' (helping staff get the job done).

The 'New Deal' for staff was instrumental in getting shop-floor workers (now called 'associates') to adopt the new working methods. Its notable features include a 'single status' for all employees (ending the monthly vs hourly paid division), everyone wearing the same 'company workwear', 'open and honest two-way communication', continued recognition for trade unions and 'enhanced' consultation with them. There is also a strong emphasis on training and employee development along with a commitment to the 'maximum devolution of authority and accountability to the employees actually doing the job'. In addition, the company promises no lay-offs and no compulsory redundancies. Everyone that wants to stay with Rover is guaranteed a job; not necessarily the job they now have, but *a* job and one for which, if necessary, they will be retrained. (Where the new job is at a lower pay scale, staff are paid their old salaries for two years.) In return for all these benefits, staff are required to commit themselves to a 'continuous improvement' of the firm's 'performance and competitive position', are 'expected to be flexible', and 'participate' in the training necessary to 'improve the processes on which we work'.

POWER AND EMPOWERMENT

It was noted at the end of the section before last, that a common theme in talk of empowerment is that it is all about realising the full potential of staff to produce at maximum efficiency and effectiveness. This can mean two things: (1) *enabling* staff to do more, and (2) *getting* them to do more. That is, making it possible for them to do more as opposed to simply requiring them to do more. In theory and in practice, empowerment involves both these things. It 'enables' staff to do more by training and development, and it 'gets' them to do more by requiring them to take on extra responsibilities in the form of functions that are the preserve of management under a command and control system. (Note these two elements in the Rover 'New Deal' outlined in the previous section, and the way they respectively parallel the 'enable' and 'authorise' senses of 'empower' discussed in the section on 'Empowerment in General'.)

It is, of course, possible to both enable and get staff to do more in ways that are not to do with empowerment: for example, by establishing more efficient working practices, by installing better equipment, a little judicious sweating, and so on. However, what analysis and examples have hopefully shown is that it is training and development along with a transfer of responsibilities which is distinctive, and even definitive, of empowerment in relation to these two ways of realising staff potential.

In reply, it could no doubt be suggested that any and all increases in the productive efficiency of staff are 'empowering' no matter what the means employed, be it more efficient working practices or whatever – after all, they all *do* give staff the power to be more productive. But then empowerment is synonymous with any and all increases in productive efficiency. It loses any distinctive application and can be replaced by 'making more efficient', or something of the sort. Conversely, what makes enabling or getting staff to do more through empowerment something distinctive is precisely because they are being achieved through the very particular means of training/development and a transfer of responsibilities (respectively).

In terms of the distinction between personal and positional power, it is clear that any increase in power through training and development involves the personal variety, while any increase through wider responsibilities would be positional. Becoming, for example, more skilled and confident through training and development is to do with a change in personal attributes. Conversely, getting self-directed work teams to take charge of quality rather than leaving it up to supervisory inspection – an example of empowerment in the form of staff taking on extra responsibilities – is all about altering organisational relationships and is, therefore, a paradigm of the positional.

It is also clear that in so far as training and development are effective, they will entail an increase in personal power for staff: they will become more skilled, more confident, or whatever. It follows then, that those who say that empowerment does not increase the power of employees are wrong in terms of the personal power relating to training and development. In terms of that particular sort of power, empowerment in the form of training and development can very well entail increased power for employees.

It is, I presume, a very safe bet that anyone who denies empowerment means increasing the power of employees is not thinking of what I have distinguished as 'personal power'. Almost certainly, they are thinking of what I have distinguished as 'positional power' and, more precisely, the organisational form which such power paradigmatically takes. What they have in mind is a denial of any suggestion that the power of managers will be diminished by employee empowerment. The point here is that it is plausible to argue that the personal power of employees can be increased without a loss of managerial power. I am not, for example, made any less powerful by someone else's gain in skill or confidence (unless, of course, it is somehow used against me). In the case of positional power, however, such diminution would seem all too possible. Being essentially relational, it would seem to be very much a zero-sum game.[17] At least in so far as they operate within the same set of social relationships, the more positional power someone has, the less for someone else. For example, if my status within a particular pecking order goes up a place, then someone else's has gone down a place.

On the face of it, such is the situation for empowerment by way of a transfer of responsibilities from management to staff. Managers are losing part of their power to command and employees are gaining the power to decide certain matters for themselves. So what is that but a loss of power for managers and a gain for employees?

Taken in isolation, this certainly is the situation. We have seen, however, that power within organisations is not unidirectionally based on a downward flow of command. It is also based on an upward flow of accountability. The crucial factor here is that while the 'command-power' of managers is diminished by empowerment in the sense of a transfer of responsibilities, their 'accountability-power' is not. In fact, it is increased. As a consequence of them taking on more responsibilities, there is more for employees to be accountable to managers for: a wider range of duties for which they are answerable to managers. For example, in being empowered to give refunds, staff at the Alliance and Leicester have become accountable for decisions about refunds. More broadly, in taking on responsibility for quality, workers at Rover have become accountable for something which would previously have been the concern of managers through the implementation of quality inspection procedures. So while the command aspect of management command and control is undeniably diminished by empowerment, the control aspect is actually enlarged. Overall, therefore, it is plausible to suggest that in contrast to what holds for training and development, empowerment in the form of a transfer of responsibilities from managers to employees does *not* increase the power of employees.[18] What would, of course, is not merely a transfer of responsibilities but a sharing of decision-making:

participation in that core sense which overlaps with democratic empowerment and therefore does involve an increase in power for employees. As far as ordinary usage goes, there is nothing to prevent this form of participation being spoken of as empowerment; after all, in overlapping with democratic empowerment it is close to the everyday sense of the word.[19] It is just that in terms of what is preached and practised in the name of empowerment as a term of managerial art, it is excluded. As a term of managerial art, empowerment can and does function independently of participation in this strong sense. In so far as empowerment of the managerial variety is a form of participation, it is so only in a very weak sense. It amounts, we can conclude, to nothing more radical than a form of job enrichment or enlargement based on delegation.[20]

MORALLY EVALUATING EMPOWERMENT

Given that it is not meant to be included anyway, it would take us too far afield to criticise the exclusion of shared decision-making from empowerment. It would amount, in fact, to an argument for redefining the term; which is a legitimate exercise, but raises wider issues than can be tackled here.

Taking empowerment as we find it, the most obvious criticism is that it involves an element of deception. Trading on the everyday sense of 'empower' it offers the promise of increased power to employees while in reality leaving power relationships within organisations altered but essentially intact. It gives the appearance of something new and radical while amounting to nothing more than old-fashioned delegation.[21]

In reply, it could be said that while, for reasons I have given, empowerment as a transfer of responsibilities from managers to staff does not lead to increased power for employees, this is not true of empowerment by way of training and development. Here, for reasons I have also given, the power of employees is increased.

The counter to this is to point out that this is not an increase which amounts to much in terms of power relationships within the organisation. Being, for example, more skilled and motivated is not going to increase the promotion prospects or bargaining power of any individual employee given that training and development will, in principle, do the same for every other employee. Moreover, given the very frequent combining of empowerment and delayering, the whole process is one of diminishing promotion prospects anyway.

Frustrated here, an advocate of the moral probity of empowerment might talk of increased job satisfaction: the increased responsibilities which come with empowerment make the job more interesting, more rewarding, and so on. All of which may be true.[22] However, the very obvious downside is that there are increased responsibilities and therefore a greater 'burden of responsibility'. Moreover, that burden is not of an essentially different form than before. What is happening is that management is being relieved of some of its 'responsibilities of command' by employees converting them into 'responsibilities of subordination'. What might previously have been a simple following of orders is now replaced by what might be broad guidelines, but this does not make employees any the less accountable to managers. What has altered is the way they are held accountable: through general guidelines rather than specific instruction. The element of subordination is no less present.

All in all, empowerment would seem to be a somewhat one-sided deal. Management gains from being partly relieved of its responsibilities while losing none of its power. Employees gain responsibilities while acquiring nothing by way of power within the organisation. More broadly, if empowerment works, then management gains by an enhancement of the productive capacities of staff. Thus, employees do more without getting anything from empowerment except the rather dubious privilege of having more to do.

Here the debate might turn towards those wider issues which I ruled out at the beginning of this section: things to do with the acceptability of existing organisational power structures and objectives. But even accepting these things as they are, there is something which experience has shown can be done to make empowerment a little less one-sided. It is for management to take on the sort of commitment to job security contained within the Rover group's 'New Deal' with its employees. Given this, and as experience from Rover shows,[23] employees can do what empowerment demands of them by way of gains in productive efficiency without the threat of working themselves out of a job. In this way the arrangement not only becomes a lot less one-sided but, arguably, a good deal more likely to succeed.

Notes

1. The favoured source for discussions of power in organisations is French and Raven (1959). For example, Thompson, 1993, pp. 88–90, offers a listing of different forms of power within organisations 'developed from a classification by Andrew Kakabadse (1982), who has built on the earlier work of French and Raven (1959)'.

2. For example: Gore (1993); Stevenson and Parsloe (1993); Worell and Remer (1992); Stewart and Taylor (1995).
3. In a business context, an equivalent would be talk of 'empowered' customers.
4. For example: in Kinlaw (1995); Brown and Brown (1994); Jenkins (1996); Terry and Hadland (1995). I should add that my sources for understanding 'empowerment' as a term of managerial art are not presumed to be definitive, or even distinguished, but rather, merely randomly representative.
5. As in Brown and Brown above.
6. See Oates (1992), where a human resource director is quoted as saying 'it took me a long time to learn a fundamental truth about empowerment. You can't give it: people have to take it.'
7. For example, the five forms identified by French and Raven, *op. cit.*
8. For a fuller discussion see Chryssides and Kaler (1996), chapter 4, where the discussion is put in the context of moral responsibility in general.
9. Correlating occupation to stress is a monstrously complex affair (for a survey, see Fletcher, 1988). Perhaps the safest contention is that there is no simple correlation, with stress being much more about the incidence of a range of factors within and across occupations rather than the occupations themselves (Fletcher, p. 5). Arguably, the most stressful situation is the combination of high demands, low support and low discretion typical of assembly-line work, with the high demand factors typical of executive work being off-set by high levels of support and discretion (Fletcher, pp. 29 and 32). The 'myth of executive stress' might be accounted for by the greater readiness of professionals to admit (boast?) they are suffering from nervous strain (Fletcher, p. 26).
10. For example: Plunkett and Fournier, *op. cit.*, for empowerment as a form of participation; and Kinlaw, *op. cit.*, pp. 2–3 and 6 for empowerment as an extension of participation.
11. See Chryssides and Kaler, *op. cit.*, pp. 99–105, for different senses of 'participation'.
12. The linkage to empowerment made by some advocates of quality is examined and referenced by several contributors to Wilkinson and Willmott (1995); for example by Wilkinson and Willmott on p. 16, L. McCardle *et al.* on pp. 159–60, and by D. Kerfoot and D. Knights on pp. 234–5.
13. See Wilkinson and Wilmott, *op. cit.*, pp. 8 and 38 for references to an original 'hard' form of quality with the emphasis on management control systems, and a later 'soft' version emphasising employee responsibility (the distinction is owed to the British Quality Association). Certainly, the founding fathers of the quality movement, Deming and Juran, seemed to have emphasised control rather than empowerment (Deming, 1986; Juran, 1988).
14. In so far as empowerment leads to productivity gains (see next paragraph), it could be said to be a response to 'downsizing' in general and not just 'delayering' in particular. That is, through productivity gains, empowerment could be a way of dealing with an overall reduction in staffing and not merely a reduction in supervisory staff. Empowerment is, however, only one of very many possible ways of achieving the required productivity

gains. In contrast (see this paragraph), empowerment seems the only possible response to delayering.
15. After saying that empowerment is 'not about increasing the power of employees', the quote by Randolph cited in the introduction goes on to say 'rather it is about releasing the knowledge and motivation that employees already have'. Talk of realising potential is a theme throughout Brown and Brown, *op. cit.*; Kinlaw, *op. cit.*, p. 7, defines 'empowerment' in terms of maximising the 'competent influence' of individuals and teams to improve organisational performance; while for Terry and Hadland, *op. cit.*, 'empowerment' and 'releasing potential' are taken as synonymous.
16. Sources for this section are: documents supplied by the Rover group; a site visit to the Land Rover plant; Donkin (1994); Arthur (1994); Pickard (1993) for information relating to Harvester; Open University (1995) for information relating to McDonald's, HarperCollins, Alliance and Leicester, and Rover group.
17. Those who deny that empowerment is a 'zero-sum game' (for example: Brown and Brown, *op. cit.*, pp. 13 and 18; Kinlaw, *op. cit.*, p. 16) are saying something which is only true in relation to empowerment as personal power.
18. It is plausible to argue that such is the increase in management control through empowerment that it actually leads to a *de*crease in the power of employees. This has been referred to as the 'empowerment paradox'. (See Gandz and Bird, 1996.) This echoes the traditional criticism of just about all forms of participation: namely, that they are tools of management manipulation which weaken the collective resolve of workers. This is typified by criticisms of quality of working life programmes, the sort of participation I have suggested is closest to empowerment (see, for example, Parker and Hansen, 1990).
19. Gandz and Bird, *op. cit.*, speak of employees sharing its decision-making as 'governance empowerment'. But given that advocacy of this sort of participation pre-dates talk of empowerment and is not even normally part of that discourse, it would seem no part of empowerment in the sense at issue here.
20. Kinlaw, *op. cit.*, p. 17, denies that empowerment is simply delegation. This is true in so far as it is also about personal power. But in so far as it is about the positional, delegation would seem to be all it does amount to.
21. A criticism cited in D. Oates, *op. cit.*, p. 34.
22. There is evidence that greater autonomy, variety of tasks, etc., can make workers happier and healthier. See Fletcher, *op. cit.*, p. 29.
23. A BBC television programme (BBC, 1995) recounts how a Land Rover worker invented a new foundry tool enabling a job previously requiring three people to be done by one person. This is only one instance among many. Since job security came in, Rover has seen a near eight-fold increase in improvement suggestions by staff, with savings up to 1995 totalling around £100 million. Needless to say, the worker who designed the new foundry tool, William Britton, said he would not have done so without the 'no compulsory redundancies' guarantee. (Voluntary redundancies are

a different matter. As I write, Rover are looking to lose 1500 jobs by voluntary agreement, with further losses being forecasted.)

References

Arthur, M. (1994) 'Rover Managers Learn to Take a Back Seat', *Personnel Management*, October, pp. 58–63.
BBC (1995) 'Working All Hours', BBC 2, 23 September.
Bound, G. (1994) *Beyond Total Quality Management: Toward the Emerging Paradigm* (Maidenhead: McGraw-Hill).
Brown, R. and Brown, M. (1994) *Empowered! A Guide to Leadership in the Liberated Organisation* (London: Nicholas Brealey).
Chryssides, G. and Kaler, J. (1996) *Essentials of Business Ethics* (Maidenhead: McGraw-Hill).
Deming, W.E. (1986) *Out of the Crisis* (Cambridge: Cambridge University Press).
Donkin, R. (1994) 'Rovers Cultural Revolution', *Financial Times*, 9 May, p. 14.
Fletcher, B. (1988) 'The Epidemology of Occupational Stress', in C.L. Cooper and R. Payne (eds), *Causes, Coping and Consequences of Stress at Work* (Chichester: Wiley).
French, J.R.P. and Raven, P. (1959) 'The Bases of Social Power', in D. Cartwright (ed.), *Studies in Social Power* (Ann Arbor: University of Michigan).
Gandz, J. and Bird, F.B. (1996) 'Ethics of Empowerment', *Journal of Business Ethics*, vol. 15, April, pp. 383–92.
Gore, J.M. (1993) *The Struggle for Pedagogies* (London: Routledge).
Hobbes, T. (1968) *Leviathan* (Harmondsworth: Penguin).
Jenkins, D. (1996) *Managing Empowerment: How to Make Business Re-engineering Work* (London: Century).
Juran, J.M. (1988) *Juran on Planning for Quality* (New York: The Free Press).
Kinlaw, D.C. (1995) *The Practice of Empowerment* (Aldershot: Gower).
Lakatos, I. (1970) 'Falsification and the Methodology of Scientific Research Programmes', in I. Lakatos and A. Musgrave (eds), *Criticism and the Growth of Knowledge* (Cambridge: Cambridge University Press).
Lorsch, J.W. (1995) 'Empowering the Board', *Harvard Business Review*, January–February, pp. 107–17.
McHugh, P. *et al.* (1993) *Beyond Business Process Re-engineering* (Chichester: Wiley).
Oates, D. (1992) 'Power to the People Who Want It', *Accountancy*, December, pp. 34–6.
Open University (1995) 'Empowerment', TV programme for T245.
Parker, M. and Hansen, D. (1990) 'The Circle Game', in W.M. Hoffman and J.M. Moore (eds), *Business Ethics: Readings and Cases in Corporate Morality* (New York: McGraw Hill).
Pickard, J. (1993) 'The Real Meaning of Empowerment', *Personnel Management*, November, pp. 28–33.
Plunkett, L.C. and Fournier, R. (1991) *Participative Management: Implementing Empowerment* (New York: Wiley).
Randolph, W.A. (1995) in L.K.R. Rothstein, 'The Empowerment Effort that Came Undone', *Harvard Business Review*, January–February, p. 30.

Stevenson, O. and Parsloe, P. (1993) *Community Care and Empowerment* (York: Joseph Rowntree Foundation).
Stewart, M. and Taylor, M. (1995) *Empowerment and Estate Regeneration* (Bristol: The Policy Press).
Terry, A. and Hadland, M. (1995) 'Reaping Benefits from Development', *People Management*, July, pp. 30–2.
Thompson, J.L. (1993) *Strategic Management: Awareness and Change* (London: Chapman & Hall).
Wilkinson, A. and Willmott, H. (eds) (1995) *Making Quality Critical* (London: Routledge).
Worell, J. and Remer, P. (1992) *Feminist Perspectives in Therapy: An Empowerment Model for Women* (Chichester: Wiley).

4 Organisational Empowerment: A Historical Perspective and Conceptual Framework

Julia M. Christensen Hughes

INTRODUCTION

The pursuit of organisational empowerment raises a number of important questions – all with ethical implications. To what extent can empowerment be achieved within organisational contexts when such entities are designed to control employee behaviour? What are the implications for empowered individuals when their personal goals and values conflict with those of the organisations they work for? What can we expect to be achieved through empowerment? In answer to the latter question, empowerment advocates suggest that it will result in many positive outcomes; 'empowerment promises to instill in our institutional life the same values of individual freedom, dignity, and self-governance that we readily embrace as a society' (Block, 1987, p. xiii). Its detractors suggest that empowerment is simply another management tool designed to provide organisations with increased control and cost efficiencies.

In exploration of these issues, this paper traces the struggle for empowerment over time. Its central premise is that by understanding issues of power and control encountered in the past, we can better understand the barriers to empowerment we face today. One critical barrier to empowerment is the fundamental tension that exists between the need of people to be autonomous and free-willed, and the need of organisations to monitor and control employee behaviour. As long as this tension remains unresolved, empowerment within organisational settings will be limited. Another key barrier is the lack of clarity that surrounds the concept of empowerment itself. In order to help address this issue, this chapter provides a conceptual framework through which multiple perspectives of empowerment may be understood. Objectives, processes and barriers are identified for five distinct types of empowerment.

A HISTORICAL OVERVIEW

Reportedly, the concept of empowerment originated with Aristotle's (384–322 BC) conceptualisation of power as potency; 'ideas and the movements of people and animals were a result of their own power' (Vincenti, 1993, p. 7). During the late 1600s and early 1700s this conceptualisation of personal power was rejected:

> With the development of positivism and experimentalism, the notion of power endowed to humans lost importance... As nature came to be understood as invariable and predictable... the notion of humans as empowered beings was abandoned altogether. This changed our conception of ourselves from active agents to passive objects. (Vincenti, 1993, p. 8)

This period of time has also been referred to as the *machine age* (Ackoff, 1974); 'those who held the mechanistic view found no need for teleological concepts – functions, goals, purposes, choice and free will – in explaining natural phenomena. Such concepts were considered to be either meaningless, illusory, or unnecessary' (p. 11). Not surprisingly, the machine age was followed by the industrial revolution, a time in which people came to be equated with 'parts' of the industrial machine; 'mechanization led to the dehumanization of man's work' (Ackoff, 1974, p. 11).

The late 1700s and early 1800s: domestic industry and the factory system

During the late 1700s and early 1800s, people who were employed typically worked in either domestic industry or in the newly-emerging factories. In domestic industry, people worked at home and were given materials by their employers to turn into finished goods. Workers were paid on the basis of their output and consequently had the opportunity to decide for themselves how many hours to work and when to work. Reportedly, they also had the opportunity to 'embezzle wool or silk, exchange poor quality material for good, conceal imperfections or devise ways to make the finished material heavier' (Marglin, 1976, pp. 93–4).

The factory system gradually replaced domestic industry in an effort by employers to increase their control over the production process. Within the factories, employees worked more regular and longer hours, product quality could be more closely monitored and production costs could be minimised. Compliant behaviour was assured through the enclosure of the factory (workers were controlled from the time they entered the factory gates until they exited) and constant surveillance (Foucault, 1977), as well as through a series of disciplinary procedures including fines and imprisonment:

> Elaborate and severe systems of fines were imposed by employers on workers who arrived late or left early, and for faulty work. If workers struck to protest against such employer-made laws, employers could take their workers to the criminal courts for breach of contract. (Friedman, 1977, p. 87)

Foucault (1977) described the power used in these settings as disciplinary power and suggested that while 'invisible' its effects were far reaching; 'it is everywhere and always alert, since by its very principle it leaves no zone of shade and constantly supervises the very individuals who are entrusted with the task of supervising' (Foucault, 1977, p. 177). By being 'enclosed' in the factory, workers and their supervisors were highly visible; 'their visibility assures the hold of the power that is exercised over them' (Foucault, 1977, p. 187).

This rigid control over people's lives existed outside the workplace as well. Writing in 1816, Tronchot described the orders given to students during a typical school day. He estimated that the pupils received over 200 commands a day, delivered by voice, bell and whistle. The start of a school day was described as follows:

> Enter your benches. At the word *enter*, the children bring their right hands down on the table with a resounding thud and at the same time put one leg into the bench; at the words *your benches* they put the other leg in and sit down opposite their slates... *Take your slates*. At the word *take*, the children, with their right hands, take hold of the string by which the slate is suspended from the nail before them, and, with their left hands, they grasp the slate in the middle; at the word *slates*, they unhook it and place it on the table. (Foucault, 1977, p. 167)

The factories employed both skilled and unskilled workers. Friedman (1977) suggested that different control strategies were used for managing people from the two groups. Unskilled labour was managed through a strategy of *direct control*, whereas *responsible autonomy* was used for the management of skilled labour (p. 78). Friedman (1977) defined direct control as 'coercive threats, close supervision and minimising individual worker responsibility'. Responsible autonomy involved giving workers status, authority and responsibility and 'encouraging them to adapt to changing situations in a manner beneficial to the firm' (p. 78). In explaining the rationale behind responsible autonomy Friedman (1977) suggested:

Skilled workers generally disciplined themselves and did not respond strongly to financial incentives... It took advantage of the much deeper attitude of craftsmen towards their work which characterised simple commodity production – self-respect, pride in certain standards of workmanship and customary rewards for different grades of skill. (p. 88)

Interestingly, Friedman (1977) also argued that responsible autonomy was a barrier to industrialisation; 'loyalty to firm, attention to good craftsmanship, expectations of a "just" wage or price were a hindrance to capitalists replacing major aspects of craftsmen's work with machines' (p. 89). Gartman (1983) argued that changes to production methods were required to maintain control over the labour process; 'capitalists are forced to constantly revolutionise production methods in order to overcome the struggle of workers generated by the contradictory class structure' (1983, p. 636).

Capitalists also sought the increasingly efficient use of labour power in order to produce surplus value. Surplus value was used for both increased consumption and for reinvesting in more productive techniques, which enabled the owner's of capital to remain competitive and to produce more surplus value in the future. Marx (1867) referred to this process as the *law of value*, whereby the capitalist is compelled 'to keep constantly extending his capital, in order to preserve it' (p. 555). Nord (1974), however, described this process as a 'vicious circle', noting that the creation of surplus value alienated workers from the output of their labour and led to the redefinition of societal values:

> The division of labor and private property generates alienation which, in turn, increases the emphasis on material products, which further accelerates the division of labor and the stress on accumulation, which results in further alienation. Capital, landed property and commodities are reified. People come to view economic events as subject to uncontrollable natural law. Man's creations – capital, machines, the economic system, and money – come to control man himself. (p. 571)

The mid-1800s and early 1900s: the era of scientific management

During the mid-1800s to the early 1900s, workers gained increased power through the abolition of Master and Servant Laws and the legalization of trade unions (Heron, 1989). At the same time, the move towards the factory system intensified. There was widespread adoption of new technology, further deskilling of workers' jobs, unprecedented economic and organisational growth, and monopoly capitalism and bureaucracy flourished. It was also at this time that Frederick

Taylor introduced his book, *The Principles of Scientific Management* (1911). Taylor advocated a form of direct control which involved managers breaking down work into its simplest components and then specifying to their employees exactly what was to be done, how it was to be done and the exact time allowed for doing it. Employers also sought ways to exert direct control over their workers beyond the factory gates. For example, in the USA Henry Ford employed social workers whose job it was to levy fines for a range of infractions including, 'inappropriate dress, non-attendance at church, swearing, visiting a pool hall, being shaved in a barber shop, accumulating debt' (Nightingale, 1982, p. 9).

In critiquing scientific management, Friedman (1977) argued that people were treated as if they were machines; 'the problem is that people are not machines. They may sell their labour power but they cannot alienate their minds or their will' (p. 94). Braverman (1974), conversely argued that scientific management was the answer to the problem of how best to control labour, and that advances in technology were an opportunity to control what previously had been accomplished through disciplinary and organisational procedures.

Friedman (1977) also criticised responsible autonomy and suggested that it was an impossible ideal given the contradiction between employee needs and the goals of the organisation; 'Responsible Autonomy does not remove alienation and exploitation, it simply softens their operation or draws workers' attention away from them' (p. 101). He suggested that worker alienation and exploitation became more apparent as business conditions required organisations 'to cut back on loyalty or satisfaction payments' (p. 101). Similarly, Gartman (1983) argued that measures such as responsible autonomy, 'generate worker consent by constituting the labor process as a "game"' (Gartman, 1983, p. 632).

In summarising his perspective on the two strategies, Friedman (1977) suggested that both direct control and responsible autonomy involve contradictions which result in a persistent, fundamental tension in the workplace:

> To treat workers as though they were machines, assuming they can be forced by financial circumstances or close supervision to give up direct control over what they do for most of their waking hours; or to treat workers as though they were not alienated from their labour power by trying to convince them that the aims of top managers are their own; both of these types of strategies involve a contradiction. People do have independent and often hostile wills which cannot be destroyed, and the aim of top managers ultimately is to make steady and high profits, rather than to tend to their workers' needs. (p. 106)

While acknowledging this tension, Friedman argued that as long as people were employed, the contradictions were difficult to avoid. Yet, workers had little option except to be employed; 'to work, one must have tools and equipment. And the tools and equipment are increasingly available only in bureaucracies' (Merton, 1968, p. 251). The task for employers was to use appropriate methods to support their preferred means of control. Direct control required 'well-defined lines of authority and a high proportion of white-collar staff' (Friedman, 1977, p. 106), whereas responsible autonomy required an 'elaborate ideological apparatus for co-opting workers' as well as 'relative employment security' (Friedman, 1977, p. 106).

Emphasising the role of ideology, Merton (1968) suggested that the, 'efficacy of social structure depends ultimately upon infusing group participants with appropriate attitudes and sentiments' (p. 252). Merton (1968) also drew attention to *dysfunctions of bureaucracy*. He argued that while concerned with precision, reliability and efficiency, bureaucracy could also be associated with *trained incapacity*, in which, 'one's abilities function as inadequacies or blind spots' (p. 252), and *goal displacement*, in which the ends of the organisation (the goals) become displaced by the means (policies and procedures). He argued that both trained incapacity and goal displacement prevented people from exercising good judgment and responding flexibly to changes in the environment; 'with increasing bureaucratization, it becomes plain to all who would see that man is to a very important degree controlled by his social relations to the instruments of production' (pp. 250–1).

The mid-1900s: the systems age

The mid-1900s have been referred to as the *Systems Age*; open-systems theory, free will, choice and teleology (the study of goal-seeking and purposeful behaviour) became integrated with our conception of science (Ackoff, 1974, p. 16). Academics began to focus on the dehumanising aspects of work and the human relations movement was born (see for example, Argyris, 1957; Herzberg, Mausner and Snyderman, 1959; Likert, 1967; Mayo, 1933; and McGregor, 1960). Several recent works trace these challenges (see for example, Ketchum and Trist, 1992; Lawler, 1986; Mansell, 1987; Nightingale, 1982; Zwerdling, 1980). A common theme in each of these reviews is that while the human relations movement sought to improve working conditions for employees, it failed to advance fundamental challenges to power relations in the workplace. For example, Nightingale (1982) wrote:

Human relations has focused on a form of participation which takes place within and is consistent with the conventional hierarchical structure of the work organization. Human relations has endeavoured to soften the effects of the command-and-obey system without requiring fundamental change to this system. (p. 14)

This criticism was answered in the mid-to-late 1900s, when fundamental challenges to organisational power structures did occur.

The 1970s and 1980s: the call for fundamental change

During the 1970s, challenges to the organisation of work became more radical; there was a growing demand for 'participation based on a substantial redistribution of power to organisation members at lower hierarchical levels' (Nightingale, 1982, p. 14). Quality of Working Life (QWL) was introduced and described as a new organisational paradigm which 'has the flexibility and the resilience to cope with turbulent environment fields' (Trist, 1981, p. 42), and as 'an explicit set of values, concepts and methods for the design of jobs and organisations in terms of direct industrial democracy – work systems in which people are directly involved in the decision making process' (van Beinum, 1986, p. 7). Others specifically advocated workplace democracy; 'power-sharing which is organisation-wide and extends decision-making rights to members at lower levels of the organisation's hierarchy' (Nightingale, 1982, p. 14).

Throughout the 1970s and 1980s, governments throughout North America began to take an active interest in these emerging concepts. Concerned with industrial conflict, low productivity, the lack of job satisfaction and the impact of these factors on the economy, the federal and provincial Canadian governments established programmes in support of QWL (Mansell, 1987). The Ontario Ministry of Labour opened the Ontario Quality of Working Life Centre, and in 1981, an international conference entitled 'QWL and the Eighties' was held in Toronto and attracted over 2000 delegates.

The US government also expressed interest in QWL. In his 1971 Labor Day address, President Nixon said:

In our quest for a better environment, we must always remember that the most important part of the quality of life is the quality of work, and the new need for job satisfaction is the key to the quality of work ... We must make sure that technology does not dehumanize work but makes it more creative and rewarding for people who will operate the plants of the future. (Ketchum and Trist, 1992, p. 30)

In 1972, a subcommittee of the US Senate Committee on Labor and Public Welfare held hearings on worker alienation, and the National Commission on Productivity and the Quality of Working Life was formed. At the commission's 1973 conference, Senator Charles Percy blamed rising job dissatisfaction on, 'an entrenched, authoritarian industrial system in which managerial and labor institutions have too often become blind to the broader needs of our society' (Ketchum and Trist, 1992, p. 31).

About the same time, several North American organisations began experimenting with QWL (AT&T, General Foods, General Motors, Proctor and Gamble, Inco Metals, MacMillan-Bloedel, Shell Chemical, Xerox). As part of their experiments, new plants were designed, organisational structures were flattened, teams were formed, rules were eliminated, and the purpose of management became redefined as 'to enable people to do work' (Ketchum and Trist, 1992, p. 20). The results of many of the experiments were described as 'phenomenal' and 'beyond belief' with productivity gains of 30 to 40 per cent, higher quality products, and lower absenteeism rates reported (Ketchum and Trist, 1992, p. 21). Despite these successes, many of the new organisational forms incited severe resistance, both inside and outside their respective organisations. Ketchum and Trist (1992) wrote:

> Given the surge of achievement and its attendant publicity and national support, one would have expected corporate managers to embrace innovations that so impressively improved the bottom line. Instead, these intelligent, sincere, dedicated, bottom-line-oriented-managers ignored, rejected, or even vigorously opposed them. (p. 32)

Several authors have provided explanations as to why power-enhancing initiatives such as QWL, workplace democracy and participative management programmes met with so much resistance. Nightingale (1982, p. 4) argued that the resistance could partially be explained by confusion with the concept; 'much of the confusion and apprehension ... arises from the absence of a precise and established definition'. Similarly, van Beinum (1986) suggested that QWL was characterised by 'confusion, misunderstanding and lack of proper definition' (p. 7). He also argued, however, that much of the confusion was deliberate:

> It is a deliberate act in the sense that the undefined and vague use of this encompassing term will allow us to avoid dealing with the political dimensions of the work situation ... It can act as a screen, as a defence mechanism against becoming personally engaged with critical issues in the real world of work. (p. 9)

The opinion of Bob White, while president of the Canadian Auto Workers union (CAW), lends further support to this perspective:

> The programs that most of the companies are promoting today are not about democratizing the workplace at all. They are about increasing productivity. They are about cutting out any time at all that the workers have for themselves and convincing workers that what is good for the enterprise is good for them... The whole fight [is] for the mind of the worker. (Estok, 1989, p. 42)

Offering a different point of view, Krishnan (1974) suggested that managerial attitudes were at the core of the problem:

> It appears that the majority of business executives... do not take the view that employees should have the right to participate, through the democratic process, in making organizational decisions. They do not even favour allowing employees direct input to the decision making process... except when the nature of the problem is such that the traditional managerial prerogatives will in no way be affected.

Lastly, Ketchum and Trist (1992, p. 39) argued, 'the concepts of paradigm and paradigm shift are central to understanding the failure of the "better mousetrap" theory – why managers, even those most oriented to the bottom line, reject the evidence of the benefits of the redesign of work and attack its successful practitioners':

> Traditional organizations serve only their own ends. They are, and indeed are supposed to be, selfish. The new paradigm imposes the additional task on them of aligning their own purposes with the purposes of the wider society and also with the purposes of their members. (Ketchum and Trist, 1992, p. 42)

In many of the companies where innovations did occur, the participating managers were ostracised by their traditional counterparts and the innovations themselves either faded away or were restricted to peripheral areas of the company. In Canada, Rankin (1986) reported that 40 per cent of QWL redesign projects did not survive beyond two or three years. In Ontario, the Quality of Working Life Centre was quietly closed. Portis and Hill (1989, p. 58) claimed that many companies that had started with quality circles or QWL programmes eventually modified or replaced them with other participation efforts 'more suitable to their businesses'. The replacements included suggestion programmes, joint management/employee task forces, work-redesign, and various communication schemes, in all of which employee participation could be more easily managed and controlled.

Undeterred by these results, the late 1980s saw a new body of literature argue that organisations needed to embrace fundamental organisational change if they were to endure the increasing competitiveness and complexity of the environment. Kanter (1983) recommended organisations adopt a 'post-entrepreneurial' model characterised by autonomous work teams and fewer layers of management. McCamus (1989) argued that organisations should be obsessed with customer satisfaction, innovation and flexibility, and could achieve these attributes through strategies of empowerment, visionary leadership and high moral values. Bennis (1989) argued that in organisations where employee potential, productivity, profitability and growth were maximised, empowerment was evident in four themes: people felt significant; learning and competence mattered; people were part of a community; and work was exciting. Morgan (1988) suggested that managers should empower others to take on leadership roles and achieve coordination and control through shared values and understandings. Lawler (1986) suggested that participative management (programmes that move information, knowledge, rewards and/or power further down the organisation), 'is an idea whose time has come' (p. 1). Citing the benefits of participative management, Lawler (1986) wrote:

> We could be a much more productive society in which work positively contributes to the quality of people's lives... We might also come much closer to matching the reality of how people are treated in our workplaces with our ideal of how they should be treated: with respect, dignity, democratic rights, individual rights, and the right to share in the fruits of their labour. (p. 4)

Lastly, Nightingale (1982) suggested, 'there is a growing conviction among Canadian working people of every description and circumstance that something is wrong at the workplace... More than at any other time in the past, we seek new forms and patterns of work' (p. 3).

The 1990s: organisations and empowerment today

Organisations in the 1990s continue to face turbulent conditions. Despite the prescriptions for fundamental change just reviewed, many organisations have responded to these challenges by aggressively pursuing overhead and labour cost reductions. Whether such strategies are referred to as 'downsizing', 'delayering', 'outsourcing', 'headcount reduction', 'horizontal loading', 're-engineering' or being 'lean and mean' they all typically involve the same things. Middle and lower-level managers are removed, and increased responsibility or 'bigger jobs' are given to those who remain.

Much of this activity has occurred under the guise of 'empowerment' which has resulted in much confusion and cynicism. In adopting a 'power-sharing' perspective of empowerment in which employees are given 'bigger jobs', many senior managers have expected their newly 'empowered' employees to feel good about the changes. Many employees, however, have complained about being expected to do both their own and their boss's jobs without being additionally compensated. They resent being told they are empowered when they have no real say in the work they do, the direction of the company or in its values. They also dislike the fact that they have little time or energy for themselves, their families or friends. Some have suggested that empowerment has become a nice word for 'slavery in the 90s'.

In applying the concepts advocated by Friedman (1977), this situation can be explained as a shift in strategy from the more obvious *direct control* to the more subtle *responsible autonomy*. As Friedman suggested, such a shift is consistent with the reduction in the number of white collar workers available to perform monitoring and control functions. In order to be successful, however, responsible autonomy requires an elaborate ideological apparatus to ensure worker co-optation. Given the extent of employee cynicism concerning empowerment, the ideology of empowerment (as it has been implemented in many organisations) has arguably been ineffective. Instead, deep contradictions or fundamental tensions that exist within organisations have surfaced. As Friedman (1977) explained, employee needs and the goals of traditional organisations are different; 'people do have independent and often hostile wills which cannot be destroyed, and the aim of top managers ultimately is to make steady and high profits, rather than to tend to their workers' needs' (p. 106). Friedman also argued that as long as people were employed by others, such contradictions would be difficult to avoid.

This suggests that the very term *organisational empowerment* may be an oxymoron. Given that it is a critical organisational function to control employee behaviour and to subvert employee needs for the needs of the organisation (which has been the case since the start of the industrial revolution), how can an organisationally-based empowerment strategy result in anything more than power-sharing in its most limited form? This concept was stated more positively by Ketchum and Trist (1992, p. 39) who suggested that organisations need to align 'their own purposes with the purposes of the wider society and also with the purposes of their members' (Ketchum and Trist, 1992, p. 42). But, is such an alignment possible?

Either through increased personal recognition of this fundamental tension, or through the lack of employment opportunities that have come about through corporate downsizing, the 1990s have seen a dramatic increase in the number of people pursuing self-employment. Over 15 per cent of working Canadians are now self-employed (Onstad, 1996, p. 32). This type of arrangement – by its very nature – provides the opportunity for empowerment. The extent and type of empowerment realised, however, may depend on the values of the individual in question. For example, drawing on Nord's (1974) arguments, we live in a materialistic-oriented society and, as such, can become ensnared in the trap of needing to generate sufficient wealth to accumulate material possessions. In other words, although self-employed, many individuals may still feel they have little control over how they spend their time and the quality of their lives. As Nord explained, 'man's creations – capital, machines, the economic system, and money – come to control man himself' (p. 571). The extent and type of empowerment realised by the self-employed may also depend on the types of relationships established with other organisations. For example, the trend towards self-employment has somewhat ironically been strengthened by the number of organisations actively replacing traditional employer–employee relationships with contractually limited ones. Self-employed people who find themselves dependent upon one or two rigidly defined employment contracts may experience the same or greater work demands, along with the increased insecurity of knowing their contract could be cancelled at any time.

Coming full circle, these contractual work relationships arguably resemble *domestic industry* in the late 1700s. They are also fraught with the same issues. While often saving labour costs, employers who contract-out production, may worry about their lack of control over raw material inventories and the quality of finished goods. They may also suspect that those with whom they've contracted aren't working as hard as they should. Unlike the 1700s, however, technology is now available to help monitor work being completed beyond the *enclosure of the factory gate*. *Constant surveillance* (Foucault, 1977) is being achieved through other means: cellular phones provide 24 hour access; lap-top computers with modems are brought on vacation; and e-mail and voice mail provide date and time logs with respect to worker activity. Within some organisations, employees who are known to check their e-mail on the weekend, late at night, or early in the morning, are perceived as being more dedicated or committed to their jobs than those who do not. Some supervisors routinely collect such information. Today, many corporate managers expect those with whom they do business to be available on an essentially continuous and immediate basis. Foucault (1977) described the disciplinary power used in factory settings as 'invisible' and 'far reaching'. For the self-employed, technology provides this type of control.

In summary, challenges to the organisation of work and prescriptions for change are not new to the management literature. Since the onset of the industrial revolution, concern has been expressed with the degree to which peoples' lives are controlled. Some progress has been made. The school system is now radically different than that described by Tronchot. Employees have more control over their lives outside the workplace today (when they have time for such pursuits) than they did working for capitalists like Henry Ford. Yet with technological advances, other more insidious types of control systems are rapidly emerging.

Over the past several decades, the call for fundamental change has intensified. Academics have called for visionary leadership and empowerment within organisational settings. In practice, however, organisations have responded to current pressures by downsizing their operations and implementing strategies of responsible autonomy. While often being labelled 'empowerment', such strategies have proven ineffective at either masking or responding to the tension that has always existed, and will likely always continue to exist, between owners of capital and those who provide their labour. Today, many people are seeking increased empowerment through the pursuit of self-employment opportunities. Given the materialistic nature of Western society, in terms of how we live our lives, the self-employed may find themselves less empowered than they'd hoped to be. History suggests these contradictions will not resolve themselves soon. Perhaps by generating a clearer understanding of empowerment and related ethical issues, some progress can be made. In the next section, multiple meanings of empowerment are explored.

EM(POWER)MENT – SOME DEFINITIONS

Several theorists have suggested that in order to understand empowerment, one must consider its root word power (see for example, Conger and Kanungo, 1988; Vaines, 1993; Vincenti, 1993). Yet, like empowerment, a precise understanding of power is elusive; 'it is difficult to define power because its meanings and related terms such as influence, control and domination are uncertain, shifting, and overlapping' (Vincenti,

1993, p. 9). Power has been referred to as 'America's last dirty word'; 'people who have it deny it; people who want it do not want to appear to hunger for it; and people who engage in its machinations do so secretly' (Kanter, 1979, p. 65).

Present-day conceptions of empowerment suggest power may be differentiated as a relational versus motivational construct (Conger and Kanungo, 1988); as a fixed sum versus a reciprocity of influence (Kouzes and Posner, 1987); as a personalised versus a socialised concern (Kouzes and Posner, 1987); and as distinct paradigmatic views (Morgaine, 1993; Vaines, 1993). The latter differentiation (distinct paradigmatic views) is particularly significant because it draws attention to an important gap in the empowerment literature. Embedded within much of the management literature is the implicit assumption that empowerment strategies should enable employees to more effectively contribute to task goals and organisational effectiveness. In this sense, empowerment is regarded as a management tool (Kanter, 1979). Within other disciplines, however, such as Home Economics, empowerment is explicitly regarded as a mechanism for fundamental social change. By incorporating the work of Morgaine (1993), Rappaport (1986), Rehm (1993) and Vaines (1993) into this review, the multiple objectives that empowerment strategies are meant to achieve are revealed.

In their seminal article on empowerment, Conger and Kanungo (1988) argued convincingly that the conceptual development of empowerment has been limited by our understanding of power as a *relational construct*; the power of an individual is seen as the net dependence that he or she has in relation to others (Pfeffer, 1981). From this perspective, the verb *to empower* is defined as, 'to give power or authority to – police are empowered to arrest people' (Oxford American Dictionary, 1980) or, 'to give legal or moral power to; to authorize' (Webster's Dictionary, 1993).

In the workplace, this type of empowerment has been described as, 'the process by which a leader or manager shares his or her power with subordinates' (Conger and Kanungo, 1988, p. 473). Participative management, delegation, decentralised decision-making, quality circles and management by objectives are some of the processes that are often equated with this type of empowerment. In their study of employee involvement programmes, Lawler, Mohrman and Ledford (1992) found that the most common goals associated with such programmes included improved product quality, productivity, motivation, morale and cost reduction. The most common barrier to successfully achieving these outcomes was identified as short-term performance pressures. In explanation, they suggested that 'employee involvement is a long-term process that may not produce short-term results' (p. 49).

Clarkson (in the forward of Nightingale, 1982) provided a somewhat different explanation. He argued that when goals such as technological efficiency and maximising profits in the short-term are prioritised, certain behaviours (obedience) are rewarded, while others are discouraged (independence and honesty), resulting in alienation and lack of commitment amongst employees. In other words, in the presence of short-term, profit maximising and cost-reducing goals, empowered behaviours are not supported in the workplace. Other barriers identified by Lawler et al. (1992), included the lack of a long-term strategy, unclear employee involvement objectives, the lack of a champion and the centralisation of decision-making authority.

Kouzes and Posner (1987) suggested that whether or not relational empowerment (power sharing) was resisted by managers was dependent upon whether power was perceived as a *fixed sum* or as a *reciprocity of influence*. When power is perceived as a *fixed sum* (if you have more, I have less), power sharing is resisted. When power is perceived as a *reciprocity of influence* (the leader and follower are willing to be mutually influenced by one another), power sharing is embraced. This latter view may be understood as a paradox; the leader has to give power in order to gain power (Kouzes and Posner, 1987, p. 164).

Kouzes and Posner (1987) also suggested that power may be understood in terms of whose interests it is meant to serve. They argued that when a *personalised concern* predominates, power is used in the service of the self, whereas with a *socialised concern*, power is used in the service of others. Adopting a personalised concern, people with power may show little self-control, exercise power impulsively and are reluctant to share it. In contrast, when a socialised power concern predominates, managers tend to be more emotionally mature and are more likely to use a participative, coaching style with their subordinates.

As an alternative to understanding power as a relational construct, Conger and Kanungo (1988) suggested that power may be conceptualised as a *motivational construct*; 'power and control are used as motivational and/or expectancy belief-states that are internal to individuals' (p. 473):

> Individuals' power needs are met when they perceive that they have power or when they believe they can adequately cope with events, situations, and/or the people they confront. On the other hand, individuals' power needs are frustrated when they feel powerless or when they believe that they are unable to

cope with the physical and social demands of the environment. (Conger and Kanungo, 1988, p. 473)

Motivational power is related to the intrinsic need for self-determination (Deci, 1975) or the belief in self-efficacy (Bandura, 1977). Wood and Bandura (1989) defined self-efficacy as the belief 'in one's capabilities to mobilize the motivation, cognitive resources, and courses of action needed to meet given situational demands' (p. 408). From this perspective, 'to empower' may be defined as 'to enable' (Oxford English Dictionary, 1989), and delegating or resource-sharing is recognised as 'only one set of conditions that may (but not necessarily) enable or empower subordinates' (Conger and Kanungo, 1988, p. 474). Accordingly, Conger and Kanungo (1988) proposed the following definition of empowerment:

> Empowerment is... a process of enhancing feelings of self-efficacy among organizational members through the identification of conditions that foster powerlessness and through their removal by both formal organizational practices and informal techniques of providing efficacy information. (p. 474)

Block (1987) described how bureaucratic contexts and authoritarian management styles encouraged powerlessness by fostering dependency, denying self-expression and imposing meaningless goals. Conger and Kanungo (1988) hypothesised that organisational factors, supervisory style, reward systems and job design all contributed to the lowering of self-efficacy belief (see Table 4.1). In order to reduce feelings of powerlessness they recommended the use of participative management, goal-setting and job enrichment, as well as removing conditions that contribute to the psychological state of powerlessness (ensuring employees have the necessary technical, linguistic and social influence skills; fostering a culture which values self-determination, collaboration, high performance standards, and meritocracy; and setting inspirational and/or meaningful goals) (Conger and Kanungo, 1988, p. 478).

Similarly, Kouzes and Posner (1987) suggested powerlessness could be overcome by ensuring people have the requisite skills and knowledge, keeping people informed, actively involving others in planning and decision-making, and giving employees important work to do on critical issues. They also advised acknowledging people's contributions and efforts, providing broad visibility for accomplishments, being considerate of the needs and interests of others and creating an atmosphere of trust, human dignity and mutual respect.

Table 4.1 Context factors leading to potential lowering of self-efficacy belief

Organisational Factors
　Significant organisational changes/transitions
　Start-up ventures
　Competitive pressures
　Impersonal bureaucratic climate
　Poor communications/network-forming systems
　Highly centralised organisational resources

Supervisory Style
　Authoritarian (high control)
　Negativism (emphasis on failures)
　Lack of reason for actions/consequences

Reward Systems
　Non-contingency (arbitrary reward allocations)
　Low incentive value of rewards
　Lack of competence-based rewards
　Lack of innovation-based rewards

Job Design
　Lack of role clarity
　Lack of training and technical support
　Unrealistic goals
　Lack of appropriate authority/discretion
　Low task variety
　Limited participation in programmes, meetings, decisions that have a direct impact on job performance
　Lack of appropriate/necessary resources
　Lack of network-forming opportunities
　Highly-established work routines
　High rule structure
　Low advancement opportunities
　Lack of meaningful goals/tasks
　Limited contact with senior management

Reprinted with permission of Academy of Management, PO Box 3020, Briar Cliff Manor, NY 10510–8020. *The Empowerment Process: Integrating Theory and Practice* (Table), J. Conger and R. Kanungo, *Academy of Management Review* 1988, Vol. 13, No. 3. Reproduced by permission of the publisher via Copyright Clearance Center Inc.

Many other authors have studied powerlessness and related constructs such as helplessness, hopelessness, learned helplessness, locus of control and organisationally-induced helplessness (OIH) (see for example, Ashforth, 1989, 1990; Garber and Seligman, 1980; Martinko and Gardner, 1982; Overmier and Seligman, 1967; and Rotter, 1966). Although more micro in orientation than the literature I have chosen to discuss within this review, additional support is found in the work of these authors for Conger and Kanungo's (1988) and Kouzes and Posner's (1987) discussions on powerlessness. For example, Ashforth (1990) wrote:

> The experience of powerlessness can be quite traumatic, entailing frustration, disruptive behaviours, feelings of helplessness, and loss of job involvement and organizational identification. Conversely... fostering a sense of control can forestall frustration and reactance, increase perceptions of organizational legitimacy and self-efficacy, and stimulate involvement. (p. 235)

In addition to the above, Conger and Kanungo (1988) hypothesised that subordinates needed to be provided with self-efficacy confirming information. Bandura (1977, 1986) suggested four sources of self-efficacy information: *Enactive attainment*, which is personally derived from the successful completion of a task; *vicarious experience*, which involves the observation of similar others engaged in successful task completion; *verbal persuasion* which includes encouragement and positive feedback; and the avoidance of an *emotional arousal state*, which involves the removal of stress and fear through such techniques as generating a supportive and trusting group atmosphere, and avoiding both information and task overload.

Bandura (1986) also argued, however, that enhancing subordinate self-efficacy was not necessarily sufficient for achieving behavioural change:

> Efficacious artisans and athletes cannot perform well with faulty equipment, and efficacious executives cannot put their talents to good use if they lack adequate financial and material resources... When performances are impeded by disincentives, inadequate resources, or external constraints, self-judged efficacy will exceed the actual performance. (Bandura, 1986, p. 396)

Underscoring the importance of subordinate identification with organisational and task goals, Bandura (1977, p. 194) stated, 'there are many things that people can do with certainty of success that they do not perform because they have no incentives to do so'. Further, 'people do not care much how they do in activities that have little or no significance for them, and they expend little effort on devalued activities' (Bandura, 1986, p. 348). Bandura (1986) cited laboratory studies in which people were paid to sacrifice quality for quantity. He found that people who subscribed to high standards, continued to strive for quality despite personal financial disincentives to do so (p. 374). In explanation of these findings Bandura suggested, 'there is no punishment more devastating than self-contempt' (Bandura, 1986, p. 374). In other words, employees will tend to work towards goals they find meaningful, regardless of those imposed by the organisation. Further, Bandura argued that employees preferred to work with others who had similar values in order to 'ensure social support for their own system of self-evaluation' (p. 375). Similarly, Bradford and Cohen (1984) found that when subordinates encountered meaningless goals, they 'retreat[ed] to a defense of their narrow parochial interests' (p. 31). Also acknowledging the link between motivation, goals and empowerment, Thomas and Velthouse (1990) suggested empowerment is based on an internalised commitment to the task itself. Empowered employees are motivated by the 'pull of the task' rather than the 'push of management' (p. 667).

Gandz (1990) suggested that in order for empowerment to be effective, organisations should redefine their objectives. Rather than focusing on net income and return on investment, he argued managers should emphasise goals that are more appealing to employees, which at the same time contribute to profit, productivity and market share growth (for example, excellence in customer service). Nightingale (1982), further argued that providing employees with meaningful goals was impossible without organisations first undergoing radical change:

> The modern work organization can never gain the moral commitment of those whose lives it rules without itself embodying a moral purpose. Unfortunately, many of the practices of the modern work organization are without moral justification; the legitimacy of these practices rests solely on economic and productive efficiency. (p. 7)

Similarly, Nord (1975) argued that it may be impossible for employees to pursue meaningful goals within capitalist enterprises; 'clearly, profits, and growth are given priority over humanization... Human welfare is sacrificed for individual advantage' (Nord, 1975, p. 180). Nord (1975) advocated a re-examination of organisational goals from a social point of view:

> We have assumed that the quality of a product and its role in serving human needs are inconsequential to the worker. However, based on a more

social view of man, we might have given more emphasis to the role of producing high quality products which directly serve central needs of one's fellow man as a contributor to a person perceiving his work as meaningful. (p. 181)

Echoing this call for fundamental change, Vaines (1993) argued that empowerment could best be understood from a framework of *multiple paradigms*. Vaines (1993) provided three 'world views' or paradigms of power. The first, she referred to as the 'no choice' or 'powerless' paradigm in which power is accepted and unexamined; 'an invisible and obvious "given" which goes unchallenged because persons perceive themselves as too powerless to change the social order' (Vaines, 1993, p. 25). The second she called, 'technical rationality' or 'power over'; 'Those in power...impose policies and politics to benefit those in power...and influence [the] distribution of limited resources. Power is hierarchical and deeply embedded' (Vaines, 1993, p. 25). Vaines suggested that people who live this world view, 'perceive themselves and others as products of society and as cogs in a giant machine' (p. 21):

> Society sets the rules, and success is gained through conformity and through competition with others who are also striving to succeed... In a technically oriented society these structures are the vehicles of power required for imposing authority over others and for controlling the distribution of human and material resources such that they are both efficient and effective... In this context, the first and most important consideration in any decision is maximization of economic growth. (Vaines, 1993, pp. 21–22)

Vaines' third paradigm was 'empowerment' or 'power with'; 'power is in people working actively together for the common good... All "authority" is challenged in view of what was, what is, and what should be in relation to what is believed, studied, experienced and done in light of social responsibilities to all living systems' (Vaines, 1993, p. 25).

The contribution of Vaines is particularly significant because it draws explicit attention to the objectives of empowerment strategies. From her perspective, the objective of empowerment is to bring about fundamental change to traditional societal structures. Similarly, Morgaine (1993) suggested that empowerment processes 'must be based on experiences designed to illuminate, challenge, and change social structures that support and maintain injustice and unequal power' (Morgaine, 1993, p. 15). In explanation, she argued empowerment should be considered on three different levels:

The first level is intrapersonal empowerment or that which is experienced within the self as efficacy, potency, or 'power within'. The second is interpersonal empowerment, or that which is experienced as a collaboration with others through dialogue and results in an increased awareness of societal power structures. The third level is community empowerment or that which involves the use of strategies for both personal and sociopolitical change leading to justice. (Morgaine, 1993, p. 37)

Lastly, Rappaport (1986) defined empowerment as a 'powerful force for change contained within ourselves, our significant others, and our communities' (p. 67). Rappaport argued that empowerment is impossible to achieve without the full development of human potential. Building on the work of Rappaport, Rehm (1993) suggested that, 'empowerment occurs when full human potential is developed through reflective thinking and critical dialogue' (p. 26).

The objectives reflected in the work of Vaines (1993), Morgaine (1993), Rappaport (1986) and Rehm (1993) are in marked contrast to those associated with the relational and motivational conceptions of power discussed at the beginning of this section. From a relational or power-sharing perspective, managers explicitly share their power to enable subordinates to contribute more effectively to the organisation's goals. No fundamental change to the organisation is implied. Even given a socialised power concern, organisational legitimacy is not questioned. Social interests, in this sense, are equated with those of the organisation.

From a motivational or enabling perspective, empowerment is positioned as a strategy for overcoming employee powerlessness and fostering self-efficacy to enable subordinate 'initiation [and] persistence of behaviour to accomplish task objectives' (Conger and Kanungo, 1988, p. 475). This perspective implies at least some degree of organisational change; bureaucratic contexts and authoritarian management styles are challenged and the importance of providing employees with meaningful goals is acknowledged. Participative management and goal-setting are advocated by Conger and Kanungo (1988) as processes for achieving this end. Implicit within this suggestion is that subordinates can pursue meaningful goals within organisational contexts. What is not clear, however, is whether this is possible without organisations undergoing the fundamental transformation advocated by Nightingale (1982) and Nord (1975). This observation is critical, because if radical change is required, motivational empowerment strategies will be frustrated in at least the short and medium terms.

EMPOWERMENT – GENERATING A NEW UNDERSTANDING

As previously argued, the empowerment literature lacks a quintessential definition. Rather than offering one new, all-encompassing definition here, I will now attempt to re-present the critical elements already discussed, within a multi-paradigmatic framework. In doing so, I will additionally draw from the work of Bradshaw-Camball and Murray (1991), who applied Burrell and Morgan's (1979) paradigmatic framework to their study of politics and power, as well as the work of Foucault (1977, 1978, 1980), in order to provide a postmodern perspective.

Bradshaw-Camball and Murray (1991) suggested power could be understood from four different paradigms (functionalist-rationalist, functionalist-pluralist, interpretive and radical). Each of these paradigms will be used to summarise the various conceptions of power, as well as the associated objectives, processes and barriers to empowerment previously discussed (see Table 4.2).

A rationalist-functionalist perspective

From a functionalist-rationalist perspective, power is regarded as an objective reality in which the formal power of top management is accepted as legitimate (Bradshaw-Camball and Murray, 1991). Perspectives of power that are consistent with this paradigm include the relational construct developed by Conger and Kanungo (1988), and the 'no choice' and 'technical rationality' paradigms discussed by Vaines (1993). Empowerment is equated with power-sharing and is regarded as a management tool (Kanter, 1979).

Associated processes involve the limited sharing of formal power through such mechanisms as participative management, delegation and decentralised decision-making. Empowerment objectives include increased quality and productivity, while barriers include management attitudes (Kouzes and Posner, 1987), short-term performance pressures, the lack of a long-term strategy, unclear objectives, and the lack of a champion (Lawler *et al.*, 1992).

A pluralist perspective

From a functionalist-pluralist perspective, power is also regarded as an objective reality. Pluralist theory, however, additionally stresses diversity in individual interests and goals, the conflicts this diversity produces, and the use of power through which conflicts are resolved (Bradshaw-

Camball and Murray, 1991). Organisational control devices, 'are not wholly effective in producing a coherent and unified set of goals' (Pfeffer, 1981, p. 28). The relative power of individual stakeholders plays a critical role in bargaining processes. Decisions seldom reflect 'the preferences of any group or subunit within the organisation', but are more likely to be based on their perceived short-term acceptability, especially with respect to powerful others (Pfeffer, 1981, p. 28). Empowerment may be seen as a vehicle for giving voice to long-silenced employee interests, but employee influence will be limited if sufficient formal power is not given. This perspective also provides an explanation as to why empowerment strategies often lead to increased organisational conflict; 'democratic decision-making practices are disruptive in the absence of consensus on fundamental goals' (Nightingale, 1992, p. 10).

Pluralist arguments are also found in theories of bureaucratic dysfunctions (Burrell and Morgan, 1979; Merton, 1968). From this perspective, empowerment processes involve enabling employees or enhancing self-efficacy through the removal of bureaucratic conditions that contribute to feelings of powerlessness, trained incapacity and the lowering of self-efficacy belief. This type of empowerment may also be equated with Friedman's (1977) responsible autonomy strategy. The overriding objective of enabling empowerment is the maximisation of organisational effectiveness. Bureaucratic contexts, authoritarian management styles, the lack of appropriate employee skills, inadequate resources and meaningless goals are some of the most critical barriers to enabling empowerment.

An interpretive perspective

The interpretive paradigm assumes reality is socially constructed and that people exert influence by constructing the meaning of what others experience through myth, symbol, metaphor and language (Bradshaw-Camball and Murray, 1991). Concepts such as organisations, structure, hierarchy and efficiency are viewed as social reifications used by people to 'construct their world' and should not be taken for granted as they are within the functionalist paradigm (Berger and Luckmann, 1966; Bittner, 1974).

From this perspective, the exercise of power involves constructing others' reality and as previously suggested, the very word *empowerment* can become part of the construction or language 'game'. Managers may attempt to draw workers' attention away from their exploitation

Table 4.2 A multiple-paradigmatic perspective of empowerment

Paradigm	Functionalist-rationalist	Functionalist-pluralist and bureaucratic dysfunctions	Interpretive	Radical	Postmodern
Power	Objective reality 'no choice' Relational construct Fixed sum/personalized Accepted and unexamined	Objective reality Motivational construct	Social construction	Deeply embedded in social relationships and monopoly capitalism	Invisible and everywhere embedded in knowledge and self-conception
Empowerment	Power-sharing Management tool	Self-efficacy To enable Responsible autonomy	Word game Ideological tool	Mechanism for radical social change	Internal state Impossible ideal
Objectives	Product quality Productivity Motivation and morale Cost reduction	Self-efficacy Organisational effectiveness	Co-optation of workers' interests	Societal effectiveness	Liberating society and the self

Process	Participative management Delegation Decentralisation	Identification and removal of bureaucratic conditions Particpative management Information-sharing Job/skill enrichment Celebrate achievements Meritocracy	Construct the reality of others	Hasten contradictions in economic and socio-cultural context Challenge assumptions of goal congruence and growth as ends vs means	Self-awareness Reflective thinking Critical dialogue
Barriers	Short-term goals Obedience vs innovation Unclear empowerment objectives Lack champion Centralised decision-making	Bureaucratic contexts Authoritarian management styles Lack of resources Lack of employee skills Meaningless goals Non-contingency rewards Narrow job design	Competing definitions of empowerment 'Independent and hostile wills'	Capitalism – division of labour and capital Labour as commodity Focus on cost-effectiveness, profit accumulation, perpetual growth	Internalised, psychological mechanics of power

(Nightingale, 1982) by providing them with an ideology of empowerment. This perspective is also consistent with the arguments of Gartman (1983), van Beinum (1986) and Bob White (in Estok, 1989) previously reviewed. Barriers to empowerment from an interpretive perspective include competing social constructions such as the definitions advocated by Vaines (1993) and Morgaine (1993).

A radical perspective

From a radical perspective, power is regarded as a relationship which is deeply embedded within the structure of society (Bradshaw-Camball and Murray, 1991). Organisations are seen as 'instruments of domination' (Burrell and Morgan, 1979), and empowerment is regarded as a radical means for overcoming this domination. Vaines' (1993) empowerment paradigm, and Morgaine's (1993) community-based empowerment strategy are consistent with this view.

Radical theories can be characterised by their critique of contemporary society and their focus on societal forces or contradictions that create pressure for social change. Contradictions cited by Weisbord (1987) included changing environmental conditions, growing uncertainty and unpredictable global connections of economics, technology and people.

In drawing attention to differences between societal and organisational values, Nightingale (1982) argued that since we live in a democratic society, workplace democracy is inevitable. Mansell (1987), however, argued that North American societal values are not in keeping with a democratic workplace and further, that 'change cannot ultimately survive at the micro level unless supported by changes at the macro level' (p. 22). Nord (1975) has consistently argued in support of the latter perspective:

> We have ignored the impact of the economic and sociocultural context in which these organizations attempt to survive and grow... This milieu induces pressures upon even the best-intentioned manager to treat people, even himself, in nonhumane ways. (p. 176)

Nord (1975) suggested that in order for change to occur, the assumption of 'high congruence' between organisational and humanitarian goals must be challenged as well as the treatment of technological and economic growth as ends rather than means. Nord (1975) advised questioning the purpose of growth; 'growth of what? For what?... we may need to make some choices about where we as a human race can afford to have growth occur' (Nord, 1975, p. 182). He also discussed the issue of formal power and the enormous barrier it represents:

> Organizational psychologists seem to have underestimated the difficulty in changing the distribution of power. We seem to forget that individuals who currently have power, whether they are in business, government or the labor movement, have an interest in not changing the distribution of power too much. (p. 184)

The radical paradigm is also home to Marxist structuralist theories. These theories focus on the inherent problems of monopoly capitalism. This perspective is in keeping with the work of Nightingale (1982), Nord (1974, 1975) and Braverman (1974), and can be summarised as follows:

> As long as competition and cost effectiveness control productive activity, the worker is only a means, not an end. Consequently, work can not play a positive role in human development; as long as the demand for labor is controlled by the laws and needs of competition, labor will be treated as a commodity. Since alienation is a product of capitalistic exchange, the end of alienation requires radical changes in the social order. (Nord, 1974, p. 571)

From the radical perspective, empowerment implies radical social change. Barriers to empowerment include the tenets of capitalism including the division of labour and capital, the treatment of labour as a commodity, the unwavering focus on cost effectiveness, and the overriding objectives of increased accumulation of profits and perpetual growth.

Braverman (1974), argued that scientific management, human relations, and QWL, 'all reflect, in their own ways, the development of the labour process within monopoly capitalism' (Burrell and Morgan, 1979, p. 381). Similarly, conceptions of empowerment from the rational, pluralist/bureaucratic dysfunctions and interpretive paradigms, serve as barriers to empowerment from a radical perspective. Once co-opted, empowerment (as with earlier power-enhancing initiatives), can no longer be effective at bringing about fundamental social change.

A postmodern perspective

Foucault (1978) introduced the postmodern conceptualisation of power in which power is regarded as neither finite in quantity nor hierarchical. According to Foucault (1978, p. 93), 'power is everywhere; not because it embraces everything, but because it comes from everywhere'. Power and knowledge directly imply one another; 'there is no power relation without the correlative constitution of a field of knowledge, nor any knowledge that does not presuppose and constitute at the same time power relations' (Foucault, 1977, p. 27).

From a postmodern perspective, empowerment remains an essentially elusive ideal. Foucault (1977) argued that while society has experienced an increase in democratic and liberating institutions and practices, these changes have been countered by disempowering, disciplinary forces that have had a much greater control over us than previous, more obvious forms. Our own values, our need to accumulate material possessions, and our willingness to be controlled by technology may be seen as barriers to empowerment from a postmodern view. Such barriers are even more deeply embedded than those identified in the radical frame. Not only are they embedded within societal relationships, but within our knowledge and our conceptions of ourselves. Empowerment involves not only liberating society from external forces such as the tenets of capitalism, but also from the internalised, psychological mechanics of power. In the words of Foucault (1977):

> It is not that the beautiful totality of the individual is amputated, repressed, altered by our social order, it is rather that the individual is carefully fabricated in it, according to a whole technique of forces and bodies ... we are neither in the amphitheatre, nor on the stage, but in the panoptic machine, invested by its effects of power, which we bring to ourselves since we are part of its mechanism. (p. 217)

Of the previous conceptions of empowerment discussed, Morgaine (1993), Rappaport (1986) and Rehm (1993) come closest to offering a postmodern view. Morgaine (1993) acknowledges several levels of empowerment including intrapersonal empowerment (power within), interpersonal empowerment (power between), and community empowerment (personal and sociopolitical change). She suggested achieving empowerment through mechanisms of enhanced self-awareness, discourse and challenges to the social order. Similarly, Rappaport and Rehm advocated reflective thinking and critical dialogue. Barriers to empowerment from this perspective include the ability of individuals to challenge their own deeply embedded values and in so doing overcome *increasingly invasive apparatuses of power*.

In summary, empowerment may be regarded as a power-sharing strategy within organisational contexts, as a mechanism for enhancing self-efficacy, as a social construction, as a mechanism for radical social change, and as an illusive ideal involving the liberation of society and the self. Each perspective carries with it its own objectives, processes and barriers. While the management literature (as reviewed in the first half of this paper) has tended to focus on functionalist empowerment perspectives, it is important to recognise that other conceptions of empowerment exist. Within organisations, if management adopts a power-sharing perspective, while employees assume empowerment will bring about much more radical change – as is often the case – conflict and cynicism will likely result.

CONCLUSION

At the root of questions pertaining to ethics and empowerment are issues of goals, values and control with respect to individuals, organisations and society as a whole. It is easy to state that within ethical enterprises employees should become more empowered. But what does this mean? Reflecting the functionalist perspective of empowerment, in many organisations employees have been given increased responsibility but within narrowly-defined parameters. Capitalistic organisational goals and values have not been successfully challenged. As such, ever increasing rates of corporate growth, profits and materialism continue to be given priority within western society over other more humanistic considerations such as family and community relationships, spirituality, and mental and physical health. For people to become truly empowered (from a radical or postmodern perspective), much more fundamental change is required. The very essence of organisations needs to be challenged. What should their purpose(s) be? What values should they uphold? How should people who contribute to their success be organized and rewarded? Yet, such questioning is unlikely to lead to successful change unless we are also willing to challenge the very essence of our lives. Collectively and individually, what is our purpose? What values should we uphold? How should we organise and live our lives? We need to engage in critical discourse and self-reflection. We need to break free from the power relations that inform our knowledge and define our self-interest. This is why the struggle for organisational empowerment and its associated ethical implications is so difficult and so profound. As Foucault (1977) stated, 'we are neither in the amphitheatre, nor on the stage, but in the panoptic machine, invested by its effects of power, which we bring to ourselves since we are part of its mechanism' (p. 217).

References

Ackoff, R.L. (1974) *Redesigning the Future* (Toronto: John Wiley).
Argyris, C. (1957) *Personality and Organization* (New York: Harper).
Ashforth, B.E. (1989) 'The Experience of Powerlessness in Organizations', *Organizational Behaviour and Human Decision Processes*, vol. 43, pp. 207–42.
Ashforth, B.E. (1990) 'The Organizationally Induced Helplessness Syndrome: A Preliminary Model', *Canadian Journal of Administrative Studies*, September, pp. 30–6.
Bandura, A. (1986) *Social Foundations of Thought and Action: A Social-cognitive View* (Englewood Cliffs, N.J.: Prentice-Hall).
Bandura, A. (1977) 'Self-efficacy: Toward a Unifying Theory of Behavioral Change', *Psychological Review*, vol. 84(2), pp. 191–215.
Bennis, W. (1989) 'Why Leaders Can't Lead', *Training and Development Journal*, April, pp. 35–9.
Berger, P.L. and Luckmann, T. (1966) *The Social Construction of Reality* (New York: Doubleday).
Bittner, E. (1974) 'The Concept of Organisation', in R. Turner (ed.), *Ethnomethodology* (Harmondsworth: Penguin).
Block, P. (1987) *The Empowered Manager* (San Francisco: Jossey-Bass).
Bradford, D.L. and Cohen, A.R. (1984) *Managing for Excellence* (Toronto: John Wiley).
Bradshaw-Camball, P. and Murray, V. (1991) 'Illusions and Other Games: A Trifocal View of Organizational Politics', *Organizational Science*, vol. 2(4), pp. 379–98.
Braverman, H. (1974) *Labor and Monopoly Capital* (New York: Monthly Review Press).
Burrell, G. and Morgan, G. (1979) *Sociological Paradigms and Organizational Analysis* (England: Gower).
Conger, J.A. and Kanungo, R.N. (1988) 'The Empowerment Process: Integrating Theory and Practice', *Academy of Management Review*, vol. 13(3), pp. 471–82.
Deci, E.L. (1975) *Intrinsic Motivation* (New York: Plenum).
Estok, D. (1989) 'Old Wounds Still Fester', *The Financial Post*, Winter, pp. 42–5.
Foucault, M. (1980) *Power/Knowledge: Selected Interviews and Other Writings, 1972–1977* (New York: Pantheon).
Foucault, M. (1978) *The History of Sexuality* (New York: Random House).
Foucault, M. (1977) *Discipline and Punish* (New York: Pantheon).
Friedman, A. (1977) *Industry and Labour: Class Struggle at Work and Monopoly Capitalism* (London: Macmillan).
Gandz, J. (1990) 'The Employee Empowerment Era', *Business Quarterly*, vol. 55(2), pp. 74–9.
Garber, J. and Seligman, M.E.P. (1980) *Human Helplessness: Theory and Applications* (New York: Academic Press).
Gartman, D. (1983) 'Structuralist Marxism and the Labor Process: Where Have the Dialectics Gone?' *Theory and Society*, vol. 12, pp. 631–58.
Heron, C. (1989) *The Canadian Labour Movement: A Short History* (Toronto: James Lorimer).

Herzberg, F., Mausner, B. and Snyderman, B. (1959) *The Motivation to Work* (New York: John Wiley).
Kanter, R.M. (1983) *The Change Masters: How People and Companies Succeed through Innovation in the New Corporate Era* (New York: Simon & Schuster).
Kanter, R. (1979) 'Power Failure in Management Circuits', *Harvard Business Review*, vol. 57(4), pp. 65–75.
Ketchum, L.D. and Trist, E. (1992) *All Teams are Not Created Equal: How Employee Empowerment Really Works* (Newbury Park, Cal.: Sage).
Kouzes, J.M. and Posner, B.Z. (1987) *The Leadership Challenge* (San Francisco: Jossey Bass).
Krishnan, R. (1974) 'Democratic Participation in Decision Making by Employees in American Corporations', *Academy of Management Journal*, vol. 17, pp. 339–47.
Lawler, E.E. (1986) *High-Involvement Management* (San Francisco, Cal.: Jossey-Bass).
Lawler, E.E., Mohrman S.A. and Ledford, G.E. (1992) *Employee Involvement and Total Quality Management* (San Francisco, Cal.: Jossey-Bass).
Likert, R. (1967) *The Human Organization* (New York: McGraw-Hill).
Mansell, J. (1987) *Workplace Innovation in Canada* (Ottawa: Economic Council of Canada).
Marglin, S.A. (1974) 'What Do Bosses Do? The Origins and Functions of Hierarchy in Capitalist Production', *The Review of Radical Political Economics*, vol. 6(2).
Martinko, M.J. and Gardner, W.L. (1982) 'Learned Helplessness: An Alternative Explanation for Performance Deficits', *Academy of Management Review*, vol. 7(2), pp. 195–204.
Marx, K. (1867) *A Contribution to the Critique of Political Economy* (London: Lawrence & Wishart).
Mayo, E. (1933) *The Human Problems of an Industrial Civilisation* (New York: Macmillan).
McCamus, D. (1989) 'A Revolution in Management Thinking', *Business Quarterly*, vol. 54(2), p. 62.
McGregor, D. (1960) *The Human Side of Enterprise* (New York: McGraw-Hill).
Merton, R.K. (1968) *Social Theory and Social Structure* (New York: The Free Press).
Morgaine, C.A. (1993) 'A Language of Empowerment', *Home Economics Forum*, vol. 6(2), pp. 15–20.
Morgan. G. (1988) *Riding the Waves of Change* (San Francisco: Jossey-Bass).
Nightingale D.V. (1982) *Workplace Democracy* (Toronto: University of Toronto Press).
Nord, W.R. (1974) 'The Failure of Current Applied Behavioral Science – a Marxian Perspective', *Journal of Applied Behavioral Science*, vol. 10(4), pp. 557–78.
Onstad, K. (1996) 'No Job? No Problem!' *Canadian Business*, vol. 69(10), pp. 30–9.
Overmier, J.B., and Seligman, M.E.P. (1967) 'Effects of Inescapable Shock upon Subsequent Escape and Avoidance Learning', *Journal of Comparative and Physiological Psychology*, vol. 63, pp. 28–33.
Pfeffer J. (1981) *Power in Organizations* (Marshfield, Mass.: Pitman).

Portis B. and Hill, N. (1989) 'Improving Organization Effectiveness Through Employee Involvement', *Business Quarterly*, vol. 53(3), p. 58.

Rankin, T. (1986) 'Integrating QWL and Collective Bargaining', *QWL Focus*, vol. 5(1), p. 3.

Rappaport, J. (1986) 'Collaborating for Empowerment: Creating the Language of Mutual Help', in H.D. Boyet and F. Reissman (eds), *The New Populism: The Politics of Empowerment* (Philadelphia: Temple University Press), pp. 64–79.

Rehm, M. (1993) 'An Aesthetic Approach to Empowerment', *Home Economics Forum*, vol. 6(2), pp. 26–9.

Rotter, J.B. (1966) 'Generalized Expectancies for Internal versus External Control of Reinforcement', *Psychological Monographs*, vol. 80 (1, whole no. 609).

Taylor, F.W. (1911) *The Principles of Scientific Management* (New York: Harper & Row).

Thomas K.W. and Velthouse, B.A. (1990) 'Cognitive Elements of Empowerment: An "Interpretive" Model of Intrinsic Task Motivation', *Academy of Management Review*, vol. 15(4), pp. 666–81.

Trist, E. (1981) 'The Evolution of Socio-technical Systems', *Issues in the Quality of Working Life*, Ontario Ministry of Labour, 2 June.

Vaines, E. (1993) 'An Empowerment Orientation for Home Economics', *Home Economics Forum*, vol. 6(2), pp. 21–5.

Van Beinum, H. (1986) 'Playing Hide and Seek with QWL', *QWL Focus*, Ontario Ministry of Labour, vol. 5(1), p. 7.

Vincenti, V.B. (1993) 'Empowerment: Its History and Meaning', *Home Economics Forum*, vol. 6(2), pp. 7–14.

Weisbord, M. (1987) *Productive Workplaces: Managing for Dignity, Meaning, and Community*, Jossey-Bass Management Series.

Zwerdling, D. (1980) *Workplace Democracy* (New York: Harper & Row).

5 Ethico-power and the City
Keith Pheby

INTRODUCTION

Why in the West, is politeness regarded with suspicion? Why does courtesy pass for a distance or a hypocrisy? Why is an 'informal' relation more desirable than a coded one? Occidental politeness is based on a certain mythology of the 'person'. Topologically, Western man is reputed to be double, composed of a social, factitious, false 'outside' and of a personal, authentic 'inside'. According to this schema, the human 'person' is that site filled by nature, girdled, closed by a social envelop which is anything but highly regarded: the polite gesture is a sign of respect exchanged from one plenitude to the other, across the worldly limit. However, as soon as the 'inside' of the person is judged respectable, it is logical to recognize this person more suitably by denying all interest in his worldly envelope: hence it is the supposedly frank, brutal, naked relation, stripped of all signalectics, indifferent to any intermediary code, which will best respect the other's individual value: to be impolite is to be true – so speaks our Western morality...

In order to give a present, I bow down, virtually to the level of the floor, and to answer me, my partner does the same: one and the same low line, that of the ground, joins the giver, the recipient and the stake of the protocol, a box which may well contain nothing – or virtually nothing; a graphic form is thereby given in the act of exchange in which, by this form is erased any greediness. The salutation here can be withdrawn from any humiliation or vanity, because it literally salutes no one; it is not the sign of a communication – closely watched, condescending and precautionary – between two autarchies, two personal empires; it is only the feature of a network.

Roland Barthes

The uniqueness of a place, or a locality...is constructed out of particular interactions and mutual articulations of social relations, social processes, experiences and understandings, in a situation of co-presence, but where a large proportion of those relations, experiences and understandings are actually constructed on a far larger scale than what we happen to define for that moment as the place itself, whether that be a street, a region or even a continent.

Places do not have boundaries in the sense of divisions which frame simple enclosures. 'Boundaries' may, of course, be necessary – for the purposes of certain types of studies for instance – but they are not necessary for the conceptualization of a place itself. Definition in this sense does not have to be through simple counterposition to the outside; it can come in part, precisely through the particularity of linkage to that 'outside' which is therefore itself part of what constitutes the place.

Doreen Massey

The political striation of space

In *Empire of Signs*, Barthes entices us to join him in the exploration of a fantasy, his fantasy. We are encouraged to interrogate 'the idea of an unheard-of symbolic relation, one altogether detached from our own' (Barthes, 1995). This system he calls 'Japan'. The idea here is to draw upon a symbolic reserve in order to release certain signifiers, especially those concerned with space, and allow them to vibrate at a different frequency. In other words 'Japan' offers Barthes, offers us, a space within which certain terms: *boundary, identity, enclosure, place, division*, can be rethought and, perhaps, re-articulated.

The pertinence of this fantasy lies in a certain failure, a failure of the West, of the western metropolis, to sustain a level of social cohesion which makes life bearable. A vending machine stands, replete with beer, wine and whisky in Iwakura; an eastern suburb of Kyoto. An insignificant observation perhaps but, on the other hand? If there is one process that pervades the western metropolis more than any other, it is that of social fragmentation. Alcoholic vending machines are no match for the desires of the alienated youth of most western metropolitan spaces. Yet they exist here in Japan. Their time may be numbered, perhaps. But in this discrete geo-political space, the necessary conditions for the possibility of their existence is ensured without, it should be added, overt policing. But how?

This chapter is an attempt to map this, *prima facie* anomaly. It represents an exploration of the type of space that can yield community. There is no Japan as Barthes describes, yet, in the movement of social encoding, there are enough gaps to tentatively hint at what a civic space might need to encapsulate if those vending machines are to survive. We will also be investigating to what extent these possible spaces can be modelled. In recent years computerised gaming-simulations have been deployed to simulate the chaotic complexity of social systems which have proved resistant to analysis by more traditional (linear) conceptual frameworks.

There is also an explicit intention in Barthes text to counterpose an ethics of the self, based upon an inherent interiority, and a view of the ethical subject as a specific moment in a network of relations. Foucault writes that 'A whole history remains to be written of space – which would at the same time be the history of powers' (Foucault, 1984). He concerned himself with many spaces – institutional architectures in particular, because 'anchorage in a space is an economic-political form which needs to be studied in detail' (Foucault, 1984). Anchoring the self in space, in a space that can ethically sustain us, is the topic of this chapter. As its title suggests, we will be exploring the relation that holds between the city (as a psycho-physical space), ethics and power.

The idea that the essence of the human subject resides in an interior self, in spatial isolation from other selves, is one of the major themes of Enlightenment and much post-Enlightenment thought. The role of rational consciousness in modern philosophy leads to the positing of the individual at the centre of the disclosure of the nature of reality. In Descartes' philosophy, rational consciousness, consciousness as representation of the real, becomes in the Cartesian meditations the guarantor of certainty and knowledge: 'something true is that which man himself clearly and distinctly brings before himself and confronts as what is thus brought before him (re-presented) in order to guarantee what is represented in such a confrontation' (Heidegger, 1973). The assurance of such a representation is certainty. What is true in the sense of being certain is what is real. Thus, Descartes will argue 'our inquiries should be directed, not to what others have thought, nor to what we ourselves conjecture, but to what we can clearly and perspicuously behold and with certainty deduce ... (Rule 3) and if man observe them (the rules) accurately, he shall never assume what is false as true, and will never spend his mortal efforts to no purpose' (Descartes, 1984). Reality becomes that which is open to the mind's act of re-presenting. The mind becomes engaged in the discursive task of differentiation, discrimination and the establishment of identities. By the distinct representation of things and the clear comprehension of the connection between things, certainty is assured. Thus relations between beings are to be conceived in the form of order and measurement: the method of 'analysis' becomes paramount. A further effect of this privileging of the 'knowing' mind is the subordination of the material body, which becomes a mere appendage; to be fashioned and controlled by the discursive intellect.

So, when this form of analysis is turned towards the human subject itself or at least towards other human subjects, it is invariably tied to relations of power and control. In our society, it could be argued that science and scientific discourse have been at the centre of this process. Power is exercised via an integrated process of normalisation, where 'normalisation' denotes the acquisition by the subject of a particular discourse. The social body becomes technologically encoded, striated and gridded. The body is subjected to a host of regulatory disciplines: medical, legal, physical and psychological. The micro-mechanisms of power determine relations at every level. These mechanisms function primarily not by virtue of legislation but far more pervasively through a technology of normalisation, which sets identities and maps the specific boundaries within which the individual body will become enclosed. Given these processes of normalisation, the individual self is but a perspective rather than a unique and autonomous point for the disclosure of the world and thoroughly situated historically within certain finite conceptual frameworks. Many of these frameworks are situated in space and are the result of a process of striation. The citizen and his or her relation to the city is merely a replication of his or her relations with other institutionalised forms of life (acts of enclosure) of which Foucault has spoken in detail. All concern discipline or what we have been referring to as 'striation'. One example should clarify this process.

The over-arching question posed by Foucault in *Discipline and Punish* is: how did the prison ('a coercive corporal secret model of the power to punish' (Foucault, 1979, p. 131)) replace the collective signifying model (for example, torture as public spectacle) for the teaching of discipline? From being an art of 'unbearable sensations', punishment has become an 'economy of suspended rights'. Foucault argues that the technology of power is the principle both of the penal system and of the knowledge of man. He construes the body politic as a set of 'material elements and techniques that serve as weapons, relays, communication routes and supports for power and knowledge relations' (Foucault, 1979, p. 28) that invest human bodies by turning them into objects of knowledge.

According to Foucault, the objective of the nineteenth century movement for penal reform was to set up a new economy of the power to punish, to ensure better distribution of control, in a way more subtle, yet also more widely spread in the social body. The core concept that will allow for the automatic functioning of power is discipline. The Enlightenment discovered the body as an object and target of power. It discovered that knowledges and institutionalised spaces were an effective mechanism for the creation of methods of control.

The notion of 'man-the-machine' appears, as Foucault argues, on two distinct yet overlapping levels: the Cartesian 'anatomico-metaphysical register' and the 'technico-political register'. It is constituted by a set of regulations and empirical methods for controlling and correcting operations of the body. The primary institutions for effecting such control were the school, army and hospital. The distinction between the useful body and the intelligible body is collapsed, the two poles conjoining through the notion of 'docility'. A body is docile that may be subjected, used, transformed and improved (Foucault, 1979, p. 136). Although, as Foucault is aware, this was not the first instance of such 'pressing investment', the scale of control and the interest in individual bodies was unprecedented. The process of 'working it individually' by subtly and coercively controlling the mechanism itself, its movements, gestures, attitudes and so on, by manipulating its internal organisation, brings into play a veritable plethora of codifying strategies. 'These methods, which made possible the meticulous control of the operations of the body, which assured the constant subjection of its forces and imposed upon them a relation of docility, utility, might be called "disciplines"' (Foucault, 1979, p. 137).

Foucault argues that it was this point in history that the 'art of the human body' was born. Subsequently, there developed a policy of coercion directed towards the body, a calculated 'manipulation of its gestures, its behavior' (Foucault, 1979, p. 137). The production of docility via a political anatomy, a 'mechanics of power', had a dual effect. Discipline at one and the same time increases the forces of the body (in terms of utility) but also diminishes its forces in political terms by creating obedience. Thus we see the establishment of the connection between aptitude and increased domination. However, this process should not be viewed as having a single, consolidated, central core. It becomes effective through a multiplicity of minor processes which variously intersect and overlap (education, hospitals, military, corporate organisations, and so on).

If we were to elicit any particular concern common to all these processes, it might be that for obsession with detail, a new 'micro-physics of power'. The meticulous observation of detail plus the awareness that people can be controlled by this information, gives rise to a complex network of methods and data. Foucault argues that discipline requires enclosure: 'the specification of a place heterogeneous to all others and closed in upon itself. It is the protected place of disciplinary monotony' (Foucault, 1979, p. 141). Following the monastic model, the machinery put into place to effect the principle of enclosure has, as its main target the notion of partitioning: 'every individual has its own place and each place its individual' (Foucault, 1979, p. 143). The model then is basically cellular.

The institution that captures these features of control most adequately is Jeremy Bentham's Panopticon: 'Inspection functions ceaselessly. The gaze is alert everywhere' (Foucault, 1979, p. 195). Its primary aim is to assure the automatic functioning of power. The inmate is an active participant. The architectural structure is designed in such a way that it is no longer necessary for those who are exercising power to be overtly manifest: 'Bentham laid down the principle that power should be visible and unverifiable' (Foucault, 1979, p. 201). The visible aspect is provided by the erection of a central tower from which the prisoner is spied upon. It is unverifiable because although he is uncertain whether he is being observed at any particular moment, he knows always that it is a possibility. Thus, 'The Panopticon is a machine for dissociating the seen/being seen dyad, in the periphic ring, one is totally seen, without ever seeing; in the central tower, one sees everything without ever being seen' (Foucault, 1979, p. 202). Confronted with the possibility of continual surveillance, the prisoner becomes the 'principle of his own subjection' (Foucault, 1979, p. 203). There is little need for corporal methods as the prison assumes responsibility for the constraints of power.

However, as Foucault points out, observation was not the only function of the Panopticon. As we have said above, the notion of discipline also incorporates training and behavioural modification. The Panopticon becomes an ideal place for experimentation. It becomes a space in which people can be analysed and in which the possibilities of transformations can be determined. 'The Panopticon functions as a kind of laboratory of power. Thanks to its mechanisms of observation it gains in efficiency and in the ability to penetrate into man's behavior; knowledge follows the advances of power, discovering new objects of knowledge over all the surfaces on which power is exercised' (Foucault, 1979, p. 204). The principle of the Panopticon then is not restricted to the prison; its scope ranges over hospitals, schools, factories and cities.

But it would be wrong to suggest that power should only be construed in terms of coercive forces. Power relations are constitutive of the social fabric and their effects can be either positive or negative, productive or oppressive and this is determined by the degree or level of normalisation operative in the particular structural mechanism within which they are manifested. We do not need recourse to the 'autarchic selves' referred to by Barthes in our opening quotation to avoid the power-oppressive aspects of social/institutional processes of normalisation. While it is true that the majority of Foucault's inquiries into the micro-mechanisms of power tend to take the form of exposés of social and intellectual structures that produce mechanisms that function through a technology of normalisation, they also offer us the possibility of constructing new mechanisms which are less pernicious. But, before turning to a consideration of the nature of these mechanisms, it is necessary to examine the ethical position that arises at the same moment this rationalised individual becomes the object of such a pressing investment. The Panopticon is only one strand of Bentham's conceptualisation of ethics. This disciplined docile body, this abstract, striated unit of utility, is then universalised to produce an equally abstract notion of society and ethical behaviour within that society. And Bentham sees this conceptual structure as the bedrock of modern democracy.

Thus, there appears, at one and the same time, two competing ethical theories. Both, it should be noted, arguing their roots in human rationality. Deontology within the atemporal, non-spatial, noumenal self. Utilitarianism finds its locus in the spatio/temporal desiring self of interests and preferences. It could be argued that utilitarianism has won the battle. However, both share an allegiance with neo-classical economic theory and its atomistic, externally related selves.

Utilitarianism, in a variety of guises, still stands as the major ethical underpinning of representative democracy. But it could be argued that, in the context of moral evaluation, utilitarianism takes a somewhat narrow view of the notion of 'personhood'. As Williams and Sen point out, persons are construed not as individuals (even contextualised individuals) but rather as 'amounts of utility'. They become 'locations of their respective utilities'. They are seen in terms of placeholders to which certain desires and preferences are predicated. Moral decision-making on the basis of this quantitative analysis can be formulated as follows: a state of affairs is judged exclusively on the basis of utility information related to that state. This reduces the collection of diverse information about the n-persons in that state into n-bits of utility with the totality of relevant information being given by an n-vector utility (Sen and Williams, 1982). Sum-ranking merges the utility bits together as one lump, losing in the process both the identity of the individuals as well as their separateness. Persons as persons have dropped out. They are totally subordinated to the assessment of states of affairs in terms of utility equations.

It is clear that closely related to the utilitarian consequentialist structure is the neglect of personal autonomy. Sum-ranking combines individual welfares for the purpose of assessing the entire unit of utility, rather than the individual. Personhood for the utilitarian thus takes the form of an abstraction. Interpersonal bonding within a domain of shared values is reduced to a quantitative operation relying on the mathematical resolution of interpersonal conflict. But if we deny the neo-classical economic viewpoint, deny the premise that conflictual relationships are inherent to the nature of man, and reinterpret the relationship between self and other in terms of an internal relationship of reciprocal bonding, then responsibility rather than self-interest becomes the main ethical concept. But, this notion of responsibility needs to be retrieved, both from the utilitarian framework, where its functions as a corrective to the narrowly instrumental interests of atomised subjects, and from the deontological predisposition to construe the notion in terms of the obligation/rights/duties axis. The term 'responsibility' signifies, like any other term, within a context, and perhaps, more forcefully, no particular context ever saturates the term's possibilities of signification.

Life, and especially organisational life, at the end of the twentieth century requires that the term 'responsibility' is freed from the eighteenth and nineteenth century construal of the notion. The neologism *ethico-power* is one such attempt to enact this process. The motivation for the type of responsibility required by *ethico-power* is not dependent upon imperatives or the imposition of moral commands. It is not generated by a code or system but is a mode of 'responding' which flows directly out of the respect for difference which lies at the heart of democracy. It is also worth noting that 'rationalism' has not always formed the basis of moral theory. Modes of ethical response change as we enter different historical epochs. Foucault writes,

> nobody is obliged in classical ethics to behave in such a way as to be truthful to their wives, to not touch boys, and so on. But if they want to have a beautiful existence, if they want to have a good reputation, if they want to be able to rule others, they have to do that. (Foucault, 1984, p. 356)

However, during the stoic period, this personal choice aspect ceases to be the primary motivation, now 'you have to do it because you are a rational being' (Foucault, 1984, p. 356). The mode of obligation is changing. With the inception of Christianity, religious instructions become the framework for ethical norms. It is the juridical aspect of religious law that is maintained when religion stops being the motivating factor. Thus, at the inception of the Enlightenment, 'the religious framework of those rules disappear in part, and then between a medical or scientific approach and a juridical framework there was competition, with no resolution' (Foucault, 1984, p. 357).

While ethical modes of obligation are subject to radical historical change, there appears to be a common element in Stoic and Christian modes: asceticism. The type of self-creation indicative of these ethical postures entails the act of 'knowing oneself' and 'knowing the "truth"':

> Even if it is true that Greek philosophy founded rationality, it always held that a subject could not have access to truth if he did not operate upon himself a

certain work which would make him susceptible to knowing the truth: a work of purification, conversion of the soul by contemplation of the soul itself. (Foucault, 1984, p. 371).

The Enlightenment constitutes a rupture, a break with the tradition. The Cartesian insistence that 'to accede to truth, it suffices that I be *any* subject which can see what is evident' (Foucault, 1984, p. 372) leads inevitably to a nonascetic subject of knowledge. The 'science of knowing' can proceed unfettered by self-analysis. Of course there were attempts to ameliorate the dichotomy. As Foucault notes,

> There was much debate in the Enlightenment as to whether these subjects were completely different or not. Kant's solution was to find a universal subject of knowledge, but which demanded nonetheless, an ethical attitude: precisely the relationship to the self which Kant proposes in *The Critique of Practical Reason*. (Foucault, 1984, p. 372)

Thus, Kant reintroduces ethics from its Cartesian exile. Descartes had driven a wedge between ethics and scientific rationality. Kant brings the two together again by a form of what Dreyfus and Rabinow term 'procedural rationality' (p. 372 in Foucault, 1984). Ethics becomes the conformity to *practical Reason*. The universal subject must obey the commands of a universal moral law. The fusion of ethics; and an instrumental notion of rationality at that!

Without wishing to unduly valorise the Greek ethical experience, certain features of this experience seem to have been neglected in post-Enlightenment thinking which, if resurrected, may serve the task of realising *ethico-power* in a civic context. In his discussion of the pleasures in Greek society, Foucault argues that

> The principle according to which this activity [sexual] was to be regulated, the 'mode of subjection', was not defined by a universal legislation determining permitted and forbidden acts, but rather by a *savoire faire*, an art that prescribed the modalities of use that depended on different variables (need, time, status). (Foucault, 1985, p. 91)

What had to be effected was an 'aesthetics of existence' in which one constituted oneself *as* an ethical subject. Foucault suggests that 'classical antiquity's moral reflection concerning the pleasures was not directed towards a codification of acts, nor towards a hermeneutics of the subject, but towards a stylization of attitudes and an aesthetics of existence' (Foucault, 1985, p. 92). A stylistics of the subject is being addressed in which the self is fashioned and not discovered. Furthermore, the successful accomplishment of this aesthetics of existence could not be achieved separately from praxis; a mode of enactment, of self-regulation. Such a posture is markedly distinct from the universal and abstract self of post-Enlightenment thought:

> The time would come when the art of the self would assume its own shape, distinct from ethical conduct that was its object. But in classical Greek thought, the 'ascetics' that enabled one to make oneself into an ethical subject was an integral part – down to its very form – of the practice of a virtuous life, which was also the life of a 'free' man in the full, positive and political sense of the word. (Foucault, 1985, p. 77)

The important point to recognise is that the moral requirements that were implied by 'the constitution of this self-disciplined subject were not present in the form of a universal law, which each and every individual would have to obey' (Foucault, 1985, p. 77). The ought aspect is missing. Virtuous acts are performed so as to give existence 'the most graceful and accomplished form possible'.

This brief consideration of ethics in Greek society is useful for the general argument of this chapter, inasmuch as it demonstrates that an ethics can be formulated without recourse to universal moral principles or divine edicts, binding upon all. It introduces a certain flexibility and evokes a pluralistic and innovative approach to how individuals constitute themselves as ethical subjects. Innovation in the field of ethics relies in part upon the readiness to dispute the post-Enlightenment belief that the moral subject is constituted entirely within the parameters of reason. Multiple rationalities or contextualised rationalities do not imply a plunge into the depths of unreason, where 'anything goes' in the moral domain. What is being opposed is a rationality, an instrumental rationality, which appears at a particular point in human history, is the result of certain socio-political and economic arrangements, has become hegemonic and which may not be appropriate to the *fin-de-millennium*. The notion of responsibility suffers from a particular lack, a depletion of its signifying capacity when it is locked within the reductionist rhetoric of either deontological or utilitarian theory. This lack becomes particularly acute when we move from a consideration of individual or personal responsibility to the organisational and civic level. When we move to the need to construct ethical spaces for the enactment of a new ethical vocabulary.

What is the nature of the metropolis? How can it be a space for the expression of ethical behaviour? How is it, that in 1997, vending machines, carrying hard liquor can exist, unhampered, in Iwakura? Difficult questions. But, much of the answer has to do with social cohesion. To what extent can it be planned for? What necessary conditions need to be in place for it to manifest itself? The structuralist leanings of this chapter would support the proposition that ethical behaviour can, in part, be facilitated by design. The metropolis as a possible ethical zone can be helped or hindered by the activities (inherently political) of the city planners themselves.

Angotti has argued that although 'urban inequalities are not created by urban planners... they are often protected by them' (Angotti, 1993, p. 204). They enact a striation of space, a strategy of segregation based upon the physical separation of land uses and social groups, inevitably leading to unequal development. Thus 'planners do not shape or control development, they codify and legitimize it with their zoning rules' (Angotti, 1993, p. 204) and usually to the benefit of the centre (central city development) and to the exclusion of the periphery. This codification of centralism and segmentarity has a long history. It arises at the same moment the state becomes the primary form of social integration, overcoming, displacing, at one and the same time a more fluid form of human interaction. Deleuze, perhaps more than any other thinker has traced the history of this movement and demonstrated the connection between spatial striation and political oppression. In *A Thousand Plateaus* (Deleuze and Guattari, 1987), he offers the following analogy:

> Let us take chess and Go, from the standpoint of the game pieces, the relations between the pieces and the space involved. Chess is a game of state, or of the court: the emperor of China played it. Chess pieces are coded; they have an internal nature and intrinsic properties from which their movements, situations, and confrontations derive. They have qualities; a knight remains a knight, a pawn a pawn, a bishop a bishop. Each is like a subject of the statement endowed with a relative power, and these relative powers combine in a subject of enunciation, that is, the chess player or the game's form of interiority.
>
> Go pieces, in contrast, are pellets, disks, simple arithmetic units, and have only an anonymous, collective, or third-person function: 'It' makes a move. 'It' could be a man, a woman, a louse, an elephant. Go pieces are elements of a nonsubjectified machine assemblage with no intrinsic properties, only situational ones. Thus the relations are very different in the two cases. Within their milieu of interiority, chess pieces entertain biunivocal relations with one another, and with the adversary's pieces: their functioning is structural. On the other hand the Go piece has only a milieu of exteriority, or extrinsic relations with nebulas or constellations, according to which it fulfills functions of insertion or situation, such as bordering, encircling, shattering. All by itself, a Go piece can destroy an entire constellation synchronically; a chess piece cannot (or can do so diachronically only)... Another justice, another movement, another space-time. (Deleuze and Guattari, 1987, pp. 353–4)

Another justice, another movement, another space-time. A questioning of the nature of boundary and identity, of enclosure and division and, *inter alia*, of the ethics of space and the space of ethics. Thus, Angotti argues that the metropolis can only be viewed as a thoroughly politicised space, serving the interests of the speculators and the transnational corporations. What is lost, is what Deleuze calls the 'nomadic trajectory' which 'does not fulfill the function of the sedentary road, which is to parcel out a closed space to people, assigning each person a share and regulating the communication between shares' (Delueze and Guattari, 1987, p. 381). This is a space without boarders or enclosure, a 'comprehensive inter-relationship of social groups, land uses and districts' (Angotti, 1993). Against the post-Enlightenment bureaucratisation of the metropolis, Angotti quotes Jane Jacob's belief that cities require 'a most intricate and close-grained diversity of use that give each other constant mutual support, both economically and socially' (Angotti, 1993).

Current urban planning follows the statist form set down by the micro-zoning indicative of nineteenth century, trajectories/strategies of imposing discipline and control – 'the eye of power'. For example, Foucault, quoting Philippe Ariès, writes that the house is until the eighteenth century an undifferentiated space, but between the 1830s and 1870s 'The working-class family is to be fixed; by assigning it a living space with a room that serves as a kitchen and dining room, a room for the parents which is a place of procreation, and a room for the children, one prescribes a form of morality for the family' (Foucault, 1984, p. 149). Segmentarity surrounds us 'and in all directions' (Deleuze and Guattari, 1987, p. 149). In every facet of our lives, to quote Doris Lessing

> I was seeing a map, a chart, of a certain way of thinking... this was a way of thought, a set of mind, made visible. It was the mind of the Northwest fringes, the mind of the white conquerors. Over the variety and change and differentiation of the continent, over the flows and movement and changes of the earth – as vigorous as that of the air above, though in a different dimension of time – was the stamp of rigidity. Cities, towns, the larger mountains, the deserts, interrupted it: but over rivers and hills and marshes and plains lay the grid, this inflexible pattern. (Lessing, 1994, p. 319)

We are zoned. From micro to macro zoning 'we are segmented in a circular fashion, in ever larger circles, ever wider discs or coronas' (Deleuze and Guattari, 1987, pp. 208–9). If we are to avoid the pernicious aspects of segmentarity, it is clear that there must be both a return and an advance. Not a mere repetition of the nomadic life but a re-integration of the fluidity and flexibility of pre-statist social organisation with the inevitable demands of metropolitan life. There is a growing awareness that the institutions of civil society can act as a corrective to the segmentary forces of national governance. We have already noted that decentralised power lies at the heart of the attempt to stay the effects of segmentalism and its corollary – social fragmentation. But how is this to be accomplished? Angotti suggests that *neighbourhood power* can offset both the inefficiencies and inequalities produced by centralised governance. However, it must be supported at the metropolitan level: '... only planning at the metropolitan level can establish policies of equitable distribution of services throughout the region. Only planning at the neighbourhood level can establish inclusionary plans for neighbourhood conservation and development. The secret to metropolitan planning is the successful integration of the two' (Angotti, 1993, p. 23).

Ethico-power: ethical systems design

The processes of enframing that encode the city and its inhabitants are subject not only to the lawgivers of the centre but also to an onto-theological interpretation as to what constitutes the human subject. Rational islands of sentience brought together by contracts. External relations between atomised subjects. Segmentarity in all directions. The resistance lies in re-thinking the human subject, re-thinking the nature of power and re-thinking the nature of ethical discourse. Perhaps Angotti's use of the idea of 'integrated diversity' can be useful here inasmuch as it is prefigured in certain systems theoretic discourse, especially the concept of *autopoiesis*.

Autopoiesis can be seen as a self-referencing system of communication which both defines relations with the outside environment and provides itself with its own mechanism of justification. The neighbourhood's relation to the metropolis can be understood in precisely this way. Living systems exhibit three principal features: autonomy, circularity and self-reference:

> living systems strive to maintain an identity by subordinating all changes to the maintenance of their own organization as a given set of relations. They do so by engaging in circular patterns of interaction whereby change in one element of the system is coupled with changes elsewhere, setting up continuous patterns of interaction which are always self-referential. They are self-referential because a system cannot enter into interactions that are not specified in the pattern of relations that define its organization. Thus a system's interaction

with its 'environment' is really a reflection and part and parcel of its own organization. It interacts with its environment in a way that facilitates its own self-production, and in this sense we can see that its environment is really part of itself. (Morgan, 1986, p. 236)

Organisations (and for the sake of what follows, cities, will be construed as a complex system of organisations) 'need to attain a certain level of self-referentiality if they are to be able to enact their own environment; to project the internal value system outward. The environment should not be construed as an amorphous mass, a singular entity, standing over and above the specific system under consideration but an intersystemic network' (Pheby, 1997, p. 77). Morgan offers the following example:

The bee as an organism comprises a chain of self-referring biological systems with their own circular organization, and lives within a society of bees where relations are also circular. Eliminate the bees and the whole ecology will change, for the bee system is linked with the botanical system, which is linked with insect, animal, agricultural, human, and social system, e.g. a decision to use an insecticide which eliminates bees as a side effect, can transform all the others. (Morgan, 1986, p. 237)

Systems, both internally and externally, are subject to complex processes of mutual causality. The act of drawing a boundary can only be seen as an imposition (such as the institutionalised boundaries of which Foucault speaks) – the imposing of a striated social/conceptual framework upon an otherwise undifferentiated space/time continuum. Thus, the system/environment distinction, so coveted by the contingency theorists, can only be maintained at the price of simplifying the intersystemic matrix. Once this idea of the fragile system facing an alien environment is overcome, we can see that all systems can be proactive as well as reactive. Providing they exhibit robust internal mechanisms capable of projecting their identities onto the matrix, they have a chance of maintaining a certain level, albeit contextualised, of autonomy. The question arises as to how we can create neighbourhoods that exhibit such mechanisms and what is to be the relationship between the neighbourhood and its citizens.

Autopoiesis suggests that just as systems, qua organisations, are intricately interwoven with other systems/organisations within the overall network, individuals (as systems themselves) bear the same relation to the particular organisations of which they form a part, a moment. The relation between these circular patterns of coherence, these integrated bundles of memories in time, and the wider community cannot be conceived as that of master and slave. 'Organisations maintain identities that are qualitatively distinct from the aggregate of individual desires and preferences' (Pheby, 1997, p. 77). They form matrices of contextualised, autonomous agencies. The self is a process. The self is dynamic. It is embroiled, implicated with other selves. It has only a *contextualised* autonomy. It is in such a relationship that ethical selves are formed. The ethical relation is premised upon the nature of this internal bonding. Before all contracts. Before the external relations of neo-classical economics – there exists the openness of self to other – this is the 'real' ethical relation.

Structuralism and deconstruction have laid siege to the edifice known as the 'sovereign individual'. Ethnology, psychoanalysis and linguistics have all played their part in showing that the human subject is not an autonomous entity with an indubitable essence but a multiplicity. Human subjects are thoroughly contextualised in the sense that they inhabit a world of meaning and significance which is not of their own making as atomised and isolated individuals. In contrast to the classical world-view, which insists on the sovereign independence of individuals and their desires, preferences and interests, we are insisting that individuals are discrete systems, yet exist intricately embroiled with other systems; other humans, semantic structures and social institutions. It is this internal relation, as we have said, that holds between individuals, through an openness to others, that already constitutes the possibility of the ethical relation.

But the possibility of this relation also requires a political intervention, an intervention into the structures of power that currently control our social lives. It is necessary to diffuse the control of the centre, wherever it appears. Push the decision-making processes towards the periphery. In the context of the city, of the metropolis – towards the neighbourhood, the community. What is crucial are the bonding processes, the fields of shared meaning capable of generating the stability required to sustain their identities. This process of reality construction should not be seen as totally closed. 'Diversity and heterogeneity are important elements in ensuring the system imports enough energy from the "environment" to secure its continued growth and development' (Pheby, 1997).

What then are the practical implications of this approach? Angotti, although it is doubtful that he would endorse the theoretical framework we are deploying here, offers some interesting possibilities.

> Community movements... give rise to institutions and strategies dedicated to community development. Community development may be equated with either growth or preservation but usually it is the former. Community

development that combines growth and preservation is more likely to encourage integrated diversity. Community development that is supported by metropolitan-wide and national policies is more likely to encourage integrated diversity. (Angotti, 1993, p. 219).

Integrated diversity, contextualised autonomy and *autopoiesis* are all a gesturing towards a mode of communication and a mode of metropolitan design premised on the ethical postulate that the individual, while preserving her autonomy is also 'one amongst many'. This type of social organisation is reflected in Angotti's examples of integrated diversity:

> Lauchlin Currie proposed a multi-level approach to neighborhood development. He outlined a program for 'cities-within-cities' with populations ranging from 400 000–500 000. They would be planned to integrate many smaller neighborhood clusters, each of which would be large enough for pedestrian circulation to be adopted as the main transportation mode. Single ownership of land, local administration, local employment, coordination with regional authorities and within a national urban policy are other key elements of his proposal. (Currie, 1976)

> In a similar approach, urban designer, Eduardo Lozano (1990) recommends: the establishment of metropolitan authorities is essential for dealing with the regional issues – subsumed under growth and development policies: the location of main centers of employment, the extension of public transit lines, the banking of land for integrated housing. These authorities should have the power to override local municipalities in order to zone land in strategic centers and corridors (though not in all metropolitan areas), to plan main public transportation lines, to acquire land for housing, and to apportion property tax revenues from land and to various municipalities... The reconstruction of urban communities must stress diversity, as both a social and visual characteristic, and ensure a variety and equality of social groups, so that no one can exert undue dominance. It must stress a rich urban mixture with economic and political balance, an environment that is resilient and fair. (Angotti, 1993, p. 231)

These models have a distinctly autopoietic flavour. In a sense, we might say that in the socio-political arena which we are addressing, they have strong federalist leanings; where federalism demands an integration of the local and the global (twin citizenship) and the belief that power belongs at the lowest level possible – subsidiarity:

> Federalism properly understood, can restore a sense of local belonging and a broader, bigger citizenship, both in our organization and in society... Nations are too big, the connections not enough, the commitment to the future not long enough. It is better to look smaller, to our now-smaller organizations, to local communities and cities, to families and clusters of friends, to small net-

works of portfolio people with time to give to something bigger than themselves. We have to fashion our own directions in our own places. (Handy, 1995, p. 114)

But, if the federalist paradigm is to be realised, subsidiarity needs to be reinforced by modes of communication, only now available:

> *The ultimate promise of the new technology is the rebuilding of community.* (Nicholas Johnson, former Chairman of the Federal Communications Commission)

Pierre Levy has argued that 'Collective Intelligence entails an understanding of how techniques of communication can unite the intellectual forces and imagination of each one of us in a greater whole'. He suggests that there is a way in which information technology can allow us to move from the industrial paradigm of representative democracy to the post-industrial paradigm of direct democracy or 'power by the people' (Levy, 1995):

> We must incorporate into our communicative life the huge potential for real-time consultation and debate. It is essential that we start exploring this positive option soon; if we don't, our worst fears about misuse will inevitably translate into reality. Fast. We will not see a Third Wave religion or ideology. That is because one of the characteristics of the Third Wave is diversity ... not just mass movements but micro belief systems springing up, and the central issue is the tolerance for diversity, which is going to be the hardest thing to achieve.
> Political discourse has long been mediated by electronic machines: the issue now is that these machines have enabled decentralized dialogue and created unique combinations of human-machine assemblages – individual and collective 'voices' that are the new building blocks of political formations and groupings. If the current media technology (television) is viewed as a threat to democracy, how can we account for a technology like the Internet, which appears to decentralize communication but enhance democracy? (Levy, 1995)

These thoughts should do much to ameliorate the 'humanist' critique of systems-theoretic discussion of communications. Certain writers have been worried, unduly, by the contentions of information theorists in particular, that communication or systems of communication can be theorised without there having to be any communicators.[1] However, a thorough contextualisation of the subject and the breaking down of the traditional subject/object distinction does not imply the disappearance of the self qua communicator but merely complicates the relation to its spatial and temporal milieu. What is communicated and how it is communicated is dependent on the way in which the observer (communicator) integrates and differentiates the message from the noise which constitutes its general context. This in turn depends upon the observers position, the site s/he occupies within the system. S/he is both observer, subject and object and so on, depending upon the position s/he occupies within an interlocking systemic reality of which s/he forms a part. In one sense, s/he is a point of view in time. But how to integrate these perspectives? How to ensure social cohesion while at the same time maintaining a respect for diversity? Mechanisms capable of generating transparency in communication, transparency of meaning, and trust are essential.

These ideas have been exploited to great effect in the Research and Development Project for 'Planner's Cockpit' for Planning Officials.[2] The theoretical postulates behind the project (outlined in Appendix A) reflect our concerns in this chapter, namely, the decentralisation of administration, the diversification of mass services for citizens and the participation of citizens *vis-à-vis* democratic institutions. Within this conceptual framework, citizens are expected to change from consumers to prosumers. This change demands a more accessible administration system in order to improve interaction between the administration system and the administrated citizens. For this reason, the structure of the administration system should become more flexible and adaptive with respect to the evolution of the municipal social system. For this to happen, it is necessary for the development of a better information infrastructure for improving the planning process within the municipal administration and enhancing communication between the administration and its citizens. It is necessary to the required structures for value coordination.

So what of Barthes' fantasy? What of the possibility of overcoming the autarchic selves of modern industrial society in favour of community. For all of us in the West, faced as we are with social alienation, social fragmentation and political impotency, such a fantasy must be an appealing option. Autopoiesis gives us the theoretical underpinnings and federalism gives us the strategy for implementing the notion of *integrated diversity*. But, we still need the mechanisms.

In the PINS project (planning information network system) Kamuta suggests that one important element in the concepts-oriented design of the planner's cockpit, is the role of interactive gaming-simulations. These allow participants to explore multiple realities, laying open blind spots of the various actors when dealing with complex social issues, and subsequently enhancing their potential for shaping social reality. The *Fractos* Gaming-Simulation,[3] described in Appendix B, was designed to provide participants with an understanding of complex patterns of connectivity and to offer the opportunity for strategic formulations in a non-hostile environment. The matrix displays the necessary conditions for the possibility of achieving an ethical and empowering metropolitan space. The various elements within the matrix are based upon the work of Thomas Angotti. However, the manner of their relationship has been devised by the author and represents the autopoietic systemic structure described above. Each element is embroiled within a complex process of mutual causality. Releasing *ethico-power* at the metropolitan level requires the construction of a civic space that can both maintain its own identity (at the level of the 'neighbourhood'), yet draw enough energy from its relationships with other neighbourhoods and the metropolitan centre which does not control but coordinates. Thus the neighbourhoods possess a form of contextualised autonomy or, to use Angotti's term, integrated diversity.

The original *Fractos* model was designed to enable both public and private organisations to maintain their identity and growth in turbulent environments. There is an explicit belief here that this can only be accomplished if the organisation in question exhibits a commitment to a generally accepted system of shared values. At the heart of this system lie the ethical notions of trust, transparency, respect for difference and power-sharing. Such systems are immensely fragile and difficult to sustain. When we are considering cities, rather than individual organisations, we are faced with an almost impossible task. Yet, it is a task we must attempt. If the arguments advanced in this chapter have any value, it resides in the belief that there exists a space for communities to shape their destiny, despite the overwhelming power and control of the centre. Information technology (if its decentralising force can be deployed) can aid our project: if only incrementally. But, as Handy has argued,

> We cannot wait for central government to give away its power, we have to do what we can without it. In the world ahead we shall increasingly have to make our own virtual city and our own virtual village. (Handy, 1995, p. 267)

Appendix A The planner's cockpit

Kamuta describes a conceptual framework called Planning Information Network System (PINS). The components of PINS are: people, communication channels, communication nodes, information storage, support tools and a social environment. The Planner's Cockpit is the so-called central nervous system for planners and planning teams at the various administrative levels. Four types of Planner's Cockpit are envisioned, namely for:

1. Intra-Public Organisation Planning (comprehensive plan formation in municipalities in Japan).
2. Inter-Public Organisation Planning (housing supply plan formation of Tokyo Metropolitan Area).
3. Inter-Citizen/Public Organisation Planning (housing district renovation programme formation via citizen participation).
4. Inter-Private Organisation Planning (urban revitalising project formation initiated by private sectors in the centre of Tokyo).

The Planner's Cockpit has not only been developed as a planning support system but also as a learning environment for the training of planners. Design principles for the Planner's Cockpit are:

1. Concepts-oriented design of the planner's work and learning environments.
2. Development of component subsystems and subsequently coupling of these systems. Relevant component subsystems are:

- requirement system;
- concept system;
- gaming simulation equipment;
- consultation or instruction system; and
- network system.

The Planner's Cockpit is used for the development of a Planning Administration Laboratory to be used for land-use planning activities of the Utsunomiya City Government and as a pilot system for intra-city government.

Appendix B The *Fractos* model for urban planning

Mechanisms

The *Fractos Gaming Simulation* consists of the following elements:

1. Tutor Facilitation Console (linked by E-mail) to the
2. Team workstations (4)
3. Printer

1. Tutor facilitation console

The tutor facilitation console enables the tutor to communicate with his/her team via the E-mail system. Depending upon organisational requirements and the number of teams, a single tutor may occupy a room or, alternatively, tutors may wish to share a room. The latter has the advantage of cross-fertilisation between tutors.

2. Team workstations

Each team engaged in playing the Fractos gaming-simulation comprises of eight members. Two members are allotted to the four directorates:

- Intra-Public Organisation Planning
- Inter-Public Organisation Planning
- Inter-Citizen/Public Organisation Planning
- Inter-Private Organisation Planning

Via their PCs and the E-mail system they will be in direct contact with the facilitator/tutor. Each of the directorates will need to concern themselves with both the operational and strategic issues concerned with the realisation of the *learning points fields*. It is suggested that the two team members of each directorate alternate between strategic and operational concerns during the two four-hour simulation sessions.

The Fractos gaming simulation assumes that these roles are interlinked and thus team members are encouraged to avoid treating them as discrete functions.

3. Printer

There will be a printer linked to the team members' PCs in each room allowing each of them to obtain a hard copy of the transactions with the tutors. Teams will also have the opportunity to print off a 'hard copy' of their progress after each of the *Fractos Audits*.

Analysis of outputs

During the two days of the Fractos gaming simulation teams are scheduled to meet with their tutors on four occasions. Two of these take place directly before each interactive session and two directly after each interactive session. The purpose of the former strategic sessions is to ensure that team members are aware of the ground rules of the simulation and are offered an opportunity to voice any issues they feel relevant. The latter sessions, the 'feedback' sessions, have three purposes:

1. A general discussion of the results of the Fractos audit.
2. Aiding the team to produce a 'cognitive map' of their planning process during the simulation period.
3. A review of the history of the mechanisms and methods used during the simulation period.

Items 2 and 3 above will serve as the basis for the *learning points presentation* which follows the conclusion of the second simulation period. Each directorate will be responsible for describing its strategy and implementation procedures to the other groups during the simulation.

NB: Figure 5.1 is a diagrammatic representation of the urban planning model outlined in this chapter, using the Fractos game-simulation mechanism.

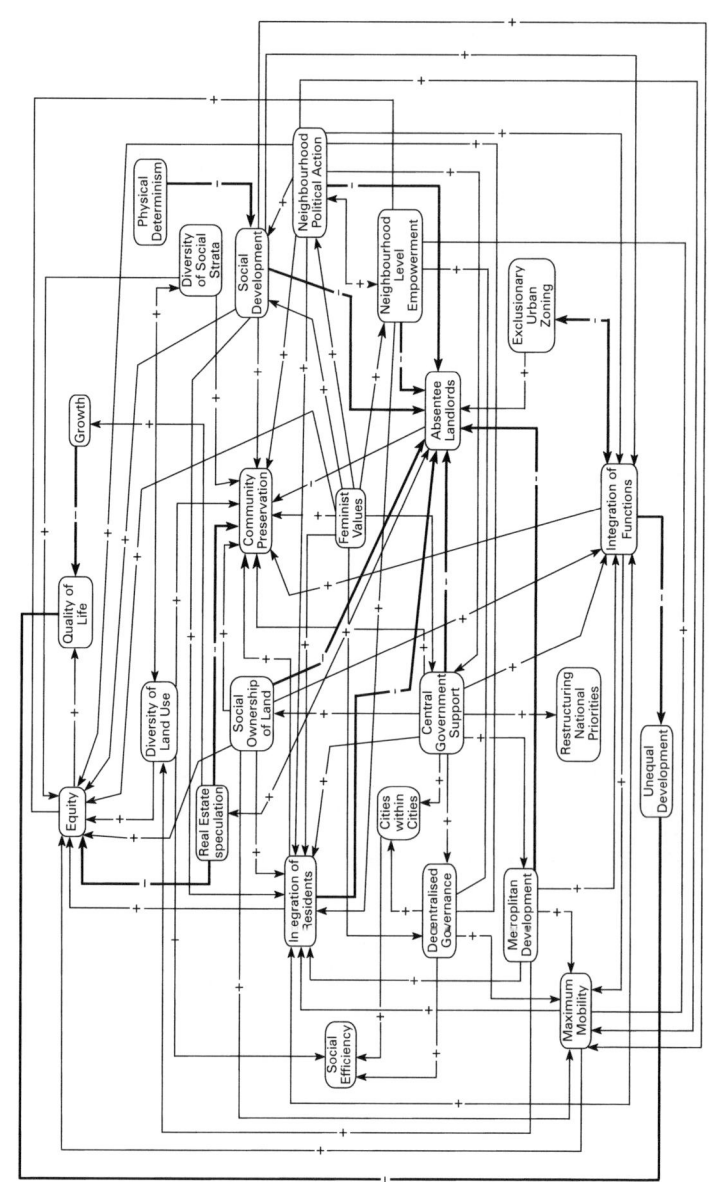

Figure 5.1 Urban planning model

Notes

1. A particularly well-argued statement of this position is given in Alan Wolfe's 'Algorithmic Justice' in *Deconstruction and the Possibility of Justice*, ed. Cornell, Rosenfeld and Carlson (1992) (London, NY: Routledge).
2. This project was developed at the Tokyo Institute of Technology in order to help municipal policy-makers in Japan to improve local planning and municipal administration. The present description of the project was offered by Y. Kamuta at the *Scope 2000* conference hosted by the Department of Gamma Informatics, University of Utrecht, and as far as the author is aware is ongoing.
3. The *Fractos Gaming-Simulation* was developed by Fractos Ltd.

References

Angotti, T. (1993) *Metropolis 2000: Planning, Poverty and Politics* (London: Routledge).
Barthes, R. (1995) *The Empire of Signs* (New York: Hill & Wang).
Descartes, R. (1984) *Rules for the Direction of the Mind: The Philosophical Works of Descartes* (2 vols) trans. E. Haldane and G. Ross (Cambridge: Cambridge University Press).
Deleuze, G. and Guattari, F. (1987) *A Thousand Plateaus*, trans. B. Massumi (Minneapolis, Minn.: Minneapolis University Press).
Foucault, M. (1979) *Discipline and Punish: The Birth of the Prison*, trans. A. Sheridan (New York: Vintage).
Foucault, M. (1984) *The Eye of Power* (Foucault Reader) ed. P. Rabinow (New York: Pantheon).
Foucault, M. (1979) *Use of Pleasure* trans. R. Hurley (New York: Pantheon).
Handy, C. (1995) *The Empty Raincoat* (London: Arrow).
Heidegger, M. (1973) *The End of Philosophy* trans. J. Stambaugh (New York: Harper & Row).
Lessing, D. (1994) *The Sirian Experiments: The Report by Ambien II of the Five* (London: Flamingo HarperCollins).
Levy, P. (1995) 'Interview with Andrew Joscelyne', *Worad*, July/August.
Morgan, G. (1986) *Images of Organisation* (Newbury Park, Cal.: Sage).
Pheby, K. (1997) '*The Psychological Contract: Enacting Ethico-Power*', in Davies, P.W.F (ed.), *Current Issues in Business Ethics* (London: Routledge), pp. 76–86.
Sen, L.A and Williams, B. (1982) *Utilitarianism and Beyond* (Cambridge: Cambridge University Press).

6 Ethics, Empowerment and Ownership
Peter W.F. Davies and Anne Mills

INTRODUCTION

Empowerment is the democracy of the 1990s. No-one is sure what the term means but we all know that it is something good and worthy, and so consequently we nod sagely when the term is presented in managerial and academic discourse. To use the arguments of Karen Legge (Legge, 1995), could it be that in keeping with wider human resource (HR) initiatives the term has entered the realms of rhetoric only? Is the reality that business at best uses the concept as yet another management tool, and at worst uses the notion as an extension of their power and control in the workplace whilst articulating the reverse? In ethical terms, *is the true implementation of employee empowerment contingent upon ownership, form and business philosophy, rather than management strategy?*

In this chapter, we shall consider the concept of *empowerment* in relation to the *degree of control* (as a matter of justice) exerted by employees over their activities in the workplace. If workplace activity can be divided into the model of 'planning, execution and control', then the traditional activities of employees at the lower levels in the organisation are associated with just the *execution* activity. But it is precisely this area (the degree of control over their work) that empowerment is supposed to extend, and thereby gain its ethical credentials.

This chapter will consider a framework of three perspectives concerning the relationship between empowerment and control. First we focus on the *pragmatic approach* to empowerment whereby control is extended to employees at the discretion of management, and mainly as a means to fulfil corporate objectives. Empowerment here is essentially an adaptive mechanism for organisational survival; the Rover car company is used as an illustrative example. This is then followed by a consideration of empowerment as a deliberate strategy to *extend management control* rather than reduce it. This view is discussed within the context of labour process theory and uses 'Japanisation' as a current example. As regards the third perspective we will argue that for empowerment to be 'genuine' it must become a human 'right' (rooted in *non*-consequentialist theory) rather than merely a discretionary tool of management. Establishing this 'right' has direct implications for changed forms of ownership, and the Scott-Bader company is focused on here as an example.

Pseudo-empowerment

The first two perspectives are what we call *pseudo-empowerment* and are premised on the typologies used by Reed (Reed, 1989, p. 14). Here, the notion of empowerment as yet another management tool is underpinned by the model of management as a 'rationally designed tool for the realisation of instrumental objectives'. Management is perceived as a 'neutral social technology' and 'is about means rather than ends'. It is very much a systems approach to the organisational thinking whereby the objective of management is to enhance the effectiveness of the organisation to ensure that it establishes equilibrium with the environment. This perspective also portrays a model of organisation as systems of hierarchical control which are 'geared to the extraction of the maximum surplus value' (Reed, 1989, pp. 2, 4, 10). Within this model, individual managers are treated as the principal 'bearers' of the inner economic logic within capitalism. This critical perspective argues that with greater internationalisation of enterprises and the growth in technology there now exists

> a sophisticated combination of rational control techniques and ideological devices (such as quality circles, briefing groups, works councils and participation schemes), which is aimed at mobilising worker consent to increase productivity, has emerged as the dominant control structure under advanced capitalism. (Burawoy, 1985, p. 150)[1]

The two perspectives stemming from this ideological underpinning are now considered in more depth.

THE PRAGMATIC APPROACH TO EMPOWERMENT

This view of empowerment is encouraged greatly by much of the plethora of populist management literature which leans heavily on the empirical 'best practice' approach. The rationale and methodology behind much of this literature is to observe a company or country which is perceived as functioning successfully against a given set of criteria, and attempt to copy their policies and procedures. In terms of the short historical perspective on such literature, Peters and Waterman highlighted the significance of human resources in *In Search of Excellence* (Peters and Waterman, 1982). The notion of radically restructured organisations and empowerment emerged again later in the 1980s in Tom Peters' *Thriving on Chaos* (Peters, 1987).

In support of the notion of empowerment in this context, Tyson (1995) argues that, in strategic and organisational restructuring terms, empowerment is a logical extension of flatter organisation structures. The wider spans of control which result from this kind of strategy have led to the granting of greater autonomy and responsibility to groups of people lower down the organisation. Additionally he argues that the major economic recession and the social and political changes of the last decade have led to a situation where

> normative purposes cannot be sustained over the varying stages in the economic cycle, and the values which management bring to their work are not constant, but are dependent upon the strategic choices which their companies face. (Tyson, 1995, p. 46)

Such a perspective clearly fits empowerment within the realms of the classical pragmatists' approach to management, and presumably empowerment as a tool could be abandoned with equanimity if it were not deemed to be in congruence with the prevailing economic situation. A determinist view indeed! Tyson's conclusions were based upon research carried out in 30 major UK enterprises. However, only the senior management and human resource professionals were interviewed. Additionally, the interview checklists stayed within a fixed paradigm of a given managerial philosophy. Despite reference to a societal and sentient level of interpretation of the survey findings, there is little evidence to suggest that the issues upon which Tyson based the above statement were researched in sufficient depth during this project to validate this initial assertion.

The case of *Rover* provides an interesting example of the scenario whereby empowerment is seen as the logical extension of organisational delayering. This delayering process and the subsequent extension of managerial spans of control led to a redefinition of the role of management and their relationship with the teams for which they were responsible. The logic of devolution of duties and responsibilities to the team by means of 'empowerment' strategies was pursued. This led to a redefinition of the roles of the human resource management function, line management, the team leaders and the teams themselves. Rover has supplemented these changes with a series of human resource and change implementation strategies. Whilst not without its problems in terms of resistance to change from some levels of management and the personnel function, Rover believe that the strategy is achieving a significant measure of success. In epistemological terms, Mike Arthur states that

> the move to teamworking has given Rover gains in terms of product quality and associate morale. We believe that empowered teams are not a fad that will disappear as quickly as other management theories. (Arthur, 1994, pp. 58–61)

There is no research information as to how the company has measured the direct relationship between empowered teams and product quality. Most research findings have been unable to establish such a causal relationship. It would also have been interesting to ascertain why they believe empowered teams to be fundamentally different from other management strategies. This is not discussed. It could be logically argued, however, that in the future (were the organisation to be dissatisfied with the strategy) there would be no apparent moral or ethical dilemma associated with abandoning it in favour of another approach to improving morale and quality within the organisation. There was no evidence of any social or ethical discourse on this issue.

EMPOWERMENT AND LABOUR PROCESS THEORY

To tackle the empowerment issue from this angle, we will use the research done under the heading of *Japanisation*, in relation here to the Nissan plant in the North-east. A wealth of literature has been produced on the success of Japanese enterprises which launched not only a whole new set of corporate strategies, but a whole new language of management rhetoric to accompany it. It seems at first sight that the more egalitarian Japanese approach might also be a more 'empowered' one. It is possible to argue however, that such supported enabling and strategies, *especially* those based on Japanese models, whilst espousing empowerment in reality promote more management control and a significant *reduction* in the degree of autonomy granted to workers. Thus it is possible to interpret the implementation of these Japanisation policies within the context of the second approach to empowerment (the critical theory of management) and so illustrate the seeming paradox outlined above.

In relation to this view Karen Legge cites the critical theorists' interpretation of the example of total quality management and just-in-time systems employed at the Nissan plant in Sunderland. In this context the critical theorists would argue that the flexibility, quality, teamwork and empowerment which are said to underpin its success are in fact based upon *compliance, surveillance* and *blame* (Legge, 1995, p. 232). They cite examples of autonomy in task re-design through quality circles as being implemented only at the discretion of management. Thus Garrahon and Stewart (1992) view the process as a game whereby employees learn to participate in the agreement of decisions which have already been made by management.[2]

Sewell and Wilkinson (1992) also stress the role of *technology* in the detection of errors which trace the fault back to those responsible. In this context employees receive red, yellow or green cards, which are clearly visible. Thus, they argue a '*blame culture*' can emerge, and management can use these signs to alter the flow of the line in keeping with the quality standards of the workers upon it. They conclude that 'the solitary confinement of Taylorism has been superseded by the tagging of the Information Panapticon' (Sewell and Wilkinson, 1992, p. 109). It is further argued that the role of the *customer* now represents a body which can legitimately reject what is not acceptable. Additionally, as arbiters of quality they function in a management role where the satisfaction of the customer is critical to the success of the enterprise, and so the control mechanism subtly changes. Thus, based on the work of DuGay and Salaman (1992), Legge notes:

> the increase of administrative controls from the centre can now be re-represented as management through customer responsiveness [and that] the image of empowerment may be used to mask an experience of reduced autonomy and labour intensification. (Legge, 1995, p. 244)

However, given the nature of the ideological basis of labour process theory which predicates the above empirical studies of empowerment and control, it is important to appreciate the limitations of this theoretical perspective within a wider context. Labour process theory is premised upon the class allocation of managers and employees into middle class and working class stratifications respectively, which is reflected in the nature of the employment relationship. However, Thompson and McHugh (1995) note the increasing complexity of organisation structures has cast managers in the contradictory functions of: 'agents of capital and salaried employees' (p. 115) who are possessed of 'operational' rather than 'allocative' control. Additionally, labour process theory can be criticised on the basis that it seeks to find a universal prescriptive rationale for behaviour within organisations in terms of control.

Thompson and McHugh also note that according to labour process theorists, 'Capital always seeks and finds definitive and comprehensive models of control as the solutions to its problems' (p. 117). The reality is that stakeholder influences, environmental issues and the nature of the employment relationship create a complex interactive model of behaviour, influence and power between groups within enterprises. To rationalise the dominance of capital within a complex environmental context in terms of variations on control strategies alone, is a much oversimplified interpretation of the nature of employment relations within organisations.

Nevertheless, it is true that the balance of power and the discretion to exercise control as outlined in the cases above clearly exists within companies. It is important to appreciate however, that the ability of managers to exercise this control varies within different organisational and cultural contexts.

Summary of the above sections

With both the *pragmatic* and *labour process theory* approaches to empowerment there is ultimately no real shift in the locus of power and control, hence our label of *pseudo-empowerment*. A rough parallel can be drawn with democracy in the UK. Having no Bill of Rights or Freedom of Information Act enshrined in the Law, the British Public have as much democracy as those in power deem expedient for the masses to have, commensurate with the power-holders remaining in power. Power can always be centralised again (and like empowerment in organisations this often happens whilst the rhetoric sells the opposite, *more parental choice, citizens' charter, and so on*), as we have witnessed in the UK in the 1980s and 1990s. It would seem then that anything that falls short of a *legally embedded* change in the locus of power and control can only ultimately be merely pseudo-empowerment.

OWNERSHIP: THE KEY TO GENUINE EMPOWERMENT

Revisiting stakeholder theory

The underlying criticism of the notion of empowerment in the above sections is that these approaches treat people essentially *as means to ends* (overemphasising ethics in consequentialist terms), rather than as *ends in themselves* (more emphasis on *non*-consequentialist ethics); as such the former is more likely to result in pseudo-empowerment. Here, empowerment is seen as a management tool, a form of motivation, to achieve the essentially unchanged organisational objectives – (profit, market share, ROCE, and so on) – albeit in the name of 'excellence', or whatever – and without any change in power-relations (and hence no real change in the spread of control). Using words like 'organisational objectives', 'power-relations' and so on immediately brings to mind stakeholder theory, and agency theory (the separation of management from ownership).

At heart here is essentially an ideological battle in which the current (and long-standing winner) is the Friedmanite view of business – the business of business is business (Friedman, 1970). Here, business should stick to a narrow brief of doing what it does best (efficiently producing goods and services in a competitive environment), and it should leave issues of distributive justice to the government. Business is happy to operate within the law, and, should people not like what business gets up to then they can get the law changed, and business will happily respond. Naturally Friedman's model fits well also with a very narrow view of who are the important stakeholders (essentially (and legally) just the shareholders, creditors and directors) and hence management should always serve primarily the interests of these groups. It is of course a very appealing view of what business should be about, and it owes its appeal to its ideological content.

In general, ideologies which are most enduring are those which (i) have a nice simple 'ring' to them appearing to be 'obvious', (ii) confuse the general with the specific, (iii) contain an element of truth, and (iv) are also quite vague (sometimes deliberately so making them difficult to pin down). Friedman's notion of 'our goal is profit' falls supremely well into this category. Many of the critiques of Friedman tend to appeal to stakeholder theory, arguing that business should take into account a broader range of stakeholders (for example see Grant, 1991). They say that Friedman's treatment of business as a separate 'game' with its own set of rules etc, does not allow for the fact that the activities of business (especially in the modern industrial world) *do* impact on a *wide* variety of stakeholders whether business likes it or not; it does not, and never can, act in isolation from a wide range of stakeholders. Such and other angles of critique of Friedman may however persuade managers *why* they should take into account a wider range of stakeholders, but it does not help them *how* to do it. This is of course one of the main criticisms of stakeholder theory; it is a great idea, but *how* does a manager weigh up the value of the relative 'stakes' of the local community, employees' livelihoods, and the environment as well as City opinion and shareholders who desire maximised dividends? The answer to this question is that it *cannot be answered within traditional forms of business ownership*; and to question these traditional forms of ownership requires us to re-examine our assumptions about the *nature, meaning and purpose of business activity*.

Stakeholder theory and five perspectives on business activity

If you believe the purpose of business is to 'maximise profit' then you will deal with stakeholder issues in a very different way than if you believe the purpose of business is, for example, to 'provide meaningful employment'. Davies (1997b) has identified five perspectives on business in the business ethics literature. Very briefly these are summarised as follows:

1. *Western Christian Theological Perspectives*: three important aspects are generally highlighted. First, is that as humans are made in the image of God, then they have inherent dignity which must be respected; this of course ties in with Kantian ethics as well as being reflected in the Universal Declaration of Human Rights. Second concerns the implications of the Fall. The ground was cursed (Genesis 3: 7–19) and from that point on economic activity (mainly agriculture) was to be come a never-ending harsh grind instead of a joyous creative activity. The point here is that economy is fundamentally about WORK, not money. This suggests that business should be ethically evaluated in terms of (quality of) work provided and not by some abstract financial measure. Third, a major theme of Christian theology is reconciliation, which points towards the importance of justice for all stakeholders.
2. *Industrial Democracy Perspective*: since the collapse of communism it seems to be generally agreed that democracy is a 'good thing', and hence by implication, also Capitalism. But attention has now turned to critiques of Capitalism, which varies considerably between such countries as Sweden, Germany, Japan and the UK (Trompenaars and Hampden-Turner, 1993). Such critiques also point to the variation of democracy *in industry* as well as in politics generally. This raises the issue of *ownership*, a much neglected area in business ethics literature. In the UK those who work in a company generally have no ownership of it, and those who (legally) own it generally do not work in it. The result of this tends to be short-termism, alienated and demotivated employees who have no reason to be loyal to the

company, and a managerial elite who act as if they own the company. Lack of industrial democracy means that there is no commonality of purpose for those involved in the enterprise, which at the very least must be inefficient (as well as unjust).

3. *Eco-Systems Perspective*: here it is claimed that the industrial system (in its present form) has come up hard against the ecological system and both cannot win. Industry is slowly but surely destroying the planet on which we all depend, and given that it is generally accepted that there is an ethical imperative for the human race not to destroy itself, then remedial action is likewise ethically obligatory. Although business has fought tooth and nail virtually every piece of environmental legislation over the last 30 years, there *can* be a win–win situation if the world is viewed by business through a different paradigm (Hawken, 1993). Organisational biodiversity (smaller, flexible and more varying organisational units) are also called for by writers on strategic management (see for example Stacey, 1996). There appears then to be a Natural Law for the survival of both businesses and the planet, and they are complementary. This means that business should raise the profile of the ecology in the stakeholder equation, and be more prepared to experiment with alternative forms of organisation.

4. *Friedmanite Perspective*: this has already been discussed and its dependence on a very tight definition of what is the legitimate territory of business has several weaknesses, not least whether you accept the tight definition in the first place. Additionally, the weakness of assuming that business is a separate 'game' has also been pointed out. Another weakness is that corrective action which depends on pressure groups getting the law changed does not take into account either the asymmetrical power between big business and smaller groups (the former have very powerful lobbying resources), nor does it adequately address the long time-lag to achieve changes in the law. Moreover such an approach does not have a very good track record so far.[3] The value of the Friedmanite perspective of course is that it keeps its critics on their toes; one continually has to ask: *why not?* and answer the challenge: *prove there's a better alternative!*

5. *Virtue Perspective*: this approach sees the flaw in all other approaches as being that you can go no further than merely expose centuries old debates between differing philosophical schools (if you are a Kantian do this, if you are an Act Utilitarian do that). Virtue ethics would state that 'being' is as important as 'doing'. It considers not so

much what is the ethical thing to *do*, but on what it means to *be* an ethical sort of person. It draws on the Aristotelian notion of 'virtue' and hence focuses on the *character* of people in business organisations. People of good character will inevitably make good decisions. So money spent on being a caring organisation is not (as Friedman might argue) theft from the shareholders, but 'the ultimate aim of the Aristotelian approach to business is to cultivate whole human beings, not junglefighters, efficiency automatons, or "good soldiers"' (Solomon, 1993, p. 180).

Underlying stakeholder theory is a vital question relating to empowerment, namely: *to what extent (and how) should others (particularly employees) take part in the general control of the firm?* (Van Gerwen, 1994, p. 74). This question will be answered differently depending on which of the above five perspectives you hold, but what the four non-Friedman ones have *in common* is that they all agree on the ethical imperative to broaden out the stakeholder base which should be the legitimate concerns of any business organisation. But doing this immediately challenges some much cherished assumptions, for example that 'organisations' as separate entities have a 'right' to survive in perpetuity at the expense of people, that financial criteria alone are the ethically legitimate measures of 'success' for business organisations, and that the current legal structure of companies is in line with basic social justice. Questioning such assumptions again points towards the neglected issue of *ownership*, but we need to justify this argument more fully.

Ownership: why is it key in the ethics and empowerment debate?

To answer this question some working definitions and preliminary points are needed first. We implied in the introduction that *genuine* empowerment requires a certain minimal *degree of control* over one's activities in the workplace. The term *'ownership'* relates to this both in terms of daily *process* (having a meaningful say in the decision-making processes), and *status* (probably by having some sort of financial stake in the company). Our definition of ownership therefore goes beyond ownership merely in terms of a mission statement to believe in – important as that may be. Furthermore, we live in a society where few people appear to question the whole structure of company ownership as simply, in ethical *non*-consequentialist terminology, *unjust*.[4] Even within the business ethics literature, it seems to strike few UK writers that it is unjust (or even just plain odd) that, as already noted, the majority of people who work in an organisation (their livelihoods depending on it) have no ownership of it, and that those who (legally) own it rarely work in it. Whenever though the ownership question is tackled in *con*sequentialist terms, it is usually in the language of motivation (means to ends again); after all, which sane person is going to leap out of bed each day full of enthusiasm to go to work to increase the dividend share of some anonymous shareholders? Moreover, if share options are seen as motivators and rewards for senior management, why not everybody else? For us then, there is little need to justify in *con*sequentialist terms the argument in favour of some form of wider ownership, so we will concentrate on the *non*-consequentialist reasons, from the angle of *justice*.

We suggest that the term *'empowerment'* should also be considered in terms of *justice* (as well as control), particularly from the point of view of a human being's inalienable right to be treated with dignity, as well as the individual's perception of justice arising out of their experience of the organisation. Both *non*-and *con*sequentialist arguments in relation to empowerment point towards the need for an acceptable degree of control over one's immediate circumstances in the organisation, which in turn depends on issues such as autonomy, being trusted, input to decisions that affect one, and so on. But it is precisely *ownership* that gives credence (both symbolic and real) to these very precious commodities of autonomy, trust, 'voice' in decision-making, task significance, and so on.

So it seems to us that ownership and empowerment are inextricably bound together via their connection with the notion of justice; in a just organisation empowerment implies ownership, and vice-versa. Empowerment is therefore only genuine when argued convincingly from a *non*-consequentialist viewpoint because otherwise it can ultimately always be disposed of via some pragmatic consequentialist calculation; empowerment here is merely at the mercy of organisational politics, management fads, and 'City' ratings. Perhaps we can contrast *pseudo-* and *genuine* empowerment as in Figures 6.1 and 6.2 respectively.

It seems strange that so much of the (UK) business ethics literature gives so little weight to the ownership issue in terms of it being a moral imperative in *non*-consequentialist language.[5] When discussed it is often only obliquely so, and in the corporate governance debates. European writers on business ethics (as for example in Harvey, 1994) do of course give a different slant on the issue of ownership because they are writing from within the context of other capitalist frameworks (for example, Rhenish), and these will be looked at later on in the chapter, drawing on the work of Trompenaars and Hampden-Turner (1993).

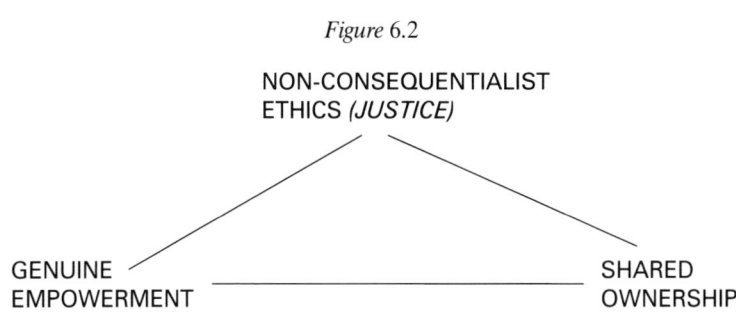

Figure 6.1

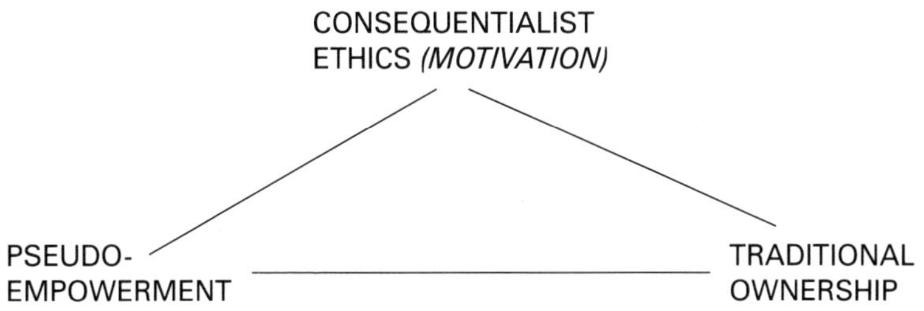

Figure 6.2

Six non-consequentialist arguments

Meanwhile, how can we support the associations and arguments as summarised in Figure 6.2? *What are the non-consequentialist arguments in favour of asserting that ownership (financial and process) are fundamental to genuine empowerment?* We suggest six points should be considered:

1. *The status and purpose of business organisations*: the traditional professions have an advantage over business here in that they have some fundamental ethical principle that underlies their reason-for-being. For example, for the law, it is justice; for medicine, it is the Hippocratic oath; for the church, it is spiritual well-being. But what basic ethical notion underpins business activity? The historian R.H Tawney also noted this need:

   > The problem is to find some principle of justice upon which human association for the production of wealth can be found. (As quoted in Goyder, 1993, p. vi)

Perhaps we can agree for a start that firms exist to produce goods and services for society at large. Although they may achieve this purpose by being allowed (by society) to be privately owned in a competitive setting, this is not the whole story. Albeit maybe *originally* established by the risked capital of some individual(s), companies soon become institutionalised requiring the cooperation of a variety of people, each with their own interests. Hence they develop a *social* character which implies that control and ownership by any *one* party is *no longer legitimate*; *all* parties have a right to participate because they contribute to the firm's continuance. *Firms are therefore social goods, not merely private commodities* (Van Gerwen, 1994, p. 75). Of course there are those who would argue the opposite, and for over 100 years their viewpoint has prevailed, and is enshrined in the law. They *do* see the company as a commodity, the implication being that employees can only then ever be seen as 'hired labour' (means to ends, no real empowerment) with no rights to ownership in the decision-making processes, or to be seen as co-equal with capital providers. However, though this may be the prevailing view, we suggest that it is unjust.

This means that Tawney has asked the right question, but we are still looking for an answer. The 1990s interest in business ethics from both the business world and academia – as well as a weekly diet of sensationalist cases in the media – seems to suggest that such interest stems from more than just a short-term knee-jerk reaction to the grab-it-all 1980s, but constitutes a more fundamental and long-term questioning of the role and purpose of business in contemporary society (Davies, 1993). There is a feeling in the wider public that business organisations with their immense power and impact on people's lives should be 'accountable', but we are struggling to decide: *accountable to whom, and by what criteria?* Such a public debate may eventually coalesce into a more tightly agreed answer, which will simultaneously depend on answering Tawney's question. Nevertherless, this does not detract from the main point that if business are 'social goods' rather than 'private commodities', then the status and purpose of business organisations requires a new (and widely accepted) ethical underpinning supported from some principle of justice.

2. *Kantian dignity and respect for persons*: people have inalienable rights and dignity, but this does not leave them just because they spend part of their lives as an 'employee'. It seems though that once we walk through that factory gate or office door, we feel

obliged to say goodbye for the day to our normal rights which we have in civilian life; the right to be consulted about decisions which greatly affect our lives, for example. Such a view certainly suggests that it is not only unjust to treat people as commodities, to be hired and fired at will, but also unjust that they should have so little say in the decisions that greatly affect their lives. *Some* form of ownership, particularly via structurally embedded participation, is *more* likely to mean that people's inherent rights and dignity will be respected because they will have a genuine say in what is going on, and be in a positive position to challenge managerial tunnel vision.

3. *Natural law*: natural law (which is above human law) also gives a basis for employee ownership. The moral philosopher John Locke wrote:

> Each individual is the owner of his own person, over which no-one else has rights. Work done with his own body and hands is his alone. Whatever man takes from the state in which nature created it, he incorporates his own work and adds to it something that belongs to him, and so takes possession of it. By removing that object from the common condition to which nature allocated it, he has – with his work – added something that rules out the common right of ownership of other men. (As quoted by Corbetta, 1994, p. 97)

There is an important distinction to note here between *natural* rights and *conventional* rights of ownership. The former are as per Locke's quote above and give rights of ownership in a situation which requires *no* social co-operation; the latter implies social interaction *is* required in order to enjoy the benefits from the assets and resources. From this viewpoint, owners (as distant shareholders) have only 'conventional' rights to ownership and therefore should consider the claims of those who have 'natural' rights in that same firm (Corbetta, 1994). This also implies that 'conventional' owners have no moral right to dispose of a firm, and also have a moral duty to share the benefits produced with those who have 'natural' rights to the firm's produce – another argument in favour of some form of employee ownership.

4. *Current company law is unjust*: the historical development of company law in the UK has established a situation (despite the Companies Act of 1980 and Consolidating Act of 1985) whereby (due to the divorce of ownership from responsibility) the requirements of justice and participation in industry are seriously lacking. Goyder states:

It is absurd that a law designed for family business a century ago should continue to apply, without substantial change, to the whole of industry today regardless of the size and purpose of the company. *This represents an abdication of the state from its responsibility to create responsible institutions.* (Goyder, 1993, p. 20, emphasis added)

In 1862, when incorporation as a company with limited liability and perpetual succession was first made legally possible, the essence of a company's existence was that *it should be for public benefit, not for private gain.* Company law lays obligations on directors principally to look after shareholder's interest; it does not *require* them to look after the interests of customers, employees, the community or require them to behave in a generally socially responsible manner.[6] The passage of time, and the phenomenal growth in the power of the money markets has drowned out the original 'public benefit' ethos as well as reducing companies to tradeable commodities (see item 1 above). As long as the law effectively sanctions the huge gap in reward and decision-making power between those who contribute their capital, and those who contribute their work, then empowerment can only remain denuded of any real meaning. Some form of wider ownership (supported by the law) can again help redress this injustice.

5. *Distributive justice*: rival theories of justice make their appeal to a number of principles for distributing wealth, such as equality, need, effort, contribution and merit. Several of these principles would support a minimum wage (a legal reality in most European countries apart from the UK – at the time of writing) as an *ethical* requirement because it enables people to live with minimal dignity, *and it therefore rightly sets an ethical baseline below which market forces should not be allowed to force wages.* That said, there is no excuse for then not ensuring a significant proportion of an employees' wages are proportional to the company profits to which they have contributed. Employee ownership in financial terms is a better guarantee of justice here than a paternalistic approach of handouts at the whim of senior managers. It is also often assumed that managers are the only ones with legitimate (derived/role) authority within an organisation, but there is also a shopfloor authority – an accumulated wisdom about how things are best done, (which some of the Japanese management ideas tap into). Distributive justice therefore also requires a just distribution of decision-making, since managerial authority depends on the willingness '...of individuals to submit to the necessities of co-operative systems' (Goyder, 1993, pp. 30–1).

At the very least then, not to include shopfloor wisdom in decision-making processes could be seen as detracting from overall performance (and hence shareholders' interests also) – as well as being unjust.

6. *Asymmetrical rights and duties*: for every employee/er right, there is a corresponding duty, and Table 6.1 below[7] summarises some of these main rights and duties. However, not all rights on one side are matched proportionately by the corresponding duty being fulfilled by the other, thus producing an asymmetry. Partly this is because our understanding and acceptance of rights is continuously evolving making full agreement difficult (witness Britain's lengthy refusal to sign the EU Social Charter). Any 'right' will essentially remain meaningless until the corresponding duty is carried out, something that usually requires legislation before it becomes an accepted and established cultural norm. The value of ownership in all this is that it promotes, and is a catalyst for, a better symmetry between rights and duties, which in turn imputes greater genuine meaning into that word 'empowerment'.

Table 6.1 Employee/employer rights and duties

Employees' rights and duties	Employers' rights and duties
• Right to work	• Duty not to discriminate in hiring
• Right to just compensation	• Duty to fair compensation
• Right to free association	• Duty to respect union presence
• Right to participation	• Duty to consult workers
• Right to job satisfaction	• Duty to improve quality of work
• Duty to be loyal	• Right to loyal co-operation
• Duty to respect legal and moral norms	• Right to correct behaviour at work
• Duty to comply with labour contract	• Right to minimal productivity

In summary, we have briefly sketched six *non*-consequentialist (deontological) reasons as to why ownership is not only an ethical imperative, but also essential to genuine empowerment. These have appealed to arguments about the purpose of business, to Kant, to Natural Law, to the injustice of current company law, to distributive justice, and to a greater symmetry between rights and duties. *But how can such ethical imperatives be translated into the practical production of goods and services?*

This question is answered in two parts. First we note that the Anglo-American version of capitalism by its very nature makes genuine empowerment virtually impossible and we suggest that other European models of capitalism are possibly more empowerment friendly. Second, we refer to Scott Bader, a 'common ownership' company, as one example which we believe provides a good example of genuine empowerment at work, albeit done more in the name of 'industrial democracy'.

LESSONS FROM EUROPEAN VERSIONS OF CAPITALISM

One of the recurrent themes in the business ethics literature (and criticisms of business ethics in general) is that in the end it all boils down to a critique of capitalism; Lippke's *Radical Business Ethics* is an example of this genre (Lippke, 1995). Whereas critiques of capitalism as a whole have some value, perhaps of more current interest is to critically examine the *varieties* of capitalism that currently exist. Trompenaars and Hampden-Turner (1993) have done just this and they identify seven fundamental valuing processes by which cultural values influence economic choices, and this has implications for empowerment (as well as business ethics issues more widely). It seems that Britain's particular historical and political uniqueness has not served it well industrially, either economically, or in terms of industrial relations – the two of course are not unconnected. In economic terms the UK is low down on several indicators compared with its European neighbours; in industrial relations terms the UK seems to be the principal protagonist against the Social Charter. All this is tied in with structural handicaps such as the power of City institutions and capital providers, as well as more 'cultural' handicaps such as short-termism and excessive individualism. The *adversarial* nature of UK (and American) culture (which is also deemed as the best way to solve problems in the judicial and political spheres as well) continues to pervade industrial relations and the structure of business in a way that makes genuine empowerment very difficult. An important point here is that if culture to a large extent drives economic choices and thereby industrial and organisational structures, then trying to emulate the more successful countries may not work because of the difficulty in trying to make another country's culture more part of one's own.

Despite this, other countries such as Germany are often analysed by those looking for clues to economic success, and concerning the theme of empowerment it is sometimes believed that such Rhenish models of Capitalism are more empowerment friendly. Trompenaars and Hampden-Turner (1993) identify cooperation at the meso-economic level (between labour, financial and industrial groups, and government) as providing a clear competitive advantage for Germany. This level of interaction hardly exists in the UK, and translates directly into a lack of genuine commonly understood purpose at the organisational level, making empowerment particularly difficult; low levels of trust, intensified by an individualist (as opposed to a Germanic 'communitarian') culture, do not encourage the 'letting go' of power.

But it seems that individualism alone is not the enemy of empowerment. Holland is a country that also scores high on individualism, and indeed only differs from the UK on one of the seven dimensions. However, for the Dutch individualism exists within the context of a more general culture of equality, and hence individualism is really only endorsed with a view *to contribution to the whole*, rather than for displays of individual power. They also share with Germany, Japan and France a more consensual (rather than adversarial) attitude towards the democratic process. Although at first sight this appears more to do with politics, it has an important lesson for industrial relations. The Dutch are aware that 'You do not make high quality products with sizeable pockets of malcontents in an organization... the costs of working with an alienated workforce are known to be high' (Trompenaars and Hampden-Turner, 1993, pp. 284–5). Voting out minority opinions in the UK with its first-past-the-post mentality may speed up the decision-making process, but instead of this process gaining the true commitment of all, it may only result in what is currently known as 'resigned behavioural compliance' (Ogbonna and Wilkinson, 1990). At the very least, then, this emphasises the importance of achieving genuine empowerment, as well as the difficulties of achieving it in an Anglo-Saxon culture. This comes over quite strongly in and Trompenaars Hampden-Turner's research, as well as the importance of the complex interaction between the many structurally embedded dimensions of culture.

In order to achieve genuine empowerment within the UK (as a culturally handicapped nation in this respect), activity is needed on two fronts. One is the longer-term task of promoting cultural and legal change at the macro- and meso-levels; for example to encourage less adversarial ways of problem-solving, and arguing for the legitimacy of a wider range of stakeholders to be involved in business decision-making. Second is to create island-examples of empowerment with and within specific organisations in the wider culture; a culture which is unfortunately not particularly conducive to it. (Indeed, Scott-Bader, focused on below, could not come into being in its present form until the law was changed in 1976 in order to enable common-ownership organisations to come into existence). Despite its criticisms, the success of 'Japanised' organisations in the UK *does* present a challenge to hierarchical and adversarial ways of organising business, and challenges the cultural mentality of 'a manager's right to manage' where such phraseology usually means hierarchical control. The more examples of successful businesses that do things in a different way, the better. Scott-Bader is another example of a business whose continued successful existence (over 40 profitable years of 'common ownership') presents a real challenge to those who say: 'there is no alternative'.

EMPOWERMENT AT SCOTT BADER[8]

Ernst Bader was a Swiss emigre who set up Scott Bader in 1920 with the sole agency for Swiss celluloid in the UK. The company now has a turnover of £100m world-wide (£60m at its original Wollaston factory in Northamptonshire), and makes polyester resin type products for use in the paints, automotive and marine industries. The way it is run provides an interesting example of genuine empowerment along the lines we are advocating. Having built up his business as an owner-manager, Ernst Bader formed the Scott Bader Commonwealth Ltd (which has no share capital) in 1951 and gave 90 per cent of the company shares to it, effectively giving his company away to his employees. The remaining 10 per cent of shares (which initially had the greater voting power – just in case this experiment in industrial democracy went wrong!) – were transferred to the Commonwealth 12 years later in 1963. Since the company shares are held in trust by the employees via the Commonwealth, they exercise ultimate control. In 1976 parliament passed the *Common Ownership Act* and Scott Bader was awarded the first certificate the following year.

Ernst Bader strongly believed that labour should employ capital, not vice-versa, and also that all are equal as human beings, thereby having the right of human dignity. His beliefs and values have become enshrined in the company's Constitution, the key principles of which include:

- Human dignity and spiritual awareness
- Opportunities for, and commitment to, personal development
- Sharing of jobs, wealth and with the wider community
- Democratic involvement and accountability in the workplace

- Management by consent, not coercion
- Responsible management of the earth's resources

The values are also enshrined in a slowly evolving *Code of Practice* which include such statements as the remit of the manager being '... to act as "catalysts for common effort" and not as authoritarian "bosses"',[9] and, 'We are conscious of a common responsibility to share our work among ourselves in such a way that it becomes a meaningful and creative part of our lives rather than merely as a means to an end'.[10] The structure of the company is shown in Figure 6.3.

Figure 6.3 The structure of Scott-Bader

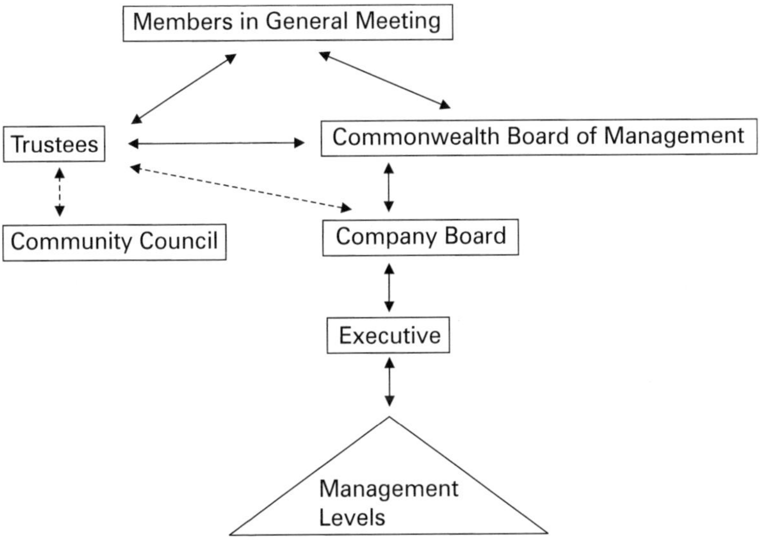

```
              ┌─────────────────────────────┐
              │ Members in General Meeting  │
              └─────────────────────────────┘
                   ↙              ↘
    ┌──────────┐        ┌──────────────────────────────────┐
    │ Trustees │ ←────→ │ Commonwealth Board of Management │
    └──────────┘        └──────────────────────────────────┘
         ↕                         ↕
    ┌───────────────────┐   ┌───────────────┐
    │ Community Council │   │ Company Board │
    └───────────────────┘   └───────────────┘
                                   ↕
                            ┌────────────┐
                            │ Executive  │
                            └────────────┘
                                   ↕
                            ╱──────────────╲
                           ╱  Management    ╲
                          ╱     Levels       ╲
                         ╱_____╲
```

The *company board*'s remit is to run the company (within constitutional requirements) and there are four elected directors from the workforce, with external directors being subject to approval by the *community council*. This second body has a monitoring role to ensure that the board run the company within the letter and spirit of the constitution and founder's values. They can discuss any issue they choose, and two members are on the company board; on matters of discipline their decision is binding. The *trustees*' remit is to safeguard the constitution, to be arbiters in the event of any serious dispute between the other bodies, and to step in if the company starts to run at a loss. However, their role to date has not been a particularly active one. The *commonwealth board of management* holds the shares of the operating company and is made up of employees. They are responsible for membership,[11] administering a charitable fund, and for 'philosophical development' – ensuring that the company is run within the parameters of the constitution.

An example of the workings of Scott-Bader can be seen in how the company handled a 'redundancy' situation in 1978–80. The *Code of Practice* states: 'We are agreed that in the event of a downturn in trade we will share all remaining work rather than expect any of our fellow members to be deprived of employment, even if this requires a reduction in earnings by all'.[12] However, the required reduction in earnings at the time to keep about 100 'surplus' people in employment proved untenable (the reduction in earnings would have meant that many employees simply would not have been able to up keep their mortgage payments). In the event, a consensus was reached for voluntary redundancies, with generous retraining packages. The number of redundancies, though, were quite substantial. In 1978 employees numbered 438; on 31 January 1979, 98 people left the company with the first voluntary redundancy package. On 31 December 1980 a further 70 people similarly left, leaving 270 out of the original 438, a 38 per cent reduction (Bader, 1981). However, the constitution was not undermined because the requirement to share 'downturns' was in the *Code* and as such is a *guideline* and not an article of the constitution. This *Code* is also under continuous development to remain relevant and appropriate in an ever-changing business environment.

In the last few years there has been a gradual watering down of some of the Scott-Bader ideals. For example, the ratio of the highest to lowest paid person within the company used to be stated clearly (it has ranged from 4:1 to 7:1) and this ratio had to be voted upon by members in a general meeting. Recently the actual ratio has been removed and been replaced by a statement that pay differentials should not be 'excessive', but it is no longer clear who defines what 'excessive' means; it seems to belong to the remit of the CEO. The voluntary element of being involved in the local community (taking food parcels to the elderly, and so on) seems also to have dwindled. Such a 'watering-down' though does not necessarily point to the inadequacy of the structural checks and balances. Ernst Bader was keen that all members should also be *accountable*, and take on responsibilities for the running of the company. It seems that many do not want this and are happy to give the CEO and senior management more power in return for secure jobs, and for not having to spend too much time and energy being involved in the various decision-making bodies.

In theory, what we have at Scott Bader is a company structure where no *one* group has overall authority so ultimately they have to move together in consensus. The idea is that, freed from the fear of take-over, and with substantial emotional security (relative to industry norms), people can spend their energy on developing the company, and themselves as individuals. As a self-governing democratic structure with all members having one vote within the *Commonwealth*, they share equally in the obligations of trusteeship regardless of their (formal) role or position within the firm. However, constant re-enforcement and encouragement is needed if, indeed, the majority of Scott-Bader employees are actually going to do the necessary work and fulfil their obligations – which are theirs for the taking due to the existing Constitution and structure.

For us, Scott Bader is a good example of 'genuine' empowerment because it is rooted in the notion of justice which is then also translated into a concrete form of common ownership. The words 'trusteeship' and 'stewardship' are often heard at Scott-Bader and these add a useful dimension to our use of the word *ownership*. They are a reminder that our emphasis on ownership does *not* imply the right to own assets *per se*, but does imply the right to use assets in terms of fulfilling the duty to be a good steward or trustee of those assets which come under one's care for a certain length of time.

There are of course other attempts at introducing 'ownership' into business organisations. Co-operatives have a long history but tend not to grow to more than about 20 people in size if they always insist on decision-making involving having consensus from everyone. Share-ownership is another attempt but involves no real shift in decision-making power or control for the individual over their workplace. Partnerships such as John Lewis, and other forms of employee participation are also attempts to give some form of wider ownership and whilst there are some benefits, they do not seem to go far enough in terms of ownership to enable genuine empowerment by our definition. All this highlights the point that ownership may be a necessary (but possibly not a sufficient) condition for genuine empowerment – and the same could be said of the Scott-Bader example. The culture of a company needs to be right and the commitment of the people needs also to be there to actively get involved in the running of the company – providing the right structure is not merely by itself sufficient. That said, whilst not perfect, Scott-Bader does at least provide a viable alternative that has stood the test of time –

and it constitutes an ever-present challenge to the prevailing Friedmanite paradigm.

CONCLUSIONS

In this chapter we have tried to make a distinction between *pseudo-empowerment* (the 'pragmatic' and 'labour process theory' approaches) and *genuine* empowerment (which requires concrete forms of ownership in terms of capital and process). As long as the underlying assumption in companies is that *'people are our greatest asset'* (seen on many a company report), then ultimately people will always be the means to ends of the owners (or more accurately in our terminology – pseudo-owners). A fundamental paradigmic shift in thinking is required to change the aforementioned trite adage to something more like: *'people ARE the company'*. This in turn will shift thinking away from merely expedient questions such as: *will it work?* to a more ethical question, *is it right?* and in particular, *is it right in relation to justice?* It is from this angle of reasoning that genuine empowerment is more likely to materialise.

Notes

1. As quoted in Reed, 1989, p. 47.
2. As referred to by Legge (1995).
3. For example the Public Interest Disclosure Bill, designed to give more protection to whistleblowers, had all-party support but it was 'talked out' in 1996 by a minority who opposed it. It *might* now become law under the New Labour government.
4. An exception to this is Goyder (1993).
5. There is a growing (non-UK) literature under the banner of 'Organisational Justice'; for example see: Singer, M. (1997) *Ethics and Justice in Organizations* (Aldershot, Hampshire: Ashgate/Averbury Press).
6. The 1980 Companies Act does however require directors to have regard to 'the interests of the employees in general' (clause 46) with a footnote to this clause stating that directors 'will need to balance the interests of various classes of members'. Such requirements though are still rather vague.
7. This table is adapted from Table 3.1 on p. 57 in Van Gerwen (1994).
8. Information on Scott-Bader is taken from the company's own publicly available information, including the 1993 company report, a copy of the Constitution, and a reprint of a 1991 paper by the Commonwealth Secretary, Mick Jones. Additional information on Scott-Bader was obtained from a half-hour telephone interview with Godric Bader (the founder's son) on Thursday 30 January 1997.
9. *Code of Practice for Scott-Bader Commonwealth Members*, part D.

10. *Code of Practice for Scott-Bader Commonwealth Members*, part C.
11. Not every employee is automatically a member of the Commonwealth; they have to have worked for Scott-Bader for at least 18 months (six months for company approval, and a further 12 months for approval by their work group and the Commonwealth Board of Management), providing satisfactory evidence that they have the commitment to participate fully in the various decision-making processes.
12. *Code of Practice for Scott-Bader Commonwealth Members*, part G.

References

Arthur, M. (1994) 'Rover Managers Learn to Take a Back Seat', *Personnel Management*, vol. 26(10), pp. 58–61.
Bader, G. (1981) 'Everyone Understands When the Crunch Comes', *Financial Times*, Wednesday 21 October.
Blyton, P. and Turnbull, P. (eds) (1992) *Reassessing Human Resource Management* (London: Sage).
Burawoy, M. (1985) *The Politics of Production* (London: Verso).
Corbetta, G. (1994) 'Shareholders', chapter 4 in B. Harvey (ed.), *op. cit.*, pp. 88–102.
Davies, P.W.F. (1993) 'Business Ethics Education: Fad or Fusion?' *Journal of European Business Education*, vol. 4(3), pp. 1–20.
Davies, P.W.F (ed.) (1997a) *Current Issues in Business Ethics* (London: Routledge).
Davies, P.W.F. (1997b) 'Business Philosophy: Searching for an Authentic Role', chapter 1 in P. Davies (ed.), *op. cit.*, pp. 15–26.
Dugay, P. and Salaman G. (1992) 'The Culture of the Customer', *Journal of Management Studies*, vol. 29(5), pp. 615–33.
Friedman, M. (1970) 'The Social Responsibility of Business is to Increase its Profits', *The New York Sunday Times Magazine*, 13 September, pp. 32 et seq; (and widely reprinted since).
Garrahon, P. and Stewart, P. (1992) *The Nissan Enigma: Flexibility at Work in a Local Economy* (London: Mansell).
Grant, C. (1991) 'Friedman Fallacies', *Journal of Business Ethics*, vol. 10, pp. 907–14.
Goyder, G. (1993) *The Just Enterprise: A Blueprint for the Responsible Company* (London: Adamantine Press).
Harvey, B. (ed.) (1994) *Business Ethics: A European Approach* (Hemel Hempstead, Herts: Prentice-Hall).
Hawken, P. (1993) *The Ecology of Commerce: How Business Can Save the Planet* (London: Weidenfeld & Nicolson).
Jones, M. (1991) *The History and Philosophy of the Scott Bader Commonwealth*, internal document, 10 pages.
Legge, K. (1995) *Human Resource Management: Rhetorics and Realities* (London: Macmillan).
Lippke, R.L. (1995) *Radical Business Ethics* (Lanham, Maryland: Rowman & Littlefield).

Ogbonna, E. and Wilkinson, B. (1990) 'Corporate Strategy and Corporate Culture: The View from the Checkout', *Personnel Review*, vol. 39(4), pp. 9–15.
Peters, T.J. (1987) *Thriving on Chaos: Handbook for a Management Revolution* (New York: Alfred A. Knopf).
Peters, T.J. and Waterman R.H. Jr. (1982) *In Search Of Excellence: Lessons from America's Best-run Companies* (New York: Harper & Row).
Reed, M. (1989) *The Sociology of Management* (London: Harvester Wheatsheaf).
Sewell, G. and Wilkinson, B. (1992) 'Empowerment or Emasculation? Shop Floor Surveillance in a Total Quality Organisation', in P. Blyton and P. Turnbull, *op. cit.*, pp. 97–115.
Solomon, R.C. (1993) *Ethics and Excellence: Co-operation and Integrity in Business*. The Ruffin Series in Business Ethics (New York: Oxford University Press).
Stacey, R.D. (1996) *Strategic Management and Organisational Dynamics*, 2nd edn (London: Pitman).
Thompson, P. and McHugh, D. (1995) *Work Organisations: A Critical Introduction* (London: Macmillan).
Trompenaars, F. and Hampden-Turner, C. (1994) *The Seven Cultures of Capitalism: Value-systems for Creating Wealth in the United States, Britain, Japan, Germany, France, Sweden, and the Netherlands* (London: Piatkus).
Tyson, S. (1995) *Human Resource Strategy* (London: Pitman).
Van Gerwen, J. (1994) 'Employers' and Employees' Rights and Duties', chapter 3 in B. Harvey (ed.), *op. cit.*, pp. 56–87.

Part II
Theory, and the Experience of Empowerment Strategies

7 Beyond Rhetoric: A Typology of Empowerment Strategies Found Within One Organisation

Julia M. Christensen Hughes

INTRODUCTION

Within the North American business community, the word *empowerment* can be found in corporate vision and value statements, product advertisements and management text books. For example, Digital Equipment's product NAS (Network Application Support) promises to 'empower your people to work together more effectively' (advertisement, *Business Week*, 20 April 1992). In *Organizational Behaviour*, Hellriegel, Slocum and Woodman (1992) assert that empowerment is an important characteristic of 'a high performance-high commitment work culture' (p. 516). Empowerment has also become one of the most popular topics for management best-sellers, conferences and seminars, management consulting services and organisational success stories. For example, the Institute for International Research (IIR) advertised a two-day seminar with the promise: 'achieve full productivity and world class total quality improvement through employee empowerment' (IIR advertisement, 1992). The National Businesswomen's Leadership Association referred to their self-empowerment seminar as, 'the key to personal success and professional productivity – bring balance, control and confidence to your life' (NBLA advertisement, 1992).

Reflecting this interest, Peter Block (1987) wrote, 'I do not know of one large organization, whether it is government, education, health care or business, that is not now experimenting with empowerment strategies' (p. xvi). Similarly, Gandz (1990) suggested the 1990s will be known as the empowerment era; 'the age when successful businesses finally take the steps necessary to reintegrate thinking and doing, thereby liberating the creative and innovative energies of employees to compete effectively in a global environment' (p. 74).

Despite these proclamations, there is a dearth of empirical research on empowerment and much confusion surrounding its meaning. According to Conger and Kanungo (1988), 'our understanding of the construct is limited and often confusing... most management theorists have dealt with empowerment as a set of managerial techniques and have not paid sufficient attention to its nature or the processes underlying the construct' (p. 471). Similarly, Thomas and Velthouse (1990) asserted that 'empowerment has become a widely used word within the organizational sciences... At this early stage of its usage, however, empowerment has no agreed-upon definition' (p. 666). Lastly, Sparrowe (1993) argued, 'it is remarkable that very little empirical research has examined the antecedents, processes, or outcomes of empowerment. Moreover, the theoretical work done to date on empowerment has not reached consensus at the level of defining the central concept' (Sparrowe, 1993, p. 2).

Within the management literature, empowerment is often regarded as a relational construct (Conger and Kanungo, 1988) whereby the power of an individual is seen as the net dependence that he or she has in relation to others (Pfeffer, 1981). From this perspective, empowerment is often achieved through decentralisation and participative management techniques. Alternatively, empowerment may be regarded as a motivational construct (Conger and Kanungo, 1988), whereby empowered individuals have an intrinsic need for self-determination (Deci, 1975) or a belief in self-efficacy (Bandura, 1977). Based on the latter perspective, Conger and Kanungo (1988) hypothesised that organisational factors, supervisory style, reward systems and job design can all contribute to empowerment. They also proposed the following definition:

> Empowerment is... a process of enhancing feelings of self-efficacy among organizational members through the identification of conditions that foster powerlessness and through their removal by both formal organizational practices and informal techniques of providing efficacy information. (p. 474)

In addition to self-efficacy, others have argued that empowered employees need to be provided with goals that are personally significant; 'people do not care much how they do in activities that have little or not significance for them, and they expend little effort on devalued activities' (Bandura, 1986, p. 348). Yet, Nord (1975) argued that it may be impossible for employees to pursue meaningful goals within capitalist enterprises; 'clearly, profits, and growth are given priority over humanization.... Human welfare is sacrificed for individual advantage' (p. 180). Further, Nightingale (1982) argued that providing employees with meaningful goals was impossible without organisations undergoing radical change:

> The modern work organization can never gain the moral commitment of those whose lives it rules without itself embodying a moral purpose. Unfortunately, many of the practices of the modern work organization are without moral justification; the legitimacy of these practices rests solely on economic and productive efficiency. (p. 7)

In keeping with this call for change, outside the management literature other conceptions of empowerment have been offered. For example, Vaines (1993) argued empowerment could be understood from a framework of multiple paradigms. The first she referred to as the 'no choice' or 'powerless' paradigm in which power is accepted and unexamined. The second she called 'technical rationality' or 'power over' in which those in power impose policies and politics to benefit themselves. The third paradigm was 'empowerment' or 'power with'; 'power is in people working actively together for the common good... All authority is challenged in view of what was what is, and what should be in relation to what is believed, studied, experienced and done in light of social responsibilities to all living systems' (Vaines, 1993, p. 25). Similarly, Morgaine (1993) suggested that empowerment processes 'must be based on experiences designed to illuminate, challenge, and change social structures that support and maintain injustice and unequal power' (p. 15). She advocated three levels of empowerment: intrapersonal empowerment (self-efficacy or power within); interpersonal empowerment (collaboration with others for enhanced awareness of societal power structures); and community empowerment (strategies for both personal and sociopolitical change). Lastly, Rappaport (1986) defined empowerment as a 'powerful force for change contained within ourselves, our significant others, and our communities' (p. 67). Rappaport argued that empowerment is impossible to achieve without the full development of human potential.

Given all of these perspectives, what does empowerment mean within organisational settings? To answer this question we must move beyond the rhetoric of empowerment. In this chapter I attempt to do so by presenting the results of an ethnographic study I recently completed on organisational empowerment. By generating a thick description of empowerment from the perspective of employees within one organisation, this research contributes to our understanding of empowerment, not as it is 'conceptualized or prescribed to be' by management theorists, not as it is 'espoused to be' by management practitioners, but how it is 'known to be' by employees at all levels of one organisation.

RESEARCH METHODOLOGY

Given the exploratory nature of this research, an ethnographic methodology was employed (Fetterman, 1989). I began by selecting an organisation in which there appeared to be a substantial commitment to *empowerment* and one in which I would be provided with virtually unrestricted access to people and information. The organisation chosen was a Canadian quick-service restaurant division of a large US-based, multinational. The Canadian home office was located in Toronto, Ontario. At the time of the study, this division had 107 company-owned and 160 franchised units, and employed 4725 people (125 at home office, 4600 in the field).

During an initial interview I was told the company had implemented an empowerment programme called the 'customer revolution'. I was also told they wanted to be a 'premiere' employer, were committed to training and had shifted their management style from 'controllers to coaches'. When I asked what the impetus for the customer revolution had been, I was told:

> We were a company that had mixed messages and seemed to go on a roller coaster ride of focusing on the customer, focusing on profits, then focusing on employees... We wanted a theme we could focus on... We did the times are good, let's do something really neat... we're going to have the look of the leader, then we'd have a couple of bad months and its forget the look of the leader, profit, profit, profit.

I was impressed by the extent of empowerment-related activity they were reportedly involved with. I was also intrigued by the underlying theme of 'mixed messages' and the lack of a clear organisational focus (customers versus profits versus employees). In a follow-up meeting with the Director of Human Resources and the Vice-president (the head of the Canadian division) I was able to secure their commitment to the research. I was subsequently given a private office and was invited to attend any meetings or events I thought would be relevant.

My research occurred over an extended period of time. I was directly involved with the organisation from January to December of 1992. For the first seven months, I spent three to four days per week at the home office. During September and October, I focused on the restaurants in 'the field'. November and December were spent refining my analysis and getting feedback to my ideas. Data-collection techniques included participant observation, interviewing, and archival data searches. In total, I was able to observe/participate in six management training courses, five market tours (visiting restaurants with Canadian and/or US executives), seven off-site meetings (meetings held away from the office often spanning several days), 59 regular meetings (all departments, all levels), nine presentations, one managers' conference, four social events and one 'mystery shopper' tour. I also spent a week working at one of the restaurants. In addition to these observations, I conducted a total of 47 formal interviews and had many informal conversations too numerous to mention. Sampling for the interviews was purposive as opposed to random (Lincoln and Guba, 1985). I interviewed the most senior managers in both the US and Canada, local cooks and servers, and people from all levels and departments in between. Although not included in my interview 'count', during management training sessions I was often given the opportunity to ask participants questions. In this sense, I was able to conduct a number of group interviews and gained the insights of many restaurant managers while at the home office.

Archival data also proved to be an extremely important source of information. The company was frequently written about in the popular business press and I found these public accounts useful points of comparison. Its culture was said to be aggressive and results-oriented; its US leaders described it as the 'ultimate capitalistic engine'. Its focus was on growth, improved operational efficiencies, and year-over-year improvements in financial measures. Growth was achieved through international expansion, adding 'points of distribution', and aggressive, value-oriented marketing promotions. Operational efficiency was achieved through vendor-prepared food products ('getting the kitchen out of the restaurant'), new technology (automating many administrative functions), restructuring (increasing management spans of control) and through the reduction in capital investment costs (finding less expensive ways to distribute food products). It was assumed that financial improvements would follow increased growth and operational efficiencies. Its human resource philosophy was said to be 'Darwinian': managers who failed to achieve expected financial results didn't survive. Other important data came from training manuals, training videos, annual reports, employee handbooks, transcripts of speeches, presentation decks (copies of the overheads used in presentations), financial statements, written reports, newsletters, memos and the results of a company 'values' survey.

THE ANALYSIS: AN EMPOWERMENT TYPOLOGY

In analysing the data, one of my first insights was that the word empowerment meant very different things to different people. Like the roller-coaster analogy previously described, I identified four types of empowerment: customer-focused empowerment, cost/productivity-focused empowerment, quality/process-focused empowerment and employee-focused empowerment (see Table 7.1). These four types provide the framework for the story of this organisation's experience with empowerment. It begins with the company's customer-focused and cost/productivity-focused empowerment initiatives. I describe the origins of these two types of empowerment, what they were meant to achieve, their processes and outcomes (both intended and otherwise). I also identify several organisational philosophies or assumptions and many organisational control systems that prevented the success of their customer-focused approach. Next, I discuss quality/process-focused and employee-focused empowerment. I also identify some of the organisational barriers that prevented these types of empowerment from being fully developed. I conclude by presenting a model which explains why any form of empowerment (beyond a cost/productivity approach) could not survive within this organisation.

Customer-focused empowerment

The organisation's empowerment initiative began with the 'customer revolution'; 'they call it the customer revolution but everyone assumes it means some kind of empowerment' (human resource manager, 8 April 1992). Its stated purpose was to generate an increased focus on customer service. Human resource managers also hoped it would replace their rigid, assembly-line approach to service, clarify the company's priorities and reduce their high turnover rates, especially in the field (7 January 1992). Senior managers ('the directors') extolled the customer revolution's importance: 'it is imperative that we start to look at things from a customer's point of view' (company documents, August 1989); 'Customers must become the obsession with us' (company documents, September and October 1989); 'The Customer Revolution is exactly what is going to give us the long-term competitive advantage' (company newsletter,

May 1991). The Vice-president outlined the challenge they faced in implementing the customer revolution; 'It's going to mean hiring the best people we can, giving them more training than ever before, and then demanding new levels of performance' (company documents, September and October 1989).

The customer revolution was introduced in 1989 through training classes, conferences, a company newsletter and a mission statement which spoke of 'exceeding customer expectations'. Managers were encouraged to 'confront the status quo' and lead rather than manage; 'challenge the process, inspire a shared vision, enable others to act, model the way, encourage the heart' (Kouzes and Posner, 1987). As a result, policies and procedures were challenged, customer service became more flexible, and employee enthusiasm grew: 'the revolution sort of opened the flood gates... We were getting all these really great service ideas... They were really having fun with their customers' (human resource manager, 16 April 1992); 'That whole year people were really talking about customer service and changing things, turning the organization upside down' (human resource manager, 16 April 1992).

Despite these positive intended outcomes, other unintended outcomes resulted. For example, the directors became concerned with the customer revolution's impact on product and service consistency; 'service was different in every restaurant, we were not consistent' (16 April 1992). More importantly, they disliked its impact on operating costs and their ability to make *plan*. *Plan* referred to the organisation's annual financial and unit growth objectives and was the single most important characteristic of the organisation's culture. Overall plan goals were imposed by the US (they were said to 'descend like tablets from the mount'). It was up to the directors to figure out how to achieve them; their bonuses and career progression depended on them doing so. One US executive explained: 'If you don't get the results you're managed out. They're not interested in what you can do in three years but what you can do tomorrow'.

Not surprisingly, this led to the assumption that *plan had to be achieved at all costs*. The Vice-president explained, 'It's not some game that's being played. We can't miss plan' (3 February 1992). Similarly, the Director of Operations told his area managers (managers who were responsible for several restaurants): 'they don't care how we make plan as long as we do' (26 February 1992); 'Just hit the number... I'm serious... It's carved in stone' (12 August 1992). He also told the restaurant managers during their annual conference that making plan meant they could 'keep their jobs' (25 February 1992).

Table 7.1 A typology of employment strategies

Focus	Cost/Productivity	Customer service	Quality/Process	Employee
Objectives	Reduce management and labour costs	Increase customer focus	Improve processes, product and service quality	Maximise employee potential and commitment
Process	Reduce head count Increase spans of control Redistribute power Delegate 'Bigger Jobs'	Adopt customer-oriented mission: 'exceed customer expectations' Hire the best Train managers: Confront the status quo; lead vs manage	Departmental meetings Re-visit organisational priorities and values Speech – communicate changes Continuous improvement	Increased focus on employees Align organisational goals and values Employee participation in establishing strategic direction
Outcomes	Intended outcomes Decreased costs Unintended outcomes Reduced managerial awareness	Intended outcomes Policies and procedures challenged More flexible customer service	Intended outcomes Clarification of organisation's priorities, vision and values Modest process improvements	Intended outcomes None – perspective was not accepted by the directors

Management task avoidance	Increased employee responsibility	Unintended outcomes Cynicism, conflict, confusion
Responsibility without skills, experience or training	Increased employee enthusiasm	Organisational barriers prevented substantial change from occurring
Emerging titles and positions	Unintended outcomes Felt loss of control	
Employees wearing management uniforms and accessing safe	Product and service inconsistency Increased cost of sales	
Declining customer service, product quality, unit sales and employee commitment		
Cynicism and distrust		

A related and equally important assumption was that in order to achieve plan, it was operations' job (the area and restaurant managers) to *drive the bottom line* (control costs), while it was marketing's job to *drive the top-line* (increase sales through value-based promotions and innovative advertising). Based on this assumption, the restaurant managers were expected to aggressively control their costs. In doing so, however, they made decisions that negatively impacted employees and customers alike; product quality, customer service and employee morale declined. Several human resource managers reflected on the conflict that emerged between the customer revolution and plan: 'We needed to beat [plan], we needed to cheat for a couple of months, and the message clearly was the revolution died when we had to do that' (16 April 1992); 'In 1989 and even into 1990 it was fine, but late 1990 we weren't hitting plan. Everything came to a grinding stop. You don't buy anything, nothing, zero...it was targets, make money' (16 April 1992).

Cost/productivity-focused empowerment

Throughout 1991, plan pressures intensified. In addition to continued pressure on the restaurant managers to control their costs, the organisation embarked on a reorganisation in which spans of control were increased and the number of managers in each unit were reduced. In order to cope with these changes the managers were encouraged to 'empower' their hourly employees to assist with administrative jobs (for example, ordering, scheduling, payroll, inventory counts and supervising other employees). The Director of Human Resources referred to this as giving employees 'bigger jobs' and argued it would provide the company with a 'fundamental competitive advantage' by helping take labour out of the restaurants. A human resource manager described the transition of empowerment from a customer-focused to a productivity focused strategy:

> The empowerment almost seemed to come about when we started talking about productivity more, in the sense that you've got to be more productive, you've got to push responsibility down and delegate... It definitely started as a customer service thing. (8 June 1992)

While some managers and hourly employees relished the additional responsibility and labour costs were decreased, several unexpected problems arose. Some area managers complained that while they were given additional pay for their increased spans, it was not as much as they had expected. The restaurant managers were disappointed with the lack of technological assistance. They had been promised a computer system to help with their administrative work, yet due to the costs involved and development delays the technology didn't materialise. During training sessions, the managers also complained that by having hourly employees do some of their work, they were less aware of their operations. Some admitted empowering employees in order to avoid unpleasant tasks themselves. Others expressed concern that the hourly employees they were to empower didn't have the necessary interest, skills or experience.

The Director of Operations also took issue with some aspects of empowerment. He was particularly concerned with the emergence of several new positions in the restaurants. 'Shift leaders' and 'crew leaders' were two of the titles given by the restaurant managers to hourly employees who assumed supervisory responsibilities. As these titles/positions were not formally recognised by head office, these new 'managers' didn't receive any corporate training. The Director of Operations also disliked the fact that these employees wore management uniforms and had access to the restaurant safes. Others in the organisation challenged the very fact that they were calling these changes *empowerment*:

> Nothing's changed, we're just getting crew members to do management's job for less money. (Area manager, 26 February 1992)
>
> The shift leader empowerment thing is potentially a formula for abuse. Shift leaders become glorified, low paid, high responsibility people... Are we trying to (a) save money or (b) are we trying to get more empowerment? (Director, 26 March 1992)
>
> I think we've got a game going on here that we don't fully comprehend... All we're doing is focusing on head count numbers and dollars. There's the appearance of flattening the structure without actually flattening it. (Human resource manager 26 March 1992)
>
> We reduced our managers from 3.1 to 1.8 [clapping hands] aren't we great... and we did it through empowerment. We don't tell them that we created a whole new layer called crew leaders who don't even go to [training] classes. (Human resource manager, 16 April 1992)

As the cost/productivity focused interpretation of empowerment began to predominate, employee cynicism and distrust grew. Many managers and hourly employees questioned what was meant by empowerment; 'are we customer-focused or cost-focused?' They also questioned whether the customer revolution was 'still alive'? When asked what the company valued, one restaurant manager said, 'The customer is what they say, but that's not what they mean...it's not. It's definitely cost-focused' (1 July 1992). Similarly, one director commented:

> As much emphasis as we put on the customer revolution, what comes down from the top...still is, if the numbers aren't there who gives a shit about what's going on from a service standpoint...we're a numbers driven company not a service driven company. (10 March 1992)

This switch in emphasis was supported by the organisation's assumptions regarding *plan*. It was also supported by the introduction of several new control systems and procedures. In the next section, the impact of these assumptions and control systems on the customer revolution are discussed.

Critical barriers to customer-focused empowerment

As previously stated, one organisational assumption was that plan had to be achieved at all costs, and a second was that plan was best achieved by operations focusing on costs, and marketing on sales. During 1992 these assumptions became even more evident. When asked what 'drove sales', the Director of Marketing said there was an 'immediate correlation' between marketing activity and sales results (25 June 1992). He said nothing of the importance of meeting customer needs or customer satisfaction levels. When I later asked specifically about these issues, he dismissed them as a 'long-term' concern.

During 1992 sales did increase, but this was achieved by adding new points of distribution. Same-store sales were actually in decline. In an attempt to reverse this trend, the marketing managers frantically introduced a whole series of in-store promotions while disregarding their impact on operating margins. Even the Director of Marketing argued there was merit in running promotions that only made a, 'penny in profit' but increased sales; 'it makes margins look bad but we have to decide which one we're going after' (27 July 1992). This established a vicious cycle which forced the operations managers to become even more aggressive in cost reduction, as they were expected to 'flow-through' a certain percentage of sales to the bottom-line.

Despite the suggestion of many managers that sales could also be increased through an investment in labour hours, improved customer service and improved product quality, this philosophy was not adopted. For example, they argued:

Any idiot can lower their prices. We have done an abysmal job on the product experience. There isn't enough of a customer orientation. (Director, 8 October 1992)

If you put on extra servers you'll have better service, you'll have a full restaurant... the customers will be happy and bottom line is your unit contribution will be higher. (Restaurant manager, 24 June 1992)

If you will give me the hours to train my people, I'll put the dollars on the bottom line. If you fix my restaurant, I'll show you what the customer's reaction will be. (Human resource manager, citing restaurant managers, 1 July 1992)

There's one simple way to re-invigorate the dining room, that's put some people in it called employees who actually have the time to actually service the customers. (Human resource manager, 19 April 1992)

We're not going to sell any desserts because our procedures say that we take the menu away from them, we don't give them another one, and we don't go back to them after we've dropped the pizza off in their lap. (Marketing manager, 2 March 1992)

The stores that have had three [manager] teams, the consistency on margins has been great, sales are growing. (Area manager, 9 September 1992)

I'd have to say we're not winning them back operationally as well as we could and I think over time that has to have an effect... We can't quantify it but there's an effect, and it's not positive. (Director of Operations, 27 July 1992)

The dine-in business is declining. I think we have made a number of bad decisions that are exacerbating the problem... we need to set a gold standard for what our product's going to be. The customers know we've been fooling around with stuff... we have customers that are literally reducing their frequency. (Area manager, 9 September 1992)

At one point (24 July 1992) the Human Resource Director confronted the Vice-president directly; 'Some people believe that if you spend some money the customer will respond.' In response, he said they did 'investment spend', but his interpretation was analogous with investing in marketing; 'The one line of the P&L [profit and loss statement] that we have never touched is marketing.' He also argued that they were 'customer-focused'; 'we have this fiscal responsibility that we have to hit and given that, we do as much as we can for the customer.' Ironically, when the customer revolution was first introduced, it had been the Vice-president who had said, 'no longer is it enough to say that we do the best we can for our customers' (company documents, September and October, 1989). As a result of his new perspective, by mid-1992 the company's stated goal of 'exceeding customer expectations' was replaced with trying not to 'violate' them or make them 'suffer'.

This perspective was reinforced by one last critical assumption; *compromising employees and customers in the short-term, supports the long-term interests of employees, customers and the company*. This assumption helped prevent challenges to their short-term orientation and was reinforced throughout the organisation. For example, the Vice-president argued that increasing prices provided customers with a long-term benefit because it kept the organisation 'in the game'. A director also stated, 'in the short-term it may not be good for the customer, but over-time it is'. A human resource manager explained:

> Sometimes we do things that are anti-customers because they're going to help us meet plan. Now, is meeting plan ultimately going to be good for customers because it keeps enabling us to stay in business and doing the things we need to do for customers?... So you compromise this customer today, because you're taking care of that customer tomorrow... It's a very complicated set of logic to go through. (16 April 1992)

Associated with plan and its related assumptions was the introduction of a number of control systems. Despite being 'empowered' the restaurant managers found themselves more controlled than they'd ever been. A director observed, 'It's hard to reconcile empowerment with a policies and procedures oriented system' (10 February 1992). These policies and procedures included the introduction of a financial audit, a QSC (Quality, Service, Cleanliness audit), and ALGAM (a labour management system that controlled the number of employee hours that could be scheduled). They also simplified the menu and increased their use of pre-prepared products. With respect to specific cost areas, they increased their focus on average wage, training, and semi-variable expenses. To help monitor the impact of these changes on the customer experience, they introduced a 'mystery shopper' evaluation programme. Lastly, all of these initiatives were reinforced by a controlling management style that pervaded the operations group. Each of these control systems are briefly described below:

The audits

The financial audits were a point of contention because managers who did not achieve the required standards were placed in the 'disciplinary process'. The managers complained about how the requirements took their attention off customer service, but to little effect:

> The stuff my boss looks at I do, the rest gets dropped... Service has slipped. It's not nearly as good as it used to be. Service is not at the level we want to see. (Area manager, 8 July 1992)

For over three years [the organization] has been teaching us empowerment as one of its basic principles... It appears to me that we may have lost our primary focus as we have nearly as many auditors and/or controllers as area field trainers or area managers. (Restaurant manager, 8 April 1992)

They also found the audit requirements to be blatantly unreasonable. For example, as part of the customer revolution, servers were encouraged to deal directly with customer complaints by offering a coupon or discounting some portion of the bill. The new financial audit disallowed this practice by stipulating that only the restaurant general managers had coupon and discount signing authority. To get around this requirement, some managers encouraged their employees to learn how to forge their signatures. One observed:

> How are we supposed to empower people when finance has got a death grip or squeeze hold on them? Assistant managers can't sign invoices or paid outs. But the [general manager] only works five shifts, not 15. (Area manager, 9 April 1992)

Eventually, the financial audit was changed to reflect some of the managers' concerns, such as allowing servers to sign coupons.

The QSC audit sent a different message as the managers were forewarned about being audited and the auditors often overlooked infractions that were considered beyond the managers' control (those that required a capital expenditure); 'that's someone telling [the auditor], we're not going to spend the money, we know it's an issue, we don't want to hear about it' (restaurant manager, 24 June 1992). The managers also expressed frustration with the audit's standards and the lack of resources to achieve them: 'It's a lot of double talk. When you get low marks and you can't do anything about it, that's what really bothers me. A lot of managers when they get low marks, they're pissed off for weeks' (23 October 1992).

Labour control

ALGAM was introduced to help minimise total labour hours in the units. Managers were told they had to achieve 100 per cent to ALGAM and like the financial audit, those who didn't were placed in the 'disciplinary process'. To achieve this objective, many managers ran short-staffed (tables per server increased from six to more than ten), scheduled themselves into staff functions, reduced their emphasis on training and cleaning and didn't pay employees for all hours worked. Managers complained about the impact of ALGAM on their ability to 'empower' employees. They also complained about the impact of ALGAM on customer service:

> I think [the organisation] is way off base with its focus on labour dollars. In the long-term you'll really suffer. (Restaurant manager, 7 April 1992)
>
> They are so short-sighted. Where's customer service in all of this? The financial pressures are ruining the business. (Area manager, 15 June 1992)
>
> Customer revolution, schmevolution. ALGAM is more important than the customer revolution. (Human resource manager, citing hourly employees, 1 July 1992)
>
> We've constantly pressured our margins, so we've got less and less labour in the restaurants to serve the customers. We've definitely deteriorated the dine-in experience. (Director, 22 July 1992)

Product simplification

In addition to these 'numerical' control mechanisms, control was further achieved through the products themselves; the *menu was simplified* and *vendor-prepared food products* were introduced to help increase consistency and further take labour out of the restaurants. While greater consistency may have been achieved, it also compromised the 'value added' elements of the dine-in business (product quality, customer service, atmosphere, physical plant), which further contributed to declining same store sales. As one director explained, 'we've taken off sandwiches, we've taken off salad bars, we've taken away a lot from the dine in experience' (22 July 1992). The area managers also complained about the quality of the vendor-prepared food products (area manager meeting, September 9, 1992):

> We are no longer going to serve our customers this crap... I personally am no longer doing this at the expense of our customers... We're losing customers, we're losing sales... We had to do it... because it was part of the plan... The stores are sick of seeing one more bag of crap come in... and what they're forced to use. It colours their approach to every product we produce, they feel a little less good about it.

A US executive similarly observed (10 March 1992): 'We have a cost of sales target and labour efficiency target and what gives is the quality of all of those products because we're not serious about the quality... It hasn't been a high priority.'

Cost control

A number of specific cost areas (average wage, training and semi-variable expenses) also came under pressure as a result of plan. Each one of these served as a further barrier to the customer revolution because they negatively affected the level of customer service achieved. For example, to help reduce *average wage rates*, managers fired long-term workers, didn't pay over-time, and delayed giving employees performance reviews (a positive evaluation was supposed to result in a wage increase). According to a human resource manager (26 March 1992), 'Here's how you manage average wage down...you fire high paid employees...They're hiring new people...hiring them in at minimum wage.' Rather than hiring the 'best,' 'empowered' hourly employees were often young, immature, transient and inexperienced. Managers similarly lacked literacy, analytical and decision-making skills. Some directors complained about the situation, but did nothing to change it. One director argued they couldn't attract 'the type of intelligent, quality people we want' (10 July 1992). Another admitted, 'we end up going with lower calibre people who we don't want running our business' (29 June 1992).

Despite the low skill level, adequate in-store *training* also wasn't provided because it wasn't accounted for in ALGAM and spending more than was budgeted conflicted with the managers' bonus objectives: 'That .1 per cent can push me into my bonus, and that's my livelihood, that's my rent cheque, that's my vacation, that's my engagement ring I have to buy my girlfriend' (assistant manager, 6 April 1992). Training in the new units was also limited in an effort to reduce opening costs:

> You've got inexperienced people trying to become very efficient very quickly. And really most importantly is the erosion of the customer base...We'll have higher turnover rates...Eight weeks arguably for management training was marginal...we're now looking at five weeks. (Director, 24 August 1992)

Semi-variable expenses (small wares and repairs and maintenance expenses) were controlled by the directive 'don't spend a penny', and refusing all requests for capital expenditures in the last four months of the fiscal year. These measures resulted in managers not replacing needed supplies (glassware, cutlery and ashtrays), not maintaining or replacing needed equipment (refrigerator seals, pizza ovens, hand dryers, pop machines, pasta steamers), and delaying needed changes to production systems. Not only did these delays impact product quality, they also affected sales and costs. A restaurant manager discussed his concerns with respect to not being able to purchase an additional phone and table to support his restaurant's delivery system (23 October 1992): 'As far as morale and productivity, it holds everything back ... It stops you from being able to build your sales up. All the complaints we get ... [customers] tell us you guys have to work on your consistency.'

At the same restaurant, servers sold bottled pop (which is much more expensive than soda fountain pop) to restaurant patrons, because they could not replace their broken pop dispenser. Due to the same problem, other restaurants couldn't serve critical menu items such as garlic bread or even their main item – pizza. A mystery shopper commented, 'it happens often enough to surprise us ... "there's no pizza available tonight" ... it's happened fairly frequently' (26 June 1992). Due to malfunctioning heating, ventilation and air-conditioning systems (and the lack of funds to repair/replace them), some restaurants were also very uncomfortable to be in. This further discouraged sales and was an annoyance to staff (employees wore parkas in the winter and customers and employees alike got overly hot in the summer). Some restaurants were heated during business hours by keeping the doors to the ovens open.

The managers summarised the impact of the organisation's control mechanisms and reporting systems: 'It's unfortunate to say but the bottom line is what counts right now, and how you attain it is, you know, might be another issue' (21 April 1992); 'Your focus after that [monthly] meeting is going to be on food costs and labour costs and nothing else.'

The mystery-shopper programme

Given all of these control systems, the mystery-shopper programme was a particular point of controversy. It involved monthly restaurant evaluations by employees of an outside organisation: the 'shoppers' were trained to respond yes or no to 30 statements pertaining to service, product quality and restaurant cleanliness. The restaurant managers argued these evaluations contributed to the decline in service by rigidly enforcing robot-like service procedures. For example, five of the service statements pertained to time ('greeted within one minute of arrival'). Meeting these standards meant the servers had no time to talk informally with their customers. Ironically, the impersonality fostered was further reinforced by the expectation that servers introduce themselves to their customers. An assistant manager explained that he made his servers introduce themselves to their customers at every table, even people they already knew, because he needed to improve his mystery-shopper rating.

Despite their lack of credibility with the restaurant managers, mystery-shopper scores were routinely tracked at home office and held up as proof of the high level of service and product quality that was being achieved. When questioned about rumours of declining service levels, the Director of Operations replied, 'It's improved. Our mystery shopper [scores] are improved.' Similarly, when I asked a US executive about the conflict between their cost-reduction focus and the customer revolution, he said that if mystery-shopper scores started to decline they'd have to rethink their approach (23 April 1992). When I asked the Vice-president about the impact of a reduction in labour hours in the units he argued that service had improved; 'Our mystery shopper scores confirm that' (16 June 1992).

In fact, while mystery shopper scores remained more or less constant (they had actually declined slightly from 1991), the number of customer complaints received by home office increased 59 per cent in the same period. Rather than focusing on the source of these problems, the restaurant managers were told by the Director of Operations to stop the complaints from reaching home office. Ideas they generated for doing so included giving out the area manager's phone number when asked by a disgruntled customer for the home office's. Although the complaints that did get through were summarised in a year-end report (which was given to the Vice-president), this information was not used to challenge the validity of the mystery-shopper scores or the often spoken premise that service levels had improved. In essence, by focusing on mystery-shopper scores instead of the increasing number of customer complaints, senior management masked the serious decline in service and food quality that was occurring.

Management style

Contributing to the restaurant managers' cost-control focus, was a controlling management style that pervaded the operations group. In the training centre, when asked how they dealt with under-performing employees, several managers figuratively advocated the 'seagull' technique ('shitting' on them). Another suggested, 'slap them in the side of the head, but not too hard, then pat them again' (8 April 1992). Area mangers, human resource managers, and restaurant managers cried as a result of how they were treated. This approach began with the Director of Operations and was passed along to his subordinates. He advocated the *Five F*s of management ('be friendly, fair and firm, if that doesn't work use fear, and if that still doesn't work they're fucked'). His techniques included espoused commitment ('I love you guys'), verbal aggressiveness ('shove it'), sarcasm (jokes about the managers' lack of sexual prowess), and control over meeting agendas (when area managers pressed for change or challenged him, they were often told, 'in the interests of time ... let's move on').

In the field, the area managers similarly controlled the restaurant managers and hourly employees. A restaurant manager said that people who 'worked hard' and kept their 'mouths shut' were favoured (15 November 1992). Another said he had been yelled at by his area manager for pointing out the conflict between ALGAM and the customer revolution; 'that's when I got the idea they don't like [feedback] ... I should keep my mouth shut.' He added that the restaurant managers were candid amongst themselves but that some said 'yes to everything the king bosses say ... Some are scared, it's their careers, they have families' (20 October 1992).

This fear was reinforced by the acknowledgement of employees at all levels that due process did not exist. When describing the relationship between her managers and their area manager, a cook observed (23 October 1992); 'either they have to kiss his ass or they get fired'. A human resource manager told me that on several occasions she had intervened to prevent the firing of employees for being candid with their bosses (25 June 1992). A director similarly explained:

> You don't challenge the growth goals. You don't say we can't do that. Instead, you figure out how to do it. If you don't do it, [the company] will find someone else who will. That's why you have to be young, have energy and never have time for your friends. (Interview, 12 March 1992)

In summary, plan, its associated assumptions, and a host of control-oriented policies, practices and procedures, negatively impacted the success of the customer revolution or 'customer-focused' empowerment in the field. While the restaurant managers found themselves caught in this conflict, home office employees tried to increase their influence with respect to the organisation's processes and strategic direction. I labelled these initiatives quality/process-focused empowerment and employee-focused empowerment. While not as dominant as the customer and cost/productivity-focused empowerment types (organisational barriers prevented them from becoming more fully developed), they played an important role in the company's experience with empowerment. In the next section, these types of empowerment are described and the associated barriers identified.

Quality/process-focused empowerment

The primary objective of quality/process-focused empowerment is to facilitate the development of a culture in which employees constantly strive for a higher level of quality in all of the company's systems, processes and products. While the restaurant managers were unable to make such changes in the field, many middle managers at the home office attempted to improve the organisation's processes by voicing their concerns to their directors. In this section I review the major suggestions for improvement and identify some of the barriers that prevented change from occurring.

Marketing

The marketing managers confronted their director with concerns about the poor downward communication of priorities, the lack of interdepartmental co-ordination, the lack of support for new product development, and unrealistic work loads: 'There is just nobody at the top that understands the level of involvement... Everybody's doing these projects as an aside when in reality they're a full time job' (25 June 1992). When the Director of Marketing advised his managers to 'push back' if their work loads were excessive, they argued that the company's culture and their fear didn't allow them to; 'You do see people in meetings quite genuinely afraid to say I can't make this happen... They're afraid to say it'; 'part of that is just getting it into the culture where it's acceptable to say [no].' The Director of Marketing shared these concerns with the senior team, and while all their issues were not addressed, the Vice-president began to clarify the organisation's priorities at monthly review meetings.

Development

The development managers also met to discuss process issues (26 August 1992). The Director of Development encouraged his group to be candid:

> While we may not be able to resolve everything today, we're not going to be able to move forward unless we address some of the underlying issues in the department and the organization... If it's affecting the group's ability to get the job done, bring it up.

During the course of the meeting, the managers complained about inefficient approval processes, the lack of tools and technology, the lack of

218   *A Typology of Empowerment Strategies*

intra-departmental co-ordination and the lack of time. One manager observed that money could always be found for social events, but couldn't be found for tools; 'I would rather have the tools to do my job properly than go to a nice Christmas party.' They also discussed the lack of commitment towards employees: 'I'm not sure to what extent there is commitment to the employees within [this organisation] with respect to job security and training'; 'Does this company put bottom line dollars before the people? I believe they do. There's always more commitment to the dollar.' He then suggested a different approach, 'If you put the commitment to the people, they'll put the commitment to the dollar for you.' Others argued that the company needed to understand, 'financial commitments are achieved through people'.

At the end of the discussion the director explained they couldn't change corporate policies or matters beyond their control. Issues he agreed they could address included holding a 'forum to voice concerns', improved budgeting for 'tools required' and holding a 'job security discussion' with a manager from human resources. One manager challenged the director on how he had limited their action plan; 'if every time we raise an issue you say "that's policy let me explain the policy" I'm not interested. I want to know if the policy can change'.

Purchasing

Although I didn't spend much time with employees from the purchasing department, I was aware that they had raised several issues (for example, they had complained about inefficient photocopiers and purchase order forms). The Vice-president viewed their complaints as trivial and was frustrated by their inability to solve the problems themselves. He suggested that all they needed to do was circulate a memo asking for input and then implement the change (23 June 1992). When I asked if they were aware they could initiate such a process, he admitted they probably were not.

Finance

Within finance, the director focused on creating process change through the establishment of a finance revolution committee made up of departmental representatives. They surveyed the department's employees concerning barriers to empowerment, job satisfaction, effective management, and training and development, and met to discuss the results. At the beginning of one meeting they talked about the lack of resources for initiating change ('we're the resource that they've allocated'), and the lack of candour ('I have never heard anyone say I screwed up, I'll fix it. There's a fear to say, I screwed up').

Barriers to empowerment they identified included the unacceptability of mistakes, lack of recognition, red tape, lack of trust, lack of information, the need for controls, controlling management styles, and the lack of opportunity to influence goals and objectives. Barriers to 'job satisfaction' included the lack of opportunities to learn, poor communication, uninteresting jobs (redundant work, low work variety), and a poor atmosphere (lack of respect, fair play and teamwork). They also complained about the hiring of unqualified individuals. Barriers to training included the lack of time, excessive work loads, spending constraints and lack of 'managerial will'. When the finance director presented these findings to his managers (8 May 1992), he began by suggesting:

> This is a great opportunity to scrap what we're doing. We're growing far too fast to have anything we developed two years ago to make sense two years from now. Put the team in charge of the process, to challenge their managers and make the case.

The managers readily acknowledged that there were problems in the department; performance evaluations were often late and there was a 'strong lack of commitment on the part of managers with respect to training, follow-up and communication'. They also argued that their excessive work loads were contributing to their lack of commitment for resolving the issues. In response, the director said it was 'management's responsibility to manage the work load. If we had the management commitment, we'd make the time'. He added, 'I'll throw it out to the group for what we can do about it, or should we leave it to the individual managers?' There was silence from the group and the director concluded, 'I guess we'll leave it to the individual managers.' By failing to address the *catch 22* his managers found themselves in, the Director of Finance inadvertently provided support for the status quo.

Human resources and training

The human resource managers challenged all aspects of the way the organisation was being run, especially the impact of plan on employees and customers:

> If every year we kill employees to make plan, there's gotta be something wrong with the plan... The root of the conflict is long-term versus short-term thinking... The numbers can't possibly be reached. We're not provided with

the training or the tools. Everyone is cynical because what is promised isn't coming through. (2 March 1992)

They also took issue with a newly proposed corporate values statement, an exercise that had been initiated by the Director of Human Resources. The directors had met on several occasions and after several iterations had come up with a list of seven values they felt represented those of the organisation (see Table 7.2). The human resource managers challenged almost every aspect of the statement. In particular, they took issue with the seventh value of striving for the 'look of the leader'. They asked, 'do you want everything to be based on how you look or what you are?' (19 February 1992). One manager similarly challenged the values process itself; 'We can do these things and rah rah them out and get a nice warm feeling...I just hope that we will take a look in the mirror... and say we're full of shit.' He later suggested that to believe

Table 7.2 Draft of values commitments (28 February 1992)

1. We are a customer driven company. Our quality, service and value will consistently exceed the expectations of each and every customer

2. We operate this company through honesty and integrity which includes respecting the letter and the spirit of the law. We encourage and respect candour and we deliver on commitments made amongst ourselves

3. We always maintain an aggressive goals and result orientation – challenging ourselves to reach beyond understood expectations. We are, as a team, fiercely competitive and maximize our success through people development and profit growth – balancing the short term with the longer term needs of the business

4. We are a performance driven company. We hire only the very best people without regard to any factor unrelated to skills and abilities. We ensure that there are no barriers to success for any individuals, and pay and promote solely on the basis of merit

5. We believe that empowered individuals and teams make a difference and provide the foundation for success. We encourage calculated risk taking. We recognize and celebrate achievements, and when mistakes are made, we learn from them and grow

6. We believe in the long term employment relationship. We respect and encourage the need to balance work with changes in personal lives. We expect our employees to work hard and are sensitive to their commitments to family and friends

7. We are proud to be a leader in the foodservice industry. We strive for 'the look of the leader' in the community and in the way we do business

your own propaganda was 'an acutely American, big corporation thing'. Other managers supported his contention: 'We are full of shit... We're not the look of the leader... the only way you go to sleep at night is to say, hey, that's [the company]... The real problem is that a lot of the directors believe, *believe*, that we're all these things they're professing.' They also challenged the manner in which financial information was portrayed. One manager described the information as a 'statistical mirage'. He argued:

> I think you've got unit growth and franchise buy-back and [management cost reduction] hiding what you all know is going on throughout [the company] worldwide, but particularly in the United States, which is, [sales] transactions are in a friggin nose dive. (1 July 1992)

During an off-site meeting (20 May 1992), they talked specifically about barriers to the customer revolution. The Director of Human Resources suggested, 'if it's dead we've got to get it on the table, and if empowerment can't happen then we've got to change the systems that allow it to'. The managers challenged back that they lacked time and senior management support. Gradually, the human resource managers came to the realisation that significant change was unlikely to happen without the complete support of the senior management team. They talked about their frustrations: 'we've been trying to change it for so long'; 'we reached the point about eight months ago where we don't believe it's going to change'; 'it's outside the bounds of our influence'. One manager observed; 'we keep struggling with this huge strategic organisational effectiveness nut, that we just don't seem to crack, because it's not ours to crack'.

The directors

When by themselves, the directors also spoke frankly about the organisation and its processes. At one meeting (29 July 1992) they met to explore organisational barriers to empowerment with the assistance of two consultants. The barriers they identified included: poor communication of the company's vision and values; rigid systems and policies; the lack of timely information; the lack of listening opportunities; the lack of follow-up to employee concerns; interdepartmental conflicts; the lack of time ('it comes back to one thing, time... People want to be involved but they have no time'); the lack of resources ('a lot of the impediments are financial'); their workloads ('fundamentally it gets down to the work load that we're all under'); and their risk averse culture and short-term orientation ('it may involve doing things differently that may affect profitability in the short-term... We make short-term decisions because of the profit pressures'). They also acknowledged that these factors had resulted in the lack of 'an emotional rah rah commitment', a lack of trust, confusion and frustration. In an earlier conversation, the Vice-president also acknowledged a *catch 22* with respect to some of these barriers:

> Time is the biggest thing stopping us from taking a step back and communicating to the key people and that leads to some of the confusion, the conflict and the cynicism... You get caught in the catch 22, recognizing that you've got to take the time to do this more effectively, but I don't have the time. (16 June 1992)

During another meeting in which they met to re-consider their values statement (30 August – 1 September 1992), the directors spoke even more frankly, to the point where they seemed prepared to challenge both the organisation's culture and its processes:

> We always... say but that's the way it's done... We need to understand what we want to do differently;
> We are in [the company] but we can still be unique;
> We have the flexibility... We use the organisation as an excuse that tells us how to run the business.

The Vice-president, however, countered these suggestions: 'The vision and values have to fit within our reality... We have to have a strong focus on margin controls. I will put a time out when I feel we're being too utopian. There are realities, economic realities'. He later observed, 'everything we do is to maximize shareholder wealth'. Another director added under his breath, 'one year at a time'.

In the discussion that followed the directors acknowledged many 'truths' about the organisation:

> We need to accept responsibility at this level for not being clear about the vision and honest about the values;
> We're so internally focused on achieving plan;
> Decisions we make fly in the face of customer needs;
> As much as I'd like to deny it, I believe what we're all about is profit;
> In the field we hire the best warm body;
> We put barriers in their way and ask them to do the impossible;
> We need to get ourselves out of this mess, whether it's tools, technology or training;
> We made plan, that's effective... the way we've made it might mean we won't make it next year, but we made plan.

They also discussed the reward system and how it shaped their behaviour. A human resource manager who was attending the meeting summarised: 'we have a system that rewards results... but there are real issues with the how'. When reflecting on his commitment to goals he didn't believe were appropriate, the Director of Operations explained, 'we've made a pact with the devil'. Interestingly, another division of the same organisation found that in order for empowerment to work for them, managers had to be rewarded on how they achieved results as well as the results themselves. This was in response to the realisation that 'the most punitive people got the best results and got the promotions' (23 January 1992). They also talked about the lack of incentive for innovation:

If I come up with an innovative idea, I may be too busy to deliver;
The first priority is getting your job done;
If I take this on, it just adds to my list and will become just one more thing that this organisation expects of me;
You don't have the time to think, innovate because the jobs are so big.

Faced with their acknowledgment of these problems, as well as mounting employee unrest, the directors eventually agreed that process change was required. To begin, it was decided that the Vice-president would make a speech to the organisation's home office employees in which the organisation's mission would be clarified and a new values statement presented (see Table 7.3). Amongst other things, the new values statement claimed: 'We are developing a focused and empowered organisation which, through a process of continuous improvement, supported by the right leadership, job design and environment, provides the foundation for innovation and success'.

In his speech, the Vice-president said they were committed to empowerment and that he was confident they would 'reinvigorate the revolution'. While most employees found the speech inspirational (to some it brought tears to their eyes), it failed to sustain their enthusiasm and was soon replaced, once again, with cynicism. One explanation is that although the Vice-president was prepared to re-visit some of their processes, he was not prepared to challenge the overall goals and objectives of the organisation, or the assumptions pertaining to plan. He also failed to address several *catch 22*s that were deeply embedded in the culture of the organisation. In the next section, these barriers are specifically explored.

Table 7.3   Values

We recognize the inseparability of our customers, employees and shareholders. Effectively managing this relationship will ensure the long-term success of our business

We are in the business of satisfying consumer needs. Our quality, service and value will consistently meet or exceed the expectations of each and every customer, both internal and external

We are a growth company that is committed to innovation. We are continually searching for better ways to do things. We are, as a team, fiercely competitive and always maintain an aggressive goals and results orientation – challenging ourselves to reach beyond understood expectations while balancing the long and short term needs of the business

We operate this company through honesty and integrity. We respect and encourage constructive candour and commitments made to each other. We all contribute to a positive team environment where individual and organizational accomplishments are recognized, celebrated and shared

We are developing a focused and empowered organization which, through a process of continuous improvement, supported b the right leadership, job design and environment, provides the foundation for innovation and success. We encourage calculated risk taking, using fact based decision making and when mistakes are made, we learn from them and grow

We hire only the very best people, based solely on skills and abilities. WE are committed to addressing any barriers to success for any individual. WE believe in a performance based long-term employment relationship in which each individual is dedicated to both personal and organisational growth. We provide regular informal and formal performance feedback and pay and promote solely on the basis of merit

We are sensitive to commitments to family and friends. We expect our employees to work hard and realize that at times the needs of the business come first; however, we respect and encourage balancing work with personal needs

Catch 22s and mixed messages: barriers to quality/process-focused empowerment

The existence of several organisational *catch 22's or mixed messages* were acknowledged by managers in the field and home office alike. For example, upon learning about some of the tactics being used to make plan, one senior US executive cautioned; 'we're not asking anybody to do anything illegal or immoral to make our 13 million'. In defence of the

Canadian operations the Director of Operations said they had fired three managers for not paying over-time. The US executive countered; 'we tell them if they have over-time they have to pay over-time, but we don't want them to have over-time. As a result they have two choices, not to pay them or not to have over-time.'

Other catch 22s were found in the field. One restaurant manager said they were told 50 per cent of their employees should be 'above target' performers (which would result in pay increases), yet they were also told to 'manage your average wage'. He concluded, 'the message is cut where you've got to cut' (terminate higher paid/higher quality employees) (8 July 1992). There was also a catch 22 with respect to restaurant security. In response to a rash of armed robberies, the managers had been told to keep their back doors locked at all times and were audited on their compliance. One restaurant manager observed, 'let's get the mixed messages straight. We were running delivery out the back door'. They suggested that if the company was serious about employee safety, they would have allowed them to install push bars on the back doors (8 July 1992).

Another, perhaps more insidious catch 22, was the expectation that employees who drew attention to serious problems (for example, the impact of cost reductions on product quality or customer service), were expected to achieve the same financial results in a different manner (without impacting customer service). Further, to admit it was impossible to do so was to admit they couldn't do their jobs. For example, one director said that when he told the Vice-president that training cuts were hurting customer service and repeat sales in the new units, he had simply been challenged to 'figure out a way to do it [reduce costs] differently' (24 August 1992). The Vice-president summarised this expectation with respect to ALGAM: 'If ALGAM isn't working I want to hear about it... But now we've got a challenge. Now we've got to figure out another way to get to plan' (22 June 1992).

Contributing to this catch 22 was the practice of blaming problems on the individuals who identified them, as opposed to the organisation or its systems. For example, in response to the suggestion by an area manager that there were operational barriers to service, the Director of Operations angrily blamed their poor service on 'the people that we have' (people the area manager would have hired). Similarly, at one senior team meeting in which they had been asked to be candid, a director stated that they were not sufficiently investing in training and development, or tools and equipment (29 June 1992). The Vice-president became visibly angry; 'that's not the organisation that says that. It boils down to the individuals.' The director then softened his position, 'I know we haven't cut it, but it's money in the bank.' Another director supported him; 'the priorities come along and the training's the first to go and we all agree that makes sense'. Seeing the Vice-president's reaction, he then adjusted his wording; 'the perception is there that training is the first to go'.

Employees who voiced contrary perspectives were also told they were being 'too tactical', 'naive', 'idealistic', 'jaded', 'cynical', not enough of a 'business man', 'not strategic', 'babies', 'heretical', 'bitchers and complainers' or 'a cancer'. Despite these pressures (or perhaps because of them), the directors' jokes were remarkably candid. The jokes concerned all aspects of the organisation including productivity ('our systems are so efficient that one person can handle the dining room', 20 April 1992); customer service ('we're a customer driven company – Not!', 30 August 1992); quality ('oh, you didn't tell me that was an issue', 21 July 1992); semi-variable expenses ('can't people eat the pizza with their hands if it's proofed properly?', 12 August 1992); how to reduce costs ('I can get him $100000 tomorrow...I can do it tomorrow with one memo' [a threatening directive to the field], 21 July 1992); their definition of empowerment ('to provide an organisational environment to create profit', 29 July 1992); and unrealistic financial projections (the Vice-president joked about not wanting to be around in the future so as not to be held accountable for achieving the targets they'd established, 30 August 1992). As one director explained, they needed to joke because if they didn't laugh they'd cry (12 August 1992).

Employee-focused empowerment

In addition to involving employees in continuous process improvement, employee-focused empowerment attempts to align employee values and interests with those of the organisation by involving employees in the establishment of the organisational goals and objectives. Some employees argued that this was, in fact, what was meant by empowerment. For example, one human resource manager asked:

> Is anybody saying... let's really have the planning process roll up? Because if not, we better redefine empowerment and the customer revolution, because people think... and I've always felt that it meant, setting our own goals and objectives and determining the means to get there. (19 May 1992)

At the senior level, this understanding of empowerment was strongly resisted. The Director of Finance explained:

We set up our mission statement, our values that's in development, our long-term vision statement, so everyone knows where we're going. That has to be top-down. That's senior management's responsibility to make sure the company's going in the way that's most profitable for the long-term. (10 April 1992)

This opinion was shared by a US executive; 'this is not consensus decision making. To have a strong strategic decision, there needs to be one person calling the shots' (22 April 1992). The Director of Human Resources similarly explained; 'you can't run a company by consensus ... I get paid to know when to say this is what we're going to do. It's a matter of expediency' (31 January 1992). The 'right' to be involved with establishing the company's direction, was linked by the Director of Finance with the ownership of capital: 'No matter who you are in the company you can't stand up and say well I think we should be doing this and then expect to have the empowerment to go do it because it's not your company, it's not your capital' (10 April 1992). The Vice-president similarly acknowledged, 'we're a publicly traded company and that drives most of what we do, the need to generate a certain percentage of earnings growth year over year over year'. He also joked that 'greed is good' and that 'profit is not a four letter word' (1 June 1992).

Rather than creating a 'strong' strategic direction as planned, the top-down nature by which the organisation's strategic direction and values were established resulted in their failure to challenge critical plan assumptions and organisational catch 22s which ultimately led to declining customer service, declining unit sales, and the inability of the company to foster employee enthusiasm and support. One human resource manager talked about the impact on her own motivation:

I know what I'm doing Period 6, I know what I've gotta do Q2 [the second quarter], but no where did I feel that I was involved in defining what those things are... So consequently I'm not bought into the vision. I'm cynical about our vision because I'm struggling between the, 'what do we want to be?' and 'what will this organisation let us be?'

Another human resource manager observed, 'the organisational need is directly in conflict with what we want our jobs to be' (27 August 1992). Yet another commented (24 August 1992) 'people are frustrated, because they're being asked to do things that they personally believe are not right, are not the best way'.

Summary of the empowerment typology

In summary, several distinct types of empowerment existed within this organisation. They began with the customer revolution (customer-focused empowerment), but with increased plan pressures soon switched in emphasis to lowering head count in the field (cost/productivity-focused empowerment). This change in emphasis was supported by the organisation's assumptions regarding plan and the introduction and reinforcement of many control mechanisms in the field. Restaurant managers who challenged the organisation's direction had little success.

Home office employees also tried to challenge key organisational processes (quality/process-focused empowerment). Some employees argued they should have greater involvement in establishing the strategic direction and values of the company (employee-focused empowerment). Organisational barriers prevented all but the cost/productivity-focused perspective of empowerment from succeeding (see Table 7.4 for a summary of the barriers identified within the previous discussion). When shown my typology the Vice-president confirmed my analysis (16 June 1992):

> The field is here [customer focused empowerment]... The office is more in the cost focused area... There's certain aspects of these [quality/process focused and employee focused empowerment] that I know we also believe in... I'm sort of moving down a track without thinking a lot about it, creating a lot of the conflict that is happening.

When I then suggested they should try to clarify their empowerment objectives he angrily replied, 'Well we do know why we're trying to achieve it... it's to lower G&A [general and administration costs], simply and clearly' (16 June 1992). Similarly, another director observed: 'If we thought having miserable people doing our bidding would make us more money we'd probably do it. We're doing this because we want to make more money' (29 July 1929). When it was suggested by a consultant that they might want to link empowerment with a quality objective, a director stated; 'If the best way to sustain profitability is to down grade our quality and sell the product at 80 per cent of where we are today, you might mind, but we'd do it.'

The multiple understandings of empowerment that existed resulted in conflict, cynicism and confusion. Decisions made 'in the name of empowerment' in one department or organisational level, often conflicted with decisions made in others. Even the human resource managers admitted that neither the word empowerment nor its processes were well-understood. One questioned, 'do we really practice empowerment or do we just pretend?' (2 March 1992). Yet another commented, 'it's all smoke and mirrors' (8 April 1992).

Why couldn't this organisation make more progress towards empowerment? In the last section of this chapter the key organisational barriers

Table 7.4 Organisational barriers to empowerment

Plan, associated operating assumptions and the catch 22s	Control and reward/discipline systems	Management style and job design	Communication and values
Plan Unrealistic/overly-aggressive Imposed goals – linked to ownership of capital Focus on maximising shareholder wealth ('one year at a time') Short-term orientation **Operating assumptions** Plan to be achieved 'at all costs' Marketing drives top line, operations drives bottom line Sacrificing customers and employees in the short-term supports the long-term	**Control mechanisms** Period by period plan review Misleading financial information – 'statistical mirage' Rigid systems and policies: financial and QSC audit; ALGAM – labour control; menu/production simplification. Expense control: average wage; training costs; semi-variable expenses. Mystery shoppers – 'proof' of service levels being achieved	**Management style** Aggressive/controlling style (the 5 F's) Fear and distrust Actively silence subordinates **Job design** Unrealistic goals Lack of meaningful goals Highly established routines Lack of appropriate authority/discretion Lack of financial resources Excessive workloads Lack of time	**Communication** Unclear priorities Confusion regarding empowerment 'type' Believe own propaganda mentality **Values** Lack of clarity and honesty Dichotomy (espoused versus practised) 'Can't say no – challenge the process' Incongruent (organisational versus employee)

229

Table 7.4 (contd.)

Plan, associated operating assumptions and the catch 22s	Control and reward/discipline systems	Management style and job design	Communication and values
The catch 22s People who identify problems are expected to achieve same results but in a different manner People who identify problems become problems Problems are blamed on the misinterpretation of individuals or their quality and not on the organisation's processes	Reward/discipline systems Director and managerial bonuses and promotions linked to plan ('Pact with the devil') Emphasis on short-term goals Ends versus means orientation Managers who fail to comply with control systems placed in 'disciplinary process' Lack of job security/due process Lack of incentive for ideas and innovations	Lack of training, tools and technology Lack of opportunity to learn Lack of professional/skilled subordinates Lack of forum for voicing concerns Poor intra- and inter-departmental coordination	

to empowerment are revisited and the connections between them are presented in a model entitled The Catch 22 and The Cycle of Denial (Table 7.5).

THE CATCH 22 AND THE CYCLE OF DENIAL

The roots of this model were first identified by a human resource manager and were further supported by the Director of Human Resources (30 August 1992):

> The people can't achieve the plan and still follow the rules, because they don't have the time, or they don't have the tools... So they execute it the best way they can, and people then close their eyes to the broken values and broken rules. Where that's happening is in the field because that's the people who have responsibility for the plan... The only problem with that is it's not possible, period. You can't make the money and not violate the customer and your people. (Human resource manager)

> People can't achieve the plan by following the rules. They won't admit they can't because it's admitting they can't do their jobs. I completely agree with you, 100 per cent... People are afraid to admit they can't do their job, because they'll get fired. (Director of Human Resources)

Table 7.5 The catch 22 and the cycle of denial

1. Plan had to be met
2. It was each manager's job to contribute to making plan. Their livelihood (that is, keeping their jobs, making their bonuses and being promoted), depended on it
3. Plan was based on unrealistic financial expectations
4. In order to make plan, managers compromised personal and/or operational integrity
5. 'Integrity' was an espoused corporate value that could not be violated
6. People who were candid about integrity violations were silenced in a variety of ways (for example, the requirement that they achieve the same result in a different manner, and being 'labelled')
7. Short of time and resources, emphasis was placed on creating the perception of a positive reality
8. In order to maintain this perception, the directors had to deny how plan was being made

The *catch 22* began with plan; plan objectives were imposed and it was assumed they had to be met. It was each manager's job to contribute to plan; managers who didn't achieve plan objectives put their job security and bonuses at risk. The assumption by managers at all levels was, 'if I can't do it, they'll find someone else who can'. Plan objectives, however, were based on unrealistic financial assumptions (for example, sales levels, managers per unit, labour costs). In order to make plan, decisions were made that negatively impacted ('violated') customers and employees. Many managers saw this as compromising personal and/or operational integrity. Integrity, however, was an espoused corporate value. It was each managers job to deliver plan results without committing integrity violations. When managers pointed out such violations, they were expected to deliver the same results in a different manner.

Ironically, candour and challenging the process were also espoused corporate values. Yet, a common home office sentiment was; 'the best thing to do is to keep your mouth shut, you just bite your tongue and hopefully someone else will take care of it' (finance revolution meeting, 10 April 1992). One human resource manager explained, 'people who raise problems become problems' (9 October 1992). Another stated:

> Keeping it quiet keeps your reputation intact... People fall out of favour. Perceptions are huge. It's face time... You do your job and be quiet, there will be times when it's acceptable to say this, but it's not in a room where there's levels of management. You don't want to be the person who continually challenges the process... Know your place... You learn your place real quick. (25 June 1992)

Short of time and financial resources to consider alternatives and with personal bonuses and careers at stake, most senior managers chose not to try to resolve core problems. Instead, they focused on creating the impression of a 'positive' reality. This was achieved through what they espoused in the values statements, mystery-shopper scores, and the financial results they tracked.

As a result of all of these factors, the Vice-president and the Directors (more often than not) denied the problems the organisation was having. At the very least, they were unwilling to challenge plan and its associated assumptions, and this made fundamental change impossible. Rather than resulting in customer, quality/process, or employee-focused empowerment, a cost/productivity-focused strategy continued to predominate. This in turn resulted in the ongoing pursuit of growth through new unit development while unit sales, customer service, product quality, and the physical plant continued to decline. Company outsiders were left questioning why the organisation continued to build restaurants when 'it was getting tougher to bring customers through the door'.

CONCLUSION

Clearly, the type of empowerment being practised most often in this organisation was a long way from the radical personal and social change suggested by Vaines (1993), Morgaine (1993) and Rappaport (1986). The limited power-sharing approach described by Conger and Kanungo (1988) came closest to matching what was found here. It was not the type of empowerment the employees wanted, but was the only type the organisation would allow them to have. And of course, cost/productivity-focused empowerment was not really empowerment at all. As one employee suggested, in this organisation empowerment 'was a nice word for slavery in the '90s'.

This study helped reveal deep cultural barriers to empowerment within an organisational setting. In doing so it has provided empirical support for the arguments of Bandura (1986), Nightingale (1982) and Nord (1975), who raised the issue of organisational goals and their influence on employee self-efficacy and empowerment. The experience of employees within this organisation additionally suggests, however, that not only do the organisation's goals and values need to be aligned with those of its employees, but so do related assumptions such as those concerning the means of goal achievement.

Lastly, the cynicism, distrust and confusion experienced by this organisation's employees helped identify a subtle yet powerful barrier to empowerment; rhetoric and confusion pertaining to the word itself. As the word empowerment became embedded within the directors' mixed messages and cycle of denial, it ironically became a barrier to its own achievement. The typology that was developed to help explain this confusion may prove useful in making sense of the empowerment rhetoric found within other organisations. By understanding these barriers perhaps other organisations will have more success at implementing customer, quality/process or employee-focused empowerment strategies.

References

Bandura, A. (1986) *Social Foundations of Thought and Action: A Social-cognitive View* (Englewood Cliffs, N.J.: Prentice-Hall).
Bandura, A. (1977) 'Self-efficacy: Toward a Unifying Theory of Behavioral Change', *Psychological Review*, vol. 84(2), pp. 191–215.
Block, P. (1987) *The Empowered Manager* (San Francisco: Jossey-Bass).
Conger, J.A. and Kanungo, R.N. (1988) 'The Empowerment Process: Integrating Theory and Practice', *Academy of Management Review*, vol. 13(3), pp. 471–82.

Deci, E.L. (1975) *Intrinsic Motivation* (New York: Plenum).
Fetterman, D.M. (1989) *Ethnography: Step by Step* (Newbury Park, Cal.: Sage).
Gandz, J. (1990) 'The Employee Empowerment Era', *Business Quarterly*, vol. 55(2), pp. 74–9.
Hellriegal, D. Slocum, J.W. and Woodman, R. (1992) *Organizational Behaviour*, 6th edn. (St Paul, Minn.: West Publishing Co.).
Kouzes, J.M. and Posner, B.Z. (1987) *The Leadership Challenge* (San Francisco: Jossey Bass).
Lincoln, Y.S. and Guba, E.G. (1985) *Naturalistic Inquiry* (Beverly Hills, Cal.: Sage).
Morgaine, C.A. (1993) 'A Language of Empowerment', *Home Economics Forum*, vol. 6(2), pp. 15–20.
Nightingale D.V. (1982) *Workplace Democracy* (Toronto: University of Toronto Press).
Nord, W.R. (1975) 'Economic and Socio-cultural Barriers to Humanizing Organizations', in C.C. Thomas (ed.), *Humanizing Organizational Behaviour* (Springfield, Ill.: Charles C. Thomas), pp. 175–93.
Pfeffer J. (1981) *Power in Organizations* (Marshfield, Mass.: Pitman).
Rappaport, J. (1986) 'Collaborating for Empowerment: Creating the Language of Mutual Help', in H.D. Boyet and F. Reissman (eds), *The New Populism: The Politics of Empowerment* (Philadelphia: Temple University Press), pp. 64–79.
Sparrowe, R.T. (1993) 'Empowerment in the Hospitality Industry: An Exploration of Antecedents and Outcomes', working paper, Roosevelt University, Chicago, Illinois.
Thomas K.W. and Velthouse, B.A. (1990) 'Cognitive Elements of Empowerment: An "Interpretive" Model of Intrinsic Task Motivation', *Academy of Management Review*, vol. 15(4), pp. 666–81.
Vaines, E. (1993) 'An Empowerment Orientation for Home Economics', *Home Economics Forum*, vol. 6(2), pp. 21–5.

8 Empowerment and Teams: Ethics and the Implementation of Socio-technical Systems
Ian McLoughlin, Richard Badham and Paul Couchman

> Ethical system design is trying for an ideal, but it also has to recognise the art of the possible. If the philosophy and actions of the systems designer ensure that the new system is 'better' in human terms than it would otherwise have been, a great deal has been achieved. Although large gains should be striven for, small gains should not be regarded as less than satisfactory.
>
> (*Mumford, 1996, p. 106*)

INTRODUCTION

Self-managing, self-directed or empowered work teams have become a core feature of contemporary organisational and work redesign (Orsburn *et al.*, 1991; Lawler *et al.*, 1995; Knapp *et al.*, 1996; Wellins *et al.*, 1996). However, their application has been controversial. For promoters of socio-technical system design they represent a radical break from 'inhumane' Tayloristic and Fordist work design and a means by which genuinely empowered and autonomous work can be brought about. For critics, team-based working represents a new and more manipulative form of management control whereby workers become complicit in their own exploitation. The apparent 'ethical ambiguity' surrounding current trends towards team-based working and empowerment raises serious questions for system designers and change agents seeking to intervene in organisations along lines promoted by socio-technical theory.

This chapter explores the ethics of intervention in the design and implementation of new work systems by examining the experiences of socio-technical researchers engaged in a project to introduce team based cellular manufacturing in three Australian firms. The project aimed to introduce 'smart' as opposed to 'intelligent' manufacturing techniques. The latter approach emphasises the use of advanced technology to replace the need for informed human intervention whilst the former stresses the optimisation of social and technical systems in a complementary relationship (hence the project became known as the 'SMART project'). We begin by noting the revival of interest in socio-technical change and review the case made recently by Enid Mumford – a leading figure in socio-technical theory and practice since the 1960s – for regarding such an approach as 'ethical'. Some critical points are then made concerning the role of system designers and change agents as conceptualised in socio-technical theory. The nature and objectives of the SMART project in the participating companies are then outlined, the improvements in employees' working lives and organisational efficiency assessed, and the role played by system designers and change agents examined. As we will show, the experience of the project revealed a process of change which was messy and political and change outcomes were uneven, limited in scope and sometimes unintended. At the same time, contrary to the 'ethical' prescription of socio-technical change theory, it became necessary for both internal and external change agents to intervene in the political and cultural systems of the organisations concerned. We conclude by assessing both the outcomes of the project and the role of change agents in relation to Legge's recent discussion of the ethics of 'human resource management' (Legge, 1996).

THE REVIVAL OF SOCIO-TECHNICAL CHANGE

Whilst socio-technical ideas are not new and have enjoyed considerable currency in the past, it is now conventional wisdom that modern production conditions – driven in particular by changes in product markets, technology and work-related legislation, favour the diffusion of autonomous team-based working far more than ever before. As a result, strategic rather than operational importance is said to be attached to team-based forms of work by management. For some this is, or at least ought to be, a key difference marking off team-based working and empowerment initiatives of the 1980s and 1990s from their predecessors of the 1960s and 1970s (Buchanan, 1994).

Team-based cellular manufacturing (TBCM) is one such initiative and has attracted considerable contemporary interest in Europe, North America and the Asia–Pacific region. In manufacturing, TBCM involves the grouping of machines (lathes, drills, presses and so on) into groups (cells) according to the particular processes and their sequence which are required to produce parts or families of parts. The 'technical' redesign of production in this way creates the potential, it is argued, for the 'social' redesign of work so that the tasks performed in the cells can be undertaken by workers operating as a semi-autonomous team. For this to occur cell members need to become multi-skilled (for example, in order to operate different machines and carry out maintenance tasks) and empowered to take day-to-day operating decisions (for example, in the planning, execution and monitoring of cell operations).

In place of the traditional first line supervisor, teams have 'leaders', who may be elected by other team members rather than appointed by management. In addition, teams may be able to stop production as and when they see necessary to discuss work-related problems and so on. In their most advanced form, team-based cells might have considerable responsibility for interfacing with their environment to the extent that they have direct contact with 'customers' both inside and outside the organisation. Ultimately they might operate, in effect, as mini-business units themselves. The upshot is an approach to the design of the technical and social aspects of production which, it is claimed, is radically different to the traditional layout of machines by function and the organisation and control of work according to the 'Taylorist' principles of a detailed division of labour and hierarchical supervision. It is this view of the characteristics and possibilities of TBCM and similar initiatives that have made them attractive to those interested in promoting more human-centred, humanised or socio-technical approaches to work redesign.

THE ETHICS OF SOCIO-TECHNICAL SYSTEM DESIGN

According to Enid Mumford the ethical basis of socio-technical systems design rests on its capacity to address the problem of increasing the autonomy and freedom of employees whilst at the same time attending to the economic and efficiency goals of the employing organisation. Following Mumford, five 'implicit contracts' which make-up the employment relationship can be identified:[1]

1. The *knowledge contract*: this addresses how the individual employee and the organisation learn or gain from learning.
2. The *psychological contract*: this addresses the employee need for non-pay rewards such as achievement, responsibility, job satisfaction

and career advancement, and the employer concern to have a loyal and motivated workforce.
3. The *efficiency contract*: this addresses the employee interest in receiving appropriate rewards (in particular monetary rewards) in exchange for performing their jobs efficiently, and the employer concern to improve productivity and performance.
4. The *task structure contract*: this addresses the employee concern for tasks which have interest, variety and are challenging, and the employer need for employees prepared to work with new technologies, techniques and forms of work organisation.
5. The *values contract*: addresses the employee interest in working for any employer whose values and ethics do not contravene their own, and the employer interest in having employees who identify with organisational goals and objectives.

Socio-technical system design is concerned with the joint optimisation of the goals of human 'freedom' and economic 'efficiency' in terms of these five dimensions of the employment contract. According to Mumford, optimising these goals generates a series of questions which system designers and change agents need to find positive answers to if the consequences of their efforts are to be judged 'ethical' (Mumford, 1996, pp. 26–9). For example, in relation to the *knowledge contract* a key question is whether new socio-technical systems allow employees to apply their skills and knowledge, for example by ensuring that appropriate training and other opportunities for learning are provided by the organisation. In the case of the *psychological contract* a critical question is whether employees perceive their new jobs and work organisation as more satisfying and employers view the workforce as more committed to organisational goals and objectives. The *efficiency contract* highlights the question of whether payment and performance measurement systems support high standards of quality and output. The *task structure contract* focuses attention on the question of whether new job and work organisation design increases the autonomy and control of employees. Finally, the *values contract* raises questions such as whether consultation, participation and bargaining over the design and implementation of systems increase employee support for change.

According to Mumford, the more system designer/change agents are able to make choices and decisions which resolve these contractual issues positively, the more human-centred and efficiency objectives are likely to be satisfied by socio-technical system design. However to achieve this, she argues, system designers and change agents need to approach their task with 'ethical integrity' represented by 'good will and sincerity' (Mumford, 1996, p. 28). In practice this means such things as: applying principles of participation to get user-involvement in design, ensuring the representation of both direct and indirect user-interests regardless of status, hierarchical position or social background and, creating circumstances in which 'good communications' can occur through 'group facilitation' ((Mumford, 1996, pp. 57–8, 87, 90). All of this adds up to a 'new role and philosophy' for the role of the system designer/change agent:

> Our human-centred systems designer will think carefully about the people aspects of system-design, will be concerned with the needs of others and will have a group rather than an individual focus. Relationships will be seen as a series of circles, loops and networks rather than as lines of authority. There will be an awareness of how events and relationships influence each other over time as part of a continuous dynamic process of innovation and change. Our systems designer will accept mistakes, problems and uncertainties as valuable learning experiences. Whenever possible, these will be brought into the open, discussed and examined without attribution of blame or penalty. Doing this will reduce the occurrence of errors in the future. (Mumford, 1996, p. 100)

Mumford realises that the moral worth of the change agent's intention and conduct does not guarantee successful implementation in itself. Where organisational circumstances are not receptive to socio-technical system design principles, perhaps because of resistance from some interest groups, she suggests the system designer/change agent has to behave tactically and 'seek the middle ground'. This may involve the offer of advice on how to improve existing systems rather than trying to encourage radically new ones, seeking to bring differences and conflicts into the open so that the change agent can act as a 'mediator' and, if possible, enrolling senior management support against 'hardliners' (1996, p. 101). Mumford also accepts that socio-technical design solutions may advantage some groups but disadvantage others, enable increased technological control of workers, increase visibility and surveillance possibilities, and even threaten jobs. Here it is vital for the system designer/change agent to establish and maintain 'trust' through openness, even-handedness and honesty. In particular the interests of one stakeholder group must not be placed above another, and if this becomes unavoidable the reasons why should be clearly explained to all. Above all, the system designer/change agent must be prepared to temper socio-technical ideals with appropriate levels of pragmatism (Mumford, 1996, p. 106).

SOCIO-TECHNICAL SYSTEM DESIGN AND ORGANISATIONAL POLITICS

The socio-technical approach has its origins in the human relations movement in the USA during the 1940s and 1950s, and the socio-technical school which became associated with the Tavistock Institute in the UK during late 1950s and 1960s (Mumford, 1996). This 'traditional' approach has long emphasised the central importance of focusing on both technology and organisation at one and the same time in the creation of new techno-organisational systems. However, in practice it has tended to focus on organisation rather than technology and has had little to say about the detailed shaping of technological change (van Einjatten, 1993; Badham and Naschold, 1994). At the same time, concepts of organisation have tended to draw on systems ideas which have stressed equilibrium and stability as the norm and competing interests and conflict as dysfunctional. Thus, for traditional socio-technical systems theory, the problem of implementing new systems has been viewed as largely one of jointly optimising given 'technical' and 'social' sub-systems (Rose, 1988). As a result there has been little systemic concern to investigate the role of local and internal political processes which serve to configure the implementation and final outcomes of change.

At worst, this supports an elitist perception of 'external' change agent activities, which include those of the organisational development practitioner or the socio-technical consultant, as the province of 'experts' engaged to initiate change in conservative and essentially passive systems. This is often combined with what has been termed the 'truth, trust, love and collaboration' (Pettigrew, 1985) approach to the 'soft' people and organisational issues in change management. This combination can foster a high-minded ethical 'God complex' amongst self-appointed change agents who downplay the inherently controversial political processes involved in the negotiation of the technical and organisational outcomes and seek to impose their 'one-best' ethical way.

To some extent these issues have been more adequately addressed by a range of continental European and other socio-technical theorists and practitioners who have broadened the socio-technical constituency considerably since the 1980s. These approaches have sought, in various ways, to develop alternatives not only to Taylorist/Fordist work design but also the now much vaunted 'lean production' model (Badham, 1994; Mathews, 1994). Here attention has been given to specifying and incorporating human-centred design principles into both technical and social systems; recognition that the application of socio-technical principles is not appropriate in all national circumstances – for example those lacking a higher skill-base or established trade union structure; and that there are substantial constraints on the full development of a human-centred trajectory, such as the resistance of existing Taylorist/Fordist forms of organisation and 'unintended' threats to jobs and working life posed by team-working, such as increased worker stress (Badham, 1994, pp. 45–8). Similarly, the role of the change agents and the politics of organisations and change has been more effectively addressed. However, the full implications of the political dynamics of organisational systems and change projects remain underdeveloped in socio-technical theory and methodology. One consequence, is that the implications for the role and expertise of socio-technical system designers and change agents of the political dynamics and context of attempting to put these ideas into practice has not been adequately specified.

We have argued elsewhere that, by their nature, socio-technical projects tend to cut across horizontal and vertical boundaries within organisations and impinge upon the interests of a broad range of 'stakeholders' who may perceive a variety of 'threats' and 'opportunities' (Badham *et al.*, 1997). More so than projects whose focus is mainly on the technical dimensions of change, socio-technical projects are characterised by political negotiations, alliances and compromises. As such, they are particularly vulnerable to organisational disturbances and micro-political disruptions. Moreover, it is this activity which can impose severe strains on project teams as apparently clear general directives become bogged down in a myriad of details and compromises. The uncertainty, frustration and potential for sabotage involved in the lengthy processes of resolving such issues is a further factor which considerably enhances the vulnerability of such projects. In our view, such circumstances mean that the final nature of implemented change and its impact on productivity, working conditions and so on will be influenced in crucial ways by how conflicts and compromises are managed and resolved during the change process.

All of this has considerable implications for system designers/change agents and the ethics of their role. One implication of our analysis, for example, is that rather than avoid as far as is possible intervention in the political and cultural systems of an organisation as traditional socio-technical theory advocates, the success of socio-technical system design may depend, in part at least, on the capacity of system designers and change agents to *actively* engage with and manage the political process which ultimately directs change and shapes its outcomes within organisations (McLoughlin, 1993). Indeed, a failure to adequately address the organisational complexities and, in particular, the political aspects of socio-technical change may well go some way to explaining the frequent documentation of the restricted impact of most work humanisation and 'socio-technical' work redesign projects (see for example, Kelly, 1982; Badham and Naschold, 1994).

THE SMART PROJECT

The focus of the SMART (Smart Manufacturing Techniques Team Based Cellular Manufacturing) project was on the practical integration of technical and organizational aspects in the design and implementation of socio-technical systems. The project was called 'SMART' to contrast it with the more conventional view of 'intelligent' manufacturing systems. According to this latter view, 'intelligent' manufacturing is identified with machines incorporating artificial intelligence which are capable of coping with complex and changing conditions, and hence refers to high levels of automation and the automatic control of production operations consistent with a Taylorist/Fordist approach. By contrast the 'SMART' approach, inspired by European human-centred socio-technical design principles (see for example Wobbe, 1995), aspired to the creation of adaptable and flexible systems that support rather than undermine the responsibility and creativity of skilled operators. Through this approach it was believed that, in the Australian context, the twin goals of increased international competitiveness and more humane work could be addressed.

The project was carried out over two years, from early 1993 to March 1995, by collaborators from four research institutions who conducted action research in three partner companies in the manufacturing sector. The companies were: Koala Irrigation a manufacturer of plastic irrigation systems; Wombat Plastics, a division of the Australian operation of an international motor company, that supplied plastics components for local car assembly; and Kangaroo White Goods, part of an international domestic appliance company that manufactured whitegoods and floor care products. The research collaborators worked in Australian universities and Federal and State government research organisations and had skills and knowledge in the areas of manufacturing systems design and organisational analysis. The overall project was funded by the companies and the Australian Department of Industry, Technology and Commerce. At the end of the action research stage a summative study was undertaken to produce case studies of the three projects. These were supplemented in late 1996 by a follow-up site visit to two of the companies and interviews with company and other personnel involved in the original project.[2]

Project objectives in each company

In each case specific objectives were agreed with the companies for the introduction of TBCM which were appropriate to their context. A key factor here was differences in terms of experience of socio-technical approaches and more generally in terms of the extent of previous innovations in work design and manufacturing methods.

Koala Irrigation

Koala was the most experienced of the three partner companies in the application of socio-technical design principles. Although a new facility built in the late 1980s, the factory was originally laid out in conventional Taylorist/Fordist form with assembly lines arranged according to function. Work on the lines was low skilled and repetitive, accomplished mainly by women many of whom, because of the seasonal and unpredictable nature of the company's product market, were on temporary employment contracts. Skilled work was undertaken by male workers in an injection moulding shop and toolroom both of which were physically separated from the assembly area. As one would expect, management and supervision were organised in a hierarchical command and control structure. The overall effect, was often described by employees as, 'you came to work, left your brains at the door'.

However, a major business crisis in 1990 prompted the introduction of TBCM in a radical attempt to 'turn around' the manufacturing operation. This was given added momentum by the receipt of an Australian Federal Government 'Best Practice' Grant for the period 1990–93. This was used by the company to further develop the programme and to contribute to the creation of semi-autonomous work groups. The ultimate goal was set out as follows:

> ... each cell will manufacture parts of a product or a whole product from given raw material as completely as possible. The necessary machinery, tools and fixtures are to be located and administered within the unit. The workteam has to be able to perform as much self regulation as possible for all kinds of work and coordination procedures, planning, decision making and control functions within given boundaries. (Internal Company Documents)

By the end of 1992, the assembly lines had been replaced by seven cells – beginning initially with two pilot cells. During this period the physical barriers between the moulding shop and the assembly area were also removed and subsequently the die setters, who set up the machines, were allocated to individual cell teams.

From the company's viewpoint, involvement in the SMART project was seen as a further means by which this already well-developed philosophy on the development of team-based working could be extended. For the SMART project, involvement also meant an opportunity to learn in the context of an already up and running programme. After an initial evaluation of the progress made towards TBCM under the 'Best Practice' programme, SMART researchers focused on the further development of one of the cells around a new product innovation. Subsequently the project researchers contributed in other ways to ongoing change at the plant, in particular in relation to the development of new performance measures and to an attempt to re-focus managerial activities on coaching cell teams.

Wombat Plastics

Like Koala, Wombat Plastics, also had prior experience of workplace innovation, which in this case extended back to the mid-1980s. This had started initially under a corporate employee-involvement programme and had subsequently been extended through a plant-based quality improvement project. This project was driven by an innovative plant manager and was reported as having made considerable progress in developing team-led quality and productivity improvements. A key element of this had been the creation of WAGs (work area groups) consisting of teams of 8 to 20 operators performing a role similar to quality circles. This and other workplace innovations had marked the factory out as a significant arena of change in the Australian automobile industry. One independent Federal Government sponsored study had gone as far as to claim the plant was a 'veritable laboratory of workplace innovation' and as 'engaging directly with the establishment of genuine self-managing teams or semi-autonomous work groups'.

The SMART project sought to take advantage of this innovative environment to redesign the assembly process for the instrument panel or 'dashboard' for a new car model being introduced by the Australian parent company. This would involve replacing a single machine-paced production line with a cellular assembly process involving autonomous teams.

Kangaroo Whitegoods

On the face of it Kangaroo Whitegoods looked the least fertile ground upon which to introduce human-centred socio-technical ideas. Manufacturing had not been the focus of such extensive experimentation and innovation as in the other two cases. Work on the main assembly lines remained labour intensive with little automation. Where innovation had occurred, for example with just-in-time manufacturing and a form of quality circle (known in the company as 'VAM groups'), success had been limited and many problems persisted. The plant's press shop rather than main assembly areas was chosen as the location for the SMART project. A key reason for this was the existence of plans drawn up internally, but which had never been implemented, to introduce a cellular layout of machinery in the shop. The objectives of the project were to incorporate socio-technical principles in job redesign models that spelt out the various options concerning how teams in the shop might be organised around a cellular configuration of the press machinery. At the lowest level this would involve no more than some enlargement of team members' jobs. At the highest levels the teams would be fully autonomous and effectively a 'business within a business' thus incorporating indirect tasks and decision-making responsibilities from other areas within the press shop and beyond.

The outcomes of change in the three companies

In each of the three companies the outcomes of change were at variance to varying degrees with those anticipated. In the case of Koala, for example, more or less from the start of the introduction of TBCM, changing contextual factors such as market conditions, alterations in head office product strategy, turnover of plant management, and other corporate changes – which culminated in late 1996 with the prospective sale of the company – all combined to either slow the pace of change, deflect it from its intended course or, stall it completely. Even by late 1996 only three of the seven cell teams could be said to be fully self-managing and functioning autonomously, and the contribution of the SMART project became obscured within an overall complex of change which was often disrupted and diverted.

At Wombat outcomes turned out to be far different to those initially envisaged. After intensive efforts in the first half of 1993, plans to cellularise the instrument panel line were eventually abandoned by the plant management. By the end of 1993 all such initiatives had officially been put 'on hold' pending broader developments in the business involving a prospective sale of the plant to another company (which eventually took place in 1995). From this point the energies of the SMART researchers were directed elsewhere to minor evaluation projects concerned with productivity improvement. Subsequently the company was to use the cell concept – but without the involvement of the SMART researchers – in the assembly process for the instrument panels of 'carry over' models (versions of the existing model that were not being immediately replaced). Ironically, this was a suggestion made by the SMART researchers when plans to cellularise the existing instrument panel assembly line were scrapped.

In the case of Kangaroo Whitegoods, by the end of the project in March 1995, one pilot cell team had been introduced and trained and the press machines moved to create four other cells. Even this outcome was often uncertain and further doubt over the future of TBCM was created by the takeover of the company and the introduction of a new senior management team. In the event these fears proved unfounded and eighteen months after the conclusion of the project the change programme had been sustained by what turned out to be the supportive approach of the new management. By this point the five cells planned for during the SMART project had been reduced to three in number. The original pilot cell, and a further cell – both of which were now seen by management to be functioning more or less as self-managing teams – and a third 'cell' which seemed to be a residual grouping of remaining staff which could only loosely be termed a 'team'.

EVALUATING THE SMART PROJECT OUTCOMES AGAINST SOCIO-TECHNICAL DESIGN CRITERIA

To what extent then can the outcomes of the introduction of TBCM in the three organisations be considered as consistent with human-centred socio-technical objectives? We can explore this by examining the nature and consequences of change in terms of the five 'implicit contracts' identified above.

The knowledge contract

To what extent did the design and implementation of TBCM in the three firms allow employees to apply their skills and knowledge and were appropriate training and other opportunities for learning provided?

In the case of Koala Irrigation the answers to these questions are largely affirmative. For example, in the five months after the first cell had been introduced, 138 shop floor employees received 7000 hours of externally sourced off-the-job training, equivalent to 26 hours per person, and at a cost equivalent to 7 per cent of pay-roll. Much of this training was undertaken in a new purpose-built training facility at the plant. However, as the change programme progressed a number of problems emerged. First, training effort had initially mainly been focused on the first three cells. However, subsequent resource constraints arising from head office decisions, meant that even by late 1996 the training of the remaining four cell teams had still not been adequately addressed. Second, the initial experience of training showed that its effectiveness required considerable learning on the part of management, in particular with regard to the assessment of training needs – a process which cell team members needed to be participants in. Finally, by late 1996 it was also becoming apparent to plant management that there was now a need to go back to reinforce the initial training, even in the original pilot cells.

In the case of Wombat the question cannot really be answered at all because of the failure to implement TBCM as planned. In fact, the reality which confronted the SMART researchers at Wombat, contrary to expectations, was rather different to that at Koala. It quickly became clear that workplace reform in the plant had not spread as widely or involved as deep a change as first thought. The WAGs, for example, had not all been implemented and those that had did not all operate successfully. Whatever the shop floor innovations that had occurred, assembly lines in the plant were still governed in the main by 'Taylorist/Fordist' principles, although 'lean production' ideas were also evident. For example, the instrument panel assembly process was accomplished on a conventional line with 24 work stations, each staffed by an individual operator and linked by a moving conveyor. Material handling on the line was automated, work tasks were fragmented and de-skilled, and task execution was machine-paced with low task cycle times (68 seconds). At the same time, the pace and output of the line was determined by the 'pull' of a just-in-time system operating on the final assembly line at the adjacent plant of the parent company. This system imposed on the line strict timescales from receipt of order to delivery as well as rigid quality and test requirements.

In the case of Kangaroo Whitegoods a considerable amount was achieved in equipping cell team members with appropriate skills and knowledge and in providing appropriate training and other learning opportunities. At the start of the project SMART researchers confronted a situation where, hitherto, no investment in off the job training for shop-floor staff had ever been made. At the same time the workforce was multicultural, some 40 non-English speaking nationalities were represented on the shop-floor, and English literacy was a major problem. The amount of training planned for cell team members – 40 hours 'off the job' spread over several weeks – was therefore way beyond the previous commitment shown by the company to investment in the shop-floor. It also lay well outside the criteria previously applied in manufacturing innovation – described in colloquial terms by one production engineer as, 'cost reduction, overhead recovery, great pay back, no investment and fuck all training'! Not surprisingly, as will be discussed below, the scope, timing and cost of the planned training programme in the press shop became a focus of significant contention. As a result, by the completion of the project only the pilot cell team members had received any training and there was considerable uncertainty as to when the training of the remaining four cell teams would commence. However, as the effects of the takeover of the company filtered though after the project had finished, a new policy which viewed training as an investment rather than a cost began to prevail. Encouragingly, 18 months after the end of the project, training of remaining cell members was continuing at a local TAFE (further education) college whilst in general the company had committed itself to raising the educational and skill level of all shop-floor employees.

The psychological contract

How far did the introduction of TBCM result in employees regarding their jobs as more satisfying and management viewing employees as more committed to the organisation?

Koala provides the best basis for an assessment of this question, both because of the scale and maturity of the change that occurred there, but also because detailed information on changes in employee perceptions and attitudes over time were collected as part of the SMART project – something which proved either impossible or not practical to do at the other two companies. The data collected consists of qualitative information from interviews conducted on the shop floor and with plant management. These were undertaken as the Best Practice programme drew to a close in 1993 and again at the end of the SMART project in 1994. Overall, this data clearly shows that the move to cellular manufacture was almost universally received favourably by the assembly workforce.

This said, it was clear that over time employee support had been subject to fluctuation and qualification. For example, the introduction of the first two pilot cells caused resentment amongst those who were not being retrained. This persuaded plant management to move more quickly than planned to implement cells across the shop floor. However, this was done in the absence of adequate engineering or training resources because of other demands also being made by head office. Concerns and some suspicions thus lingered amongst some assembly workers over the demands made upon them by team working as opposed to line working, in particular in relation to their and others' competence to work as members of a team. Around this time management introduced a number of commitment generating changes to their human resource policies and practice. For example, clocking-on was scrapped, and random searches of staff leaving a shift by an armed security guard were stopped. Changes to sick leave provisions and new equal opportunities and child care policies were also subsequently implemented.

However, a major blow to the progress that had been made occurred as a result of a headquarters' decision in early 1993 to make 39 redundancies at the plant because of poor predicted demand following unseasonal weather. This was followed by a process of product rationalisation and the decision – widely opposed in the plant – to import certain products. This affected 90 per cent of the products produced by the second pilot cell whose staffing level was reduced to just two people. These events raised severe doubts in the minds of the workforce as to the real benefits of TBCM. The situation recovered later in the year when it it became apparent that head office marketing forecasts had significantly underestimated the strength of both domestic and export demand. As a result a programme of re-hiring was commenced which doubled the workforce. Nevertheless, at this time the change programme had effectively been stalled and it was early 1995 before forward momentum was to be fully established again.

Finally, it should be noted that, all these developments notwithstanding, trade employees in the moulding, toolroom and maintenance areas remained throughout to varying degrees resistant to the cells concept and the idea of being allocated to cell teams. Concern was expressed, in particular, over loss of status associated with doing assembly work. The gender split between the two groups was also important. For example, the women complained about the male die setters' reluctance to integrate within the teams, their bad language, and the numerous unscheduled 'smokos' (smoke breaks) that they took. The die setters also had unresolved concerns regarding the implications of 'multi-skilling' (which would open them up to doing assembly work in the cell) for pay and career paths.

At the start of the SMART project in Wombat many of the dysfunctions of the assembly line were manifested in operator attitudes and behaviour, and in the general climate of management-employee relations in the plant. On the instrument panel assembly line the operators were seen by management to lack discipline, be poorly motivated, have low commitment to the company, be resistant to change and have high absenteeism rates. It also soon became apparent to the SMART researchers that the extent to which the quality, team work and other involvement innovations were 'voluntary' was also suspect and it was reported that in practice severe industrial relations problems had accompanied their introduction. As already noted, by the end of the project, there was little evidence of major change on the main instrument panel assembly line. More generally the atmosphere in the plant was one of caution and uncertainty in the wake of the planned sale to another company and of revived industrial relations conflict arising from a broader dispute in the Australian automotive sector as a whole. However, the changes to the 'carry over' instrument panel assembly process were reported to have resulted in improved operator commitment and morale.

At Kangaroo, as the SMART project commenced, morale and employee relations in the plant were poor. Trading conditions were difficult, employment levels were frozen and levels of uncertainty had been increased by a major reorganisation of the business that had just been completed. Within the press shop, production management regarded productivity as a major problem and external consultants had been brought in to conduct an efficiency review. This exercise had a further adverse effect on morale in the shop and had never been completed. The failure to implement the existing plans to cellularise the shop were also put down in large part to anticipated industrial relations problems. By the end of the project morale in the shop had significantly improved with members of the pilot cell having been won over to TBCM. At this point the remaining cell members were anxious to begin their own training. Some 18 months later, commitment to TBCM was said to be high amongst those in cells one and two. Some employees in the third 'cell team' were more resistant. Here, according to the shop supervisor, there were still 'hard nuts to crack' if everyone was to be won over to the concept. Outside of the cells, other supervisory staff had adapted well to their new role of supporting the teams, although toolmakers remained resistant to and outside of the cellular way of working.

The task structure contract

To what extent did the design and implementation of TBCM in the three firms increase task variety and employee control over their immediate work environment?

At Koala the assembly tasks in the cells remained repetitive and low-skilled after the introduction of TBCM but team members were now able to allocate tasks and rotate jobs as they saw fit. Increased empowerment also required them to take on more indirect functions, such as production planning. Management at the plant were engaged in a continual process to encourage the teams to take responsibility for solving problems rather than refer them elsewhere for solution. However, there was reluctance amongst some team members to fully engage in this process. This broadly reflected the differences in levels of training noted above and as a result the extent of team working and self-management across the cells was varied. At the same time, the integration of the die setters into cells remained problematic. The toolroom remained separate from the assembly area and outside of the cellularisation process. However, in late 1996 organisational changes meant that plans to allocate toolmakers to the cell teams were being contemplated as a first step in the process of integrating the 'toolies' into the cells.

Initially at Wombat, in collaboration with the SMART researchers, a set of evaluation criteria were developed by company engineers. These incorporated human-centred design principles which were then used to assess alternative production system options. These ranged from a modified single moving assembly line through to a cellular approach were each panel was assembled in full by one team member. Options such as the latter would have to be 'decoupled' from the just-in-time system of the main assembly line by 'buffer stocks'. An immediate and never resolved difficulty that this kind of option involved was caused by the size of the new instrument panel itself (two metres in length) and the number of variants that had to be made (over 20). This meant that cellular assembly would need to be accompanied by large areas of floor space to accommodate finished and part-finished panels and the full range of components to assemble each variant. Alongside this, company engineers on the redesign team were never fully convinced that the cellular approach had inherent advantages over the moving assembly line and no commitment to move to cellular manufacture was ever agreed. However, it was accepted that the design solution should allow operators to hold unscheduled meetings of a maximum of 30 minutes duration without upsetting delivery requirements dictated by the just-in-time system.

Ultimately, in the context of impending corporate changes but also a pressing implementation deadline for the 'ramp up' of production of the new model, none of these ideas were to be implemented. Instead, the existing conventional assembly line was slightly modified to incorporate a four-work-station cell which was set up to carry out initial stages in the assembly process. There were no buffers introduced and the pace of work was still dictated by the 'pull' of the parent plant final assembly line. Moreover, in practice, anecdotal evidence suggested that the line's WAGs were rarely if ever able to call unscheduled stoppages of the line. In contrast, the new assembly process for 'carry over' model instrument panels comprised a single station where one of four operators (one team leader plus three operators) built the panel to completion. Operators were responsible for carrying out their own inspection and quality control and the team leader communicated directly with the final assembly line customer on matters concerning quality and delivery. The cell layout permitted communication between cell members who were free to collaborate on work tasks and to discuss and resolve production problems.

In the case of Kangaroo, press operation after cellularisation also remained a low-skill activity requiring dexterities such as good eye, hand and foot coordination, and for the operation of the larger presses, considerable physical strength. However, whereas prior to cellularisation operators had little discretion and worked under a management hierarchy of leading hands, foreman and a shop supervisor, a considerable expansion in task range and discretion had taken place within two of the three cell teams. For example, operators now undertook material management tasks in the cell, some maintenance work and were also now responsible for quality. The cell team leaders also had responsibility for machine set-up, scheduling, maintenance and involvement in other boundary management tasks.

The efficiency contract

What were the implications of the introduction of TBCM for quality performance and productivity in the three plants? How far did employees enjoy financial rewards as a result of the changes that occurred?

Since it opened, the Koala plant had not become profitable. One problem had been the transfer of production from another plant and a lack of planning and training had resulted in severe supply problems and strained customer relations. This had resulted in warranty problems and the loss of some major contracts. Within the plant performance information and controls were rudimentary and chaotic, labour utilisation was poor, quality problems were acute, and there were millions of dollars of work in progress (WIP) and finished goods stock scattered throughout the plant. From a head office viewpoint the plant was 'something they had to have but a bloody nuisance'. At the same time, increasing availability of cheap and good quality imports offered an opportunity to place more emphasis on the marketing strengths of the business by buying in products under the company brand. For plant management, the success of the introduction of TBCM was vital if the manufacturing capability within the company was not to be severely circumscribed or even discontinued.

By the end of the SMART project, considerable improvements in performance had been achieved and profitability had returned to the company as a whole. However, headquarters accounting methods meant that the benefits of TBCM were not fully recognised outside the plant. These methods were seen by plant management as too concerned with counting 'golden eggs' and insufficiently concerned with improvement being made to the 'health and well-being of the goose'. For example, headquarters saw labour efficiency (measured as variance in time taken to actually perform work from the standard times produced by work study measures) as the key performance measure. One difficulty with this was that it militated against attempts at sustaining continuous improvement activities within the cell teams since time spent on such work would increase labour variances, whilst any benefits were not necessarily reflected in the way performance was measured or directly attributable to the efforts of team members. Thus many real improvements seen by management at the plant went unrecorded and unrecognised at head office, whilst cell teams had poor feedback and ambiguous information with which to assess their own efforts. Partly as a result of work conducted by the SMART researchers, a number of new key performance indicators and procedures were eventually introduced at plant level – although not fully endorsed by headquarters – to more accurately assess the effectiveness of the cell teams and to feedback information to them.

At Wombat, the existing assembly line was recognised by management to be badly balanced, overmanned, prone to quality problems and subject to too many highly expensive unscheduled stoppages. These efficiency problems were exacerbated by the punitive costs of such stoppages – a one minute stop costing in the order of $5000. In addition, through the just-in-time system the mother plant applied stringent requirements concerning quality of the finished product. The company had not allocated funds as part of the new model launch to redesign the instrument panel assembly process and, although other resources could have been redirected to this activity, no consensus over the priority to do this – for example to free floor space to allow initial training of staff or to permit cellularisation of the assembly process – was ever reached.

Ironically the cell responsible for assembling the 'carry over' model panels, after a 'teething' period in which a number of operational, delivery and efficiency problems were encountered, achieved several efficiency gains. These included greatly improved product quality, cheaper initial build costs, and reduced absenteeism. A change from JIT production to batch production was now planned to improve operator productivity – 70 per cent of that of the old assembly line. The change to batch production would eliminate the need for a 'stockman' to replenish stocks since this task would now be accomplished by the team. The result was predicted to be productivity levels consistent with the old assembly line.

In the case of Kangaroo the productivity problem within the press shop was largely a function of inappropriate measures and inaccurate reporting within a management information system which was fragmented and ineffective. This argument, however, proved a difficult one to win in the context of a highly conventional manufacturing management and reporting structure. For example, devising new performance measures for the press shop cell teams was identified as a key non-technical redesign objective. In the event the deliberations over this were highly abbreviated by a production engineer who saw no reason to spend time on the issue. Subsequently, however, the cell teams were given the task of devising appropriate performance measures. More generally, after the project finished the new management team introduced changes which streamlined the management reporting system and made it more transparent. One result was a clear devolution of accountability to areas where responsibility for action was located within a framework of much tighter financial controls.

In all three cases, reform of the national industrial relations framework underpinned workplace level change,[3] and also brought rewards to the workforce as a whole in each plant. For example, in the case of Koala, the changes facilitated by enterprise bargaining meant that, by the end of the SMART project, shop floor rates were now 10.5 per cent above those in the national award. Subsequently, in recognition that the link between rewards and performance improvement made through TBCM was still weak (for example a loading had been negotiated for members performing the team leader/spokesperson role but this was a 'rate for the job' rather than performance related), new performance measures were linked to a gain-sharing scheme based on a one-third split between employee bonus, new investment and profit. At Wombat agreement between employers and unions to vary the national award covering the industry as a whole resulted in an initial across-the-board 3 per cent increase in wages, followed by a further 3 per cent once productivity enhancing negotiations were completed. Similarly, at Kangaroo agreement was reached at enterprise level to provide for an immediate 1.5 per cent increase followed by three further phased increases of 1.5 per cent in return for acceptance of important enabling clauses that permitted a move to team-based working. However, subsequent problems in reaching new classifications for team leaders and cell operators – the former issue in particular being a longstanding one – meant that the anticipated upgrading of these jobs had still not been achieved some eighteen months after the project's conclusion.

The value contract

How were employees consulted about the design and implementation of TBCM in the three companies and how far did communication, consultation and negotiation improve employee support for the change process?

At Koala the Best Practice programme was endorsed in a Memorandum of Understanding between the company and the site union that outlined the direction, goals, objectives and key issue to be confronted by the project. In addition, plans for the implementation of the project were developed in consultation with shop stewards and a joint union and management project team began work full-time on the actual implementation. As a precursor to reaching the agreement a negotiating committee was formed. This consisted of the plant manager, human resources manager, the senior shop steward, four other union members and one non-union employee. The employee side attended a one day training session which gave them an overview of enterprise bargaining and the negotiating process.

The extent and significance of these formal mechanisms of joint participation were, however, qualified. For instance, there were fears (initially at least) amongst local union officials that collaboration over issues of organisational change between the shop stewards and management at the site might result in 'co-option' if the relationship became too close. Some shop stewards at the plant drew a distinction between the role of the consultative committee and the negotiating committee. The former had been established first and was perceived as 'anti-union' and as a forum in which management 'shot down' employee contributions. The latter, established in response to the national move towards enterprise bargaining, was viewed as a forum within which management 'think more about what we say'. In addition, nominations for elected employees to the consultative committee excluded those serving on existing committees thereby excluding most shop stewards. Hence the union role was seen by the stewards as too limited. This view was endorsed by some employee members of the committee who also suggested that information and communication about change tended to be restricted to the cells themselves. Finally, the joint project committee set up to implement the Best Practice project never became established and was dissolved by management after only a few meetings.

This latter point is significant since it is clear that from an early stage the focus of employee participation in the move to TBCM was the cell teams themselves. This was manifested in a number of ways. First, team members – who had all initially been volunteers – were able to design the layout of their cells. This was facilitated considerably by the simple nature of the assembly processes in which they were engaged, but nevertheless gave a strong sense of 'ownership' at an early stage in the change process. Second, the cell teams' preference for having no appointed team leader and, instead, to elect their own spokesperson was endorsed by management (albeit reluctantly and with some subsequent regret). Third, cell members were trained and involved in bench marking activities. Three operators were twice included in subsequent bench marking visits to companies in the USA. The first trip was informed by a list of questions compiled by the consultative committee from inputs by cell teams and others in the plant. Cell members were also involved in bench marking activities with companies located in Australia.

As the cell teams became established it was recognised by plant management that, although at different levels of development, each was 'well advanced' in the day-to-day management of cell activities and were now seeking more information and support from management. At the same time cell members were increasingly performing 'dual roles' engaged in both production tasks and coordinating and linking activities within and between cell teams and with management. In response, a review of management organisation was conducted, facilitated by SMART researchers. The result was a proposal for a new 'cluster' organisation structure based upon five 'task groups' covering production scheduling, material co-ordination, quality control, administration and communications. Each task group would comprise one member from each cell and a management 'coach'. Cell members would be expected to rotate task groups every 6 to 12 months and would be provided with appropriate training and career paths. Anticipated benefits from the change included improved employee understanding and wider knowledge of manufacturing functions; a shift from reactive to pro-active decision-making; and improved control for the cell members and flexibility for the plant.

However, the new structure did not prove a success. Most of the task groups failed to establish a meaningful purpose and managers had difficulty coming to terms with their role as 'coaches'. One early consequence was that the communications group, in management's eyes at least, effectively replaced the consultative committee since the former provided a far more effective means of passing information rapidly to cell teams and also increased communication between day and afternoon shifts. Within the cells views were more mixed. Some saw the new roles in the task groups as taking the stress away from the spokesperson role as the representative of the cell as a whole. Others were critical of a new division of labour which would lead to specialisation in the cell and tended to make the representative on the scheduling task group the *de facto* leader. Eighteen months after their initial implementation attempts were being made by plant management to persuade the coaches to re-activate their task groups.

At Wombat the design and implementation of the new instrument panel assembly line was the responsibility of a project team which was to include representation from the line. In addition, a stakeholder group was established which would also include the representatives from the lines, a line supervisor, and a union representative. In the event the assembly line representatives were unable to attend the initial meetings of the team, partly because of the fact that time could not be taken off the line to attend meetings. The problem was resolved by rescheduling the project team meetings for late afternoon, once production on the shop floor had stopped for the day. However, none of the assembly line representatives had experience of performing such a role and none spoke English as a first language. This made establishing dialogues with other team members difficult, although towards the end of the team's abortive deliberations the line representatives were able to contribute more effectively as they became familiar with the issues and the role that they could play. The stakeholder group, on the other hand, never met.

Finally, at Kangaroo, the Enterprise Agreement had envisaged that the major vehicle for employee involvement in the move to TBCM would be a reactivated consultative committee (whose constitution was redrafted by one of the SMART researchers). In the event the committee had little influence on the introduction of TBCM in the press shop. Initially press shop employees were informed of the planned changes through a formal presentation by management and SMART project personnel in the works canteen. This was followed-up subsequently – after staff had been selected by the press shop supervisor and put into cell teams – by discussions in the shop VAM groups. One difficulty here was that it proved difficult to obtain the active involvement of the press shop employees in these forums since they had little prior experience of consultative exercises, a lack of training and there were language difficulties.

Significantly, despite representation on the project implementation team and a key sub-group concerned with job design, union representatives did not play a proactive role in the identification of the opportunities and dangers posed by the project. In fact, it was left to the proposed pilot cell team leader, who was co-opted to the project implementation team, to play a vital role in representing the press shop operators and keeping them well-informed on developments. This contributed greatly to the effectiveness of the project team and was viewed by most participants as a major factor in translating the concept of team-based working into practice in the press shop. More generally, despite their lack of direct influence, all parties agreed that the early and full consultation with the trade unions had been an essential and critical factor in the acceptance of change by the workforce.

Summary

The reality of the socio-technical change programmes in the three companies was clearly a messy one where change outcomes were uneven, limited in scope and sometimes unintended. Clear-cut judgements concerning whether the changes achieved improved conditions for employees whilst increasing efficiency and profitability are difficult to make. In terms of our interpretation of Mumford's five implicit contracts there is considerable variation in the degree of improvement that was achieved. The case of Koala showed the most change on the most dimensions, although even here unevenness and a disrupted pattern of change was evident. Kangaroo, always regarded as the most difficult case given the relative lack of prior experience with socio-technical change at the company, showed significant change on several of the five contract dimensions, although again change was more limited in scope and extent than might have been hoped. Encouragingly though, the changes that were achieved looked as though they would be sustained. Finally, in the case of Wombat, despite initial expectations given assumptions made on the basis of the reported history of workplace reform at the plant – the least was achieved. However, even here unintended outcomes did point to improvements in line with socio-technical principles in the assembly of the 'carry-over' instrument panel.

What is clear is that in each case, generic models of the optimum relationship between technical and social systems under TBCM had to be adjusted and altered in a process which configured them to the real and practical circumstances in which they were to be adopted. In these circumstances what might have been ideal from a socio-technical viewpoint was not always obtainable, or even at the forefront when choices and decisions effecting outcomes were made. This draws attention to the considerable amount of what we have termed local 'configurational' activity required on the part of system designers and change agents in order to adapt generic models of socio-technical change such as 'cellular manufacturing' and 'teamwork' to the particular production and organisational environment of a specific enterprise (Badham *et al.*, 1997). It also brings us to the role played by system designers and change agents, both internal to the company and externally in the guise of the SMART researchers themselves.

THE ROLE OF SYSTEM DESIGNERS AND CHANGE AGENTS

As may now be apparent, in each company the application of human-centred design principles proved radical enough to expose conflicts of interest across a variety of horizontal and vertical demarcations within each enterprise. Whilst much of this activity is concerned with what has been termed the *content* and *control* agendas of change – to do with adapting technical systems and managing the project – in vulnerable change projects a *process* agenda also assumes as much if not more importance (Buchanan and Boddy, 1992). The process agenda is partly concerned with the management of the 'people' dimensions of change – communication, trust building, involvement – something frequently recognised in socio-technical theory (note Mumford's position outlined earlier). However, this agenda also addresses the legitimation of both change itself and the role of the change agent through the mobilisation of power resources to intervene in political systems, and the use of symbolic resources to 'manage meaning' in order to influence how these aspects are represented in the organisation's cultural system. Indeed, in each of our three companies the extent to which such legitimacy was established varied as a consequence of the effectiveness of system designers/change agents political activity.

At Koala, for example, the impetus and legitimacy of change were well founded through the actions of in-company change agents prior to the start of the SMART project. The need for change had been identified and initiated through the earlier response of a number of managers to the crisis facing the plant. They formed a broad-based team embracing both key managers at head office and different levels of management within the plant. In its initial stages they actively promoted and supported the move to TBCM, each making different kinds of contribution at key points to the change programme. For example, the Group Manufacturing manager brought experience of cellular manufacturing from the automotive sector. He ensured that the plant was given enough 'space' within the organisation to proceed with radical change. A new plant manager was a major 'driver and motivator' intervening wherever he thought was necessary in leading the implementation of the change programme. He was ably supported in this by other managerial staff, in particular the engineering manager and special project co-ordinator who became well versed in socio-technical theory, and a young head office human resources manager who had novel ideas concerning training.

The significance of these contributions was underlined when, for various reasons and at different times, the chief executive, group manufacturing manager, and plant manager either moved on within the company or left altogether. Increasingly, lacking support from head office, and with an unsympathetic plant manager in charge, the change programme stalled after the end of the Best Practice programme. The appointment of the special projects coordinator as plant manager in late

1994, supported by the engineering manager, was a critical factor in the revitalisation of team-based working that occurred at the plant in the latter stages of the SMART project. Eighteen months later it was clear that whilst head office constraints largely remained, the continuity that had been experienced in plant management since late 1994 was a crucial factor sustaining the changes that had occurred and in the regaining of forward momentum.

In the case of Wombat a rather different situation existed. Much of the earlier change at the plant, as well as the initiation of involvement in the SMART project, had come at the behest of an innovative and enthusiastic plant manager who had established something of a 'guru' reputation in the industry. However, he retired just as the project commenced (to be followed quickly by the recognition of another influential supporter of workplace reform) and was replaced by a more technically focused individual who had a much more 'mechanistic' view of production. The objectives and legitimacy of socio-technical change had to be 're-sold' to this new manager. This proved very difficult for the SMART researchers who had few well-placed allies within the company. It soon became clear that the new manager was never likely to wholeheartedly embrace the proposed change in the manner of his predecessor. Thus the impetus of support for an alternative approach to workplace innovation from the plant's senior management was lost at an early stage. One consequence of this was an absence of clear-cut directives from senior level concerning the redesign of the instrument panel assembly process to the engineering manager and other production engineers. As a result, no clear brief for the project team to pursue socio-technical objectives in collaboration with SMART researchers was given. The latter thus had the status of 'outsiders' whose purpose was never fully realised or understood by system designers and change agents within the company.

This was far from the ideal position from which to challenge the strong engineering and production culture within the company. This saw the moving assembly line as the most efficient design solution for mass production. In the absence of directives to do otherwise, company engineers were inclined to construct problems and seek solutions to them in ways which were consistent with their past design experience. This was particularly so where individual career interests were unlikely to be served by proposing and championing non-standard approaches that ran counter to standard procedure and practice. Thus, even where individual company engineers on the project team developed an empathy for socio-technical objectives they quickly 'reverted to type'.

Socio-technical design principles were ultimately labelled as either intangible, unworkable, or as having benefits which were far outweighed by their costs. Indeed, unknown to either the SMART researchers or the company engineers on the project implementation team, the engineering manager set up a separate group of company engineers to design a more conventional assembly process. The deliberations and existence of the 'official' project team were brought abruptly to a close by the revelation of the design solution proposed by this group. Ironically, this surreptitious attempt was subsequently vetoed by the plant manager since its implementation assumed additional space becoming available following the move of an adjacent production line to another facility. At this point the plant manager imposed a 'fall back' option, as described earlier, of only a slight modification of the existing assembly line.

At Kangaroo Whitegoods, a similar situation initially presented itself. Earlier attempts at manufacturing innovation had been championed by an enthusiastic manufacturing director aided by a young and ambitious production engineer, with an energetic and confrontational style, who led the SMART project implementation team. One immediate achievement of this individual was to intervene in the enterprise bargaining process to ensure that important enabling clauses were inserted in the agreement that would facilitate the move to TBCM. However, when as a result of company re-organisation the manufacturing director left the company, responsibility for the project fell to a new manufacturing manager. His initial views seemed to many not to be supportive, especially as a more or less immediate act was for him to move the confrontational production engineer off the project. At this time he also disbanded the Project Steering Committee whose first and, as it turned out, only meeting coincided with his arrival at the company. For some, these changes did not appear to auger well for the future of the project.

Again, at this point concerted attempts to enroll the new manufacturing manager in the project were made by the SMART researchers. On this occasion, the effort paid off and the new manager appeared to underwrite the project. However, the implementation phase was to prove much slower and the outcomes far more limited than hoped for. In particular, a 14-month delay occurred between the movement of the press machinery into cellular configuration and the commencement of training for the pilot cell. Objections were raised over the cost of the programme, its extent and the effect on press shop productivity of taking operators off the job to train. Many in the project team put the blame for delay on the new manufacturing manager. However, others saw the 'blockage' as being at more senior levels in the organisation, albeit a function in part of the former's failure to promote the project to them. This said, the new manager did play a key role in overcoming initial strong resistance from the human resource manager to industrial relations issues being placed on the project team's agenda (the HR manager's concern was to protect the integrity of the existing regulatory framework rather than have it challenged by the change programme). It is also noteworthy that the new manufacturing manager provided the budget for the training programme, a cost and a risk the human resources manager was happy for him to take. Finally, he provided renewed legitimation for the SMART project team itself in the wake of the departure of their previous 'champion' within the company.

Other sources of resistance and blockage also had to be overcome during the project. At various points the industrial relations manager, press shop supervisor and, in particular, production manager responsible for the press shop sought to frustrate, divert or delay the project. In the former two cases attempts to enroll support and involve these individuals brought positive results, especially in the case of the press shop supervisor who became a key promoter of change both in the latter stages of and beyond the end of the project. In the case of the industrial relations manager, whilst he was successfully recruited to the project team, he was also instrumental in delaying and ultimately frustrating the resolution of the team leader and operator classification issue. In the case of the production manager it was recognised by members of the project team that a failure to address his blocking activity – much of which went unnoticed at the time – had been a major error. Difficulties also emerged with company engineers on the project team using 'technical arguments' and 'local knowledge' to frustrate the pursuit of human-centred objectives, whilst there was a tendency for some key decisions to be taken outside of the team altogether.

As noted above, socio-technical theory views a key role of system designers and change agents as one of building an understanding of the needs of those affected by change. The ethics of this approach demand that any engagement in the political and cultural systems of organisations should be minimised, and the use of such tactics as threat and manipulation as means of establishing the legitimacy of change should be avoided. In contrast, we would contend that whilst gaining trust in order to achieve collaboration are important features of the role of system design and change agency, and were in the three SMART project partner companies, the 'vulnerability' of this type of change programme means that, in reality, an active engagement in organisational politics is also required. In the three SMART companies internal and external change agents spent much of their time engaged in the activities of selling and re-selling the project, convincing potential supporters and allies, building team commitment and blocking or seeking to avoid resistance. The extent to which these activities were successfully engaged in goes some considerable way to explain the nature and extent of the change achieved in each particular context. Thus, at Kangaroo and Koala relatively successful engagement with the process agenda created space in which socio-technical design objectives could be pursued. At Wombat, a far less successful engagement meant that such issues and concerns were effectively squeezed off the change agenda.

THE ETHICS OF SOCIO-TECHNICAL CHANGE

Given the 'messy' and 'political' nature of the SMART project, to what extent can socio-technical change of this type be regarded as 'ethical'? As Legge (1986) notes the answers to such a question is highly contingent upon the particular ethical position one adopts. For example, at first sight, Mumford's concept of a socio-technical ethics is founded upon what is noted by Legge as a 'deontological/Kantian' view (see Legge, 1996, p. 11). That is, for Mumford socio-technical change is ethical because it is based on the universalistic notion that in all circumstances humans are valued as an end in themselves and are not means in the pursuit of self-interested ends. Even if, in practice, the desire to treat humans and ends in themselves is also used as a means to serve self-interested organisational goals of competitiveness, profitability and productive efficiency – as long this does not become exclusively the case – then the socio-centred approach can claim to be ethical. The problem, as Legge notes, is that such an idealised state of affairs, even in this modified form, is unlikely to occur very often in practice since the conditions facilitating their attainment are highly contingent (1996, p. 12). In similar vein Adler and Cole (1994) observe in their critique of Volvo's erstwhile human-centred strategy and defence of the more conventional Toyota-GM NUMMI plant established in the USA.

> It would be wonderful if we lived in a world where every job could be an opportunity for Maslovian self-actualization. But when products are fairly standard and mass produced, and when automation is still not cheap enough to eliminate labour-intensive methods of production, then efficiency requires narrowly specialized job assignments and formalized standard methods – a form of work organization that precludes the very high intrinsic work satisfaction that would, for example, stimulate workers to come in without pay on a day off to tackle a production problem. (Adler and Cole, 1993, p. 92)

It is perhaps in recognition of this that Mumford appeals to pragmatism, observing that on many occasions small gains may be all that is possible but that this is justified by the improvement that it brings.

In evaluating the achievements of the SMART project it is tempting to adopt a similar stance. Radical goals were striven for but the realities, practicalities and contingent circumstances of change meant that more modest gains were all that could be realistically achieved. It also allows us to point to a tendency to view socio-technical changes in terms of either an 'autonomy doctrine' – where teamwork is seen as key to the progression to genuinely autonomous humane work – or a 'control' doctrine which views teams as a new means of management control in the inevitable conflict between capital and labour (Badham and Jurgens, 1997). An alternative approach – suggested elsewhere by one of the current authors – suggests that team autonomy should be conceptualised in terms of a multidimensional model based on different types of task-based decision-making. The kind of team autonomy that develops along these various dimensions is contingent upon organisational capabilities and constraints specific to the situation (Badham and Jurgens, 1997). What constitutes a team and team autonomy is therefore not given by generic socio-technical models but is situationally specific. For such an approach, there is no 'one-best' or 'one-worst' form of team-based working and empowerment. There is merely the development of team-working along different dimensions, each of which will be politically contested and evaluated differently by different groups.

In some ways such thinking appeals to a more 'utilitarian' position on ethics (Legge, 1996) in that a given degree of team autonomy and empowerment along one or more of these dimensions might be judged an 'ethical' outcome provided the greater good – for example the long-term survival of the business and therefore employees job security – is served. Certainly, the utilitarian position has some comforting aspects. In particular, the fact that the TBCM concept was not extended to all workers in the SMART companies, was experienced unevenly and often in contradictory fashion by those to whom it was, and the failure to attend to the problems and issues which effectively excluded some groups (such as skilled trades) from the assumed benefits, might all be excused by the view that benefits of both a human and efficiency kind (although in the latter case not always officially recognised) were more or less achieved to the extent and for the largest number that was possible in the circumstances. However, a critical response might be that almost any claim to have increased worker empowerment through team working in this way could be justified as long as it appeared to ensure the longevity of the organisation by some degree and to fit some arbitrary definition of what is the 'greatest good' for the 'greatest number'.

Clearly, a stronger test of the ethical status of the outcomes of socio-technical change programmes designed to increase team autonomy is needed. One such test might be to stress the degree of participation by end users in change, or the degree to which they exert real governance over decisions about change (Badham and Jurgens, 1997). Thus rather than the outcome per se being the basis of ethical judgements, the means by which this was arrived at is the key criterion.

A focus on participation of users in shaping socio-technical outcomes in this way has strong resonances with what Legge terms a 'stakeholder/Rawlsian' approach to ethics. As long as the stakeholder groups concerned are party to the decision-making which determines an outcome, even if there are some who benefit more than others, or the actual changes achieved are slight, then the process can be seen as ethical in the sense that the consequences have been arrived at in a 'just' way as far as those involved are concerned (Legge, 1996, p. 11). On this count the ethicality of the achievements of the SMART project stand quite well. Even in the case of Wombat plastics it was possible to achieve a broad constituency of stakeholder interests in the system design stage, albeit an abortive process. In the other two cases much more was achieved in respect of engaging stakeholder groups and in terms of the overall level of governance that was achieved for employees – in particular the cell teams themselves. In the latter case the end result was a marked improvement on the situation that prevailed prior to the introduction of TBCM.

However, there are two main dangers with the 'stakeholder/Rawlsian' position which lead us to temper our observations here. Firstly, as Legge notes, the assumption that a free and equal plurality of groups can be given full representation within hierarchical capitalist organisations is a weak one – this certainly cannot be claimed to have been what happened in the three SMART project companies even within the favourable 'neo-corporatist' national industrial relations framework that existed in Australia at the time (see note 3). Secondly, the political interventions of change agents in identifying the opportunities and issues for involvement and the stakeholder groups who should be engaged in, and excluded from, this process may be largely unguided and unjustified. Certainly, in the SMART companies these were highly localised and pragmatic decisions influenced only by the broad principle that employees and their trade unions should be key stakeholder groups and have a significant influence over the design, implementation and outcomes of change.

On this last point some arguments in justification of intervention by system designers/change agents in the political and cultural systems of organisations is given by Buchanan and Boddy (1992, pp. 84–6). They make the following points in 'ethical' defence of such interventions:

- First, what is ethical in this respect is situational and not universal. In given circumstances (for example the 'vulnerability' as we have described it of socio-technical change), engagement in politics in organisations can be seen as acceptable, appropriate and necessary as a means to a given end.
- Second, on pragmatic grounds, in so far as organisations are political systems, it would be foolish for the change agent to seek to ignore this, whilst the act of engagement in such systems usefully exposes for discussion and debate an aspect of organisational life which is normally hidden and denied.
- Third, the utilitarian argument, that apparently unethical political behaviours may be necessary to serve the greater good and preserve the long-term future of the organisation for the greatest number.
- Finally, the contingency argument, that the 'truth, trust, love and collaboration' approach to participation is only a practical proposition in certain organisational circumstances, for example where the timescale of change is long and not a matter of urgency. In circumstances where more urgency is needed in the change process more overtly political methods, for example in overcoming 'blockers' and resistance, may be necessary if change is to be achieved at all.

Such arguments do not, however, resolve key issues of how to guide and assess the political activity of socio-technical change agents as they 'weave, wheel and deal' their way through the organisation. This remains a serious challenge for a 'new socio-technical ethics'.

CONCLUSION

The experiences of socio-technical change outlined in this chapter do not give us very clear and conclusive answers to questions of whether team-based working and empowerment are ethical or not, or what constitutes an ethical approach to the management of and implementation of such socio-technical change. Whilst not claiming to have resolved the 'ethical ambiguity' surrounding teams, empowerment and system designers/ change agents, we would though suggest the following on the basis of the SMART project experience:

- First, it should be quite clear from the experiences in the three partner companies that socio-technical change, like any other form of change programme, is in reality about the 'art of the possible'. In each case the outcomes of change fell short of what was planned in many respects and certainly what might ideally have been desired. In each case at least small gains were achieved. In terms of Mumford's five implicit contracts these were, at least in some respects in each case, demonstrably better in human and efficiency terms than the circumstances which preceded. However, we would argue that what is or is not an ethical work system design or outcome is not a simple 'black or white' judgement that can be made against generic models of the optimum relationship between technical and social systems or any universalistic notion of what constitutes an 'ethical' outcome. Such judgements are highly context dependent and must accept the politically negotiated nature and representation of change outcomes in particular situations.

- Second, it should be evident that what was achieved came about to a significant degree through engagement in the cultural and political systems of the three organisations by system designers and change agents, including the SMART researchers. Where this activity was least effective in securing the legitimacy of socio-technical design principles as the basis for change, and in particular the engagement with and involvement of stakeholders directly effected by it, the smallest gains were made. Where it was most effective, the largest gains were made. Rather than undermining the ethical position of the change agent, we would argue that, such engagement is a necessary response to the vulnerable character of socio-technical change projects. This inevitably heightens the necessity for *active* engagement in organisational politics and the management of meaning by change agents. Whilst not rejecting the need for good communications, trust-building and participation of users, in our view, this vulnerability would seem to call for something stronger to be added to the socio-technical system designer's and change agent's armoury. As one of the authors has argued elsewhere, to achieve their objectives, those concerned with implementing socio-technical change may require some 'power-assisted steering' (Badham and Buchanan, 1996). The ethical implications of this for the change agent and system designer remain an open question.

Notes

1. For the purposes of the following analysis and to clear up some ambiguities and overlaps in Mumford's own formulations, we have slightly modified the five contracts and the types of questions for system designers and change agents that they highlight.
2. Badham and Couchman were the principal social scientists involved in the action research phase of the project, and Badham co-ordinated the project as a whole. McLoughlin was commissioned to conduct the summative case studies and post-project follow-up visits.
3. From the 1980s onwards, productivity-enhancing reforms of the highly-centralised pay-determination system through national and state awards had been set in train by the Australian Federal Government. These focused – in a framework of neo-corporatist relationships between the incumbent Labour Government and the trade unions, if not the employers (see Boreham *et al.*, 1996) – on the development of skills and productive potential through workplace innovation. Initially this occurred through a process of award restructuring and latterly through full-blown enterprise level bargaining (see Hancock and Rawson, 1993). The importance of this process in setting a framework for change, although not in determining its outcomes, was evident in all three companies. In each case, agreements were reached at either industry, company or plant level to permit, *inter alia*, changes to job classifications, the relaxation of job boundaries and demarcations, multiskilling and team-based working.

References

Adler, P.S. and Cole, R.E. (1993) 'Designed for Learning: A Tale of Two Auto Plants', *Sloan Management Review*, vol. 34(3), Spring, pp. 85–94.

Badham, R. (1994) 'From Socio-economic to Socially Orientated Innovation Policy', in G. Aichholzer and G. Schienstock (eds), *Technology Policy: Towards an Integration of Social and Ecological Concerns* (Berlin: Walter de Gruyter), pp. 1–66.

Badham, R. and Buchanan, D. (1996) 'Power-assisted Steering and the Micropolitics of Organisational Change: A Research Agenda'. Paper presented to the Australian and New Zealand Academy of Management Conference, Wollongong, NSW, December.

Badham, R. and Naschold, F. (1994) 'New Technology Policy Concepts: Some Reflections on Technology and Work Humanization in West Germany', in G. Aichholzer and G. Schienstock (eds), *Technology Policy: Towards an Integration of Social and Ecological Concerns* (Berlin: Walter de Gruyter), pp. 125–60.

Badham, R. and Jurgens, U. (1997) 'Frontiers of Autonomy and the Dynamics of Team Work: A Critical Approach to New Forms of Organisation Control'. MI-TOC Working Paper, Department of Management, University of Wollongong.

Badham, R., Couchman, P. and McLoughlin, I. (1997) 'Implementing Vulnerable Socio-technical Change Projects', in I. McLoughlin and M. Harris (eds), *Innovation, Organisational Change and Technology* (London: ITB Press).

Boreham, P., Hall, R. and Harley, B. (1996) 'Two Paths to Prosperity?: Work Organisation and Industrial Relations Decentralisation in Australia', *Work, Employment and Society*, vol. 10(3), pp. 449–68.

Buchanan, D. (1994) 'Principles and Practice in Work Design', in K. Sisson (ed.), *Personnel Management* (Oxford: Blackwell), pp. 85–116.

Buchanan, D. and Boddy, D. (1992) *The Expertise of the Change Agent* (London: Prentice-Hall).

Einjatten, F.M. van (1993) *The Paradigm that Changed the Workplace* (Assen: Van Gorcum).

Hancock, K. and Rawson, D. (1993) 'The Metamorphosis of Australian Industrial Relations', *British Journal of Industrial Relations*, vol. 31(4), pp. 489–511.

Kelly, J. (1982) *Scientific Management and the Labour Process* (London: Macmillan).

Knapp, K., Erwin, P., Park, R. and Ieronimo, N. (1996) 'Teams in Australia's Automotive Industry: Characteristics and Future Challenges. Paper presented at the Employment Research Unit Annual Conference, University of Wales, September.

Lawler, E.E., Mohrmann, S.A. and Ledford, G.E. (1995) *Creating High Performance Organisations* (San Francisco: Jossey-Bass).

Legge, K. (1996) 'Ethics and HRM'. Paper presented at conference on HRM – The Inside Story, Milton Keynes, April.

McLoughlin, I. (1993) 'Organisational Politics, Advanced Engineering Systems and Human Factors', *International Journal of Human Factors in Manufacturing*, vol. 3(1), pp. 37–52.

Mathews, J. (1994) *Catching the Wave: Workplace Reform in Australia* (Sydney: Allen & Unwin).

Mumford. E. (1996) *Systems Design: Ethical Tools for Ethical Change* (London: MacMillan).

Orsburn, J., Moran, L., Musselwhite, E. and Zenger, J. with Perrin, C. (1991) *Self-directed Work Teams: The New American Challenge* (Homewood, Ill.: Irwin).

Perrow, C. (1983) 'The Organisational Context of Human Factors Engineering', *Administrative Science Quarterly*, vol. 28, pp. 521–41.

Pettigrew, A. (1985) *The Awakening Giant: Continuity and Change in ICI* (Oxford: Blackwell).

Rose, M. (1988) *Industrial Behaviour* (Harmondsworth: Penguin).

Wellins, R., Byham, W. and Wilson, J. (1991) *Empowered Teams: Creating Self-Directed Work Groups that Improve Quality, Productivity, and Participation* (San Francisco: Jossey Bass).

Wobbe, W. (1995) 'Anthropocentric Production Systems: A New *Leitbild* for an Industrial Symbiotic Work and Technology Culture in Europe', in J. Benders, J. de Haan and D. Bennet (eds), *The Symbiosis of Work and Technology* (London: Taylor & Francis), pp. 13–24.

9 Negotiated Reality: The Meaning of Empowerment
Edna Ojeifo and Diana Winstanley

INTRODUCTION

In this chapter four different perspectives on empowerment are identified, the participative, the organisational, the critical and the differentiated. The perspective adopted here is based on the meaning of empowerment as constructed and enacted by those most affected – the 'empowered' employees themselves. The research is taken from case study material at Technon (a pseudonym), where empowerment practices have been in place for some time. We take an analytical approach focusing on the perspective of the individual, which fits in with what we term the 'differentiated' approach.

We propose three ways of examining empowerment which may be useful to help us to interpret the meaning of empowerment for the individual. These are:

1. The way in which the environmental context interacts with the introduction and implementation of empowerment – the *context dimension*.
2. The expectancy of outcomes, and the calculations an individual engages in as to whether or not these have a positive effect on their experience of work, careers and rewards – the *expectancy dimension*.
3. The interaction of the individual with the experience of empowerment, where initial experience creates core constructs which may diverge widely from the espoused definitions in managerial rhetoric and literature – the *experience dimension*.

Our interviews raise these three areas as being crucial to whether the meaning of empowerment espoused is that received by those involved. These move the locus of interest away from the giver or manager, and towards the receiver, or the one being 'empowered', and this shift has implications for our definition of empowerment. We suggest that a full understanding of empowerment should take into account how empowerment is constructed in the minds of the individual, rather than take for granted the espoused rhetoric of those creating the practice. If empowerment is not seen as such by those affected, then the espoused concept is neither valid nor likely to be successful in practice.

Through examining the employees perspective, it is possible to distil out some of the practical actions which are required to put empowerment into practice. In particular there are three types of information needs which effect the experience of empowerment. One is the design of software and use of information technology (IT) to enable empowered teams to have access to up-to-date information about key data and performance that will enable them to take better decisions. Another is to do with being made aware of what is going on in the organisation, the issues being discussed at the more informal level within management, so that any decision is not negated due to key aspects of emergent strategy being hidden. The third is the appropriate support and training required to enable employees to put it into practice. The case reveals some reluctance within management to 'give employees the tools to do the job', which is exacerbated by a context of downsizing and work overload.

FOUR PERSPECTIVES ON EMPOWERMENT

We should question whether the notion of empowerment is new at all. As one commentator has suggested, new fads can coin words which are essentially 'old wine in new bottles' (Donkin, 1994). Perhaps empowerment, is merely a new term for something which has already existed for sometime, namely employee involvement or employee participation.

Model 1   Empowerment and employee participation: the individual perspective

Empowerment, from this perspective, has been defined as a

> process of giving people more scope and power to exercise more control over and take responsibility for, their work. It provides greater 'space' for individuals to use their abilities by enabling them to take decisions close to the point of impact. (Armstrong, 1995)

Empowerment has its roots in Theory Y (McGregor, 1960), in the assumption that workers will, given the chance, work hard. They want to take responsibility and be involved in decision-taking. A humanistic view of the organisation would suggest that, in any case, employees should be given the chance to participate in decision-making in order to satisfy their own needs and motives. Employee participation has its beginnings in concepts derived from industrial democracy and the human relations movement going back as far as Mayo (Roethlisberger and Dickson, 1964 and Herzberg, 1968). We can distinguish between different forms of participation (Pateman, 1970), such as collective and individual, indirect, representational and direct, and even financial. Thus, for example, suggestion schemes are a form of individual and direct participation, union representation at the bargaining table or on a works council are forms of collective and indirect participation, quality circles are a form of collective and direct participation, and profit-sharing or share-ownership are forms of financial participation.

It is more useful to identify the extent of participation, and Pateman (1970) proposes three levels depending on power: psuedo – where the aim is to get workers to accept a decision which has already been made; partial – where workers can influence a decision; and full – where they have genuine decision-making power. Geary (1994) alternatively separates consultative from delegative participation, where in the former employees make their views known, and in the latter they are empowered to implement action. Delegation differs from empowerment in its association with individual processes, whereas, as we show below, empowerment has become more widely associated with teams and work groups. Delegation is also imbued with the gift from above; that is A, the boss, delegates to B, the employee, whereas empowerment has a flavour of being something which is in the power of B to take – 'a fundamental truth about empowerment, is you can't give it; people have to take it' (Wright, quoted in Price Waterhouse Change Integration Team, 1995).

Participation is clearly a very broad term ranging from minimal involvement such as in attitude surveys, through to full workplace democracy and the allocation of 'voting rights'. Higher and lower-level participation can also be distinguished where the former relates to decisions impacting the whole organisation, such as with investment and marketing, and the latter are merely concerned with work scheduling and activities within a specific area. Alternatively we can suggest the following levels:

1. *Awareness/information giving.* Here the organisation creates awareness by providing the employees with data on their performance. It is one-way, top-down communication.
2. *Dialogue/involvement.* The management take time for two-way discussions and the pace of change tends to be slow with input from the

employees. The organisation is seeking feedback. It is still one-way but is down-up, for example suggestion schemes.
3. *Participation*. The level of interaction between the employees intensifies, the emphasis being on team work. The employees are allowed to make decisions with respect to issues that directly affect them. The management take on the role of leaders and facilitators. The consultation is first-hand and the decisions are devolved to those who are empowered to decide.
4. *Empowerment*. The emphasis here is on accountability and the organisation is structured in such a way to facilitate this. The employees need a skills-base which will enable problem-solving as well as the ability to cope with high levels of personal responsibility. The company may also have profit-sharing and employee ownership policies. The role of management is to provide the working conditions under which the employees can do the best job and therefore have the best performance. The management will be monitoring as opposed to having direct input in the decision-making process.

There have been many proponents of participation, ranging from national and international governments and organisations, through to pressure groups, trade unions and individuals. The European Commission is one such supporting group which has been grappling for a long time with various efforts to introduce a European framework within its member states to support worker participation, for example through the Vredling Directive 1980, and more recently the incorporation within the Social Chapter of the directive on works councils and employee consultation. The French government have likewise introduced legislation to give workers the right to express their views, and successive social democratic governments in Germany have supported such work reorganisation. In addition codes of practice have been set up by the Institute of Personnel and Development (IPD) and the Involvement and Participation Association (IPA).

Empowerment is a more recent term than participation, but it could be suggested that it is merely one form of participation, and one which largely concerns individual, lower-level decisions – a form of partial participation lying somewhere between consultative and delegative participation. However, it is not totally individual as we shall see at Technon and many other companies who have implemented empowerment programmes, where they are introduced largely in the context of high performance work teams.

This history suggests, therefore, that empowerment is nothing new, it is an extension of a form of participation which has been in existence for a long time, what has changed is the label and the industrial context. Generally, as with participation, it has been viewed favourably, with more literature extolling its virtues than criticising its practice, although with some notable exceptions (for example Claydon and Doyle, 1996, and Geary, 1994).

Model 2 Empowerment and the organisational perspective: a tool for organisational effectiveness

In this model empowerment is

> The process of achieving continuous improvement in an organization's performance by developing and extending the competent influence of individuals and teams over the areas and functions which affect their performance and that of the total organisation. (Kinlaw, 1994)

Empowerment is about increasing the ability of employees to create and communicate new ideas, to be apt at problem-solving, through the 'synergetic interaction of team members' (Kinlaw, 1994).

It is even suggested that 'The survival of companies today depends on the day to day mobilization of every ounce of intelligence' (Richard Pascale 'Managing on the Edge', quoted by the Price Waterhouse Change Integration Team, 1995).

Model 2 definitions of empowerment provide a very different rationale. One of the reasons for the recent interest in empowerment has been the need for organisations to reduce overheads and to become more efficient in order to maintain competitiveness. Meeting the needs of customers in increasingly global and highly competitive marketplaces has led to rapid development which due to the necessity of speed cannot only be achieved through the use of management, hence the need to empower employees. Shareholder demands for increased financial performance has focused attention on productivity improvements, and costs-cutting. The main cost-cutting strategy which has led to empowerment has been the delayering and downsizing of organisations.

Companies may not have started out with empowerment as a goal, but because of the issues above they may end up with it. Even with advanced levels of IT it is difficult to run a delayered organisation using control and command methods. Managers have to trust their employees because their workload has increased enormously. They are responsible for a large number of employees who report directly to them, often through empowered self-managed teams. Business/economic conditions more than anything else have forced managers to empower their employees (Bolger 1995, quoting Bob Dixon of the Industrial Society).

In the UK, many empowerment programmes are associated with job and organisational redesign to create more team-based structures and decision-making processes. This in part is linked to the introduction of Japanese management practices which revolve around teamwork. For example, a form of empowerment exists for Rover's form of 'cell management' (Walker, 1991), and at the Digital plants studied by Buchanan and McCalman (1989) and Garavan and Morley (1992), all of which have a number of common practices, including:

- delayering of hierarchy;
- a move away from functional and towards project-team based organisational structures;
- self-managing, self-organising and self-regulating teams;
- multi-skilling, shared skills, knowledge, experience and problems;
- shared responsibility and authority;
- skills-based and more flexible payment systems;
- peer selection, peer review;
- open communications systems and layout;
- mutual respect and trust between individuals;
- commitment to human resource development and new ways of facilitating and rewarding learning;
- managers as coaches and facilitators rather than directors; and
- visible commitment to quality.

It is no coincidence that there is a preponderance of examples drawn from the car and the electronics industries, areas which have been particularly hard hit by Japanese competition, influenced by Japanese style management, and which have been suffering from the general decline of the manufacturing sector in western countries. In terms of overall coverage, semi-autonomous work groups have been found to be in existence in somewhere between 2 per cent (WIRS3 – workplace industrial relations survey) and 20 per cent of firms (Batstone, 1984, and Geary, 1994).

Rather than seeing empowered teams as a product, it may be better to view empowerment as a process. Cohen et al. (1996, p. 647) identifies the contributing features for self-managing work-team effectiveness and identifies a number of relevant variables related to group task design, group characteristics, encouraging managerial behaviour, and the employee involvement context which work together to create effective outcomes. Our case study will show that Technon's empowerment programme has some of these but not all, and where there are gaps this has caused problems as outlined in the section on context below. Although the way some of these practices have come together is different to the forms of workplace management and control which preceded them in the UK, there are still a number of examples elsewhere where some type of group participation and decision-making systems have been in existence for a long time, as in the case of Volvo's Kalmar plant's use of autonomous working groups, and at Alfa Romeo and Olivetti in Italy.

Despite widespread endorsement, there are still a few who sound a note of caution over empowerment and Japanese-style management. Garrahan and Stewart (1992) suggested that the 'virtuous circle' created by the mobilisation of 'quality, flexibility and teamwork' at Nissan, in fact 'represented a form of powerlessness for many workers, and even 'control, exploitation and surveillance'.

Model 3   The critical perspective

Not all, then, see empowerment like participation as 'motherhood and apple pie' and something which is inherently good. Its two origins cited above result in a tension which is exploited by critical writers, and is even seen as a deliberate clouding of the issue to conceal 'hard' pills in 'soft' packaging.

On the one hand the approach drawn from its 'participation' origins, sees empowerment as something to be pursued because like 'participation' it is good in itself, it motivates and satisfies workers, and may even be seen as a basic right. On the other the organisational perspective sees empowerment as a means to an end, the end being organisational efficiency. Motivating and satisfying workers' higher-level needs for opportunities, for autonomy and decision-making, although worthy, are pursued largely as a method for improving productivity and as a way of cutting costs and increasing output. Therefore it can become seen as a cynical form of work intensification which has nothing to do with meeting the needs of workers at all.

The pursuit of the two different perspectives in theory and practice could result in confusion; for example with relation to whether empowerment is a means or an end. When organisations concentrate on the individual definition of empowerment they are concentrating on the *'degrees of freedom'* given to employees. On the contrary, organisational empowerment does not strive to have more people involved in the decision-making process, but to encourage the use of the minds of people to make sure that the best decisions are made.

A third and more critical perspective on empowerment can also be identified, as represented by Legge (1995, p. 174). Legge posits it as one aspect of the move in contemporary human resource management away from compliance and towards commitment, as a managerial control strategy. As Willmott (1993) puts it, 'high-trust' policies 'by enabling employees to derive a sense of meaning and purpose from using their discretion to put corporate values into place' enable 'non-rational aspects of organisation' to be 'colonised by management'.

A critical perspective identifies a distinction based on hard and soft human resource management (HRM) (Claydon and Doyle, 1996) where the soft form of HRM is associated with participation, involvement, communication and learning, whereas the hard form is associated with cost-cutting. Claydon and Doyle (1996) point out there is no questioning as to whether the 'win–win' view of empowerment – it being good for the individual and good for organisational effectiveness – is sustainable. The two approaches are not necessarily compatible, and can become blatently contradictory. Some research from the critical perspective has also attempted a more differentiated view by taking into account the employee's perspective as well as examining the managerial strategy, as in the case of Claydon and Doyle (1996). However, our model separates these two out for conceptual simplicity, and to enable us to identify a framework which explores the individual level of experience.

Model 4   A differentiated perspective

The fourth framework proposed, is similar to the critical perspective in that rather than being prescriptive, that is concerned primarily with ensuring empowerment can meet the objectives set (as in the case of the individual and organisational perspectives), it is more interpretive (aimed at understanding the reality of what empowerment means in practice to those involved). However, whereas the critical perspective tends to focus more on the managerial strategies associated with empowerment, the approach here is primarily orientated towards understanding the meaning of empowerment for the individuals being empowered, and this area is the least well-understood when rhetorics are compared to realities.

Although theoretically it is possible that the individual and the organisational perspective may not clash, in practice the use of the critical framework helps to tease out some of the contradictions, and the differentiated view elaborates on these further. The information provided in the case study below explores the incompatibility of pursuing the individual and organisational perspectives simultaneously, from a more differentiated perspective. For example the imposition of the organisational perspective can impact employees' perceptions in a negative way, particularly in the context of cost-cutting, and make it more difficult for the aims of the individual to be realised. Likewise, an approach which is aimed to redistribute power may not necessarily be compatible with one which is aimed at improving effectiveness.

A topology of these four approaches to empowerment is provided in Figure 9.1.

Figure 9.1 The four perspectives on empowerment

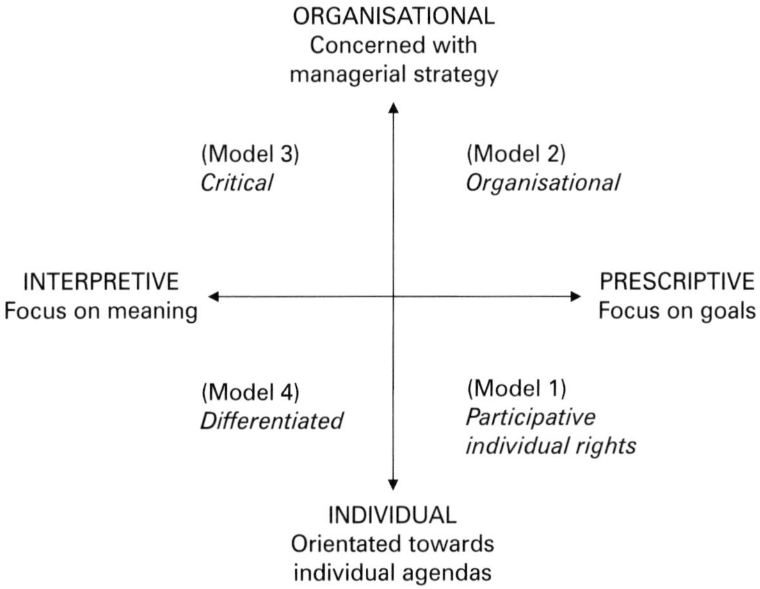

ORGANISATIONAL
Concerned with
managerial strategy

(Model 3)
Critical

(Model 2)
Organisational

INTERPRETIVE
Focus on meaning

PRESCRIPTIVE
Focus on goals

(Model 4)
Differentiated

(Model 1)
*Participative
individual rights*

INDIVIDUAL
Orientated towards
individual agendas

CASE-STUDY: TECHNON AND ITS EMPOWERMENT PROGRAMME

Technon is a diversified multinational company, one of the world's largest suppliers of office equipment. Technon UK Limited was established in 1972 as the UK sales and support subsidiary of the international company

Technon Plc. Technon UK Ltd employs over 4000 people in 50 locations and generates an annual revenue of over $500 million. It markets Technon products and services in the UK and Ireland through a direct sales-force and an indirect sales network through Technon Office Services.

In order to understand the development of its the empowerment programme it is necessary to place it in the context of the evolution of such programmes at Technon. Technon evolved through a competitive benchmarking exercise in the 1970s, employee involvement and quality leadership programmes in the 1980s, and Concept 2000, the empowerment programme, and lastly the business excellence initiative in the 1990s. Its quality leadership programme was particularly influential on the subsequent implementation of empowerment, and this was launched in 1983. The focus of this strategy was to ensure that total customer satisfaction and total quality became the focus for every employee within the organisation. This led to a reconsideration of its organisational structure and the way that it remunerated its employees. At the time the ethos was:

> It is hard to distinguish customer satisfaction from employee satisfaction. You can't have one without the other. (Managing Director, Technon)

The programme was developed mainly because of the need to focus on cost and competition as other companies began to make office equipment that competed directly with Technon in quality and price.

A major part of their implementation programme was to create 'high impact cross functional teams'. They extended the 'Team Technon' philosophy to include not only internal staff but also customers and suppliers. To further improve on teamwork ability 'process team coaches' were assigned to assist and implement continuous learning, thus enforcing the LUTI (learn – use – teach – implement) corporate paradigm; these coaches consisted mainly of line managers rather than staff professionals.

The involvement of individuals was seen as a crucial part of Technon's quality leadership strategy. Not only did Technon want to encourage employee involvement, they wanted to go one step further with employee empowerment. This is something that, as a Technon manager said, 'is sensible since employees are the ones who best know their jobs'. Technon did not only want to *involve* staff in decision-making, they wanted to empower staff to *make decisions themselves*. As a Technon manager said:

> Managers especially needed to behave in ways that recognized that they had more to gain by empowering employees and holding them accountable for how they use that authority, than by making decisions themselves.

It is this which underlay the strategy of Concept 2000, which extended the quality leadership strategy. This was a strategy aimed at developing an empowerment framework based on self-managed teams. Technon's reasons for doing so had been highlighted by the statement made in a recent company report:

> We are pursuing growth and productiveness by doing work for our customers in simpler, more effective ways. We have made a number of changes in the last few years aimed at unleashing the power of our people and aligning our collective energies for the common purpose of satisfying our customers. We have refined our organization to make it more flexible, responsive, market driven and customer focused. We are building a special community where Technon people contribute, grow and have fun.
>
> Our community is based on the principles of ethics of personal responsibility, the need to anticipate and adapt to change, our commitment to quality, the ability of each of us to draw what we need from our community and the company's obligation to respond to our need for information. This is an 'empowered workforce' that is team orientated and line driven, in which each of us reaches for more and contributes the maximum. We are market driven, action orientated and committed to absolute results. Technon people are developing a deep understanding of customer needs creating value and doing what is right for the customer. We will add value at the right time and in the right way for customers and shareholders.

Concept 2000 was building on customer-orientated services and was a restructuring exercise aimed at taking the team-based approach further. It highlighted issues of employee motivation and employee satisfaction. Under Concept 2000, customer service improvement teams were set up; these 20–30 teams looked at everything from the work environment, to how the teams were structured, benefits and compensation, and a whole array of employee-related issues. One of the common themes to come out of this was that the engineers wanted more freedom in decision-making, more say in their day-to-day work, and closer links with the customer. Comments such as 'we understand our environment, therefore we are the best people to make decisions' were common. As a result of this, Technon recognised a need for a vehicle to enable cultural change and it was felt that self-managed work groups enabled this, making for a more fluid organisation rather than one which was rigid and bound in red tape.

In setting up empowered teams, managers claim that Technon had the following principles:

- *Vision*: there is a vision of where Technon is headed and its values.
- *Communication*: there is effective two-way communication.

- *Education*: there is a commitment to train and develop people so they can be enlightened to make good business decisions, and they understand how they fit into Technon.
- *Focus*: the focus of empowerment is based on the relationship with external customers, not just internal ones.
- *Standard processes*: there is standardisation, documentation and communication of key work and management processes so that boundaries are defined that free people to use their creativity.
- *Trust*: trust supports empowerment by Technon trusting people to operate and make calls to customers which require judgement and decision-taking, without having to get authorisation. At the same time employees are responsible for the consequences of their actions.
- *Role of managers*: the role of managers is to help and support without removing responsibility from their teams. Managers are coaches and facilitators who enable the release of the creative energy of their teams. Role modelling starts at the top.
- *Support for front-line people*: the people in the front line with the customers have the support of all the functions within Technon.
- *Self-managed teams*: the aim of empowered self-managed teams is to foster commitment, accountability and ownership with less dependence on the second level of management.
- *Reward and recognition*: recognition for empowerment, coupled with reward for results and process improvements, are fundamental to the empowerment programme at Technon.
- *Breakage and risk*: there is an awareness that mistakes and errors will be made, but Technon intend to learn from productive failure. It is believed that the benefits from releasing the creative energy will more than offset the breakages.
- *Investments*: it is recognised that the transition to a fully-empowered organisation will require investments in training and other enablers.

Technon started with a feasibility team in 1991. Examples of empowered teams up to this point in time had been more in the manufacturing area, Japanese car plants based in the UK, Rover, Volvo, Deck and Digital all had some kind of work group. Technon wanted a field-service-based organisation where their culture and processes were an aspect of differentiation when benchmarked against by other companies. Unlike with manufacturing, for service engineers it was not so easy to see the processes, they were less tangible.

Technon's overall stand on empowerment within the organisation was summarised in their coined phrases: desired state and empowerment principles. Technon's long-term aim for the organisation seemed to be that of empowerment based on organisational effectiveness. This is not to say that Technon's empowerment framework did not concern itself with employee rights, but motivation was used as a stepping stone to achieve the true goal of organisational effectiveness. This can be seen by the following long-term aims of Technon:

1. The customer perception is that front-line employees can quickly take action to support and meet their needs, thereby making it easy and pleasant to do business with Technon. Namely, the customers see employees as 'The Technon Advantage'.
2. The employee perception is one of 'I can do what is needed, subject only to the boundaries of morals, ethics, laws, process capability and price exposure'. Enabling employees to take pride in what they do, take responsibility for their actions, and are motivated and willing to act.

RESEARCH FINDINGS AND THE EMERGING THEMES

In this section, we summarise some of the findings on the employees perspectives on empowerment based on primary and secondary research carried out within Technon. The primary research method took the form of one-to-one interviews and observation of working environment and practices with the following: senior management including the group resources manager, the regional manager, a regional area support executive and a sample of 15 service engineers – the sample of engineers included 2 team leaders and 2 advanced engineers.

From the research it was found that there seemed to be the emergence of three themes which were relevant to our understanding of empowerment. The themes (identified in our introduction) can be classified as:

Context
Expectancy
Experience

Context

The research found that there were several issues which needed to be considered relating to the organisational context of empowerment.

These contextual factors have an impact on an employee's perception of empowerment, and three are highlighted here: headcount reductions and downsizing, the allocation of resources to the programme, and the extent to which empowerment is supported or contradicted by other programmes, policies and procedures. Conger and Kanungo (1988) have elsewhere elaborated further on contextual factors which undermine the move to empowerment, through their lowering of an individual's belief in self-efficacy.

Headcount reductions and downsizing

Empowerment at Technon as well as other companies has been as a result of streamlining and downsizing to make the organisation more efficient. In this sense, Technon take a model-2 perspective on downsizing according to Figure 9.1. Downsizing by its nature has meant that there is a reduced headcount and a removal of a greater part of the support infrastructure.

Technon expected several benefits from empowered teams. Initially they wanted to improve employee motivation and through that to improve customer satisfaction which in turn would lead to improved business results. However, due to the downturn in the economy in the early 1990s, productivity became the major concern, the key driver. Businesses were failing and growth was not as expected. Customer satisfaction thus became ranked higher than employee motivation, and productivity became the major issue as the workforce was being reduced.

Frustrations with empowerment stemmed back to the introduction of empowerment as part of a strategy for organisational stringency and cost-cutting:

> the engineers are only empowered to save money not to spend money ... we are not given the control we were initially led to believe.
>
> empowerment might die a death unless we have the resources to carry out the job properly.

In downsizing various layers of management were removed or reduced from 1991 to 1995. The first stage of change meant the removal of one layer of management, the area managers (AMs), although there was an increase in regional assistant managers (RAMs) and regional managers (RMs) to offset this change. The RAMs were selected for their skills in the coaching area, as with empowered teams they would need to move decisions to either a higher or lower level. In the next stage the total number of senior and middle management was reduced from 50 in 1992/3 to 37 in 1994, and further reduced to 33 in 1995. The number of engineers was also reduced from 1350 in 1991 to 1200 in 1995 (leading to a ratio of 1 manager to 35 engineers). Engineers were now to work in self-managed work teams where they were empowered to run their teams in the way they saw fit subject to boundaries of morals, ethics, laws and process capability.

One contradiction is that empowerment can need more support rather than less in terms of advice, coaching and feedback. The visibility and approachability of management is an important support for empowerment. For example one engineer said: 'It is not for managers to be unapproachable it is part and parcel of their job to be out and about.' There was also a concern that with the thinning of management, regional support managers had not got the time to provide the back-up required from teams.

Allocation of resources

The extent to which sufficient resources exist to support empowerment can have a crucial effect on perceptions and success. Without such resources, employees at Technon felt overworked and unable to perform their fundamental jobs, let alone the additional tasks that their new jobs required. The engineers felt that even though they were empowered they could not achieve tasks to the standard they would like:

> They need more bodies basically. I can understand pruning dead wood, as they like to say, but there is too much work, so it does not get done properly or it does not get done on time. Nobody is there to inspect the process. They are losing money now because they are being inefficient.

Lack of staffing was perceived to have caused excessive workload which meant engineers were finding it hard to cope when jobs were not being done properly or did not get done on time, which was causing some demotivation to offset the motivating aspects of empowerment:

> The most demotivating thing in this job is coming in Monday morning and there is something like 30 jobs on the system and knowing that we don't have the manpower to deal with it.

Employees now had additional responsibilities as well as their specialist roles and so more support in the form of coaching, facilitation and training was required for these to be successfully enacted. There was generally an appreciation of the training facilities which were provided by Technon which were seen to be excellent. However it was not enough for facilities to be in place, there also needed to be the full commitment of senior management to self-development for employees, and the provision of times for training and development to be conducted:

> I think the training is good but we are tied down, as with all of these things, by the manpower problem because the three days off {holiday leave in a period} includes training.
>
> The training is there, it is available but there is no encouragement to let people go and do it.

Thus the practicalities of actually getting training was viewed to be difficult due to the scarcity of staffing.

Contradiction with other policies and procedures

Historically, performance appraisal had been something which senior management implemented and employees had to conform and adhere to. The removal of the supervisors left the problem as to who was going to carry out appraisals. As a result, the Team Appraisal Process was launched, where input was solicited from the team and collated by the regional manager and then relayed to the team member. As well as being administratively intensive, it raised the question as to whether they would get honest feedback, as the managers claimed the teams would avoid conflict especially as the majority of rewards came from the individual and not the team as a whole.

Although Technon's decision to allow the teams to design their own performance system (league tables) proved to be one which gained approval from the engineers, the engineers were not happy that they had to allocate rewards on the basis of these league tables. Some engineers had 'taken rather than been given' empowerment:

> Performance is evaluated using a league table – we had one which was given by the managers but we thought that it was unfair so we have designed one ourselves. Everyone is in agreement so you cannot argue when the pay comes out because you agreed to it before. Before it was just the supervisor who had a certain amount of money and he divided it up using a set of data. It was more subjective, he did have the figures to go by but he need not take any notice of them.

Others found they were prevented from doing what they wanted which was essentially to have all the resources pooled instead of having to use the league tables. The fact that senior management would not allow this led to the following view:

> I agree with other people having input but would rather that the resources were pooled [within the team] but management will not allow it. It seems to me that management are promoting individual competition within the teams which goes against what empowerment is all about.

Within Technon it was felt that the ground rules and the reasons for the current systems had not been adequately communicated, or understood, or accepted by the engineers, and this had led to a feeling of disenchantment. In certain cases it was thought that the league tables were biased to favour certain team members which had led to a feeling of inequity, and some of the measures were viewed to be contradictory, such as number of calls versus reliability.

There were some areas where the procedures and processes at Technon had culturally changed to be more complimentary with the empowerment teams, in a bottom-up way, rather than from formal change of the procedures. For example, in the area of disciplinary procedures and absenteeism there was an enormous amount of peer pressure when it came to sickness and time-keeping in teams. One manager said:

> If Joe Bloggs goes sick today, the whole team will phone him up in the morning telling him to get himself in, we know that you went out last night, or that Scotland was playing England! That would never have happened with the supervisor, they would have always been reluctant to make that call.

However the experience of teamwork varied across the organisation, and certainly some engineers at least felt that some teams did not have sufficient cohesion.

There were also examples of where empowerment through teamwork clashed with the needs of the organisation when it came to dealing with excessive workload. The empowerment principle required the unit of workload to be focused around teams, but there were times when this was overridden:

> (Empowerment) is where you are given an area full of equipment and it is down to us how we go about answering calls and fixing them, in an ideal world. In reality it is slightly different... In reality Technon is bigger than just a city, we like being in charge of our own businesses but we end up having to help out on other areas.

Helping out in other areas can undermine a team's management of its own performance, for example:

> There is the general thing like holiday planning, we are allowed 3 days off for holidays and training and we as a team stick to that pretty rigidly, we're good at that part. Then all of a sudden we get a call out and one of us is pinched to

another district, so as far as we are concerned other teams are not as good at controlling themselves as we are. This often causes a lot of bad feeling.

There was also considered to be a contradiction in terms of team responsibility and performance. For example:

> Because our team does well the only recognition we get is being asked by other teams to help out and there is no recognition for the extra help you give them.

There are other areas where there had been an attempt to change systems to be more complimentary with the empowerment approach. For example in IT, in the past Technon's information systems had been geared to support the management team, such as performance statistics, cost statistics and customer satisfaction data. The information would go to the manager, and the supervisors would get the information from the manager that was deemed relevant. For the work groups to manage themselves it was thought that they would need on-line systems, and this was set up and called 'Axis'. The aim was that the work groups could go to any touch-down site and have access to the system and any data needed. One manager's view was that

> there was a degree of secrecy, we only let them see what we wanted them to see, it was a great breakthrough, though it is still not used to its full potential.

However the experience, as shown below, is that IT cannot support all the information needs of the team, and that highly-relevant information was still not passed down to the teams, who were then inhibited in their decision-making.

Expectancy

There are three ways in which employee's expectations can effect their perception of empowerment. First, there are expectations based on an individual's understanding of the organisation's aims and purpose with relation to empowerment. Second, there is the calculation an employee engages in to identify the likely results of empowerment in terms of how they effect the employee, and the value of these expected outcomes, in accordance with classic expectancy theory (Vroom, 1964). Thus, if an employee believes that empowerment will result in greater work intensification, and they value this negatively, then all other things being equal they will view the empowerment negatively. Alternatively, if they expect empowerment to result in more interesting work, and this is something they value, then they will have a positive view of empowerment. The third type of expectation is over the organisation's ability to deliver the changes promised. This is related to trust, to previous experience of other change programmes, and to do with the perception as to whether other organisational members will be willing to make the change. Research at Technon found considerable scepticism from engineers over management's ability to change.

Understanding of the aims and purpose

The research found that on the whole the engineers had an understanding of what empowerment meant to Technon and how it should, theoretically, be working, for example:

> Being able to make your own decisions rather than being dictated to by someone away from the field.

> The ability to change the way we do things and to be constructive about it.

> Being left to make my own decisions.

For some, they suggested that this had always been the case:

> Empowerment is having the ability to make decisions without getting authority from managers. That is it in the broad sense. You can just make your decisions there and then, it does not slow down the processes, you don't have to go through any red tape to get things done. We as engineers are on the front line with the customers, so we need to make decisions which suit the customer at a given time particularly as there are not many people left within the company who know what that job is... There has not been any sudden impact because it is really part of the job.

Expectations leading to positive perceptions of change

A manager or engineer's expectations of empowerment relate to their 'own comfort zone', their personal characteristics and preferred work styles, and their expectations as what the outcomes of empowerment will be for them and their jobs (and for others), and whether these are desired or unwanted as in traditional expectancy theory.

The employees' views of empowerment, their expectations over it, and their readiness to accept it seems to be dependent on their perspective, particularly with relation to age and position within the organisation. The research found that two groups held predominately positive views of empowerment. One group were younger and more ambitious employees looking to advance and prove themselves within the organisation. The other were those who had gained team leadership and advanced engineering positions within the organisation and were more optimistic about empowerment, the benefits and its potential future. However, even for these groups there was a strong element of resignation to the inevitable:

> I think it is here to stay because most organizations are going the same way.

Where they were unsatisfied with issues they came forward with suggestions on how to improve matters. What was not clear was whether these groups took up the empowerment mantle because they felt this was how one gets on in the organisation (supporting new initiatives, being conformist) or in their career, both of which are self-interested positions; or alternatively whether they genuinely thought it a good thing for the organisation as well as themselves (a mix of altruism and self-interest).

Expectations leading to negative perceptions of change

There were also two groups who were predominately negative about empowerment. One group were those employees who had a generally negative view of both the organisation and empowerment, and were critical of many aspects of organisational systems and structures and ways in which they were expected to work. Another were those employees who generally felt that it was down to management to put things right and not part of their own jobs. A strong theme in respondents' answers here was that if they could only just keep their heads down it may eventually go away:

> I think it will just meander along, we will just flitter from one subject to another, the flavour of the month syndrome.
>
> It might die a death unless we have the resources to carry out the job properly.
>
> It will go straight out the door when we start losing market share.

Where team leaders were found to be amongst those who were negative about empowerment, this particularly had a negative impact on the performance of the team and the view of empowerment held by employees.

Expectations over the manager's ability to transform

Interestingly, there seemed to be more concern at Technon that manager's would not be able to make the change, rather than the engineers themselves. Engineers wanted to have access to senior management, and to work with them in an atmosphere of trust, hopefully reducing the fear of reprisals and getting constructive feedback. The engineers wanted to feel that they could approach management at any time. However they had expectations that management wouldn't be able to deliver in these new roles, as it would be difficult for people to step outside the boundaries of their jobs, if they were not given support, and:

> You step on them first time they do it.

This may be a particular challenge for those in management who had achieved positions under the older style of management. It has been suggested that if a manager believes the classification of Theory X (that people do not like work, avoid it, have little ambition, try to avoid responsibility and need firm direction, control and coercion), then they will have great difficulty in endorsing empowerment as opposed to those Theory Y managers who believe that under the right conditions people not only work hard, showing commitment and talent but also seek increasing responsibility, challenges and empowerment.

Experience

There was some satisfaction with the empowerment programme expressed by employees. For example:

> Empowerment gives you greater pride and responsibility. There is more of a wider understanding. There is greater or more credibility with the customers, they take more note of what you are saying.

The findings of the employee satisfaction survey quoted below were broadly positive. However, here we will concentrate on some of the problems in practice with empowerment for employees.

Empowerment oversold – 'pulling back the reins'

The transition to empowerment has been a gradual process. There was a widespread feeling that empowerment had been oversold by Technon and as a result this had lead to an inflated perception about what they actually could/would be allowed to do. One field manager reported on how empowerment was launched:

> Being a field manager at the time, I had 3 field supervisors and about 3 engineers. Someone from the feasibility team came along and said they wanted to talk to me about empowered teams, it was sort of sold to me but I did not have to do anything. The majority of people saw the gems within the programme but there was no force, no pressure. Empowered teams are the soft areas of the business and to change the culture of the organisation it was not going to

happen overnight. The easiest thing to do is to change all the hardware and then the software will follow. Six months went by and we expected it all to happen but it didn't. Having said that we did raise awareness in the field, so to say nothing happened is not strictly true, but in terms of tangible results nothing changed.

Various managers interviewed with hindsight concurred with these views. After the initial training it was said somewhat flippantly that the work groups felt that they would be: 'Off recruiting engineers and giving themselves big pay rises.'

One example of the way in which hopes had been dashed was when in some cases people tested the reality by attempting to take decisions, and found they were not put into practice. For example, decisions which had been reached by the team had been overruled by senior management:

> We were asked to redefine the boundaries of our work areas in London, what we thought was a sensible solution was reached within 2 hours when management had set aside 4 afternoons over 4 weeks. One week later they came back to us and told us that it could not be done. We spent the next 3 weeks wrangling over a new solution. We were never told the whole picture and in the end it caused resentment.

The managers had been told that it was the managers of yesterday that had to control and it was the managers of today that had to coach, encourage, motivate and facilitate. Some respondents reported that the result of this was that the managers let go and the work groups tried to take over everything, and that there was chaos and a degree of customer dissatisfaction. One engineer said:

> I think empowerment has gone full circle, we have gone through the application process we have now come around to saying that it has worked as effectively as it could have done, so now we have to rework the process. Some of the key elements have been attitude and behavioural elements, lack of boundary setting and lack of inspection. A lot of the problems have been that there was no boundary setting in the first place, managers washing their hands say well its self managed work groups now and get on with it, we have gone full circle now in that there is a lack of direction.

If positive outcomes are expected by engineers, and then not realised in practice, the effect can be extremely demoralising. Alternatively, if their fears are found not to be justified, then an employee may adjust their perception of empowerment in line with their changed perceived reality. What seemed to happen was a bifurcation of views, where managers concerned at rising disorganisation and customer dissatisfaction felt they needed to 'pull back in the reins', but engineers interpreted this as the inability of management to change.

'Old habits die hard'

In terms of outcomes, some of the employees' fears over the inability of management to change their style were realised – for example, the views:

> Decisions are being made whatever we decide.
>
> When the going gets tough management revert to type.
>
> At the moment I have not been affected a great deal, we are sharing out what used to be the supervisors role, management are still controlling what is happening... We are still being governed, there is no full empowerment. You can only go so far with the running of the team. Some decisions which have to be made such as getting rid of machines can only be taken by management and while this decision is being made the customer gets extremely frustrated.
>
> There are suggestion schemes, but generally management don't listen, they are blinkered. An example of this is the parts manual which has been requested on numerous occasions only for us to be ignored and not given an explanation why they were stopped or an acknowledgement of our request even.

Some team leaders were also thought to have not successfully made the transition. One employee who found that some team leaders lacked commitment to the role commented that:

> What dissatisfies me is the petty empire building that goes on with certain teams and the organisation as a whole, the small mindedness, the inability for functions to work together – still a them and us attitude.

More support needed for role clarity, information transfer, training, coaching and career development

It is clear from some of the examples above that a great deal of support needs to be provided for information transfer to the empowered teams. Although Technon had achieved this in part through the IT provision 'Axis' mentioned above, which met some requirements for monitoring performance statistics, more difficult was the information transfer over more informal information and decision-making so that people could know 'what was going on' in the organisation that might affect their own area of decision-making.

Another big problem which has negatively impacted the employee's view of empowerment was with relation to how it had been communicated and how much was revealed of its aims and extent. Also empowerment had led to a lack of clarity so that people had lost sight of what exactly they were supposed to be doing. The lack of transparency and consistency was believed to be increased by organisational politics and the pursuance of different agendas. There was a feeling that what was needed was greater communication of clear boundaries and guidelines for the level of empowerment that was expected within the teams. This is confirmed by research by Payne (1990) which showed that teams have difficulty functioning when team members had unclear and changing goals and low communication levels.

Some engineers felt the lack of clarity was not just over role, but also over feedback and what was happening in the company. One engineer said:

> I would like more contact as you don't know what is happening within the company until you get a newsletter. Its hard to say whether comments are taken on board, not having the contact makes it difficult.

Other dashed expectations arose when promised resources did not match up to what was needed in practice; for example, in the area of training. Technon spent a great deal of money on training and had invested in a learning resource centre. It was felt that engineers had had sufficient and effective technical training but Technon's training had been less effective where the softer skills were concerned, the coaching, counselling and facilitation skills, and skills to help individuals tackle new roles in teams:

> The company spends X amount on training. I think within our team we have had sufficient and adequate technical help with the new products that are coming down the line but once you start going down into the soft skills, the coaching, etc. there is not the facility there. We have been told by HR that there will be courses for team leaders which would incorporate a few days in the field to practice these skills but it does not seem to happen. The knowledge is there within the company but it does not get imparted. Sometimes you put the guys down for courses and it may be 15 months before something comes up, they are not quite as reactive as I would like or you would expect.

> We have a person who is dealing with the holiday planning and it is difficult for him to see that he does not have to stick so rigidly to the rules, I don't think he understands that the way his is acting is causing certain reactions, he needs to be able to sit down with someone [a trainer] and analyse what he is doing and give him guidance on how to deal with confrontations etc.

The length of time taken to get on courses had also caused frustration. Employees were requesting training that they had not received, or were receiving it too late, and as a result they felt disillusioned, especially as the issues of concern needed real-time responses. There was also a belief that no-one was looking at successful teams and finding out why they were successful and why poor performing teams were the way they were.

Training within an empowered organisation, such as Technon, can be divided into two time periods, the short term and the long term. Short term covers staff training on the meaning of empowerment and the processes to be used; Technon had this in place but there still seemed to be a certain level of confusion. Long-term training covers the skills required to be effective and competent within teams, and it was in this area that the engineers at Technon wanted greater input and availability, for example knowing when to make exceptions to rules. As Kinlaw (1994) states:

> Everyone needs training for empowerment but they need training which looks more like education or even professional education. They must acquire a body of knowledge that permits them to operate without constraints of a chain of command and without the limitations of traditional job descriptions and organizational charts.

It has been argued that the development of cognitive and non-cognitive skills of employees increases their flexibility and adaptability to a changing organisation (Steedman et al., 1991), and also encourages employee motivation and commitment to organisational goals (Rainbird, 1994).

Another dissatisfaction with training for empowerment, was that it was largely being conducted 'in your own time' because: 'There is not a lot of flexibility due to the manpower situation, there are not enough hours in the day.'

In a genuinely empowered organisation, the trainers should ideally take guidance on courses to run from the team and its individuals. The engineers at Technon knew what skills they needed or required to be a valuable contributor and they felt this knowledge could have been further utilised. The engineers would have liked regular contact with the trainers on an informal basis who would then have been able to gauge their requirements more accurately, maybe building up an individual profile for each engineer.

The issue of the time available to have training is also important, as the Price Waterhouse Change Team (1995) note: 'If the organization is too busy to improve, nothing will change.' The level of encouragement the engineers received at Technon may have affected their perception of the training available. The engineers knew the training facilities were available but there was no 'pressure' to use it.

Finally another area where some engineers were suffering from disappointment was in the perceived disappearance of clearly defined career progression, which for some individuals was a key motivation factor. Technon had begun to write career maps to give the engineers a horizontal career development path based on skills and experience. However it still remained an issue:

> You sit down with an engineer and say – well you don't aspire to be a supervisor anyway, and he will say that is not the point – I always knew that I could, and I will say well you never did, and the reply is that is not the point. I don't think we will ever get anything back to replace it.

Problems within teams

Some engineers had a disenchanted view of empowerment due to the problems which arose within teams. There were frustrations within teams leading to personality clashes and 'a bad atmosphere, with work colleagues where you don't feel part of a team'. This is again an issue which perhaps could have been dealt with more effectively in training. For example:

> The team seem to be run by 2 people and management. There are few open discussions, agreements tend to take place behind closed doors. We are going back to having supervisors.

Formal employee feedback on empowerment

Ultimately the main form of feedback Technon had on employee satisfaction was via the Employee Motivation Satisfaction Survey (EMSS) which was carried out annually. The results reported here were compiled for 345 employees in 1995. Although it is not possible totally to separate out the effects of the empowerment programme, we can get a general view as to how much the workforce felt they had been empowered from other indicators.

A majority (60 per cent) of employees including 51 per cent of service engineers believed that there was greater opportunity and scope to make their own decisions, and 62 per cent of sales/service and support functions and 51 per cent of service engineers believed there had been an increase in job satisfaction and ability to stand by one's judgement which had made Technon a better company to work for. Sixty-six per cent of employees and 55 per cent of engineers felt that they were encouraged to identify better ways of working. However on the negative side a minority still felt that they were not encouraged to expand the boundaries of their decision-making authority, and only 34 per cent of engineers felt that there was the right balance between managers making decisions and the work group being allowed to make decisions.

Although a majority felt there were sufficient opportunities to receive training to improve their skills, only 25 per cent of engineers claimed the same for personal development, and about half of the employees felt that management supported them in continuous learning. These findings on training reinforce the need to get the balance within the support systems right, as mentioned above.

Some employees were also cynical about the survey:

> There is a survey once a year but the comments are not taken on board, this is shown by the wage issue where management were dictatorial, there only seems to be lip service from the managers.

CONCLUSION

A number of issues are raised in this chapter which contribute to our understanding of empowerment. The first is that this research confirms the widespread finding in critical human resource management that there is a substantial gap between the rhetoric and the reality (Legge, 1995). There are various reasons for this. It is partly due to timescale, in that there is inevitably a lag between the announcement of an initiative and its full scale practice. It is also due to a lack of willingness on behalf of some mangers and some engineers to change, and also through empowerment being undermined by an unfavourable context, and conflicting policies and practices. Information provision has also been shown to be key, and where this was relinquished and made available to engineers in Technon empowerment had taken place to some extent, but where it was withheld engineers were left feeling powerless.

More fundamentally, the gap between rhetoric and reality is reinforced by the pursuit of different meanings and the experience of multiple perspectives, as we have attempted to gauge in this chapter. Organisations such as Technon see empowerment as a means to an end and expect that in the process there will be positive effects in motivation, whereas employees experience it in the context of cost-cutting and downsizing when it becomes harder for them to see their own personal benefits and an increase in personal power and participation, particularly when there is a 'reining back' of control. The context of high-performance teams means that peer pressure may replace top-down control, and the tight performance management processes mean that empowerment becomes an illusive chimera. The meaning and reality of empowerment is negotiated through an engagement in the experience of it, and the pursuit of one's own goals within it, within a context of wider organisational practices. The day-to-day experience of empowerment, and the extent to which people experience support in trying to take decisions, crucially affects their view of empowerment.

The third issue is that empowerment can in practice be a much narrower concept than we are led to believe. Returning to the discussion of the extent of participation, empowerment is something which is not as one writer has suggested 'taken rather than given', but in practice is tightly bounded by constraints. For organisations introducing empowered teams within a manufacturing or engineering environment the experience of empowerment is so far only partial, and we may have to turn to other groups such as various professional groups to get a clearer idea of it.

Therefore we may be better to opt for a processual view of empowerment, rather than a prescriptive one, as this allows us to see, as with participation, that there is a scale of practice which ranges from minor changes in jobs through to full-scale decision-making. For example, Conger and Kanungo (1988) suggest that empowerment is a five-stage process which moves an employee from being powerless to being self-managing.

This chapter has also highlighted the contradictions of pursuing a model-1 and model-2 approach to empowerment simultaneously (Figure 9.1), as we have seen that there are clearly times when these two approaches, based on individual participation and on organisational effectiveness respectively, clash.

Note

The name and certain other identifying details of this organisation have been changed to ensure anonymity.

References

Armstrong, M. (1995) *The Handbook of Human Resource Management* (Oxford: Blackwell).
Batstone, E. (1984) *Working Order* (Oxford: Basil Blackwell).
Bolger, A. (1995) 'Empowerment for Workers?', *Financial Times*, 27 February.
Buchanan, D. and McCalman, J. (1989) *High Performance Work Systems: The Digital Experience* (London: Routledge).
Claydon, T. and Doyle, M. (1996) 'Trusting Me, Trusting You? The Ethics of Employee Empowerment', *Personnel Review*, vol. 25(6), pp. 13–25.

Cohen, S., Ledford, G. and Spreitzer, M. (1996) 'A Predictive Model of Self-Managing Work Team Effectiveness', *Human Relations*, vol. 49(5), pp. 643–76.
Conger, J.A. and Kanungo, R.N. (1988) 'The Empowerment Process: Integrating Theory and Practice', *Academy of Management Review*, vol. 13(3), pp. 471–82.
Donkin, R. (1994) 'Empowerment in Virgin Territory', *Financial Times*, 25 May.
Gandz, J. and Bird, F. (1996) 'The Ethics of Empowerment', *Journal of Business Ethics*, April, vol. 15(4), pp. 383–92.
Garavan, T. and Morley, M. (1992) 'Organizational Development and Change: Introducing Flexible Working Groups in a High-tech Environment', in D. Winstanley and J. Woodall (eds), *Case Studies in Personnel* (London: IPM (now IPD)), pp. 284–91.
Garrahan, P. and Stewart, P. (1992) *The Nissan Enigma: Flexibility at Work in a Local Economy* (London: Mansell Publishing).
Geary, J. (1994) 'Task Participation: Employees' Participation Enabled or Constrained', in K. Sisson (ed.), *Personnel Management*, 2nd edn (Oxford: Blackwell), pp. 634–61.
Herzberg, F. (1968) 'One More Time: How Do You Motivate Employees?', *Harvard Business Review*, vol. 46, January–February, pp. 53–62, and reprinted.
Kinlaw, D. (1994) *The Practice of Empowerment* (London: Gower).
Lawrence, P.R. and Lorsch, J.W. (1967) *Organization and Environment* (Boston, Mass.: Harvard University Press).
Legge, K. (1995) *Human Resource Management: Rhetorics and Realities* (London: Macmillan).
McGregor, D. (1960) *The Human Side of Enterprise* (New York: McGraw-Hill).
Marchington, M. (1988) 'The Four Faces of Employee Consultation', *Personnel Management*, May, pp. 44–7.
Pateman, C. (1970) *Participation and Democratic Theory* (Cambridge: Cambridge University Press).
Payne, R. (1990) 'The Effectiveness of Research Teams – A Review', in M.A. West and J.L. Farr (eds), *Innovation and Creativity at Work* (New York: Wiley), pp. 101–22.
Price Waterhouse Change Implementation Team (1995) *Better Change: Best Practices for Transforming your Organization* (London: Price Waterhouse, Irwin).
Rainbird, H. (1994) 'Continuing Training', in K. Sisson (ed.), *Personnel Management*, 2nd edn (Oxford: Basil Blackwell).
Ramsey, H. (1992) 'Commitment and Involvement', in B. Towers (ed.), *The Handbook of Human Resource Management* (Oxford: Blackwell), pp. 208–37.
Roethlisberger, F.J. and Dickson, W.J. (1964) *Management and the Worker* (New York: John Wiley).
Steedman, H., Mason, G. and Warner, K. (1991) 'Intermediate Skills and the Workplace: Redeployment, Standards and Supply in Britain', *National Economic Review*, vol. 136, pp. 60–76.
Vroom, V.H. (1964) *Work and Motivation* (New York: John Wiley).
Walker, D. (1991) 'Creative Empowerment at Rover', Chapter 33 in J. Henry and D. Walker (eds), *Managing Innovation* (London: Sage/Open University). pp. 277–86.
Willmott, H. (1993) '"Strength is Ignorance, Slavery is Freedom": Managing Culture in Modern Organizations', *Journal of Management Studies*, vol. 30(4), pp. 515–52.

10 Empowerment in a Government Agency
Barbara Goodwin

INTRODUCTION

A case study in public-sector empowerment

This chapter considers how a policy of empowerment within a public-sector organisation has affected employees' sense of personal responsibility and their perception of ethical issues. It derives from empirical research, based on lengthy interviews, in a government 'Next Steps' agency created in 1991, one of several government agencies concerned with the distribution of welfare benefits. 'The Agency' has espoused a policy of empowerment in the last few years, and its employees have actually experienced *double* empowerment: the move out of the conventional civil service was widely viewed as a liberation in itself, and the internally propagated empowerment movement has further revolutionised the role of employees. The empowerment policy did not initially form part of my own agenda during the interviews, but it was frequently raised by the participants and evidently coloured their own view of their work. This chapter presents their perceptions, which are all-important in considering how empowerment works and whether it is working.

The second section of this chapter explores what is meant by empowerment in the context of the agency and how people see it; the third deals with the conflict between empowerment and targets, and the fourth section highlights some ethical issues raised by participants in the study which indicate that empowerment has not affected crucial aspects of their service to the customer – and perhaps never could do so. The fifth section, for the purpose of contrast, details some research findings on the empowerment process in some private sector organisations, and the final section offers conclusions about the difficulties of achieving empowerment in rule-governed organisations.

Empowerment – rhetoric or reality?

The 'pyramid-flattening' movement has been common to many businesses and public-sector organisations in Britain, the United States and other advanced industrial countries in the last decade. Flattening the pyramid of management means, essentially, stripping out much of the middle management and devolving its responsibilities to lower levels. The process is, as often than not, described as 'empowerment' for lower-level staff. Is this a cynical exploitation of lower-paid employees, a mere management fashion or a justified drive for internal economies – or is it based on a genuine perception of the value of empowering people, to facilitate better decisions and products and, incidentally perhaps, to create greater job satisfaction for lower-level employees? The tenor of analytical writing on empowerment, by contrast with the upbeat approach of the consultants who extol empowerment to managers, has been sceptical.[1]

The issue of empowerment is closely related to two other topical organisational issues: *responsibility* and *accountability*. A related idea, even an ideal, more often considered by philosophers than by managers, is the idea of *autonomy*. 'Responsibility' has various connotations: it can be associated with accountability – that is, the duty to answer to someone for one's actions – and culpability, or else with autonomy, control and freedom of choice. Although these connotations are evidently interconnected, the same word can be given a very different emphasis. Both public and private-sector organisations have been emphasising their differing accountabilities in recent years: public-sector organisations are essentially accountable to tax-payers, via the relevant Minister and parliament, while private-sector organisations primarily stress accountability to shareholders. The notion of accountability to business stakeholders has also been increasingly recognised, although the recent hijacking of the term by some British politicians has blurred its meaning. 'Autonomy' can be applied with different force to organisations and to individuals. Government agencies such as the one considered below have become relatively autonomous in the last few years, ridding themselves of years of civil service accretions and being relatively free from government direction and interference, as long as they carry out government policy satisfactorily. The idea of autonomy for individuals working in large organisations is necessarily relative: just as no-one who lives in society can be perfectly free, no worker can be entirely autonomous. The term 'autonomy' is generally used in the empowerment context when individuals (and teams) are given greater scope to make decisions at their own discretion and to determine their own pattern of work – in short, when their control over their own work processes and/or products is enhanced.

A distinction can usefully be made between process empowerment and product empowerment. Process empowerment would give employees a larger role in the processes of the organisation; it is essentially an inward-looking reform, which changes the matrix of responsibility and control within the organisation. Product empowerment denotes greater employee input into the product, or service, itself; workers might, for example, be encouraged to propose changes to the product or innovations in the service. Organisations which are open to product, as well as process, empowerment may have systems of suggestion boxes and competitions and offer prizes and other incentives for innovative ideas. Product empowerment is, however, unlikely to be feasible in large companies with well-defined and established products, and is similarly unfeasible in public-sector service organisations where ultimately the government determines the service to be delivered. This is so with the agency which forms the case study of this chapter: the focus there is on process empowerment.

Other chapters in this volume (*vide* Christensen Hughes, for example) explore the different kinds of motivation which cause managers to adopt empowerment policies. This chapter describes how such policies – whatever their underlying motivation – impact on employees. The fact that many 'empowered employees' tend to be sceptical of the process of empowerment should not lead too directly to the conclusion that such processes are a sham: empowerment requires a culture change (often unwelcome) that takes time. This is especially so in public-sector organisations or in recently privatised businesses which were formerly run on quasi-bureaucratic lines, where responsibility was always passed upwards.

The research context

My research in the agency formed part of a study of eight public and private-sector organisations undertaken to discover how people working in large organisations perceive their personal responsibilities, and whether they experience moral dilemmas as a result of a divergence between their personal moral values and the values of the organisation.[2] Next Steps agencies were constituted during the late 1980s and continued to be created during the 1990s as part of the Conservative government's policy of reducing the size of the civil service and public sector and of privatising as many administrative functions as possible. Their staff remain civil servants, at least for the time being. In theory, the agencies are responsible for the operational side and carry out government policy, while the relevant Minister retains responsibility for policy. While in principle such agencies have an unprecedented degree of budgetary freedom and autonomy, in practice they are still very much subject to government regulation and intervention. Episodes such as the dismissal by the Home Secretary of the Director General of the Prison Service, Derek Lewis, in 1995 – purportedly because of the escape of prisoners from Parkhurst and other issues of prison management highlighted in the Learmont report – indicate that the supposed autonomy of these institutions is questionable. The agencies are, of course, run more on business lines than the conventional civil service and have correspondingly absorbed many modern management and organisational doctrines – including empowerment, teamwork and incessant restructuring and reorganisation.

This agency study was based on lengthy, in-depth interviews with a relatively small sample of staff within the agency – in other words, it is *qualitative*, not quantitative, research, although where several participants made similar points they may be thought to represent prevalent views. A description of the sample appears in the endnotes to this chapter.[3] The study provides a snapshot of attitudes to empowerment in the agency at a particular time (late 1995) and does not comprehend the development of the empowerment process (cf. Christensen Hughes's study in this volume, which has a longitudinal element).

The structure of the agency is as follows: there is a headquarters ('the centre'), where the chief executive and the major support departments, including personnel, operate. Nationwide the agency takes the form of a pyramid structure composed of a number of quasi-geographical groupings: the territorial, the area, the district and the branch. The managers at each of these levels is answerable to a manager at the next level. Below the managers are senior executive officers, higher executive officers, higher clerical officers (supervisors) and clerical officers.

The research took place in two area offices and five district offices, including branch offices which deal directly with 'customers' (that is, benefit claimants). The sample (see endnote 3) was slightly skewed towards the management grades, but did not include the better paid, and often more senior, managers at headquarters because the study was directed towards those engaged in the operational side of the agency. The participants had been employed for between five and 36 years in the agency or its predecessors (that is the former Department of Health and Social Security (DHSS) which became the Department of Social Security (DSS)). They were therefore in a good position to contrast the workings and ethos of the new agency with those of their previous employer. Most participants had been in the civil service for most of their working lives (however long), although three had joined from the private sector. Two had degrees, the majority had come from school and most of those had come with A-levels. Thus, the participants still exemplified the life-long career pattern typical of a traditional civil servant despite the move to agency status, although two senior participants were actively considering early retirement because the ethos of the agency now seems to favour a different kind of manager, more business-orientated.

EMPOWERMENT IN THE AGENCY

The agency's own publicity material does not name empowerment as an explicit policy. However, publicly available documents include the objectives of ensuring management responsibility and ensuring that authority is 'extensively devolved'; 'empowering staff to take responsibility for dealing with problems and to make improvements when and where opportunities occur'; also, 'developing confident visible leadership throughout the organisation'. Seen thus from the outside, the public statements apparently relating to empowerment verge on the platitudinous.

How is empowerment perceived?

These quotations indicate how the empowerment process is perceived by staff at various levels in the agency:

> The Agency has been reorganising, de-layering, reducing the management tier and giving power to lower levels. (District manager)

> [An ex-army colleague] said that the Agency should be like the army. I said that modern organisations are not like the army: with empowerment, solutions should come from the workers themselves. (Branch manager (higher executive officer))

> Lower grades are now more empowered and confident and can manage staff better than they used to. There are training courses on empowerment for [higher-grade clerical officers], which gives confidence, makes you a better person, and better qualified. (Higher executive officer)

> Staff are empowered to take routine decisions and even if I disagree with the decision I'll back them up because I don't want to undermine them in front of the customer. (Higher clerical officer)

To summarise, staff are empowered to take decisions appropriate to their own levels; lower-grade staff take on more of a management function and staff are (in theory at least) encouraged to propose solutions to perceived problems at their own level, rather than having these imposed by managers.

Contrasts with the previous system

The following comments highlight the different climate in the agency, compared with that within a typically bureaucratic, civil service structure:

> Since becoming the Agency we've embraced empowerment. Before, it used to be 'I tell you, and you tell them.' (Higher executive officer)

> Under the old command and control system, the person at the top would have been telling people how to do their jobs and in the case of a foul-up they could say 'I was obeying the boss.' Now such people will be sanctioned if there's a foul-up, and this approach is more likely to prevent mistakes. (Area manager)

Empowerment and management

Area and district managers commented:

> [Previously] everything was pre-ordained and there was no room to manage – you had to ask permission from the highest level to employ a clerk. In the mid-1980s things began to change for the better, with more autonomy being vested in managers. Now my managers each have budgets of between three and five million pounds and can determine their own staffing and recruitment policies. (Area manager)

> I believe in empowerment for my managers and let them get on with it. If I started interfering with them, they'd start laying blame on me! (Area manager)

> My Deputy and I talk a lot about what he and I need to know. He has almost total empowerment from me and I don't think we have any doubts about whether something is his or my responsibility, there's a distinct line between Operations and Strategy. (District manager)

For managers, then, the benefit is being free to manage better and to be able to empower the managers below them. However, a number of instances were cited where their power to manage staff (and in particular to discipline or dismiss recalcitrant staff) had been restricted or undermined by the centre's personnel department, which had given advice or rulings on individual cases, usually advising against disciplinary procedures or dismissal for poor performance or misbehaviour. The advice was supposed to impose a uniform practice throughout the organisation but was often felt inappropriate for the staffing difficulties experienced in London offices, which suffered especially from discipline and recruitment problems.

Resistance to empowerment among staff

Resistance to empowerment occurs at the lower levels of the agency where it is seen as a threat or imposition – as some of these comments suggest:

> We're trying to empower staff, to get the clerical officers to take more responsibility, work above their grade. But staff and unions see empowerment as 'dumping' because they are not paid for the new responsibilities. I'm doing it to make their work more interesting. (District manager)
>
> Nobody seems to want to take responsibility for things, yet we have a Core Value of 'bias for action' and empowerment. (Higher executive officer)
>
> With empowerment, some people think they're delegated *more* work. (Higher executive officer)
>
> In the wrong hands it can lead to disastrous results, with managers delegating tasks they would formerly have done themselves. (Higher clerical officer)
>
> The [Agency] is trying to devolve power to the lowest level, whether to save costs or whatever I don't know. They are taking part of the adjudication from the managers and giving it to the people doing the work. It's good in that the managers are not so used to dealing with the public, but the down side is that some people are doing work that they haven't experience of and can't do. (Clerical officer)

Two district managers said that empowerment also caused worries at the higher levels:

> A lot of district managers are not comfortable with this and would rather be given instructions. (District manager)
>
> Some people can't cope with changing from an organisation where if you stuck to the rules you couldn't go wrong to one of devolved responsibility and accountability – they just can't cope. (District manager)

Some managers in their fifties were actively considering early retirement, although this was because they felt that they did not suit the new managerial climate, rather than because they could not cope with empowerment policies.

Teamwork

Empowerment is often implemented through enhanced teamwork. Most of the agency participants who had experienced teamwork were positive about it and pointed out its advantages: that it makes colleagues more appreciative of each other; they feel a shared responsibility if things go wrong (although the team leader may still receive the criticism); everyone contributes, is more committed and more work is done; colleagues trust each other; not letting down the team is an incentive; it is better for staff morale. One supervisor emphasised the importance of leading the team by example, for example by staying late to cover work if necessary. But clerical officers working in reception teams (which deal with the public) said that because the receptionists' work is with individual clients, although they may feel responsible to the client, they feel no responsibility to the team; they will not, for example, help out when customers are waiting. The receptionists' back offices have display boards which show the numbers of customers still waiting, but these seem not to counteract this attitude. The impression was that reception 'teams' are so in name only in some branches.

It is hard for an outsider to assess the *reality* of empowerment in the agency from these comments alone, but evidently a culture change took place in the DSS from the mid-1980s onwards, with increasing empowerment at the managerial levels; within the agency this has now culminated in a drive to empower the clerical grades. No-one gave examples of how empowerment had actually changed the nature of the clerical and customer-related work of clerical officers, which is so constrained by procedures and rules that it is doubtful whether such work can ever be made less routine and more responsible. A gesture towards product empowerment is the 'one-stop' philosophy, which encourages (or empowers) front-line staff to 'take ownership' when they receive a customer inquiry and to follow it through; however, this is prejudiced by the fact that a number of different processing units are involved in the treatment of claims, some located in different parts of the country. (Furthermore, in these days of advanced communications, correspondence between the units is still mainly by post.) Certainly, clerical officers did not feel that they had more influence or empowerment with respect to the running and the processes of the agency, although managers clearly felt that to be true for themselves. But the empowerment initiative seemed to inspire ambitious higher clerical officers and to be widely accepted as desirable by higher executive officers and above.

Statements about how empowerment relates to personal responsibility are of particular interest in the ethical context. In the conventional civil service, responsibility was strictly passed up the line by and large. In the agency, according to participants:

1. responsibility is more clearly defined;
2. people lower down are reprimanded for mistakes and cannot use the excuse of obeying orders; and
3. managers feel entitled to blame higher managers if they interfere and matters go wrong.

But the devolution of responsibility may also be more apparent than real. Discussing empowerment and Total Quality Management [TQM], Kerfoot and Knights (1995) have stated that 'anxieties within a hierarchically coordinated organisation remain, because of the question of ultimate responsibility resting with senior management. For passing responsibility down the hierarchy is no guarantee that it will stay there.' In the agency, this statement is borne out by the effects of the target-setting process.

On a different plane, *the customer's* perception of who has responsibility may be entirely different from the view within the organisation and may not relate to the actual structure of authority within the agency. An officer applying the rule governing a claim *to the customer's detriment* will often be seen, and blamed, as responsible because he/she is at the customer interface, whereas he/she actually has no option or discretion. (In fact, the only area where staff have real discretion about payments is where payments from the 'social fund' for customers' urgent or special needs are involved – and these in turn are severely constrained by limited resources and a system of prioritisation.) Given these constraints, it must be asked whether empowerment is chiefly an internally-orientated policy, devised to improve working practices, and perhaps following a current management fashion (that is, *process empowerment*), rather than something which directly affects – or could even improve – the service to the customer (that is, *product empowerment*).

EMPOWERMENT AND TARGETS

There is no such thing as a free lunch. Where empowerment walks, targets stalk not far behind. The setting of targets is a familiar process to those working in large organisations in the public sector – not least to academics. In many British universities, the system of devolved budgeting has led to targets (for example for student numbers and research income) which must be met by departments or faculties. Sanctions are often invoked against those who fail to meet the targets. Such systems are closely interlinked with the *quality* approach which, perhaps inappropriately, sets rather crude *quantitative* targets, even for services or functions which are notoriously difficult to measure. This approach has been common to public sector organisations in the United Kingdom for a decade or so (Pollitt, 1990). The concrete achievements sometimes appear trifling or inconsequential: at a mundane level, for example, most local authorities now have commitments or targets about answering the telephone and replying to letters within a given time period.

The quality movement has in turn been deliberately and explicitly associated by government policy with the doctrine of greater empowerment for government agencies. But these agencies must implement government policy and are ultimately under government control; crucially, they are (for the most part) entirely funded by government. A key controlling device is therefore target setting, to ensure the highest performance within limited resources. In some public service organisations where output is hard to measure, performance indicators are the chosen yardstick; but in the agency there is a multiplicity of *targets* which are quantitatively defined. One definition of their purposes was offered by on area manager: 'What targets do is to manage people's perceptions and the customer's expectations. I'm very target-conscious and discuss them with my managers at most of our meetings.'

The main problem with targets from the manager's perspective is that meeting targets remains his or her entire responsibility, while their actual fulfilment relies on the activities and cooperation of staff at a much lower level. Research in the agency reflected this.

Targets can be seen as the downside of *empowerment*: you are given more freedom but are constrained to achieve specific results. In the agency, their effect is felt even by clerical officers: the team leaders have their own targets to meet and have to collect statistics about the numbers of customers dealt with and claims processed. Individuals' appraisals may be affected adversely if targets are not reached, even when they are not in a position to ensure target achievement. Although some participants had mentioned targets with approval when asked about how the agency had changed, criticisms of the system's operation (although not necessarily of the target principle itself) were made by participants at all levels, and their comments are set out below. The lack of control bothered most people – in other words, they were held responsible and could be blamed for shortcomings beyond their personal control. To them, the outcome of the policy did not *seem* like empowerment. Some of the actual targets were also outside the control of even the most senior managers, because they were set by government:

> As District Manager, I'm set tasks and targets but I'm at the mercy of people delivering them. I have some power to ensure that they do things, but they could also shoot me down in flames. My manager's appraisal of me depends largely on the District's performance. (District manager)
>
> I have no control over that... my targets are tied into customers filling in forms. Or the targets may be tied into something done – or not done – by another Department, such as the Department of Employment. (Area manager)
>
> I'm responsible for hitting targets. I haven't much control over this except that I can chase people, and report on my managers as to whether they hit their targets or not... Any manager is in the hands of the staff where meeting targets is concerned. (District manager)
>
> The Secretary of State's targets are out of my control. The local target is to clear 80% of the office within one hour. I cannot control the number of callers and the number of staff sick on a particular day. The staff are individuals and may choose to cooperate or not. I don't think I should be held accountable but as a manager I am responsible. (Higher executive officer)
>
> We have 20 or 30 Secretary of State's targets and it's not me personally paying the benefits. Other people are determining my fate if they perform poorly. That's a principle of accountability inherent in management, the buck keeps going up. (Higher executive officer)
>
> If the team does not perform then my targets are affected. (Higher clerical officer)

All these comments reflect the paradox of being accountable while lacking control over the outcome of others' contributions. The distinction between accountability and responsibility (discussed in the Introduction, above) is implicit in some of the comments: to the participants whose used the terms, being accountable had the negative connotation of being called to account, while being responsible denoted the duty to get particular things done.

Policies imposed from above can lead to the sense that empowerment is rather notional:

> The Chief Executive has signed us up to good treatment of customers – better access, privacy, comfortable surroundings – and in some buildings you can't offer this. *We're caught in the middle, we have freedom but the rope suddenly pulls tight.* (Higher executive officer, my italics)

Some participants considered that the target system had adverse effects on staff:

> I have concerns about staff treatment because of the stress and pressure we put them under to achieve performance targets. (District manager)
>
> It would be nice to be better (properly) resourced. It would demonstrate more care for the employees and reduce the pressure. *It is not ethical to under-resource and then hold staff and management accountable for not achieving targets.* (Senior executive officer; my italics)

Adverse effects on the customer were also identified:

> Some people feel as if they're there to stop people getting benefits. It may be coming from the management trying to run this as a business; we have targets (which mean nothing to me in my job) and are trying to save money, cut running costs. (Clerical officer)
>
> For years the regular [home] visits weren't carried out because we got kicked harder if we were not meeting our clearance targets. (Higher executive officer)
>
> Those claims which can be done quickest get done first because that's the easy way of reaching the target. (Higher clerical officer)

The last two comments are indicative of the distortions introduced by the target process into the normal work of the agency; activities which can be measured and easily accomplished are more likely to be undertaken than more time-consuming procedures, such as visiting clients at home to assess their needs, or any changes in their circumstances. Ironically, cutting back on home visits makes benefit fraud – another 'target' of government policy – more likely to occur. (Elsewhere in this volume, Christensen Hughes makes a similar point about the audit process, quoting a manager as saying 'The stuff my boss looks at I do, the rest gets dropped'.)

Agency staff would be the best judge of whether these comments reflect some injustice and real problems or whether they merely represent a healthy 'kick against the pricks', a resistance to being so closely monitored. What *is* indicative, however, is that when participants were asked if they had ever been requested to do something morally wrong in their job, several cited having been asked to falsify statistics to meet targets:

> I have had a manager telling me to alter my statistics because performance had been lousy; I was team leader, I did it. But I whistleblew and wrote to *his* boss, accepting my own culpability as well. (Higher executive officer)

I have been asked to massage the figures in a previous job... I did so to take pressure off the team. (Higher executive officer)

In a previous job we sometimes made up the statistics, so I asked what was the point of keeping statistics. They explained to me the benefits of doing that – for example, we could get more staff. It was my instructed job so I did it. If it had been my responsibility, I'd have done the statistics differently from the beginning. (Clerical officer)

All these examples were carefully put in the past tense, but can one doubt that statistics are still manipulated, here or in any organisation which sets stringent targets for staff performance or output? Agency managers' offices have coloured bar charts on the walls comparing relative target achievements between different districts and areas. Each group gets a regular performance rating out of 9. Referring to these, one manager said that he could not understand why some districts in the agency kept achieving ratings of '8' while he found it hard even to get a '2'.

Empowerment plus targets is thus a prescription for a degree of in-built moral corruption in an organisation, which affects both managers and lower level-staff, as the above comments illustrate. Indeed, as target setters must know, the classic line of defence taken by 'target subjects' is to falsify the statistics – a lesson well-learnt by those working in directed economies, for example by industrial managers in the former USSR and by the managers of farming collectives in China during the 'Great Leap Forward'.

The consequences of achievement or under-achievement for agency staff are not negligible. At the operational level, shortfalls mean being starved of resources for extra staff. The appraisal process takes target achievement into account. One area manager said 'my manager marked me down at my appraisal in terms of my overall effectiveness, because the Area had slipped below par on performance in 1993/4. It hurt my pride because *I* didn't work less hard that year. It also affected my performance pay. I'm here to deliver a service and because it fell short I was sanctioned'.

Targets raise serious moral issues: a manager may feel that staff will suffer if there is a shortfall and so be tempted to massage the figures. Honesty vies with loyalty and responsibility to employees and self-interest may also enter the equation. Dishonest behaviour has further consequences as those who massage statistics (even for the best reasons) may deprive more honest managers, and their staff, of much needed resources. Resource allocation based on target achievement is a regular battleground:

I'm strictly honest about budgets. I had to say at the Area Team [meeting] that we would *not* make do with less than we deserved on an earned basis, and I won. The staff at District level understand we're responsible for the budget and they need to know that we have been given what we earned. I had moral indignation about [the attempt to give the District less than we had earned]. (District manager)

While target subjects find the area a moral minefield, there are also practical issues for *target-setters* about their ultimate usefulness. Stringent limitation on the allocation of resources within which an organisation has to meet its targets, which is common to the whole public sector, may also make the target exercise self-defeating, because of self-preserving behaviour. Certainly, it makes it frustrating for managers and staff.

It is hard not to conclude that empowerment constrained by blunt or crude targets is something of an organisational sham. Discretion is given with one hand and taken away with the other. In the case of the agency, the targets follow directly from government policy and are indeed set by the Secretary of State (or, more precisely, by the civil servants in the DSS). Targets are then devolved from the centre to areas, districts, branches and down to the teams dealing with customers and paperwork. Of course, managers in all organisations have always had responsibility for meeting product output or other measurable output. But the application of the target principle is more difficult in organisations which do not produce measurable outputs, or where the 'output' relates to unpredictable customer demand. For example, in the agency, a higher clerical officer may be held responsible for ensuring that her team sees all the customers who come to the office in one day, and for ensuring that no customer has to wait for more than half an hour. An unexpected rush of customers, or several difficult customers, may make that impossible; more resources (that is, funding for a larger team to meet unpredicted demand) are not on offer. Thus, *product empowerment* may be impossible without better resourcing, although constrained resources may enhance *productivity* – which is a measure of efficiency rather than of product quality. It is also noteworthy that some branches of the agency had greater problems with staffing and staff discipline than others – especially London branches – so that country-wide targets became virtually impossible to meet in those branches.

Morgan and Murgatroyd (1994) have argued that empowerment really means being licensed to realise the policies and strategy already determined by management. 'Individuals are therefore being empowered in terms of how they can achieve the goals set, not in terms of what the goals might be'. This argument can apply to target-setting, as well as to the processes and products of an organisation; certainly, it is an apposite comment on empowerment in the agency.

EMPOWERMENT AND ETHICS IN A RULE-GOVERNED ORGANISATION

Can empowerment help employees resolve the substantive moral dilemmas encountered in their working lives? In the world of social security, the necessity of following legislation and fixed criteria, come what may, when dealing with people in need, presents a major ethical issue for agency staff, at both clerical and managerial levels. Indeed, many managers have worked their way up from clerical duties and are still keenly aware of the problems facing the counter staff, who deal directly with the public. When asked what ethical issues most concerned them in their work, participants in the study offered the comments below. Paying benefits to the wrong people and not to the right people are paramount concerns; the fact that the rules sometimes seem to favour the wrong people is also an issue:

> The main trouble for a civil servant is that he delivers what he's told to deliver. In the social security empire you deliver things against your better judgement. There are people I pay money to I wouldn't choose to, and vice versa. (District manager)

> If the government of the day's policy is to do something, that's the law. The conscience clause gives people protection from doing things they think are wrong. But sometimes on the counter you feel you'd like to help people but the system won't let you. (District manager)

> The biggest [ethical issue] is helping the right people. Are we giving money to the right people? People really in need slip through the net but we have to pay the ones who are playing the system and satisfy our criteria. (Higher clerical officer)

> I have some major disagreements with social security policy. Some of the ethics of paying the 'undeserving poor' lead to scruples, but I have to sweep them away. People who don't need benefit get paid, others who do, don't... The moral dimension of our work does not appear much in the in-house literature, which concentrates on prescription and policy; training is very mundane and technical. (Higher executive officer)

> We do very bureaucratic things which don't seem fair. Most of the time when I'm an adjudicator [determining the outcome of benefits claims], I must deal with the facts and keep out emotion. (District manager)

> I disagree with many rules, such as the benefit rates for homeless persons ... We're up against White Papers etc. and have no discretion. (Clerical officer)

> The people at the top (e.g. politicians) can make decisions regardless of the staff on the front line, and you have to go out there and serve it up to the customer. We don't always agree with the rules and regulations. People are desperate ... and there's nothing you can do. (Higher clerical officer)

> [One ethical issue is] the legislation governing the benefits we pay and how we pay them. I don't have control over that but I see the results. (Higher executive officer)

Thus, empowerment does not, and because of the nature of the agency's work, *cannot* resolve the main moral dilemmas which staff encounter in their work, because they are applying rules. But, by contrast, a minority of participants saw the existence of rules (while they might not agree with particular rules) as a protection for the customer and for themselves:

> I may have personal views about the levels of benefits and may get into arguments with people about these; my defensive position is 'That's the law'. It's all about evidence. I have some areas of discretion and may follow my own moral code. *But I see so many people each week that I have to have cut and dried guidelines for fairness.* (my italics) (Higher clerical officer)

> There are areas of legislation I don't agree with as a person, but we have a clear responsibility for upholding the law and that's a better protection for the public than if we had a greater degree of discretion in awarding benefits. (District manager)

> [One ethical concern is] that everything is fair and open. We've got equal opportunities and other policies; I see that we don't circumvent these policies and deal with people fairly and openly. (Higher executive officer)

> We have guidelines and the law. I do not allow my personal beliefs to come into the job, but investigate the customer impartially, whoever it is. (A fraud investigator – higher clerical officer)

Rules versus empowerment?

Can empowerment ever be meaningful in an organisation which works strictly to rules? In the agency it succeeds – up to a point – at the higher managerial levels, as the participants agreed, but leaves the lower-level staff with the frustrations and moral dilemmas which they have always encountered in dealing with customers. The rules themselves raise ethical issues for those who have to operate them, as does the government policy and legislation on which they are based. Empowerment may make a difference in organisational terms, i.e. it may involve a redistribution of responsibility and powers, but it scarcely touches on the primary function of the agency, which is to distribute benefits according to set criteria. In this respect, the position of the agency's staff may not seem so different from that of employees in a private-sector organisation – for example, the workers in a car manufacturing company have to make cars according to specified standards, however great (or small) the degree of empowerment in the organisation. The significant difference may be that, for agency staff, the criteria (c.f. standards) to which they work are determined outside the organisation and often do not coincide with the employees' own perception of what is ethically right, because of political and humanitarian considerations.

By contrast, the car workers might well agree with the standards set by the company (concerning safety, for example, being car drivers themselves and often driving their own company's cars), even if they find the standards irksome because they create additional work. In neither case does empowerment give employees a completely free hand in how they do their work, but in the agency there are supervening moral considerations in the work itself. Many of those working there do so because of a desire to help the deprived members of society. They would like to improve the *product*, but have no power to do so because of the rules. Process empowerment, if it has genuinely happened, has had little effect on the product.

A COMPARATIVE PERSPECTIVE

For contrast, I discuss here some of my research findings in other organisations where empowerment was also a declared policy: a large accountancy firm, a bank, an airline company and a water company (Goodwin, 1995, 1996).[4] All these organisations had recently experienced restructuring and a redefinition of the responsibilities of staff, and in most there had been a degree of pyramid-flattening. Empowerment was most meaningful where the staff were most skilled or professional, which is not the case with lower-level workers in the agency.

An accountancy firm

This large accountancy firm, like other 'Big-Six' accountants, is largely staffed by people with university degrees and professional qualifications, the training for which includes a course on ethics. Empowerment might therefore seem particularly appropriate in such an organisation, where each employee has in principle the capability of using discretion and working with some degree of autonomy. In the firm in question, some participants mentioned 'empowerment' as a new policy, stating that the firm was trying to move more responsibility downwards, delegating work and giving juniors more responsible tasks. No-one made it clear precisely how this was affecting working practices or duties, except in the specific case of audit managers being recently required to be involved in marketing, in that they were now expected to spend some time – both work time and leisure time – in attracting customers to the firm and making useful contacts. This was seen as an unwelcome intrusion into their normal duties and as a devolution of what had by custom been the marketing duties of the partners.

This may suggest that empowerment is more a doctrine of convenience than a reality. But it was also said that clerical staff might soon be employed on the routine audit tasks, leaving more time for professionally qualified staff to get on with the more complex aspects of auditing, insolvency and tax. Auditors and other accountants generally work in small teams: the question of empowerment was therefore connected with a question as to whether working in a team gave people a different sense of responsibility. The spontaneous reaction of some participants was that the teams actually had hierarchies within them and were not teams of co-responsibles. The only disadvantage of teamwork noted was that lazy people can more easily delegate work to others. Several advantages of the team system were suggested in the answers: loyalty to the team and the relevant partner; a sense of belonging; greater fulfilment; more responsibility and a broader understanding of the job, and stronger motivation. In this respect, teamwork as a working method seemed to encompass some of the proclaimed advantages of empowerment. The high calibre of staff in the firm was also a factor:

> Within this Firm you are dealing with highly motivated and intelligent professionals. You point people at a problem and they do it. When running a company you have to motivate people and stand over them. There is a big difference between here and the 'nine to five' mentality found in companies.

This degree of dedication, ambition and interest in the work, which makes empowerment a reality, could probably not be expected in all organisations at all levels.

A clearing bank

In a parallel study in a clearing bank which was undergoing major restructuring, employees clearly associated the stated policy of empowerment with an increase in personal responsibility, in the sense of *accountability*:

> The Bank is going more towards individual responsibility. Previously the manager was held responsible for everything, if something went wrong. Now, everyone has a job description and is responsible for doing it.
>
> The Bank is now making people personally responsible for their work, which I believe is correct.

Formerly, the bank had operated on a rigid employee-grading system which was detrimental to the sense of personal responsibility at the lower staff levels, but this was now being dismantled as part of the empowerment drive. Participants in managerial or supervisory posts were ready to accept responsibility (and blame) for their staff's errors or failings, but were less happy about accepting blame for matters beyond their control, especially matters relating to internal costs and targets. All expressed a strong sense of responsibility to customers, echoing a message which the bank has communicated strongly in recent years to its staff.

Increased team working was said to be reinforcing a sense of collective responsibility, and the new emphasis on teamwork was seen as very positive by most participants:

> It definitely gives people a collective sense of responsibility... I don't think junior people appreciate what a team can achieve – for a lot of them it's just a job, done for the money.
>
> The work is done better because you can discuss it with the team and try to solve it instead of going to the manager. There's loyalty to each other. When they're ill they'll ring in to ensure cover. They go home at the same time. If someone has a queue they'll all jump up to serve. They seem to want to help each other more than they did.

The problems with teamwork were 'non-team-players', who were said eventually to isolate themselves (but perhaps not before damaging the team), and the enhanced possibilities of skiving. Good team management was the solution: 'Looking at the junior members of staff in the Customer Service section, when people are in a team they're more willing to avoid responsibilities on the basis that "If I don't do it, someone else will." It depends on how the team is managed; in my team we all know our responsibilities.' Against these trends, an aspect of banking which disempowered staff was the increasing reliance on computers to make judgements on customers and risks:

> I don't like the way Loans is going; formerly you got someone to sanction something, now you put it in a machine. You've still got to pass judgement on what comes out of the machine; it's difficult if you know the customer well but the machine says 'No'.

Again, this reflects the limiting effects on staff empowerment of the rigid application of internal rules. The fact that the rules in this case are enforced by the computer also makes their restraining effect seem less humane and more frustrating to staff who would like to make a moral – or practical – judgement on a customer's case.

A water company

The water company which formed part of my study had also flattened the management pyramid after privatisation; there had been many redundancies, especially among middle management. Following these changes, there was a new project to empower staff, described by a senior managers and a board member in these terms:

> We are increasingly trying to give people control over their destiny. The IT programme has increasingly given people power over their own lives. In 10 years time there will be hierarchical systems, but far fewer of them. Project Breakthrough is a method of manpower reduction in the white collar area. The method is to give people local empowerment. Local Network Services will have its own finance managers and so on.
>
> Project Breakthrough means to move from centrally-driven command or control economy, to encouraging people to accept their own destiny within their control. The dilemma is, would this empowerment work to the company's advantage? I say, only if so empowered they would deliver a different effort or product. I think that won't happen *unless we change some of the people with the public sector ethic* (my italics) [which meant that] your idleness was pinned on the sense of respectability of what you were doing... But the main object of a utility business is still to serve customers.

By contrast, empowerment was greeted by some operational workers with a degree of puzzlement: 'The project leader has taken courses on team empowerment: he thinks the team should be leaderless'.

As was said at the start of this chapter, responsibility has various connotations and the same word can be given very different emphases. For example, the written material on Project Breakthrough emphasised responsibility enforced by 'zero-based budgeting', a concept which seems close to the notion of *accountability*. However, the in-house literature also advocates that employees should take more responsibility and have a say in determining the support services they needed and should be involved in service level agreements (which help to avoid endless wrangling between different departments in an organisation about who should have done what, and when, and who is to blame for shortcomings and errors). This is closer to the idea of responsibility as autonomy. The problem in the water company was to get the message through to operational workers who had been more used to taking orders than taking responsibility.

An airline company

The airline company, in another parallel study, was promoting new attitudes towards duties and a degree of empowerment. Its Code emphasises qualities such as honesty, fairness, responsiveness and integrity and also encourages staff to subscribe to corporate values. It promotes *individual empowerment* and consultation with colleagues on difficult decisions. My research coincided with an empowering initiative to encourage cabin crews to be more spontaneous and less rule-bound in their work: 'throwing away the rule book' was the theme. Cabin staff and ground staff had recently been empowered to give (relatively small) gifts or payments to unhappy customers which they viewed as a form of empowerment and increased control over their work, since dealing with customers who are dissatisfied, for whatever reason, is a quotidian task of the employees of any airline. The airline is moving towards flexibility and self-management, as far as this is possible in a business which is necessarily governed by strict regulations and safety procedures. The staff – most of them well-qualified and highly trained – understand and welcome this empowerment and are willing to go beyond their formal duties.

Any airline must perforce empower its operational staff to an unusual extent since its major operations occur in the air, hundreds or thousands of miles from any management headquarters. Furthermore, teamwork is an integral part of the airline business. As one pilot observed: 'flying is teamwork because I can't do it by myself. The problem with us as teams is that we don't often meet colleagues, so we can't engender team spirit'. He explained that he would often only meet the flight crew just before take-off and might not know any of them personally. One participant (with experience of the engineering division of the company) drew an instructive distinction between real teamwork and more nominal teams:

'in the Shuttle we worked in teams, on shifts. At the end of the day you're handing over the responsibility to another shift team and can forget it. Here there are four of us who have to get the task finished and we all muck in. In my days at the Shuttle I didn't realise how marked the difference is between shifts and real teams.' This illustrates as well as anything the relationship between *real* teamwork, responsibility and empowerment.

'Customer empowerment' in the public sector

Similar research in two local authorities did not reveal much explicit commitment to empowerment. This may be because – despite contracting out – the remaining core of local government is still organised internally on a quasi-civil service basis, and retains a fairly hierarchical structure, although there has been considerable restructuring and a number of redundancies. Some local authorities take part in the Investors in People (IIP) initiative and I interviewed one manager (in charge of manual workers) who had successfully encouraged her workforce to apply for BS5750 certification; the latter, however, might be viewed as a system of external scrutiny rather than as internal empowerment.

But a different dimension of empowerment – not so far discussed here – was mentioned by some local authority participants, who remarked that the public now has different expectations of local government. Some participants saw this as *empowerment of the public*, and therefore good and some saw it as a regrettable development:

> People now have different expectations, they expect that organisations will *serve* them. I'm totally against all these Charters, but I think they're having an effect.

> The *'Me* society' means we have a more aggressive clientele and has changed the way we go about our jobs. We can get challenged because people pursue selfish objectives against the will of the community and they use local government to do it.

The Charter movements in the public sector, reflecting the marketisation and customer-service orientation in the private sector, are intended to be developments in *customer empowerment*: but whether such initiatives have radically changed the products and services on offer is beyond the scope of this chapter.[5]

Like many local authorities which have 'service promises' and 'quality commitments' to customers, the agency has a Customer Charter: its language has changed to denominate benefits claimants as customers, and attempts have been made – where resources permit – to improve waiting areas and speed of service. One recent customer-orientated initiative by the chief executive was to make the offices dealing with claimants open earlier in the morning: there was (I was told) no proven customer demand for this service, and it created strong resentment among staff and union resistance. But, even if the service were of poor quality and offered at inconvenient hours, ultimately the agency's customers are no more able to withdraw their 'custom' than the customers of a local authority, unless the latter can afford to move out of the borough. Customer empowerment in the public sector has inherent limitations.

One import of this section is that empowerment is more of a reality, the more professional staff are, a point exemplified by the accountancy firm and the airline. The agency's staff do not generally possess the kind of skills or special training which employees in these other organisations boast, although many of them, especially the managers, can claim long experience in the work. The clerical officers and, below these, the administrative assistants who have only temporary jobs, may not be sufficiently skilled to *be* empowered, from the perspective of higher management.

EMPOWERMENT – AN IMPOSSIBLE ASPIRATION?

> [Becoming an Agency] has made a difference because work is devolved downwards with more accountability. But it's no easier to be accountable for policies which we do not make. (District manager)

Although the managers interviewed regarded themselves as empowered by comparison with their former situation in the DHSS and DSS, this empowerment has important limits. To extend the comparison with business organisations made earlier one stage further, the senior managers in a car manufacturing company may decide to redesign the product or even to build trucks instead of cars: but here the analogy with the agency breaks down entirely. Senior managers cannot change their 'product', that is, the benefits paid; at best they might hope to influence the government on benefits policy. This is, however, difficult since governments have manifesto commitments and political agendas to pursue: recent benefit changes like the Habitual Residency Test (1995) – to prevent non-residents from claiming benefits – and the Job Seekers' Allowance (1996) – to encourage the unemployed to seek work – were both, apparently, introduced precipitately (for political reasons) and against the advice of the agency managers who would be administering the benefit and who could foresee fundamental delivery problems. So even the top management of government agencies are radically disempowered because they are not, and cannot be, in charge of their 'product'.

While the empowerment initiative within the agency has emphasised its departure from the traditional 'command and control' system of civil service organisation, it has been closely linked both with internal target-setting – undertaken perhaps to live up to the government's requirement that Next Steps agencies should correspond more closely to business organisations and also as part of the Charter movement – and with external target-setting (for example the Secretary of State's targets). Managers and staff are constrained both by targets and strict control of resources. This scenario produces certain 'internal' ethical dilemmas, as exemplified by requests to falsify statistics. This leads to a question about the *ethics of empowerment* – is it ethical to tell people they are empowered and then to regulate their behaviour so strictly in terms of targets?

The move to empowerment in the agency has also not resolved the ethical problems experienced by those who interact with customers on a regular basis, because empowerment is in turn constrained by the criteria for allowing benefits claims. This contrasts with one aspect of empowerment in the airline company, discussed above, where cabin crew and airport staff had been 'empowered' to make small *ex gratia* payments or give presents to dissatisfied customers, to improve customer relations. For all the agency's talk about 'customers', its clients are still basically *claimants* – and the money being spent is public money and cannot be used merely to alleviate dissatisfaction. Although the agency is in many ways a unique organisation, it is questionable whether here or elsewhere empowerment can significantly change the work practices of employees who have to follow strict rules in their work.

The application of rules solves many problems: rules are (we hope) impartial between cases and consistent and fair in their application. A rule may therefore be better and more just than an individual's moral judgement. There are also necessarily limits on what degree of empowerment or discretion is acceptable for staff in *any* organisation. If agency employees started to pay extra benefits when they felt sorry for someone, or when they thought that the rules were unfair to someone, the benefits budget would be in ruins and other customers would be unfairly disadvantaged, unjustly treated, by comparison. Furthermore, agency staff operate in conditions of imperfect knowledge; the most plausible and heart-rending case might be exaggerated or fraudulent. The rules prevent compassionate staff being hoodwinked. There is also the issue of whether empowerment *should* empower staff to take decisions which bend or disregard rules and procedures. The agency's customers might prefer to be dealt with by staff following fixed rules rather than by individuals exercising discretion. Uncouth or difficult customers would almost certainly lose out in the latter case.

Another further important point is that adherence to rules – although contrary to empowerment – protects staff, to some extent, from their daily moral dilemmas about how to adjudicate between people in need. In some contexts empowerment might be a curse, not a blessing:'I see so many people each week that I have to have cut and dried guidelines for fairness'.

Many of these points can be generalised from the agency to other organisations: adherence to rules and standards is a fundamental part of delivering the organisation's promised product or service. The cook at a McDonald's cannot add a few red chillies to a standard hamburger because she thinks this would make it tastier. Customers require a predictable product – this includes those who claim benefits. The move to empowerment is therefore likely to be confined to the processes within an organisation rather than to affect its products or services. Nevertheless, this study demonstrates that there are particular problems for government agencies pursuing empowerment policies. First, they have to dismantle the bureaucratic accretions that characterised their operations when they formed part of the civil service; second, they are not in charge of their 'product', that is, the service which the government pays them to provide. These are formidable obstacles to achieving meaningful empowerment.

Notes

1. John Kaler's article in this volume exemplifies and documents the sceptical approach to empowerment. For another subtle and interesting analysis, see Tuckman (1995).
2. I would like to acknowledge here the support of the Society for the Furtherance of Critical Philosophy, which gave me a two-year Paul Branton Research Fellowship to undertake this research.
3. Twenty-four people participated in the study, 14 men and 10 women. Three were from ethnic minority groups (2 Asian, 1 Afro-Caribbean). The age range was as follows: 20–29 (2), 30–39 (8), 40–49 (8), 50–59 (6). The participants' grades were as follows: clerical (operational) (4), higher clerical (supervisory) (6), higher executive officer (junior management) (7), senior

executive officer (middle management) (1), district manager (middle/senior management) (4), area manager (senior management) (2). Interviews were semi-structured and lasted between one and a half and two and a half hours.
4. The material on which this section is based has been published in Henley Management College's Research Working Papers series (HWP). See Goodwin (1995 and 1996).
5. There were early indications that the various Charters had little effect and were used primarily as a management tool; see Pollitt (1994).

References

Goodwin, B. (1995) 'Perceptions of Moral Responsibility and Ethical Questions: A Study of a Water Company', Henley Working Paper 9511 (Henley on Thames: Henley Management College).
Goodwin, B. (1996) 'Ethics and Responsibility in a London Borough (I)', HWP 9602 (Henley on Thames: Henley Management College).
Goodwin, B. (1996) 'Ethics and Responsibility in a London Borough (II)', HWP 9603 (Henley on Thames: Henley Management College).
Goodwin, B. (1996) 'Ethics and Responsibility in a Large Accountancy Firm', HWP 9601 (Henley on Thames: Henley Management College).
Goodwin, B. (1996) 'Ethics and Responsibility in a Bank, HWP 9613 (Henley on Thames: Henley Management College).
Goodwin, B. (1996) 'Ethics and Responsibility in an Airline Company', HWP 9619 (Henley on Thames: Henley Management College).
Kerfoot, D. and Knights, D. (1995) 'Empowering the "Quality" worker', in A. Wilkinson and H. Willmott (eds), *Making Quality Critical: New Perspectives on Organisational Change* (London: Routledge).
Morgan, C. and Murgatroyd, S. (1994) *Total Quality Management in the Public Sector* (Buckingham: Open University Press).
Pollitt, C. (1990) 'Overview: Root and Branch', in M. Cave, M. Kogan and R. Smith (eds), *Output and Performance Measurement in Government: The State of the Art* (London: Jessica Kingsley).
Pollitt, C. (1994) 'The Citizen's Charter: A Preliminary Analysis', *Public Money and Management*, April 1994, pp. 1–5.
Tuckman, A. (1995) 'Ideology, Quality and TQM', in A. Wilkinson and H. Willmott (eds), *Making Quality Critical: New Perspectives on Organisational Change* (London: Routledge).

11 Ethics and Empowerment: Managerial Discourse and the Case of Teleworking

Christopher Moon and Celia Stanworth

INTRODUCTION

Empowerment is not only currently fashionable 'management speak', but also has important material implications for the situation of the workforce. It can be analysed as part of the postmodernist paradigm, as emancipatory, or as a new and more subtle manifestation of traditional managerial control. This chapter explores the discourse and outcomes of empowerment in work organisations, and in particular focuses on the idea as it is applied to telework. The premise of the chapter is that empowerment is being interpreted in many different ways, but is generally related to the ideas of 'excellence' held by managers, rather than to unequivocal rights to liberation for the workforce, so that the promise of self-actualisation for workers is at best a secondary consideration compared to 'bottom-line' outcomes. Thus it does not follow that empowerment is currently a basis for strengthening employee rights. A discussion is provided of ethical issues as they relate to the empowerment literature and to that on telework.

USE OF THE TERM EMPOWERMENT

According to Ledwith and Colgan (1996) the concept of empowerment has its origins in the women's movement of the 1960s and 1970s, when women began to demand a much greater degree of control over their lives and to make their own decisions free of patriarchy. This change is encapsulated by Fauldner *et al.* (1976) who state 'Women are now, and will continue to be, taking a much fuller part in the decisions which affect their lives'. Empowered, women's locus of control moved from external to internal, and they felt in charge of events rather than being at the mercy of outside forces in their life decisions. They felt empowered by information, by joining groups and by reading and acting on the ideas contained in radical feminist literature such as Greer's *The Female Eunuch* (1970). Empowerment meant breaking free from the shackles of oppression.

More recently, Colgan and Ledwith (1996) conclude that women collectively can work within organisations to effect transformational change and 'that women's activism can be a focus of resistance and a force... which empowers creativity and resourcefulness' (p. 299). However, despite many notable advances in the position of women, if we look at labour market statistics and at women's experiences within work organisations, there is little to suggest that all women have achieved equality with men. Recent figures suggest that in the UK women's salaries are on average 72 per cent of those of men – £14 030 versus £19 479 (Central Statistical Office, 1995) representing a 28 per cent differential. There are over 10 million women workers in the UK, but there are more than double the number of women than men in the low-paid areas such as sales, personal services and clerical work.

Worker empowerment as a process was first referred to by Juran (one of the early gurus of total quality management (TQM) in 1979). Empowerment was a crucial part of any total quality system, whereby the delegation of responsibility for quality to those at the point of production meant that they would become accountable to their 'customers' with the goal of zero defects (Sewell and Wilkinson, 1992). Since then, and especially in the 1990s, there has been a flood of managerial literature on empowerment, and this interest can be traced back to its interpretation by Peters and Waterman's *In Search of Excellence* (1982) which has sold in millions both in the US and Europe. In the view of some, including academics in the human resource management (HRM) area, it has become widely misused as a tool for manipulation. It has become a term which provokes derision, often amongst those who have themselves been told they are 'empowered', but not least amongst those who may in future be called upon to empower others – namely future personnel or human resource managers.

At a recent university conference for part-time students on courses leading to Institute of Personnel and Development (IPD) membership, empowerment was mentioned by the keynote speaker, and the audience collapsed into uncontrollable laughter. Away from the workplace the students may have felt able to express dissent, or such behaviour could mean that they were not yet fully enculturated. Sisson's (1994) view is that language, as well as metaphor and symbol, are being used to try to make us think that things are different from what they really are, and words which have become the everyday language of managers may be interpreted differently by those on the receiving end. His list of such semantics depicts empowerment as 'making someone else take the risk and responsibility' (1994, p. 15). Postmodernists would counter that it does not much matter because rhetoric is in effect reality. The importance of this view is that, bogus or not, empowerment is being used as a rhetorical device which translates into material changes which are affecting the lives of many workers (du Gay and Salaman, 1992). As Fielding concludes:

> The temptation is to write empowerment off as a reliably and unremittingly vacuous notion suggesting we would be as well to just get on with our lives by ignoring it, making grudging allowances for it, and/or regarding the speaker with appropriate suspicion. None of these responses is appropriate. However fatuous or pretentious its utterance, empowerment is neither trivial nor trite in its ambitions or consequences. (1995, p. 1)

So, what are these ambitions or consequences for empowerment in work organisations? There are a number of themes from the literature, and practice from cases, which will now be explored.

Empowerment and the postmodern organisation

Using the postmodern paradigm, Joyce and Woods (1996) discuss the changes necessary to bring about the postmodern organisational form. Top managers reject rigid hierarchy and expect all workers, however humble their role, to display innovative behaviour, spontaneity and creativity – in other words to become empowered. In contrast, the manager in the modernist mould, would expect workers to follow the organisation's procedures and fulfil objectives – a much more top-down focus. The postmodernists see empowerment as vital because of the idea that we are living in a time of accelerating, indeed chaotic and unpredictable change which is affecting work organisations in the late twentieth century. This discourse of chaos runs through academic literature, but is most evident in books and articles which are more likely to be read by senior managers and articulated by management gurus such as Tom Peters and Charles Handy.

The 'truth' of this external turmoil is taken for granted, but, real or not, cannot be understood without considering the impact of the relative decline of western developed economies, and the threat which particularly British and US senior managers feel is posed by 'nations their countries once defeated in war' (Legge, 1995, p. xiv). The function of the term empowerment is to form part of the rhetoric concerning how employees should be managed in order to achieve competitive advantage, and this is just as important as its practice (Legge, 1995). The actual management of people is less crucial than the management of meaning, and empowerment promises to give meaning back to workers in the service of the profit motive. Managers are exhorted to embark upon a much more ambitious project than before: they must now 'redesign human understanding to fit the organisation's purpose' (Keenoy and Anthony, 1992, p. 239), rather than design the organisation around human needs.

Control by the customer

Amongst the drivers for organisational change presented by postmodernists is the differentiation of demand. This is a powerful push towards the empowerment of employees, as discerning active consumers are said to want ever more customised and novel products and services delivered by staff who are not merely compliant but committed. Customers must not just be served, but must now be 'delighted', and du Gay and Salaman (1992) have identified the 'cult of the customer' as the most important environmental factor in the postmodern discourse. The idea of the discerning customer is not just a fact of life (it may not even be a fact of life), but its importance is that it is an idea which has provoked much organisational change.

Particularly (but not exclusively) in service industries the customer is made to exert control over employees by means of satisfaction measures such as customer surveys, 'mystery' customers and the development of sophisticated 'service indicators' (du Gay and Salaman, 1992). The demands of customers are used as leverage for employees to become empowered. Bureaucratic controls are being replaced by cultural change as a means of control, though the latter seems to some academic observers to be just as oppressive. Heery (1993, p. 285) quotes some examples from the US:

> These include surveys of customer satisfaction, focus group discussions on levels of service, freephone numbers which enable customers to deliver a verdict on employee responsiveness and the use of anonymous shoppers to gather information on employee behaviour. Such techniques are also being used in Britain.

There are now agencies here which recruit 'mystery' shoppers to assess the performance of shop, banking and building society staff on a regular basis.

This customer orientation is not confined to the private services sector, but through Citizen's Charters and the development of internal markets has been extended strategically by government to the public sector. As du Gay and Salaman point out, patients and clients as well as passengers have all become customers, and require empowered employees of the public services to respond to their ever more sophisticated and changing needs. Market relationships are now considered superior to hierarchical ones in all public services, and this extends to transactions within organisations '... departments now behave as if they were actors in a market, workers treat each other as if they were customers' (du Gay and Salaman 1992, p. 619). In local government, for example, service level agreements have been introduced between departments which means that service quality is assessed and monitored by one group of employees on another. The creation of internal markets may be empowering in a situation of economic upturn, but the public sector is also having its resources squeezed, which means that workers may not feel empowered but overburdened.

Budgets may also be devolved further down the organisation to individuals or groups, and this may be empowering in terms of a liberation from the imposition of decisions from above. However, if the resources are insufficient or become scarcer over time, holders may feel that they have responsibility without power, and that 'ownership' of the negative consequences of a lack of resources may also fall on them rather than their superiors. Local management of schools, devolved budgeting and G.P. fund-holding in the NHS, have all been accompanied by a centrally-imposed emphasis on quantitative delivery standards designed to cut costs (Legge, 1995). Failure to meet these standards and any shortcomings in the services provided are now more publicly displayed, but the responsibility for failure is now firmly placed at the level of the budget-holder, who has little or no power to effect budgetary changes.

Self-managing teams

The need for responsiveness to customers and to 'delight' the customer has led organisations to empower workers, by increasing employee involvement through devolving authority to self-managing teams. Ripley and Ripley (1992) define a self-managing team as a group of interdependent people who agree that the best way to achieve a goal is to work together, who are empowered by being given decision-making responsibility, and trained to perform multiple functions. This, it is claimed, leads to increased commitment to organisational goals, and responsiveness to customers. The CBI in Britain relates continuing economic success to the psychological development and self-actualisation of employees:

> people want to do a good job, to have opportunities for self-development, to contribute their thoughts as well as their physical skills to the teams and firms for which they work, and to be recognised and rewarded for their whole contribution. (Quoted in du Gay and Salaman, 1992, p. 625)

Cases cited in the literature include Cadbury's, OCS Smart's Group (laundry), Harvester Restaurants, Ciba UK and Frizzell's. Looking at how 'empowered' these teams are in practice it appears that it is considerably more modest than the discourse would suggest. Workers are given authority to make fairly minor decisions and to decide upon the allocation of work between team members. At Frizzell's teams 'are empowered to draw up rotas, organise their workload and provide ideas for improvements'. Ciba UK has a policy of 'pushing the responsibility for problem-solving onto the front-line workforce'. Teams may have the power to share out the least-liked tasks: at Harvester cleaning out the pudding service area is done by two or three people who now 'muck in and help each other' (Pickard, 1993). The material changes seem to be more in the direction of work-intensification than multi-skilling through training. It is the feeling of being empowered, rather than any objective increase in power amongst employees, that is the required outcome. Peters and Waterman argue that 'the fact... that we think we have a bit more discretion leads to much greater commitment' (quoted in du Gay and Salaman, 1992, p. 625).

Total quality management (TQM) has a similar rhetoric of 'empowerment, trust and mutual dependency' which can be compared to the reality which some researchers have found of 'pervasive regimes of constant electronic and peer group scrutiny' (Sewell and Wilkinson, 1992, p. 98). The self-managing teams under TQM and just-in-time (JIT) systems are very different from the autonomous work groups of the 1960s and 1970s, which were set up to give workers greater control (Legge, 1995). Teamworking is much more intensive, the pace relentless, and described as 'management-by stress' (Parker and Slaughter quoted in Legge, 1995, p. 230). Garrahan and Stewart found peer surveillance operating at Nissan which encouraged workers to identify defects caused by other workers. This had the effect of creating pressure on individuals not to let down other team members, and encouraging competition between teams to increase output (Garrahan and Stewart, 1992). Mitsubishi encourage teams in their production plant in Livingston to adopt pop-culture names to differentiate themselves from competing teams, and display each group's weekly performance ratings to encourage greater effort towards meeting performance targets (Allen and Massey, 1988). The workers accept these conditions because of the mutual support and excitement of collective competition, and the promise of keeping their jobs. It is not immaterial that most inwardly-investing Japanese companies have chosen greenfield sites in high unemployment areas to set up their factories.

Demand by the worker

There is said to be a demand for empowerment from certain types of employee. Nykodym *et al.* (1992) argue that those now entering the workforce have much greater expectations of participating in management decisions, and this will have to be harnessed by organisations who wish to remain competitive. The 'information age' (to which we will return later in the chapter) will be one in which the bulk of jobs will be cerebral, performed by 'knowledge' workers who are highly educated and articulate (Bell, 1973). Thus it is not only the sovereign consumer, but also the self-directed, sophisticated worker who will force employers to increase participation in decision-making, and to provide a working milieu which supports self-actualisation and self-development. 'One measure of a "civilised" organisation is the degree to which its employees direct, maintain and co-ordinate their activities without external coercion' (Ripley and Ripley, 1992, p. 38).

Many of the workers of the future information age will be professionals who will demand autonomy within the employment relationship, which is part and parcel of the creation and protection of professional status. 'The origin of professional power stems from the ability to retain autonomy and occupational control within organisations' (Sewell and Wilkinson, 1993, p. 42). But will future organisations enable the professional to exercise self-control through the medium of the professional group, with standards of ethical conduct maintained through peer, rather than organisational, controls? There is a long and troubled history of the relationship of the employer and the professional employee. Professionals are defined by management as only contingently loyal to the company or organisation, and in the age of the 'sovereign' consumer, are often seen as bastions of protectionism which impede customer responsiveness (Heery, 1993). Recent attempts to control such groups have included exclusion from organisational influence, new contracts of service to increase customer contact time, and appraisal and performance-related pay in order to link service standards to reward. Heery (1993) feels that these moves may in fact be counterproductive, because the creation of low-trust may further diminish the customer responsiveness of the professional worker.

Limited empowerment

This raises the question of the limits to worker empowerment. If employers increase the discretion of their employees they must still be monitored and their performance measured through 'robust systems' (Ripley and Ripley, 1992), unless or until the employees become truly self-directed in which case the role of the manager must either change or become redundant. Legge (1995) argues that if employees become 'responsibly autonomous' all employees in effect become managers, exercising self-control in the service of the employer, and in theory the need for centralised and cascaded control falls away. This is a threat to middle management in particular, who have already been downsized and delayered, not only because of technical change, but also in the wake of Business Process Engineering (BPR) and the introduction of TQM systems (Rodriguez, 1992).

Amongst those who do not wish to be empowered, or resist the devolution of power and authority to lower levels, are the middle ranks. Using a 'zero-sum' model of power in organisations, this reaction can be understood as a perception of disempowerment as lower ranks take on managers' former responsibilities. Empowerment in work organisations may also involve the middle manager being required to make a fundamental change in role from being a bureaucrat to a 'coach-consultant' who is versed in behavioural science and interpersonal skills, able to empower those below, but at the same time becoming personally empowered.

Another aspect of the literature concerns the view that empowerment, where it exists, is most likely to be something that top management creates for other managers, but is often not extended to lower-order workers. Echiejile (1992) feels that those most needing empowerment are usually those who are excluded from it, and advocates the creation of empowering groups representing the disadvantaged at work – for example black workers and women. Such groups are more akin to those arising from the women's' movement in terms of battling against oppression, and they would be unlikely to be tolerated within many workplaces. Ezzamel *et al.* (1992) discusses the finance industry and concludes that managers may be empowered but the workers are *de facto* still managed in a top-down way, in fact ever-greater control of them is necessary to extract more work from them. Cressey and Scott (1992) researched the banking industry and found that technical change and reorganisation in the banks has created advantaged groups who could be said to be empowered, but at the same time has debased the work of others such as data entry clerks and direct banking staff, who are exposed to more factory-like conditions ('paperless factories'), with their performance closely controlled through computer technology.

Participation and empowerment

There is a strong thread throughout the literature on empowerment linking it to participative styles of management, which can be traced back to the management writers of the 1960s such as Vroom, Likert and Argyris who argued that of all the styles of management, the participative style was most likely to motivate workers to increased performance. Nykodym (1992) discusses empowerment in these terms. Participative management is also an attractive concept because it reflects the democratic ideals of western society. Carr (1992) argues that the essential difference between empowered and traditional organisations is that the former value autonomy as an end in itself, which enhances the 'bottom-line' but at the same time contributes to the self-fulfilment of individuals and the advancement of democratic ideals. Thus empowerment is not only worthwhile in terms of profit outcomes, but is also an ethical endeavour for the organisation. The strong appeal for managers of the empowerment literature can be understood by this agreeable fusion of the economically and ethically desirable.

Empowerment and ethics

There is a strong moralistic theme in the literature on empowerment (Claydon and Doyle, 1996). The CBI (1988) emphasises the right culture which must be present if individuals are to become empowered. It cannot be created of itself, but managers can provide the high trust, supportive conditions which must be in place before people can become committed, capable and ethical. This suggests that empowerment should not be imposed by managers, but is something which employees come to learn to value through this supportive culture, and gradually adopt and internalise in terms of personal growth: '...empowerment, like education, can be viewed as a process of enculturation. This is like the internalisation of community norms and standards (i.e. beliefs, values and the like)' (Ripley and Ripley, 1992, p. 31).

The moralistic theme sees empowerment as a 'win–win' situation for employers and workers. It can lead to an individual becoming a better worker, and through that becoming a more virtuous and better person. Commitment to the goals of the organisation is good in itself and also pays off for the individual in increased rewards. There is a convergence of the personally moral and the economically desirable (du Gay and Salaman, 1992) which is attractive to the management cadre: it gives an ethical basis to their strivings for competitive advantage. However, Singer (1992) brings in a note of caution to the debate in that too much empowerment may be ethically good but may not necessarily be profitable – there may be a loss of control over workers who may not always behave in profit-enhancing ways. Empowerment may therefore be tolerated only insofar as it is of benefit to the business. Self-determination and personal growth must take second place to the needs of the business and may be curtailed if necessary – a teleological approach.

Most of the literature does not countenance the possibility that the needs of the employee and those of the business are not completely congruent – the discourse goes beyond unitarism and becomes monism. If there is non-alignment of profit or competitive advantage with empowerment, then the enterprise must continue to change and improve its ability to provide what the customer wants until there is. The literature emphasises that the development of empowerment within the enterprise is an ongoing task, that it may be imperfect at the moment because of the baggage left over from the evils of bureaucracy or hierarchy. For instance 'the command and control model of management continued in business to restrict exploration of new structures of organisations or new styles of management' (Ripley and Ripley, 1992, p. 23), or 'commercial organisations must continually struggle to become ever more enterprising' (du Gay and Salaman, 1992, p. 623).

Continuous change and improvement in work organisations is necessary both because of the chaotic environment and the ever-changing needs of the consumer of the goods or services provided. Perhaps, then, the students mentioned at the beginning of the chapter who laughed at empowerment were from organisations where the journey towards empowerment had only just begun?

TELEWORK AND EMPOWERMENT

The International Labour Office (1990) define Telework as a form of 'flexible' work which involves distance work, remote work or telecommuting which is dependent upon the use of information and communications technologies (ICTs). Teleworkers may be working at home in a so-called 'electronic cottage' (Toffler, 1980), in satellite centres away from the central organisation, or be mobile workers linked via electronic communications (di Martino and Wirth, 1990). Much of the literature on the development of telework links it with the coming of the 'information age' in which it forms part of a dramatic change in how work is organised in future society. The organisation fixed in time and location gives way to the 'virtual' organisation which ultimately exists in cyberspace. The conventional office with its hierarchical relationships is replaced by the 'elusive' office (Huws et al., 1990). One of the major issues in teleworking is the question of control of workers at a distance, and whether telework is always empowering to the individual.

Empowerment, self-actualisation and personal growth is a mainstream preoccupation of writers on telework, which is mostly in the post-modernist vein. The received view is that telework has a pay-off for both employer and teleworker (see for example Toffler, 1980; Employment Department, 1993). The employer gains by the increased motivation of the worker released from commuting stress and freed from the distractions of office life, and the literature is full of examples of the increased productivity of the teleworker (Kinsman, 1987; Judkins et al., 1985). The teleworker wins because of increased autonomy, independence and ability to organise his/her own time, to combine work with domestic and community activities (Toffler, 1980) and to enjoy easy access to peers and superiors, and above all to information, through the technology. There is also assumed to be considerable discretion in how the hardware and software is manipulated by the teleworker (McGrath and Houlihan, 1996).

Managing teleworkers

Given the assumption of teleworker independence and empowerment and the reduction or absence of the need to control, there is a surprisingly large literature about the problems of control and management of teleworkers. A national study of employed teleworkers by Huws (1993) found that this problem had often been overcome because those selected for work at home were usually employees of long standing who were often higher than average performers, measured by performance management systems. Thus they could be said to be thoroughly enculturated and had internalised the norms and values of the organisation. Managers expressed reservations about teleworkers brought in straight from the labour market, who would not be socialised into the corporate culture. They would need special induction programmes to overcome the problem of not being physically present at the work place, where it would be far easier to enculturate them.

Potential managers of teleworkers often express concern about the lack of control which they are able to exert over remote workers (Huws, 1993: Gillespie *et al.*, 1995) or expect to spend more time controlling teleworkers than conventional on-site workers (Haddon and Lewis, 1994). Management resistance is seen as one of the greatest barriers to the development of telework in the UK as well as in Europe. Such recalcitrant managers are perhaps not yet themselves empowered, and have not yet transformed themselves into the developer-consultant role envisaged by Ripley and Ripley (1992). Managers who have had experience of managing teleworkers tend to be more positive about the possibility of high-trust relationships between them and their remote subordinates. This may not only be because teleworkers have been chosen from the 'best' employees, but also because the teleworkers under discussion tend to be high-status employees, technical specialists, professionals or indeed managers, with intrinsically interesting jobs, who may be assumed to have internalised the corporate culture and/or ethical systems of behaviour.

Despite the assumption that all teleworkers are 'responsibly autonomous', managing telework is still often seen as a severe test of management competence. Rothwell (1987) sees managing at a distance as orchestration or facilitation rather than close control. Managers who are incompetent are those who are unable to adopt the more sophisticated and 'hands-off' style which is deemed necessary to support teleworkers, and the experience of managing teleworkers often quickly sorts the managerial sheep from the goats. There is much discussion of managing by output, or by milestones, and a rejection of over-formal checking systems and Tayloristic methods, which are a relic of the bureaucratic organisation of modernism. Managing telework is therefore congruent with empowered management, and there are resonances with the postmodern organisation where command and control systems have been superseded.

Virtuality and empowerment

'Virtual' organisations which are totally outsourced, or consist of a minute core of employees surrounded by a myriad of suppliers, 'project-focused, collaborative networks uninhibited by time and space' (Birchall and Lyons, 1995) are seen as the high-tech organisations of the future. The employment status of the teleworker is often unclear, but short-term relationships based around self-employment are inferred. If so, the need for the 'management of meaning' and absorption of the culture of conventional organisations may pass away, replaced by pure market relationships between empowered self-employed individuals. It has been suggested that teleworkers may tend to become self-employed and work on contract to the organisation, because it is easier to control remote workers through the market than by hierarchical control (Child, 1987).

The move of some workers from employment to self-employment through outsourcing in the IT industry has also been equated with empowerment (Stares, 1993), which is a postmodernist analysis, emphasising the positive aspects of moves away from outdated hierarchical relationships. The discourse of the enterprise culture and the elevation of self-employment as superior to conventional employment which was so much a part of the Thatcher ethos is still evident. Small enterprise is usually described as pioneering and risk-taking, in contrast to large bureaucratic firms which are seen as 'dinosaurs in the flexible, fast-changing emerging global economy' (Curran, 1996). Self-employment in the literature is sometimes considered the purest form of empowerment, as the individual is released from the shackles of the conventional workplace, and is enabled to take control of his/her own destiny.

Those who have the skills to produce knowledge from raw information are considered to be the crucial resource of the information age, and many of the new jobs created are predicted to move beyond existing routine information work (such as data entry) towards high-level knowledge work (McGrath and Houlihan, 1996). If teleworkers are employed they will be empowered through decentralisation, where 'core' employees operate from remote locations equipped with the latest technologies (McGrath and Houlihan, 1996). The available empirical evidence supports this, with teleworkers who are providing highly specialised or professional services being the most likely to be empowered. Huws' study of telework in Britain (1993) found that teleworkers who were managerial or professional staff were more likely to be fully integrated into the company enjoying high-trust relationships involving a high degree of discretion.

The literature on telework and virtuality assumes that there will be a reduction in the numbers of routine, lower-status teleworkers, employed or self-employed, such as data-entry clerks, or word-processor operators who may work at home or in telecentres. The information age may lead to an increase in highly-qualified 'cerebral' workers, but at the same time the authors feel that the numbers of 'drone' workers, who input information into the networks, may well increase. These workers are far less likely to become empowered, and more likely to feel disempowered, because their work is often monitored closely through the technology which can measure key strokes, error rates or the time taken to answer telephone calls, or check whether the correct words and phrases have been used with customers. Therefore close 'Tayloristic' style control can be exercised over routine workers who are physically remote, in terms of an 'electronic panopticon' (Zuboff, 1988). The promise of autonomy for workers to decide their hours of work is least likely with these groupings. The British Telecom Inverness experiment, which used video computing to link home-based directory enquiry staff with the office centre, showed that the teleworkers were just as tied to their workstations at home as they would have been in the conventional workplace, and requested meal and comfort breaks through the technology.

The 'drone' workers of the information age have much more easily replaceable skills and a much weaker labour market position than cerebral workers. For the former, telework is likely to be low-paid and careerless, with none of the advantages of primary employment or self-employment. The segmentation of the present labour market may be re-created in the information age, and, because women workers are likely to be over-represented in the secondary segment, the gender divisions may continue. Teleworkers whose skills are in demand may be more likely to have their preferences about how work is organised around the technology taken into account, but there is some evidence that all teleworkers may be vulnerable in periods of economic downturn to the erosion of their terms and conditions and of their discretion, because they are isolated individuals rendered more powerless by their remoteness from the workplace (Stanworth, 1996).

The worst-case scenario would result in a polarised workforce 'consisting of a "core" of secure office-based employees, and a "periphery" of lower-paid, insecure employees based at home' (EIRR, 1996). Even highly-qualified teleworkers have had to work longer hours, become constantly available through the technology, and some have been moved involuntarily to home-based work or from employee to self-employed status (Stanworth *et al.*, 1993). A business environment of uncertainty is just as likely to lead to cost-cutting and casualisation as it is to empowerment. Thus the rhetoric that teleworking is always empowering is highly questionable.

CONCLUSIONS

The difference between the promise of empowerment and how it has actually been used in work organisations has led to its falling into disrepute. Workers in the US are said to be increasingly disillusioned by empowerment (Moats Kennedy, 1992) because it has been oversold and ignores the political reality of most workplaces. Moves to empower have often followed layoffs and delayering, and workers feel powerless to resist what many interpret as work intensification. Rapid change in work organisations has meant reductions in headcount, which tends to erode high trust relationships needed to make empowerment work. Workers are obliged to become empowered under JIT or TQM systems (Legge, 1995), and the introduction of teamworking in the cases from the literature has often followed the 'culling' of employees who are deemed not to be amenable to the new 'empowered' way of working. Empowerment is thus often an obligation rather than a right, and has been imposed where resistance is low. If empowerment is to be ethical, it should not be enforced by management, but seen as a right which workers may exercise if they wish to. The most disillusioned view held by Sisson and Legge is that the postmodernist discourse of empowerment seeks to obscure the underlying reality of capitalist conspiracy where managers say one thing and workers experience quite another.

Employer rights to be as competitive as possible appear to be at odds with the rights of employees to be empowered (Moon and Stanworth, 1997). Personal growth may not necessarily lead to the expected outcomes – just as high morale amongst the workforce does not always translate into better productivity. Despite the ideas of the excellence literature, in which the empowering of employees is a pre-condition for bottom-line success, empirical evidence tends to support the conclusion that at best worker empowerment is tolerated insofar as it contributes to profits, and at worst is a mechanism to persuade workers into the false belief that they have been given more discretion, so that they feel more committed and will work harder. In postmodern organisations all should become empowered, whereas in reality empowerment may be experienced only by a privileged minority, whether a certain group of managers or an elite group of teleworkers. Other workers may be excluded from empowerment, and may in fact feel more oppressed under empowering regimes.

The discourse of ethics may provide a mechanism for change. Transparency in Foucauldian terms (Townley, 1994) could offer an opportunity for more liberating forms of employment in the genuine sense. Teleological analyses of working practices may highlight the costs and benefits of new work forms for both parties, and a deontological approach may identify the respective inviolable rights and duties of employers and workers. If work organisations wish to present themselves as moral communities there must be a moral basis for the presentation (Anthony, 1994). If they fail to impress, then workers will give only lip-service to the requirements for commitment, and will remain only calculatively involved. If work organisations have only survival or profit maximisation in mind, and this undermines fair treatment for employees, then rights and obligations for workers will continue to have to be imposed on employers by employee collectives and/or outside agencies.

References

Allen, J. and Massey, D. (eds) (1988) *The Economy in Question* (London: Sage/Open University Press).
Anthony, P. (1994) *Managing Culture* (Buckingham: Open University Press).
Bell, D. (1973) *The Coming of Post-Industrial Society* (Harmondsworth: Penguin).
Birchall, D. and Lyons, L. (1995) *Creating Tomorrow's Organisation: Unlocking the Benefits of Future Work* (London: Pitman).
Carr, C. (1992) 'Empowered Organisations, Empowered Leaders', *Training and Development*, March, pp. 39–45.
Central Statistical Office (1995) *New Earning Survey* (London: HMSO).
Child, J. (1987) *Organisation – A Guide to Problems and Practice*, 2nd edn (London: Harper & Row).
Claydon, T. and Doyle, M. (1996) 'Trusting me, Trusting you? The Ethics of Employee Empowerment, paper presented to conference Ethical Issues in Contemporary HRM, Imperial College, London, April.
Confederation of British Industry (1988) *People – The Cutting Edge* (London: CBI).
Cressey, P. and Scott, P. (1992) 'Employment, Technology and Industrial Relations in the Clearing Banks: Is the Honeymoon Over?, *New Technology, Work and Employment*, pp. 83–96.
Curran, J. (1996) 'The Role of the Small Firm in the UK Economy', paper presented to Kingston University Faculty of Business, June.

Di Martino, V. and Wirth, L. (1990) 'Telework: An Overview in Conditions of Work', *Digest*, vol. 9(1).
Du Gay, P. and Salaman, G. (1992) 'The Cult(ure) of the Customer', *Journal of Management Studies*, vol. 29(5), September, pp. 615–33.
Echiejile, I. (1992) 'Empowering Disadvantaged Employees', *Empowerment in Organisations*, vol. 2(1), pp. 31–8.
European Industrial Relations Review (1996) 'Teleworking in Europe', parts 1–3, *Teleworking International*, EIRR 268, 17–20 May; 18–21 June; 18–23 August.
Employment Department (1993) *'Be Flexible'* (UK: Employment Department Group).
Ezzamel, M., Willmot, H and Lilley, S. (1994) 'Changing Management Practices in Financial Services', *Journal of General Management*, Autumn, pp. 22–9.
Faulder, C., Jackson, C. and Lewis, M. (1976) *The Women's Directory* (London: Virago).
Fielding, M. (1995) 'Empowerment: Emancipation or Enervation?' International Conference on Educational Reform: its theory and practice (Cambridge: Institute of Education).
Garrahan, P. and Stewart, P. (1992) *The Nissan Enigma: Flexibility at Work in a Local Economy* (London: Mansell Publishing).
Gillespie, A., Richardson, R. and Cornford, J. (1995) *Review of Telework in Britain: Implications for Public Policy*, Newcastle Programme on Information and Communication Technologies, CURDS, University of Newcastle on Tyne, February.
Gray, M. *et al.* (1993) *Teleworking Explained* (Chichester: Wiley).
Greer, G. (1970) *The Female Eunuch* (St Albans: Granada Publishing).
Haddon, L. and Lewis, A. (1994) 'The Experience of Teleworking: An Annotated Review', *International Journal of Human Resource Management*, vol. 5(1), February.
Heery, E. (1993) 'Industrial Relations and the Customer', *Industrial Relations Journal*, vol. 24(4), pp. 284–95.
Huws, U., Korte, W. and Robinson, S. (1990) *Telework – towards the Elusive Office* (Chichester: Wiley).
Huws, U. (1993) *Telework in Britain* (London: Employment Department).
International Labour Office (1990) *Conditions of Work Digest: Telework*, vol. 9(1) (Geneva: ILO).
Joyce, P. and Woods, A. (1996) *Essential Strategic Management: From Modernisn to Pragmatism* (Oxford: Butterworth-Heinemann).
Judkins, P., West, D. and Drew, J. (1985) *Networking in Organisations* (Aldershot: Gower).
Keenoy, T. and Anthony, T. (1992) 'HRM: Metaphor, Meaning and Morality', in P. Blyton and P. Turnbull (eds), *Reassessing Human Resource Management* (London: Sage).
Kinlaw, D. (1995) 'Employee Liberation', *Management*, May, pp. 11–14.
Kinsman, F. (1987) *The Telecommuters* (Chichester: Wiley).
Ledwith, S. and Colgan, F. (eds) (1996) *Women in Organisations: Challenging Gender Politics* (London: Macmillan).
Legge, K. (1995) *Human Resource Management: Rhetorics and Realities* (London: Macmillan).

McGrath, P. and Houlihan, M. (1996) 'Conceptualising Telework: Modern or Post-modern?' Paper presented to the conference on the New International Perspectives on Telework: From Telecommuting to the Virtual Organisation, Brunel University, 31 July–2 August.

Moats Kennedy, M. (1992) 'Empowered or Overpowered?', *Across the Board*, April, pp. 11–13.

Moon, C. and Stanworth, C. (1997) 'Ethical Issues of Teleworking', *Business Ethics: A European Review*, vol. 6(1), January (UK: Blackwell Business).

Nykodym, N., Simonetti, J., Nielson, W. and Welling, R. (1992) 'Employee Empowerment', *Empowerment in Organisations*, vol. 2(3), pp. 45–56.

Peters, T.J. and Waterman, R.H. (1982) In Search of Excellence: Lessons from America's Best-Run Companies, (New York: Harper & Row).

Pickard, J. (1993) 'The Real Meaning of Empowerment', *Personnel Management*, November, pp. 28–31.

Ripley, R. and Ripley, M. (1992) 'Empowerment, The Cornerstone of Quality', *Management Decision*, vol. 30(4), pp. 20–43.

Rodriguez, C. (1992) 'Empowerment Participation and Empowerment Programmes', *Empowerment in Organisations*, vol. 2(2), pp. 29–41.

Rothwell, S. (1987) 'How to Manage from a Distance', *Personnel Management*, September.

Sewell, G. and Wilkinson, B. (1993) 'Human Resource Management in "Surveillance" Companies', in J. Clark (ed.), *Human Resource Management and Technical Change* (London: Sage).

Singer, A. (1992) 'Can a Company be too Ethical?', *Across the Board*, April, pp. 17–23.

Sisson, K. (ed.) (1994) *Personnel Management*, 2nd edn (Oxford: Blackwell).

Stanworth, J., Stanworth, C. and Purdy, D. (1993) *Self-Employment and Labour Market Restructuring: The Case of Freelance Teleworkers in Book Publishing* (London: University of Westminster Press).

Stanworth, C. (1995) 'Remote Control: Managing Freelance Work in Publishing', Henley Future Work Forum, 27 March.

Stanworth, C. (1996) *Working at Home – A Study of Homeworking and Teleworking*, Institute of Employment Rights, June, London.

Stares, M. (1993) 'Empowered Freedom', *The TQM Magazine*, October, pp. 27–30.

Toffler, A. (1980) *The Third Wave* (London: Collins).

Townley, B. (1994) *Reframing Human Resource Management: Power, Ethics and the Subject at Work* (London: Sage).

Zuboff, S. (1988) *In the Age of the Smart Machine: The Future of Work and Power* (Oxford: Heinemann).

Part III
Business and Society: The New Empowerment Responsibility

12 Empowering Consumers through Co-operatives
Johnston Birchall

INTRODUCTION

In a predominantly capitalist economy, in which firms are owned by shareholders who are distinct from the producers and consumers of the product and whose primary interest is in profit, how can the consumer interest be safeguarded? From a market-liberal perspective, it is enough to ensure that markets are relatively free so that consumers have a choice of product and of supplier. Because markets do not always work in the way that classical economic theory requires – because there is a danger of monopoly supply, asymmetry of information between consumers and producers, negative externalities, and so on – a range of safeguards have, in practice, had to be set up. In Britain for instance, there is a growing body of consumer law which protects consumers from the entry of dangerous or counterfeit products into the market, which regulates the conditions of sale, and enables complaint and redress (Lowe and Woodroffe, 1995).

Local government is deeply involved in market regulation, both through trading standards officers and public health inspectors. There is a growing interest in advice and advocacy on behalf of consumers who are in debt. There is a range of statutory and voluntary organisations at national and local level which provide consumer information and advice. Companies respond to the demand for 'fair trading' with their own safeguards in the form of customer charters and complaints procedures, sometimes overseen by regulatory agencies set up by the industry itself. In the public and voluntary sectors which rely predominantly on state funding for services, there is a peculiarly difficult set of circumstances under which consumers are more difficult to identify and elaborate procedures are necessary so that in lieu of their ability to choose a supplier, their collective voice is enhanced (Deakin and Wright, 1990). In the privatised utilities which are monopoly suppliers there are particular problems, with powerful regulators set up to see that the interests of consumers are protected.

Very little of this activity empowers consumers, in the sense of enabling them to take part in decision-making, to exercise collective leverage over suppliers, or to share in the profits made out of the transactions in which they participate. Yet between the 1840s, when consumer co-operatives first began to flourish in Britain, and the 1960s, when their influence began to wane, a sustained attempt was made to involve consumers in both ownership and control of businesses which were major retailers and which (through the Co-operative Wholesale Society and various joint ventures) had gradually moved back through wholesaling to become manufacturers of all the basic necessities of life. Until the founding of the Consumers' Association in 1957, the main source of organisation for consumers was in fact the UK Co-operative Union, a federal body which represented 10.5 million people (around a fifth of the British population, who were members of their local co-ops), and which through the Co-operative Party in Parliament, and its own membership of many government advisory committees, exercised considerable influence on behalf of consumers (Carbery, 1969).

This chapter will explore the contribution of co-operatives to consumer theory, and the conviction of their advocates that through ownership and control of the means of production, distribution and retailing, the 'sovereign consumer' could become the dominant interest in a modern economy. It will show how the movement failed to achieve its aim of a 'co-operative commonwealth' in which co-operatives would eventually become the dominant form, but how having a large market share in some staple products did enable consumer-owners to exercise real power over the market. The chapter will end by considering what this experience of consumer control has to teach us about the role of consumers as stakeholders in the governance of contemporary businesses.

There is no agreement among historians about when Britain became a 'consumer society'; a case can be made out for any time between the seventeenth century and the 1980s (Benson, 1994). Raymond Williams says the term 'consumer' was used pejoratively in the sense of someone who destroys or wastes resources, until late into the nineteenth century (Williams, 1988). Polanyi shows why this was; the concept reflects the way in which 'modern society' grew out of, and destroyed, a pre-industrial society in which for the common people production and consumption nearly always went hand in hand (Polanyi, 1957); cottage industries had to be replaced by the factory system, subsistence and payment in kind by money wages, before consumption was sufficiently alienated to be seen as something in itself. On the other hand, McKendrick *et al.* declare that 'there was a consumer boom in England in the eighteenth century' which in the third quarter of the century reached 'revolutionary proportions' (1982, p. 9). Yet, as they show through quotations from the time, the phenomenon was referred to not as consumption but as 'luxury', and one has to take a very optimistic view of living standards during the early industrial revolution to see it as being important to the working classes of the time.

Producers, consumers and the early co-operative movement

The perspective of the working class 'co-operators' who set up and nurtured the early co-operative movement supports Raymond Williams' view; the idea of the consumer emerged only gradually, towards the end of the nineteenth century. There were three attempts at consumer control big enough to be called 'movements'. The first began in the 1760s and lasted well into the next century; shipwrights at several ports set up their own flour mills and bakeries in opposition to local cartels of millers and bakers. These were attempts to solve a particular problem of market failure and, so far as we know, only in one case did this extend into general retailing. Then there were two attempts to set up a mass movement of co-operative shops. The first of these, occurring between 1826 and 1833, was really a blend of producer and consumer cooperation; in fact, we can only make a distinction between the two with the benefit of hindsight. The second, beginning in Rochdale in 1844, was outstandingly successful and formed the basis for a worldwide movement (Birchall, 1994). Though this was not so apparent to the participants, it quite quickly became a *consumer* movement; as we shall see, the theory of consumer sovereignty took much longer to develop than did a fully-fledged consumer co-operative sector.

The story begins in 1760 with the dockyard shipwrights of Woolwich and Chatham, who set up their own flour mills and at Chatham (probably also at Woolwich) their own bakery. We can see why from a book published in 1767 which complains:

> Millers have indeed within a few years raised immense fortunes, and with incredible expedition; and bakers in general thrive and get rich in a proportion far beyond what is seen in other trades. (Quoted in Potter, 1899, p. 42)

In discussing the reasons for food adulteration, Burnett says monopoly was 'not a factor of general importance' during the industrial revolution, but it *was* prevalent in flour milling (1989 p. 95). Millers were able to supply inferior, adulterated flour at high prices because production was based on water and wind power which were obviously limited in their supply and allowed for local monopolies. Bakers, on the other hand, were one of the most depressed, overcrowded trades, with very low profit margins, but where millers had taken over bakers' shops and put journeymen in to run them, monopoly could become complete (Burnett, 1989).

We know about these experiments in consumer ownership because there are court records showing that the Woolwich mill was burned down and the local bakers suspected of arson. When the outbreak of the French wars led to a sharp rise in the price of bread, a similar venture was begun in 1795 at Hull, where it was known as the 'anti-mill'. A second mill opened at Hull in 1801, and the movement spread at least as far as Whitby (1812) and Devonport (1816), and probably a lot further, with baking societies becoming quite common in Scotland (Cole, 1944). In 1816 the skilled artisans of Sheerness, 'indignant with the general practice of adulterating flour with china clay' (Potter, 1899, p. 43) opened their own bakery which later expanded into shop retailing, a foretaste of what was to come. It is likely that these societies had a simple structure, asking members to subscribe share capital but then selling as near as possible to cost price; they were consumers' societies rather than a means of investing capital. That they were successful is in no doubt: apart from the arson attack on the Woolwich mill, there was an attempt by local millers to indict the Hull mill as a nuisance. Beatrice Potter tells us that a 'Yorkshire jury considered poverty a still greater nuisance' and found in the consumer-owners' favour (Potter, 1899, p. 43). The society continued for another 36 years without further hindrance.

The next development was a more broadly based movement of co-operative societies which began in 1826 in Brighton and which by 1833 had spread all over Britain and even to Ireland. To understand it we have to know more about the beliefs and goals of the two men whose ideas underpinned it: Robert Owen and William King. Owen was an industrialist and philanthropist, known worldwide for his pioneering work at New Lanark in primary education, and in creating humane conditions for his workforce. King was a doctor in fashionable Brighton, who had helped to found a local mechanics' institute. The starting point for both was the problem of subsistence, the inability of working people in a rapidly changing industrial society to make a living. King put it this way:

> The rate of wages has been gradually diminishing for some hundred years, so that now it is not above one third of what it used to be ... the same causes, continuing to act, the wages must go on diminishing till a workman will not be able to maintain a family; and by the same rule, he will at last not be able to maintain himself. (Quoted in Birchall, 1994, p. 8)

Owen's solution was a plan for villages of cooperation, in which the working classes could live and work, producing for themselves and exchanging goods with other villages on a co-operative basis. At first he found great interest in the idea among the aristocracy, who saw it as a way of cutting down the rapidly growing cost of providing 'outdoor relief' to the unemployed and low-paid workers. When they failed to back him he turned to the working classes, but they had no capital. When the workers set up co-operative shops he was at first sceptical, declaring that a community might set up a shop, but a shop could never set up a community.

It was King who, through practical advice given in his magazine *The Co-operator*, showed how by opening shops Owen's supporters could use surpluses to save towards their own emancipation. King's analysis began from a simple labour theory of value, seeing capital as really stored labour, and arguing that only by amassing capital could labour gain its freedom. Like Owen, he had in mind an eventual self-sufficient community in which the workers would produce to meet their own needs, buying land to set unemployed workers to work, providing sickness benefits and so on (in fact his vision has largely come true in the Mondragon co-operative sector in the Basque region of Spain). But, unlike Owen, he realised that the benefits of cooperation could be realised within the existing society; he advised that if his readers wanted to set up co-ops within an existing town, then this was also a legitimate goal. The means to either end had to be a shop because 'We must go to a shop every day to buy food and necessaries – why then should we not go to our own shop?' (quoted in Birchall, 1994, p. 28). Members would do two things: they would buy goods in bulk and sell to each other, thus ensuring a saving on retail prices, and they would bring goods they had made to the shop to sell.

The movement which began in Brighton in 1826 was under Owen's spell, but was taking King's advice. Some co-op members were saving in order to set up an Owenite community (which they did at Orbiston in Scotland), some in 'union shops' to provide an outlet for their own products, which Polanyi describes as 'more in the nature of producers' co-operatives' (1957, p. 168). The consumer element in their experiments was there – the simple expedient of buying a bag of flour and dividing it was a common device among working-class people so that they knew the advantages of bulk buying. But it was not theorised; for both Owen and King the problem remained one of employment and a fair return to labour. They both opened labour exchanges to facilitate the exchange of goods from trade union and co-operative workshops;

working people could come and sell their products at a fair price which reflected the work that had gone into them. A formula was adopted of taking the average time taken to make a product, priced at sixpence an hour, and adjusted upwards for more skilled work. This accepted the market rate for labour, but in every other respect attempted to establish labour as the source of all value (Cole, 1944, p. 31).

Owen invented a new currency, 'labour notes', which were measured in labour time and circulated widely. The exchanges and the notes were quite successful for a time, and G.D.H. Cole reckoned they only collapsed because of a general repression by government and employers against trade unions which ended with the collapse of the whole movement (including the co-op shops) in 1834. Beatrice Webb, writing 50 years before Cole, disagreed. Her analysis is that they failed because co-operators held to William Thompson's labour theory of value in its crudest form. Thompson ignored

> an all important factor in the exchange value of commodities – I mean the demands of the market, representing the manifold wants, the changing desires, and shifting fancies of the whole body of consumers. (Potter, 1899, p. 49)

She argued that, with the benefit of half a century of successful co-operative trading behind them, co-operators had finally 'been taught sound economics' and 'owe their success to a full realisation of *utility* as a determining factor in value' (1899, p. 49). As we shall see below, Webb was arguing on behalf of the consumer interest in a late nineteenth century battle with a group of influential co-operators who believed in worker profit-sharing, so she was not a disinterested historian. She attributed the failure of the exchanges to the fact that they were soon choked with articles priced according to the labour expended, and not according to consumer demand. Speculators bought up all the goods priced below market value and resold them at a profit. From the consumer point of view, her explanation seems more plausible than that of Cole.

The first co-operative movement, which began in 1826, had spawned somewhere between 300 and 500 shops. By 1833, it had virtually collapsed. There are several reasons for the failure: there was the general collapse of trade unionism due to repression by government and lockouts by employers, and a downturn in trade which plunged co-op members into poverty. But more significant from our point of view is that they did not know how to distribute the profits, and so members had to dissolve their societies in order to be paid out. The success of the movement started in Rochdale in 1844 was largely attributable to their use of the dividend on purchases to reward members not as workers but as consumers. To those who wished for a new world order of Owenite communities this was a disappointment; consumers would get their reward in this world not the next. Polanyi argues their case eloquently when he says of Owenism:

> That its impetus was lost – or rather was maintained only in the peripheric sphere of the consumers' movement – was the greatest single defeat of spiritual forces in the history of industrial England. (1957, p. 169)

To those who value the idea of consumer empowerment, the most interesting experiment was only just beginning.

Rochdale and the establishment of consumer sovereignty

By the 1840s, Rochdale was a small town of 25 000 people, surrounded by hamlets containing another 40 000. The area was heavily dependent on the woollen and cotton industries, with hand-loom weaving being the predominant occupation. The decline of the weavers, from being among the aristocracy of labour to being virtually destitute, is one of the most tragic stories of the industrial revolution (Thompson, 1968, chapter 9). A combination of the invention of the power loom, capturing of the market by large middlemen, and a collapse of the apprenticeship system leading to an influx of new weavers, had led to their wages declining from 30 shillings a week to just a penny an hour (Burnett, 1989, p. 40). Combined with the appallingly insanitary state of the town, this meant that at the time the Pioneers began their shop, life expectancy in Rochdale averaged just 21 years (Birchall, 1994 p. 35).

Before they turned to shopkeeping, the Pioneers had tried several solutions. Some were Owenite socialists who had put their money into the last of Owen's model communities, Queenwood, and it had become obvious that this would not solve the problems of all but a privileged few. Some were Chartists, agitating for the vote and a political solution, but by 1842 the movement was beginning to collapse, 'its leaders jailed or transported, its supporters demoralised' (Birchall, 1994 p. 40). Some were active religious leaders, or teetotallers, whose prescription was to live an austere and virtuous life, though their chosen brand of unitarian methodism was the most down to earth of all the sects. Finally, they were committed trade unionists, and had experienced the wave of strikes of 1842, a confrontation which the weavers had eventually lost. They seriously considered emigration, but then decided to switch the two pence a week they had been paying into the weavers' union to a fund to set up a co-op shop. They had had one before, from 1833–35, but it had failed, probably through giving too much credit to members. This time they got it right; the way they structured their society ensured not only that they prospered but that the movement would grow rapidly throughout Britain.

Their aims were much broader than that of a consumer society. They wanted to establish a store, build houses for their members, and employ members suffering from unemployment or wage reductions in their own factories and workshops. They did all of these, but their land and building company ran into trouble when tenants could not afford the rents (see Birchall, 1996), and their manufacturing society, which contained an element of worker control and profit-sharing, was eventually taken over by outside shareholders. These experiences led them to build their own housing estate and to go into manufacturing for themselves, but as a consumer co-operative. Their eight famous principles ensured both consumer sovereignty and commercial success:

- The first was *democratic control*; members gained only one vote each, regardless of the size of their shareholding.
- The second was *open membership*; anyone could join at any time, for a small down payment.
- The third was a *fixed and limited interest on capital*; they needed investment, but gave it just as much reward as was necessary to secure it and no more.
- The fourth was *distribution of the surplus as dividend on purchases*, the famous dividend principle.
- The fifth was *cash trading*.
- The sixth a commitment to providing only *pure and unadulterated goods*, something which to a consumer-owned society should come easily.
- The seventh was a *commitment to education*.
- The eighth to *political and religious neutrality*.

The combination of open membership and the dividend principle meant that the movement grew rapidly. The combination of democracy and the limited rewards to capital meant that it remained a consumer movement. The combination of the exercise of democracy in general meetings and basic education meant that the members were wise enough to run their society well. The commitment to neutrality (we would call it equal opportunities) meant that they mostly avoided unnecessary controversy. Curiously, the application of the sixth principle caused the Pioneers some trouble. They produced flour from their own mill and refused to add chemicals to whiten it. The members rejected the flour, but after much discussion were brought to see that it was purer. G.J. Holyoake, a shrewd historian of the movement, put it this way:

> The members had become more intelligent; they had learned the nature of good flour when they had it; their tastes were better educated than that of many gentlemen of the middle class, and the Directors were able to tell the purchasers in a reckless manner 'If they wanted to adulterate the flour they could do it themselves.' (Quoted in Birchall, 1994, p. 60)

Adulteration of food, shoddy clothing and shoes, were a fact of life until government regulation began to have an effect towards the end of the century. But co-op members became used to high quality and plain dealing, something which both enhanced the reputation of the movement and, because of the refusal to adulterate and the commitment to cash trading, limited its appeal to the better-off working classes.

Twenty years on, there were around 100 000 co-op members, with a combined turnover of about £2.5 million. Another twenty years on there were over half a million members in 971 societies, with sales of nearly £15.5 million. By the end of the century, membership had grown to over 1.7 million, with 1439 societies, and a turnover of over £50 million. By the end of the first world war, in which the movement had distinguished itself by campaigning for rationing and against profiteering, membership stood at over three million, with a turnover of £88 million. How did they manage to grow so quickly? Some coincident factors helped the movement's early growth: the founding of the Rochdale store coincided with an upturn in the economy, the development of railways and the invention of the penny stamp, all of which enabled the idea of cooperation to spread rapidly. But two features of their own business strategy were responsible for the rapid growth, one which came about by accident and one which they deliberately invented.

The first was the device of the branch store. At the time when the Pioneers started, retailing in Britain was lagging behind the huge movements of population which rapid urbanisation had caused. It was characterised by weekly markets, small shops specialising in giving credit at high prices, itinerant peddlers and direct sales through small workshops. Few traders had more than one outlet (Jeffreys, 1954). When the Pioneers began, they assumed that people wanting their own store would form their own society. But members insisted that branch stores be opened, and the movement rapidly learned how to run chains of stores; it was in effect the first multiple retailer.

The second feature was the development of integrated co-operative wholesaling and manufacturing through a Co-operative Wholesale Society (CWS). The Pioneers began wholesaling for other societies, but as soon as they could have the law altered to allow it, in 1864 they set up the 'CWS', which became a model for a wholesale society in Scotland, and later for similar societies in many other countries (see Birchall, 1994, chapter 9). At a time when wholesalers were expensive and inefficient, the CWS and Scottish CWS virtually invented modern retail distribution. They grew in three ways. Firstly, they organised the distribution chain. They imported cheap food from abroad, organising distribution chains for Irish butter, Danish bacon, Indian tea and Canadian wheat, owning depots in the exporting countries and in the process helping indigenous agricultural and consumer co-operative movements. They went as far back in the supply chain as they could, owning tea plantations, processing foods either in Britain (for example flour milling) or in the country of origin (for example bacon factories). When ship owners put up their prices, the CWS simply began its own shipping line. The result was that the British public got the benefit of regular supplies of pure, cheap foods, with minimal distribution costs and all the profits handed to them in dividend.

Secondly, they became manufacturers of all those basic products that working-class people demanded in regular quantities: boots and shoes, clothing, soap, furniture and processed foods. In setting up production for a guaranteed market, they were able to use all the latest techniques in their factories (such as roller milling), staying ahead of the competition. Because the market was guaranteed and stable, they were able to become largely self-sufficient; they even had a factory producing the string for the parcels that CWS sent out to retail societies. Thirdly, they took over many ailing productive societies set up by retail co-ops and worker-owners and integrated them into their network.

Consumer versus worker

The entry of the CWS and Scottish CWS into manufacturing was not seen universally as a good thing, and their taking over of productive societies was highly controversial. It is a strange fact that most of the promoters of the consumer co-operatives were more concerned with the role of the workers than that of consumers. This is not surprising, since no less a thinker than J.S. Mill had identified the antagonism between capital and labour as the main problem in society, and had seen worker control of industry as the way to overcome it:

> The form of association...which, if mankind continue to improve, must be expected in the end to predominate, is not that which can exist between a capitalist as chief, and work people without a voice in the management, but the association of the labourers themselves on terms of equality, collectively owning the capital with which they carry on their operations, and working under managers elected and removable by themselves. (Mill, 1985, p. 133)

He also enthused about the consumer co-ops, showed great interest in the Rochdale system and the founding of the CWS, but saw a need to rationalise the 'class of mere distributors', so that people would be set free to become producers. He said:

> By limiting the distributors to the number really required for making the commodities accessible to the consumers – which is the direct effect of the co-operative system – a vast number of hands will be set free for production... This great economy of the world's resources would be realised even if co-operation stopped at associations for purchase and consumption, without extending to production. (Mill, 1985, p. 138)

Yet he looked forward to worker co-ops as a 'moral revolution in society' which would transform the 'standing feud between capital and labour'. He saw them primarily in moral terms, as having the ability to 'combine the freedom and independence of the individual with the moral, intellectual and economical advantages of aggregate production' (p. 140).

Mill referred to 'a band of friends, chiefly clergymen and barristers' who had helped to found worker and consumer co-ops (p. 136). He meant Christian Socialists such as E.V. Neale, Thomas Hughes, Charles Kingsley and J.M. Ludlow who, having steered through changes in the law which helped the consumer co-ops to prosper, began in the 1850s to set up self-governing workshops, and later co-partnership enterprises in which workers had a share in the ownership and in the profits (Norman, 1987). They opposed the CWS's setting up of its own factories, and in 1872 forced it to introduce an annual bonus to labour. This was unpopular with the workforce, and was abolished in 1875 (though it continued for some time longer in the Scottish CWS). Through speeches at co-operative congresses and the polemical writings of G.J. Holyoake, they kept up the pressure and in 1882 formed the Co-operative Productive Federation (CPF) to promote new enterprises part-owned by the workers. When they realised their cause was lost in the consumer co-operative movement, they turned to a wider audience of wealthy businessmen and campaigned for labour co-partnership in the utility companies and other private industries. By 1903 the CPF had had a modest success, increasing the number of productive societies to 126.

Ranged against the advocates of producer cooperation were Beatrice Potter (later Beatrice Webb), who had written the first definitive history of the movement, and J.T.W. Mitchell, longstanding chairman of the CWS. Webb's arguments were both theoretical and practical. On the theoretical side she challenged the advocates of worker profit-sharing over the distinction between production and distribution. If a factory worker weighed and packaged tea, this would be production; but if a shop worker did it, would it be classed as production or distribution? If a farmer harvested a crop it would be production; but if he took it to market would this be part of the production process or distribution? The point was that both added value to the product, and were in practice impossible to divide. She went on to question whether consumer co-ops made profits in the first place, since the return of dividend effectively eliminated profit from the price paid by consumers. Finally, she questioned whether the labour theory of value made sense, since it was consumers who decide what value to put on a product.

Her practical arguments were just as devastating. She showed that the most successful enterprises, the co-operative flour mills, had gradually been converting from joint ownership to outright ownership by consumer societies. Worker ownership had two flaws: workers tended to interfere with management and to be ill-disciplined, and when they were successful tended to deny membership to newcomers. Of the 54 productive enterprises in existence in 1890, she found only eight genuine self-governing workshops. Even in the 13 co-partnerships, retail societies were in control and no workers had got on to the management committee (Potter, 1899). Her vision, later elaborated with her husband Sydney into a 'Constitution for a Socialist Commonwealth' was of an economy run by consumer co-ops, with local authorities running public services (what she called 'compulsory co-operation') and trade unions protecting the interests of the workforce (B. and S. Webb, 1975). There was no room, and no need, for worker empowerment.

With hindsight, we can see flaws in Webb's argument. The advocates of worker profit-sharing had weakened their case by insisting on the distinction between production and distribution workers; had they argued for profit-sharing for all co-op workers their case would have been stronger, though they would then have had to give up the particular argument for worker control of factories. The weaknesses she found in worker control can be overcome, though it requires a complex 'control architecture' such as the Mondragon co-ops have developed (Turnbull, 1997). Because she argued against quite specific points, the broader arguments for worker control tend to remain intact.

What made Webb's argument even stronger was the support of J.T.W. Mitchell. As chairman of CWS, he had fought off the calls for profit sharing, and had been forced to think about the wider significance of the consumer co-op. Overseeing the continual expansion of the CWS, he could see no reason why the sovereign consumer could not be the basis of all growth in the co-operative sector. After all, they organised production, distribution and retailing efficiently on behalf of all citizens as consumers, basing production on a known and stable market, avoiding wasteful competition, and eliminating profit by returning surpluses to customer-members. Since everyone is a consumer, it was a way of liberating everyone. Mitchell's biographer puts it like this:

> the working class was to become its own employer. The Movement would move through education, biscuits, newspapers, merchant ships etc into the National Debt, the railways and everything else. It constituted a society, or set of societies which were capable of becoming Society itself. Such societies constituted a world, a way of life, and, through co-operative insurance and the funeral service, a way of death too. (Yeo, 1995, p. 46)

Mitchell was a practical man. He could say with pride 'Our movement was no longer a theory. It was a great fact' (Yeo, 1995, p. 40). Yet the breadth of his vision of what sort of society could follow from consumer empowerment was greater even than that of Beatrice Webb.

The First World War and emergence of a Co-operative Party

By the end of the nineteenth century, the co-operative movement was really beginning to make its presence felt on behalf of consumers. It was estimated that members had benefitted from £50 million in returned dividend. Where it was strong enough – in tea importing and flour milling for instance – the CWS acted to prevent price rings from extracting excess profits from the customer. Their coastal ships broke up a shipping ring in 1885, and in 1906 public indignation at a soap manufacturers' trust led to the doubling of production at the CWS works, and then the building of two new soap works. In staple goods such as coal, milk and bread, they were the market leaders, and effectively kept other suppliers' prices down.

But it was the First World War that really showed the value of a co-operative sector to the consumer. There was a foretaste of just how capable the consumers' movement had become in 1913, when a transport strike threatened food supplies for the people of Dublin. Within three days the CWS had chartered a ship, made up 30000 food parcels, enough to feed a hundred thousand people for several days. The Dublin and Belfast co-operative societies baked 12000 loaves for distribution. 'The lesson of the food ship was that the British Co-operative Movement had greater resources than any other organisation for meeting emergency needs' (Birchall, 1994, p. 110). During the war, the CWS worked flat out to provide equipment for the army at as near to cost price as possible. Co-op shops sold all their stock at normal prices, while other shops were hoarding and speculators were buying up co-op goods and making a fat profit. They found that their loyalty was not reciprocated. While the government dragged its feet on food rationing, the co-ops introduced their own. While the co-ops supplied one in seven of retail trade, to one in four customers, there was 'studied neglect' from the government, and the co-ops were excluded from emergency committees set up to regulate prices and supplies.

Local traders had always loathed the co-ops, and had periodically attempted to persuade customers to boycott them. In 1902 for instance, a St. Helens traders' association had financed anti-co-op candidates in local elections and had vilified the local society in the press. They had done the movement little damage, but now they took hold of local war-relief committees and military service tribunals, sending co-op employees to the trenches while exempting their own workers. Then to cap it all, the government introduced an excess profits tax and applied it to co-op surpluses which should have been returned as dividends to customers. A historian of the times sums it up:

> Every action of the Government seemed to indicate a 'latent hostility' to co-operators, and an assumption that the only system for the distribution of commodities was that of the private merchant, wholesale dealer and shopkeeper. (Elliott, 1937, p. 63)

Other historians think it was not so much hostility as ignorance on the part of upper-class civil servants who were simply unaware that such a large working-class consumers' movement existed. The Co-op's credentials were eventually recognised and the movement was well represented on the Ministry of Food and on a new Consumers' Council set up to advise the minister. But even at the end of 1917 while 12 per cent of the members of local food committees were private traders, only 2.5 per cent represented the co-ops. Coming out of the war there was a universal feeling of betrayal and anger among co-operators, so much so that in 1917 they took the bold step of forming their own Co-operative Party.

In the 1918 election, ten candidates stood for the co-operative movement and one, Alfred Waterson, was elected. In 1922 four independent co-operative MPs were elected. In co-operative strongholds such as Kettering, where Waterson was MP and practically the whole local economy was co-operative, the Labour Party had entered into a loose agreement not to oppose them. It took until 1927 before a proper agreement was worked out, and the Co-operative Party would only ever agree to an 'alliance' with the Labour Party rather than full affiliation, but in the end the compromise was made to work. A predominantly consumers' movement had elbowed its way into a permanent 'Labour and Co-operative' alliance which lasts to this day.

After the first decade, there was no doubt that the Party had considerably increased the influence of the movement in politics: A.V. Alexander, a CWS director, was appointed secretary to the Co-operative Union Parliamentary Committee. Carbery, historian of the Party, sums up his career from this time onwards:

> Within a year and a half he was in Parliament; within two and a half years in the Government; within seven and a half years he was in the Cabinet. He ended up with an earldom, a Companion of Honour and Leader of the Labour Peers in the House of Lords. (Carbery, 1969 p. 29)

But the impact of the Party in general was much more muted. Carbery heads his chapter on the period 1930 to 1945 'the wasted years'. There was much that a consumers' political party had to do. Unlike capitalists' businesses, which demanded and got protection from government, the Co-op had no need of support; it survived the booms and slumps with remarkable ease, because it was supplying commodities to meet basic needs, and its assets were never subject to the valuation of the market. The CWS only once made a loss, of £3.5 millions in 1921. The movement was in an excellent position to protect consumers, breaking apart price rings such as that orchestrated in soap by Unilever, which controlled 80 per cent of the market; the Co-op controlled 15 per cent of the total weight of soap manufactured, but it only cost 9 per cent of the total wholesale price.

By 1924 the bulk of flour milling was in three hands, but one of these was the CWS, and by 1930 it was supplying 17 per cent of the market, at only 15 per cent of the wholesale price. Co-op bakeries stood out against local rings and kept down the price of bread. Where prices were fixed by marketing boards, the Co-op could offer dividend; by 1935 it controlled 22 per cent of the milk trade. As the world's largest distributor of tea, the English and Scottish Joint Wholesale Society was able to prevent a price ring from emerging, and to force other producers to exclude the weight of the packet from the cost of the tea. In response, the press was almost uniformly hostile, so the movement bought its own weekly newspaper, the Reynolds News. Manufacturers boycotted the Co-op, so wholesale societies were stimulated to further production of such lines as the 'Defiant' radio.

But what was the contribution of the Co-operative Party? In 1933 it could not prevent the government taxing co-operative surpluses, something the movement had been avoiding by arguing that the surpluses were not profits. Carbery says there was a 'dreadful lack of clarity as to the political philosophy of the Party. Indeed, it was not only the philosophy which was vague – so too was its programme' (1969, p. 35). Mostly it simply followed the Labour Party's lead. This meant that no-one was arguing for co-operative forms of social ownership, an omission which was to have grave consequences for the role of consumers in the nationalised industries of the postwar period. Carbery states boldly that by 1939 'nothing had been achieved' (1969, p. 49). In 1938 a group of economists wrote a long and detailed examination of the movement's current strengths and weaknesses. They identified it as a 'consumers' trade association' and stated 'It is not easy to understand why the Co-operative Party should have been founded' (Carr-Saunders *et al.*, 1938). The movement would have been better off serving consumers outside of parliament as a pressure group rather than inside, being emasculated by the alliance with the Labour Party.

The Co-operative Women's Guild

It is worth comparing this comparative failure to represent consumers with a much more successful co-operative institution, the Co-operative Women's Guild. The symbol of the CWS was 'the woman with the basket', but the experience of women in the co-operative movement was more mixed. Alice Acland, founder of the Guild, put it this way:

> What are men always urged to do when there is a meeting ... to start co-operative institutions? Come! Help! Vote! Criticise! Act! What are women urged to do? Come and *buy*. That is the limit of the special work pointed out to us women. (Quoted in Birchall, 1994, p. 97)

Some societies limited membership to one person in each family, and this was usually the man. Where more than one were accepted, it was usually the man who attended the quarterly meetings. A male oligarchy ruled, and women had a long struggle to make their presence felt. They were helped by the Guild which, founded in 1883, was led for 32 years by a formidable general secretary, Margaret Llewellyn Davies. Determined not to let the local guilds degenerate into 'sewing classes', she turned it into a campaigning organisation using Fabian tactics: they would do research into an issue, discuss it in the branches and then, when they had a mandate from what was in effect the largest movement of working-class women in the world, run a nationwide campaign (Gaffin and Thoms, 1983).

Gradually, women began to be elected to local government and to co-operative committees, though it was only after the first world war that a woman made it to the CWS board. The Guild ran a campaign to persuade societies to set up shops in poor areas, and experimented with a 'people's store' in Sunderland. More successful was a campaign to commit the movement to a minimum wage scale for women workers. Outside the movement, they campaigned for women's trade unions, for maternity benefits (which they got in 1911), improved health care for mothers and children, and just before the war had their entire programme adopted by central government and implemented by local authorities. They made a strong stand in favour of liberalising the divorce laws and, though they lost their Co-operative Union grant over the issue, stood firm. During the postwar period their campaigning became more diffuse, but they continued to be a strong influence on behalf of working-class women.

A long decline?

For a movement that was already old in 1914, the Co-op could hardly be expected to retain the vigour of the Rochdale Pioneers, or of the early Women's Guild. In fact, during the interwar period the movement showed what one historian has described as 'a vitality and adaptability remarkable for so old, widespread and complex a movement' (Bonner, 1970, p. 174). It had survived a world war and deep depressions and nearly tripled its membership and retail trade, holding an 11 per cent share of the market. It had serious weaknesses: it had failed to diversify in the nonfood sectors, had fallen behind in staples such as clothes, shoes and household goods, and had failed to plan for its growth, growing in an organic way in areas which it was already strong. Researchers agreed that at its best it could be outstanding, but at its worst could be parochial, unimaginative, complacent and badly-managed (Carr-Saunders et al., 1938).

Entering the Second World War, the movement consisted of 1100 societies controlling 24000 shops, having 40 per cent of the market in butter, 26 per cent of the milk, 23 per cent of grocery and provisions, 20 per cent of tea, sugar and cheese, and so on. When rationing was introduced, 28 per cent of the population – 13.5 million people – registered with the Co-op (Birchall, 1994, chapter 8). It employed a quarter of a million people in retailing, with another hundred thousand in production and distribution. With 155 factories, the CWS was easily the largest consumers' self-supply organisation in the world. This time round, the potential contribution of the Co-op to the war effort was recognised, and the movement got its fair share of the goods and was fully represented on the right committees. The war did some terrible damage – in the V-bomb raids of 1944 alone, 1100 shops were destroyed or damaged – but the mutual nature of the relationship between societies, and the availability of a national distribution network, meant that they were able to recover much more quickly than were conventional retailers. The war did some less tangible damage as well: the disruption to social life meant the Women's Guild was never the same again.

After the war, there seemed no diminution in the self-confidence of the movement. The CWS planned 36 new productive works, and by the early 1950s wholesale trade almost doubled to £400m, of which their own productions reached £114m. The Co-op was in the lead with new forms of retailing: it pioneered self-service and then its corollary, the supermarket; out of 50 supermarkets open in 1950, 20 were co-ops. The prospects for the Co-op looked bright. However, an underlying revolution in retailing was occurring, which was going to work to the advantage of the multiple stores. By 1950, most of these had ceased to be family firms and had become public limited companies, able to raise money on the stock exchange (Jeffreys, 1953). They began to concentrate this new capital on acquiring town centre sites, selling a narrow range of goods and, where the Co-op was strong, aggressively cutting prices.

They soon became large enough to dispense with wholesaling altogether and to deal direct with the manufacturers. Gradually the vertical chain which the Co-op had built up became less of an asset, more a liability. Retailers dictated terms and the manufacturers responded by becoming more efficient and producing to low prices on a large scale. The small retailers responded by beginning to join voluntary chains which brought them some of the benefits of cooperation. By the late 1950s the Co-op had a membership of over 12 million, turnover was nearly a billion pounds, there were over 30000 shops and 250 factories, it had 60 per cent of the self-service outlets, but had finally *stopped growing.* Its share of retail trade was steady at 11 per cent, but in a rapidly growing market, that of the multiples had risen to 22 per cent.

Between 1953 and 1964 there were four major enquiries into the state of the movement, including one chaired by the leader of the Labour Party, Hugh Gaitskell (1958). The movement's strength had always been in its decentralised, autonomous, small-scale democracies of consumers, but in the face of national and regional competitors, this now became a fatal weakness. The Co-operative Union was a federation which carried some authority but lacked real power to compel societies to merge. No-one could force nearly a thousand independent societies to buy loyally from the CWS, and so the movement's buying power was dissipated. The rest of the story is one of gradual amalgamations, and takeovers of ailing societies by the movement's 'ambulance', the Co-operative Retail Services (and then by the CWS which, rather confusingly went into retailing to protect its wholesaling business). Recently the CWS has sold its productive business, to concentrate on competing with the multiples in superstores. There are now around 50 societies, but the largest three have half the movement's £7 billion turnover. The market share is now down below 4 per cent, and the movement has been overtaken by Sainsbury and Tesco as the largest food retailer.

Can co-ops still empower consumers?

There are several bright spots in this general decline. Firstly, after decades of struggling to keep open, and reluctantly closing, loss-making small shops, the movement discovered the convenience store format and, through rapid conversion to this new style of trading began to reverse the process; in fact, between 1989 and 1993 the rise of the small store arrested the more general decline (Birchall, 1987).

Secondly, where the Co-op is still strong – in funeral services and the travel industry – regional societies have done outstanding work in breaking price rings and guaranteeing quality. Thirdly, two auxiliary businesses owned by the CWS have taken off. The Co-operative Insurance Society is one of the largest and most successful insurers, and it regularly distributes dividends to its policy-holders. The Co-operative Bank has experienced spectacular growth owing to its widely advertised ethical policy, in which it has emphasised its openness, its willingness to make long-term guarantees to customers, and its refusal to do business in areas it defines as unethical. Fourthly, on several occasions recently the CWS has been able to align itself with consumers, going further than other retailers and manufacturers in putting factual information on its products, offering guarantees that animals have been humanely treated and so on.

Some initiatives have come from co-op members; during the period of apartheid they insisted on a boycott of South African goods. Some have come from managers; top managers of the two largest societies, CWS and CRS, have launched very successful membership drives recently, and have begun seriously to see membership as an asset. Some societies are experimenting with an electronic dividend card, though they have been upstaged by retailers such as Sainsbury and Tesco who have introduced a similar loyalty card; the fact that the latter is a trade discount rather than a genuine return of surplus to members is a fine point which is lost on the public.

All this may be too little too late. And there is an underlying problem of democratic deficit. Turnout at elections for directors of societies and at general meetings has always been relatively low. Studies done in 1933 and 1954 show that in small societies with 1000 members or less the percentage of members voting declined from 5.11 per cent to 3.43 per cent, and that in large societies of over 50000 members from 1.65 to 1.56 per cent (Banks and Mears, 1984). In 1974, a survey found that there were between 4000 and 5000 lay leadership positions in the Co-op, representing 0.5 per cent of the membership. Their average age was over 60. Participation rates have continued to decline, with some societies becoming virtual worker co-ops in that only employees, managers and their relatives tend to be elected to the board. However, two factors have stemmed the decline. The amalgamation of societies has meant that fewer directors are needed, and their quality has recently been improving, helped by training from a new Institute of Co-operative Directors. Membership drives by societies, and renewed interest by people who discover the co-operative through activism in other kinds of co-ops (notably worker co-ops and credit unions) have brought in some new leaders. Elections are now much more often contested.

Whether this is enough to make up the democratic deficit is open to doubt. Furthermore, there is a fundamental problem in the relationship of boards to the wider membership and of lay directors to managers. So intense is the competition with the multiples that very few decisions can be identified as stemming from the membership rather than from an embattled management. The logic of the market can tend to weaken the directors' sense that they have real decisions to make. On the other hand, there are lively and successful regional societies whose boards are strong and confident. There are regional structures to the national societies which encourage genuine democracy. There is a growing recognition that customers must be turned into members, and some members into activists, if the Co-op is to survive.

Meanwhile the idea of consumer sovereignty finds its way into new channels. Recently around 70 per cent of the UK building societies have opted to demutualise. But the remaining 30 per cent have begun to think out a strategy for capitalising on their membership, which involves rewarding members for their loyalty and using their lack of investor-owners to show they are more efficient than the banks. They are also rethinking the lack of democratic participation of members (Coles, 1997). Other types of co-op are showing that the idea of consumer ownership and control works well in some contexts; credit unions and food co-ops are growing quickly in Britain in some of the most disadvantaged communities. Dissatisfaction with the performance of the privatised utilities has led to calls for their reconstituting as a form of consumer co-operative (Kay, 1996). Important lessons can be learned from the experience of the British consumer co-operative movement. It is the longest lasting and most successful consumer movement the world has ever seen.

References

Banks, J.A. and Mears, R. (1984) *Co-operative Democratic Participation* (Milton Keynes: Open University Press).
Benson, J. (1994) *The Rise of Consumer Society in Britain, 1880–1980* (London: Longman).
Birchall, J. (1987) *Save Our Shop: the Fall and Rise of the Small Co-operative Store* (Manchester: Holyoake Press).
— (1994) *Co-op: The People's Business* (Manchester: Manchester University Press).
— (1996) 'The Hidden History of Co-operative Housing in Britain', in A. Heskin and J. Leavitt (1996) *The Hidden History of Housing Co-operatives* (Davis: University of California).
Bonner, A. (1970) *British Co-operation* (Manchester: Co-operative Union).
Burnett, J. (1989) *Plenty and Want: A Social History of Diet in England from 1815 to the Present Day* (London: Routledge).
Carbery, T. (1969) *Consumers in Politics* (Manchester: Manchester University Press).
Carr-Saunders, A.M., Florence, P.S. and Peers, R. (1938) *Consumers' Co-operation in Great Britain* (London: George Allen & Unwin).
Cole, G.D.H. (1944) *A Century of Co-operation* (London: George Allen & Unwin).
Coles, A. (1997) 'The Future of Mutuality', *Journal of Co-operative Studies*, vol. 29(3).

Deakin, N. and Wright, A. (eds) (1990) *Consuming Public Services* (London: Routledge).
Elliott, S. (1937) *England, Cradle of Co-operation* (London: Faber & Faber).
Gaffin, J. and Thoms, D. (1983) *Caring and Sharing: The Centenary History of the Co-operative Women's Guild* (Manchester: Holyoake Press).
Gaitskell Report (1958) *Co-operative Independent Commission Report* (Manchester: Co-operative Union).
Jeffreys, J.B. (1954) *Retail Trading in Britain: 1850–1950* (Cambridge: Cambridge University Press).
Kay, J. (1996) 'Regulating Privatised Utilities: The Customer Corporation', *Journal of Co-operative Studies*, vol. 29(2).
Lowe, R. and Woodroffe, G. (1995) *Consumer Law and Practice* (London: Sweet & Maxwell).
McKendrick, N., Brewer, J. Plumb, J.H. (1982) *The Birth of a Consumer Society* (London: Europa).
Mill, J.S. (1985) *Principles of Political Economy* (Harmondsworth: Penguin).
Norman, E. (1987) *The Victorian Christian Socialists* (Cambridge: Cambridge University Press).
Polanyi, K. (1957) *'The Great Transformation: The Political and Economic Origins of our Time* (Boston: Beacon Press).
Potter, B. (1899) *The Co-operative Movement* (London: Swan Sonnenschein).
Smith, G. (1982) *The Consumer Interest* (London: John Martin).
Thompson, E.P. (1968) *The Making of the English Working Class* (Harmondsworth: Penguin).
Turnbull, S. (1997) 'Stakeholder Co-operation', *Journal of Co-operative Studies*, vol. 29(3).
Webb, B. and Webb, S. (1975) *A Constitution for the Socialist Commonwealth of Great Britain* (Cambridge: Cambridge University Press).
Williams, R. (1988) *Keywords* (London: Fontana).
Yeo, S. (1995) *Who was JTW Mitchell?* (Manchester: CWS Membership Services).

13 Empowerment in a Community of Purpose
Richard C. Warren

INTRODUCTION

Is empowerment an ethical management practice in business? This chapter presents a virtue-theory perspective on the ethics of empowerment. It begins with a consideration of what empowerment is, and how it is implemented inside the firm. Empowerment strategies are often portrayed as a neutral set of techniques for improving the efficiency of the firm, but it should be recognised that they are also underpinned by normative assumptions which should be open to scrutiny. The persistent criticism made about the exploitative nature of empowerment is considered and partly rejected. The chapter also examines the argument made in the empowerment literature that the common purpose of business is the generation of shareholder value. An alternative conception of business as a community of purpose is proposed as both a more realistic and a useful idea, and one that can hold out the prospect of real empowerment for employees. Some criteria for thinking about the ethics of empowerment according to its effects on character and the common good are then outlined. Finally, in this chapter, suggestions are put forward regarding the institutionalisation of business in society such that it can operate as a community of purpose which contributes to the common good.

WHAT IS EMPOWERMENT?

There is a wide and varied literature on empowerment in business and management containing many different themes and approaches to its practice. As a general concept, empowerment may be understood as the re-delegation of power and responsibility throughout the organisation, which has (in the past) tended to over-centralise its control processes. To say that employees need to be empowered is to concede from the start that they are disempowered or lack the necessary independent agency in the organisation. Evidence that the centralisation of control and the removal of employee discretion about their work has occurred in the past is well-documented in management literature (Fox, 1985). After all, in a fundamental sense there are only two basic strategies for managing a large organisation: to build on the formation of employees' virtues a sense of engagement and responsibility for what they are doing and the way that it is done in relation to the purpose of the whole organisation (responsible autonomy method); or to render these virtues less necessary and rely on close supervision, rules and technology to control the working process and reward the employees for an instrumental commitment to their allocated task (direct control method) (Friedman, 1977).

At a key point in the industrialisation process, the majority of employers in industry decided to pursue the later course in the design and management of their organisations, together with a utilitarian ideology of *laissez faire* as its moral justification (Hawkins, 1972). Some employers took the former approach, but despite its apparent effectiveness it lacked an acceptable moral ideology to justify its widespread implementation and so did not gain political support. However, in recent times employers, in the face of global competition, have begun to see the inadequacies of the direct control method and to recognise the apparent advantages of the responsible autonomy method for productivity and quality (Friedman, 1977; Lorenz, 1992). And, whilst, the idea of empowerment has been implemented by managers, what is often lacking is their understanding that the moral underpinnings of this approach also have to be embraced for the system to work. In other words, there has to be a movement from the ideology of utilitarian self-interest towards an ideology of virtuous conduct and a shared commitment towards a common purpose. The reasons why this is the case, together with the evidence supporting them will be explained in detail below.

THE EMPOWERMENT DEBATE

It should be remembered that ideas about empowerment are not new, the perennial problem of efficiency and effectiveness and how to achieve it have been with us for some time. In the 1920s, Mary Parker Follet noted that power was a 'self-developing' capacity which needed to be dispersed throughout the organisation if 'creative integration' was to be made possible (Follet, 1941). Her advice to managers in industry was to avoid putting themselves in power over others, and, instead, to seek to share power with their subordinates. Her strategy for empowerment is encapsulated in this quotation:

If the first rule for giving orders is to depersonalise the order, for the order-giver and the order-receiver together to find the law of the situation, and if the second rule is to replace orders as far as possible by teaching the technique of a job, a third rule might be to give reasons with the orders. The fourth is that, the firm should find a way of making its employees share in a common purpose. (Follet, 1941, p. 131)

Her key theme is that the employee needs to understand the task in relation to the purpose of the firm as a whole, so that they can use their discretion and take responsibility for its execution and the results.

This theme of empowerment is similar to, or has much in common with, those concepts previously described under the guise of participatory management, theory X and theory Y, job-enrichment and enlargement, and improving the quality of working-life programmes. Today, a new spur to the revival of these old ideas has been the influence of the Total Quality Management movement and the need to emulate the conspicuous success of Japanese business (Fukuyama, 1995).

Alan Fox is perhaps one of the most articulate exponents of the challenge that faces British management to change its management practices (Fox, 1985). He has characterised British industry as suffering from a 'low-trust' syndrome of mutual antagonism between workers and management. This relationship can only be set right by a movement towards the 'high-trust' model of employment, where employees are offered participation and discretion in defining their organisational roles. The point of this change is to begin to treat employees as moral participants in the collective enterprise of the firm as opposed to instrumentally attached hired hands.

The argument supporting the change in approach towards employees might be summarised as follows. If a business is to flourish in a highly competitive market, it has to be efficient, innovative and quality conscious. As markets are volatile, firms need to be able to respond to market demands quickly, and so the management of change becomes a vital factor in maintaining the firm's competitive advantage against the competition. The response of employees towards change has a big impact on the success of the change management process. In the 'high-trust' model of employment employees are thought to be prepared to respond positively to change: they are willing to be retrained or redeployed, they will be quality conscious and prepared to use their initiative and cooperate fully in the new tasks to be achieved. Employees in a 'high-trust' relationship with the firm are productivity conscious in a self-controlled way rather than made productive by management control and close supervision. This is because the organisation offers them full membership involvement and expects them to exercise responsible discretion in the roles they help play to fulfil the collective purpose of the enterprise. The other advantage of the high-trust system is that it allows managerial time and effort to be focused on the businesses' competitive profile in the market rather than on the industrial relations problems of labour control and the inefficiencies of instrumental employee motivation.

In recent years, whilst modern writers on empowerment often acknowledge the pedigree of the idea of gaining employee involvement and participation in the organisation, their innovation is to note that not enough systematic attention has been paid to making this a reality at every level in the firm. The 'new' empowerment literature concentrates upon making as widespread and as deep an impact as possible on actual management practice by presenting clearly and simply the key concepts in a practical and readily comprehensible way, often by using the literary devises of fables, allegories, and stories. Check lists and mantras are formulated for busy managers to memorise and implement in their own organisations, and consultants offer to run extensive support programmes for companies who wish to embrace these prescriptions.

Let us examine Byham and Cox's book, *Zapp! The Lightning of Empowerment*, as a representative of this genre, which in addition to being a best-seller has enjoyed widespread corporate support (Byham and Cox, 1988). In this fable, empowerment's common purpose is sold to the notional employee (Joe Mode) as the idea that in competitive markets a business needs to keep up the search for constant improvement of its products and services, and that all employees need to be involved in this search process. Empowerment strategies are designed to harness the creative energies of employees toward constant improvement of products and services. Employee involvement, they claim, cannot be imposed but must come from employees taking ownership themselves of the processes involved in the organisation. The economic task for managers of the business is to re-energise the organisation to realise a fuller development and value added from its human capital. Great importance is put on the process of creative thinking and problem-solving which can make use of the employee's knowledge to serve customer needs more effectively. To empower people requires an increase in autonomous agency or giving employee's greater discretion within their allocated roles so that they become more self-controlling and willing to accept delegated responsibility for performance targets.

The main emphasis in the book is on the need for widespread and thorough training in the 'how' of empowerment for all employees. The recommended steps for managers to empower employees are prescribed as follows: always maintain or enhance a person's self-esteem; respond to employees' problems with empathy; ask for help in solving problems, or with new innovations; offer help to employees but without taking responsibility away from the employee; delegate and share responsibility as widely as possible in teams; and remember people need coaching on how to do their jobs. The empowered (or Zapped) organisation requires energetic management direction, knowledge, resources commitments and continual evaluation on the basis of measurement and extensive feedback. Importantly, all employees need to be connected to the common purpose but little is said about employees having a say in helping to define this purpose. Business is assumed to be a nexus of mutual self-interest united around the task of survival in a competitive market.

EVALUATING EMPOWERMENT

From the conception outlined above it would appear that empowerment is just a neutral tool in the hands of management, which if applied rigorously will generate improved results for the business. The underlining assumption is that mutual self-interest is a sufficient bond to drive and sustain a collective enterprise: employers improve competitiveness and employees are rewarded with secure jobs. The moral foundation of this approach is utilitarian because the good of the whole system depends upon the collective maximisation of individual material interests. Empowerment strategies are often advocated in terms of the means justifying the ends: the need to improve productivity justifies extensive intervention to change the employee's attitude to work. On the whole, little consideration is given to the impact of these intervention strategies on character formation, nor are questions asked about how the common purpose of the firm is to be decided upon.

The main criticisms of empowerment tend to come from radical opponents to liberal capitalism, who claim that little real trust is given in exchange for the employees commitment and taking of responsibility at work (Claydon and Doyle, 1996; Grenier, 1988; Blyton and Turnbull, 1992). These critics characterise empowerment as fundamentally manipulative and exploitative in both intention and practice. Consequently, empowerment strategies constitute just another humiliation for the worker in the struggle of labour against capital. This critique tents to condemn the whole programme out of hand, and does not attempt to distinguish degrees of exploitation, or more or less acceptable forms of subordination from an ethical perspective. This can be illustrated by an examination the work of Barbara Townley who has used the approach of Michel Foucault as a platform from which to criticise the aspirations towards empowerment contained in the rhetoric of human resources management (Townley, 1994).

TOWNLEY'S CRITIQUE OF EMPOWERMENT

Barbara Townley uses her mastery of Foucaultian scholarship to build up a formidable critique of human resource empowerment policies and practices. The coherence of this critique very much depends upon the validity of Foucault's rejection of the modernist, positivist tradition in the social sciences, and Townley's own analysis of how empowerment is applied in practice. Foucault's reputation was built upon studies which took a new look at some fascinating backwaters in history: the evolution of social attitudes towards madness; the history of proto-modern medicine; the conceptual underground of biology, linguistics and economics, and the identity and sexuality of the human subject. These studies are full of ambition and build into a multi-stranded programme aimed at identifying the historical conditions of the rise of reason in modern civilisation. His early works embraced both Marxism and phenomenology before he developed his own Nietzschean-inspired brand of historico-philosophy which has been labelled as an 'anatomical gaze' for its careful dissection of the genealogy of the human condition (Rabinow, 1984). In essence, Foucault attempts to reveal hitherto unrecognised forms of domination, especially forms obscured or justified by the myths and pretensions of liberalism and rationalism. In his view, power invades our intimate social worlds and is deeply constitutive of our personalities; networks of power and strategies of control and acts of resistance are the fundamentals of the human condition.

Townley employs some of Foucault's key concepts to analyse human resource management as a system of domination in organisational relationships, and in particular at the relationship between power and knowledge. She considers empowerment concepts to be a body of disciplinary techniques which help to operationalise power and constitute the employees experience of work. Townley tries to reveal the 'how' of power at work as opposed to the 'what' and the 'for whom' of power, by focusing upon the everyday activities in the empowerment process as an administrative apparatus. The key power relationship is the employee's contract of employment and the gap between what is promised and what is realised by way of effort and commitment to the organisation under that contract.

Townley analyses the administration of employment processes using Foucault's concepts of enclosure, partitioning, ranking, taxinomina, mathesis, examination, confession and the disciplinary matrix. Three aspects of knowledge are said to be needed by those who seek to empower employees: knowledge of the workforce or population; knowledge of the activity or labour undertaken; and knowledge of the individual worker or subject. This knowledge is then used to actively order and create the reality of work and make it manageable. Empowerment is analysed as just another form of discipline in both senses of the word: as techniques of meticulous regulation and surveillance and as a form of knowledge which is the handmaiden of power and social control. Order is still imposed on employees by physical segregation into factories, offices and shops; they are still monitored closely, and their activities are routinised by prescribed timetables and procedures; they are corrected when deviations occur from a plan and inspected at all times by hidden supervisors and technology.

In this analysis the regime of the modern prison is central to industrial discipline, as Townley claims, 'The seemingly mundane and innocuous techniques...form a panopticon' (Townley, 1994, p. 139). Moreover, this knowledge is not neutral, it is intimately bound up with the desire of management to advance their own influence and domination. The language of empowerment by classifying and helping to interpret the world begins to govern the employees' ways of thinking and what they take for granted. Domination is achieved with the use of an empowerment rhetoric; and liberation only by challenging the prevailing structure of knowledge and understanding by showing it to be historically contingent and essentially arbitrary.

Townley claims that this puts the nature of information in empowerment strategies under the spotlight as the key resource of those who seek to use power to control the workforce. There is therefore no separation of the strategic from the administrative aspects of empowerment, the mundane practices of recording, ordering and inscribing are vital processes in maintaining organisational power. By focusing the analysis on the micro-politics of organisations this puts the emphasis on the political nature of organisations and the question of gender by highlighting the social construction of these practices. Townley attempts to build upon this critique an emancipatory view of empowerment based upon certain feminist ideas: the importance of voice and visibility, the rejection of technocracy, respecting the integrity of the individual and their experiences, the importance of difference, the relational nature of knowledge and a rejection of hierarchy and privilege.

Townley's optimistic prescriptions are dependent upon the assumption that the world can be improved and a point of view exists which stands outside of the corruption of patriarchal society from which critique can be made. Demystifying social practices only makes sense if we preserve a standard of truth capable of telling theory from ideology, and knowledge from rhetoric. But Townley's project is untenable because of the contradiction of trying to build a feminist prescription upon a Foucaultian critique which does not offer any foundations upon which to reconstruct this preferred alternative. At best Foucault's philosophy may be described as irrational nihilism: rebellion without a cause. His view is that history is only a secession of dominations and so no point of view exists which will allow an objective critique to be made of the present nexus of power and knowledge.

When Townley applies this perspective to empowerment her refusal to recognise empirical variation in the perspective of domination makes it impossible to make sense of freedom, authenticity and community in employment. If all empowerment is an attempt at subjection, then attempts at improving conditions and social justice by both employers, state and trade unions are ignored and opportunities for progress rendered useless. To equate all empowerment strategies with domination means that we cannot distinguish those aspects of discretion that give coherence to life and sustain autonomous projects from techniques of control that regiment, denude and degrade. We must consider how people experience and interpret their roles because the just claims of authority and the practical urgencies of subordination are very different in prisons and businesses, and they are different for different people within each institution.

For the thoroughgoing Foucauldian the human will to power is the essence of human nature; there can be no improvement, only a new regime of power which has an equally illegitimate claim to authority. Foucault is deeply suspicious of truth claims and distrusts reason; to him all knowledge, and in particular social science, is a tool of the will to power. Moreover, this apparatus of rules, techniques and knowledge can be use to further the will to power of any social group, even feminists. Townley's attempt at a marriage of Foucault and feminism is therefore flawed. There are simply no better philosophies of empowerment from the Foucaultian perspective, they are all manifestations of the will to knowledge.

This attempt to condemn in blanket fashion all empowerment initiatives because of their use as a management control tool is misguided because there are ethical criteria that can be used to evaluate these strategies. Not all values are relative, nor are all ethical norms derived from corrupted social structures. Virtue ethics judges conduct on the basis that human virtues depend upon deep facts about human needs and human nature which don't tend to vary significantly over time or merely reflect a historical epoch (Jackson, 1996). And, whilst there is an element of world relativity in our conception of the virtues, this should not destroy our faith in the fact that we can and do make objective value judgements. Hence, if there had been no human tendency to give in to certain temptations through the ages, there would be no point in calling temperance a virtue. Virtue theory provides ethical criteria that can be used to distinguish between different types of empowerment, and can help to specify some objective requirements for the evaluation of empowerment strategies. It is argued here that ethical empowerment needs to pay particular attention to the conception of common purpose that unites those engaged in the enterprise, and to the impact of the empowerment practices upon the characters of the organisation's participants.

EMPOWERMENT AND VIRTUE

It was noted earlier that the moral underpinning of many empowerment strategies is a utilitarian bond of self-interest uniting employer and employee, delivering efficiency in return for job security. However, Emile Durkheim pointed out long ago in *The Division of Labour*, that a cohesive group cannot exist on the basis of individual interests alone, least of all individual material interests, and that material interests cannot on their own operate as an effective driving force of successful cooperation (Durkheim, 1933). As he noted, in the case of contracts of employment, if the laws underpinning the system of individualised exchange were to be effective, the law itself had to be supplemented by a vast body of customary rules, beliefs and sentiments. In short, the utilitarian ideology of laissez faire is not up to the task of maintaining the moral basis of market transactions or organisational behaviour.

If the utilitarian justification of empowerment is inadequate, and radical critics condemn empowerment as just another system of domination, can another ethical perspective help to underpin empowerment? Virtue ethics provides a useful set of moral concepts against which the practice of empowerment can be judged and the degree of moral progress or regression can then be evaluated. The questions asked by virtue ethics are what kinds of characters will be developed in the empowered organisation, and what is the contribution of the firm towards the common good? These questions can only be answered by empirical investigation of empowerment practices and the purpose of business in society. Let us begin with an analysis of the function of business organisations in society because if employees are to be encouraged to identify more closely with the aims of business, then they should be worthy and inclusive aims.

EMPOWERING WITH A PURPOSE

In much of the empowerment literature the function of business is assumed to be obvious and widely accepted, and consequently can be unproblematically posed to employees as a uniting common purpose. However, this presumption about the purpose of business is erroneous and misleading, and can often lead to the frustration of the empowerment ideal. This point can be illustrated by an examination of the arguments presented in a recent book that has sought to clarify, in ethical terms, the defining purpose of business in society. Elaine Sternberg's *Just Business*, is the latest in a long line of statements on the function of business in society begun by Adam Smith and vigorously defended by Hayek and Friedman in our century (Sternberg, 1994). What unites these commentators is the basic contention that business is a specific and limited activity that has to function within the constraints of the law and established ethical norms, but that apart from respecting these constraints, business is about profits for shareholders and has no other obligations or responsibilities.

Sternberg claims that by introducing conceptual clarity into business ethics she will provide solid arguments for rebutting 'trendy, but unethical demands for social responsibility in business' (Sternberg, 1994, p. 1). To do this she uses a philosophical framework based upon the metaphysics of Aristotle which identifies and explains human activities by reference to their ends or purposes or essences. The central questions of business ethics are to be answered by clearly defining the purpose of business. When the nature of business is understood then the ethical questions surrounding its practice can be answered. Sternberg then goes on to argue that business is a very specific, limited activity, whose defining purpose is 'maximising owner value over the long term by selling goods or services' (Sternberg, 1994, p. 32). Consequently, business is not about providing social welfare, spiritual fulfilment or full employment, nor is the company to be thought of as a family, a club, a hobby or a sort of government. Emphatically, 'the purpose of business is not to promote the public good' (Sternberg, 1994, p. 36).

Having identified the purpose of business she is then in a position to identify the key principles of business ethics; the conditions of practical conduct which will enable business to flourish. Two requirements are held to be necessary: distributive justice and ordinary decency. Her book then goes on to offer a model for ethical decision making using these principles. If we take Sternberg's view seriously, business is not an amoral activity, but its demands for moral conduct are very basic and its purpose is very limited. Consequently, empowerment initiatives are just techniques that management use to improve the efficiency of the business, and as long as they are introduced with regard for basic decency and the requirements of a just distribution of rewards are respected, then they are not to be considered to have infringed any other moral criteria. Ethical questions about the exploitation of employees, or the detrimental effects upon their moral character do not arise. Empowerment is not a prescription for improving our business conduct, nor should it be considered to be so intended, it is just a management initiative for improving employee motivation and productivity.

The foundational flaw of Sternberg's conception of business purpose is that it is based upon erroneous metaphysical assumptions about the nature of the world which are now untenable and need to be discarded. Popper labelled these metaphysical assumptions essentialist because of their claim that there can be universal terms which identify real essences to which they refer (Popper, 1945). So, in the context of business, is there, an essence to business which is distinct, as opposed to individual businesses such as the Ford Motor Company which denotes a particular business? Essentialists such as Sternberg, would deny that we first collect a group of single things and then label them with a universal term; rather she claims we label a thing with a universal on account of a certain intrinsic property that it shares with other things with this universal property. This property, 'business', denoted by the universal term, is regarded as an object which deserves investigation just as much as the individual things (businesses) themselves.

Sternberg then attempts to strip away the accidental or superfluous and penetrate the essence of the purpose of business which is something universal. But the problem is that the essence of business stripped of its connections to a time and a place leaves us with an abstract and unreal universal which has nothing to tell us about the real world of business as a historically situated practice. Instead of recognising the multifaceted nature of language and its relation to social practices which inevitably means a good deal of particularity, the craving for generality leads to the development of misleading metaphysical theories which fail to shed any light on the social practice of business.

According to Popper, we have to study societies as social practices in the world, with all their particularities rather than in the ideal realm of logical abstraction. There are no *a priori* reasons for action, no *a priori* principles of practical reasoning which can be identified independently of the particularities of context and practice. Objectivity is internal to context and there is no context free standpoint from which we can evaluate the world and its social practices. This is the perspective that Popper called nominalism. It looks at things as they are and how they manifest themselves in society. The task for those who study business then becomes: how do businesses function in society and how do people doing business actually behave? 'Business' is not a common element of business practice, what links the particulars falling under this common term is, in fact, the family of resemblances between them, the crisscrossing interrelationships rather than a necessary definition. The purpose of businesses are diffuse, changeable and multiple, to find out what they are we have to study the actions, experiences and interpretations of people in business.

Sternberg's essentialist approach to the study of business purpose effectively screens out the most interesting ones and hinders our understand of its wider social and moral purpose. Business conduct is ethically relevant, and so new ideas and practices in business have to be evaluated in ethical terms; in terms of how characters are formed in the institutions of business, and the actual problems and dilemmas faced in business life. It has to be prepared to cross boundaries and to consider the realities of business life as it is lived as a matter of empirical investigation not as an armchair, logical thought programme. Indeed, Adam Smith made it plain that it was prosperity not profits that constituted the goal of the free-market system (Smith, 1976). To single out 'long-term owner value' rather than prosperity or public service as the common purpose of business activity is a falsification of most people's motives in business. Consequently, if we adopt too narrow a vision of what the common purpose of business is, we are likely to misunderstand business practice and lose its sense of cooperation, community and integrity of its participants.

The task of business ethics is to clear the way through these dangerous misconceptions which obscure rather than clarify the underlying norms which make business possible. The idea that conduct which is commercially successful may be bad for the character or add little to the common good is unfamiliar to modern business but must surely be brought into any ethical consideration of business practice. Virtue ethics requires that we ask of all social practices what is their contribution to the development of character and the identity of the community. All aspects of activity are to be considered in this regard, even those that are under the corporate veil. Corporate governance cannot be neutral towards the moral characters of its employees, or the ends they pursue, it must undertake to form their character and foster the public virtues upon which society depends. Participants in a business may be there to make a profit, to earn a living, to make life interesting, to gain status; for a multiplicity of purposes which cannot be defined out of the analysis at its outset. As Beatrice Webb put it so tellingly back in 1886:

> Now one of the many mischievous results of (Political Economy) abstract and deductive method has been the underlying assumption, used as a premise for its deductive reasoning, that pecuniary self-interest is, in fact, the basis of modern business enterprise, all else being ignored as merely 'friction'. Thus it is assumed that all the activities of profit-makers are inspired solely and exclusively by pecuniary self-interest. This is, to my thinking, to do them injustice. Public spirit and personal vanity, delight in technical efficiency and desire for power, political and social ambition, the spirit of adventure and scientific curiosity, not to mention parental love and pride of family, even racial prestige, all contribute to the make-up of the dominant personalities of the business world. (Webb, 1938, p. 484)

ETHICAL EMPOWERMENT'S PURPOSE

The first moral test of empowerment strategies is to evaluate whether employees are being asked to strive for an inclusive and worthy common purpose: the narrow self-interests of shareholders or the wider interests of all stakeholders? Serving the interests of shareholders is certainly not immoral, and, indeed, does some good, but serving the needs of a wider community of interests undoubtedly makes a greater contribution to the common good. All too often, empowerment rhetoric ignores the possibility of the stakeholder conception of business purpose or tries to distort the employees perception of this reality. In the UK, empowerment initiatives are often introduced by management to gain even greater control over all that happens in a business organisation. Every delegation of responsibility is made only within the parameters of the task and only if strictly monitored against performance targets by sophisticated surveillance systems. Such power can be used in a way which is authoritarian and leaves very little discretion or dignity to the moral agency of the subordinate.

Our record in Britain, in terms of industrial relations tends to show that this 'low trust' empowerment strategy towards employees generates resistance and can result in low motivation on the part of its still essentially powerless subordinates (Millward, 1994). This is then responded to by employees with an unwillingness to show initiative and creativity in work, and an instrumental commitment to the purposes of the organisation. Moreover, this low-trust empowerment strategy has become increasingly overbearing and difficult to sustain in the conditions confronting many firms in the competitive markets of the 1990s (Fukuyama, 1995). Many organisations are now willing to acknowledge that most employees are willing to give more to their jobs when they are granted a higher degree of individual freedom, discretion and control over their work, and that the opportunity to be involved and to participate in the decision making process of the organisation can lead to greater personal satisfaction and to the taking of more responsibility for their actions. In this respect British business in its attempts to empower employees can profit from the European lesson where we can see that 'subsidiarity', a principle of Catholic social philosophy, is applied to good effect in the context of business to limit managerial prerogatives and share decision-making power (Lorenz, 1992).

The implication for British managers is that power should be spread throughout the firm at all levels and in varying degrees, from the directors to the workers on the shop floor, such that no-one can make a contribution to the running of the firm without being accorded some degree of power and responsibility as a valued member of the community of purpose. The systems for distributing management power do not need to be prescribed in a mechanistic fashion. Several methods and levels of empowerment may be appropriate including: increasing the range of collective bargaining; increasing joint consultation and the coverage of works councils; increasing worker representation in the board room; increasing participative management processes; and increasing job autonomy. Empowerment for a common purpose that contributes to the prosperity of the community is potentially a worthy cause around which to involve and invigorate employees. Business then will begin to function as a true community of purpose.

BUSINESS AS A COMMUNITY OF PURPOSE

To justify this alternative conception of business as a community of purpose we need to begin by considering the wider community and its social order, and then go on to consider the narrower issue of how we should regard business within this order. The great sociologist Emile Durkhiem saw society as an ever expanding division of labour which was integrated by the mutual interdependence of the individuals in society (Durkheim, 1933). However, the relationship between the individual and the state needed to be mediated by smaller organisations so that the individual does not become isolated or lost in the face of such a complex society. Social order is maintained by families and communities which lay down the foundations of our sense of responsibility and civic obligation. It is in these close associations and affiliations that people learn and practice responsibility, to understand the mutuality of the social bond and to discover the nature of the good that they seek in common. However, Durkheim maintained that in addition to these close affiliations we also need a set of intermediate associations in which we can become involved and against which we can make claims (Durkheim, 1957).

Today, however, it is apparent that families and local communities are in decline leaving us only temporary and conditional affiliations to fill in the gaps. Our range of commitments has been narrowed and our sense of who we are and what we stand for has been eroded (Selbourne, 1994; Sacks, 1995). What is needed is a regeneration of the institutional framework in which moral behaviour and self-esteem can be rebuilt. A whole range of communities need to be enlisted in the education of our citizens in civic duty, the schools, churches and voluntary associations. Perhaps, society ought now to recognise that business organisations also have a part to play in this revitalising process. The moral order of society has to be maintained and enhanced by a community of communities all playing their part and acting as supports and mediators between th individual and the state.

Whilst the contribution of business companies is not likely to be the most important of these communities especially on the formation of the young citizen, its role in the moral order should not to be down played or undervalued. For many people in modern society, this can often be their most important sense of community that they experience in their adult lives. And it is in communities and through group affiliations that virtues are acquired, practised and become habitual. So we should be careful not to dismiss or discount business as an important source of moral development and the contribution it can make as a school of virtuous conduct and civic duty. We have already noted

Durkheim's suggestion made at the turn of the century that corporate associations were needed to connect the individual with an intermediate body between themselves and the state, well the business corporation may not be what he had in mind, or be its nearest equivalent, but it is one of the most enduring institutions available, and in actuality often fulfils this function. As Alexander Hamilton, remarked 'economic institutions teach and form us as effectively as schools and families do, if not more so' (Bellah, *et al.*, 1991, p. 101). Consequently, an examination of the moral underpinnings of empowerment strategies is important because of the impact they can have upon character and identity, and it is important to assess their potential for improving the moral climate of society.

This is not to argue that everyone participates in business for the same reasons or that business represents a harmony of interests, or indeed that it should do so. But the fact remains that inside companies there are often elements of community and shared conceptions of conduct and standards of behaviour that are remarkable. Too many studies of business have ignored the accounts given of conduct as it is practised as opposed to how it was thought to be practised. As Anthony notes in his discussion of the distinction between official management theory and the real theory of empirically based studies of organisations:

> at least in real theory accounts of their inhabitants behaviour, [organisations] can be seen as communities; that they are held together by informal moral relationships that may be stronger than the moral order that the hierarchical superstructure seek to impose, and that moral and social relationships are cemented by myth, symbol, culture and narrative. (Anthony, 1976, p. 188)

It may be useful if a new term is coined to describe this moral property of community which can be found in the business organisation: that the company is 'a community of purpose'. The term 'community of purpose' draws upon the work of John Macmurray who distinguishes between a community of purpose and a community of love (Macmurray, 1961). The latter is a more intimate and therefore enriching association, and is the foundation of the purpose of life. The community of purpose is a more transitory and less significant association, and is there to serve a more instrumental purpose. Clearly, the company is of the second kind but that it is a form of community and therefore has some of the valuable properties of community should be noted.

CHARACTER FORMATION IN THE COMMUNITY OF PURPOSE

The concept of a community of purpose can be used to analyse the contribution that empowerment strategies make towards the development of virtuous characters. A community is of moral significance when in Selznick's terms it requires from its participants 'core' involvement as opposed to 'segmental' involvement (Selznick, 1992). Core involvement means that people are not free floating but are connected to others in specific personal relationships with a strong sense of identity and autonomy. From such bonding people develop stable lives and characters of depth and durability with a sense of moral obligation sustained by the appropriate motives and self discipline. Core involvement is one of the foundations of moral competence. A company that functions as a community of purpose is therefore characterised by the following features: people relate to whole persons rather than to segments; each participant is perceived as having intrinsic worth; communication is open and founded upon trust; obligation is mutual, diffuse and extended; there is a sense of belonging together and sharing a common identity; and personal development, security and satisfaction are important. Evidence that these features can be encouraged in empowerment programmes is provided in Watson's study of a manufacturing firm, where an empowering manager is described by a subordinate in these terms:

> He made you feel involved. He kept me informed, made me feel that my opinion was being taken into account, is interested in me as a person. He involves me in his thought process, confides in me. He makes clear what he wants from me and if I have problems with this helps me achieve what he requires. He was not afraid to let me do things on my own and let me have visibility. (Watson, 1994, p. 174)

Empowerment initiatives requiring only segmental involvement or a limited investment of the self are more likely to undermine moral competence than it enrich it, and are likely to weaken personal responsibility. No doubt many businesses only require this form of involvement and this may be of little concern if the assumption is made that well-socialised workers, from stable families and local communities, do not need to find psychological sustenance in less-intimate, more impersonal settings. But are these presumptions still correct for many people in today's society? Many empowerment programmes can and do offer much more than this, in fact the communities of purpose they help to create add bright threads to the moral tapestry of society. Empowerment can help us to think of work as a meaningful activity with almost a sense of calling, itself a source of the good life. As Bellah *et al.*, has expressed it:

> In a calling... one gives oneself to learning and practising activities that in turn define the self and enter into the shape of its character. Committing one's self to becoming a good craftsman, scientist etc. anchors the self within a community of practice. It connects the self to those who teach, exemplify and judge these skills. It ties us to still others whom they serve. (Bellah, *et al.*, 1985, p. 24)

There are many more studies by social scientists of business organisations which can be used to support this conception of empowerment in a community of purpose. The nature of the moral community in a company is described in the classic study by Burns and Stalker of the management of innovation:

> Every firm is a community, with its own particular flavour, its own social structure, its own style of conduct. Newcomers are very conscious of this quality of uniqueness. Indeed, they have to be, since they have to learn the culture, and until they do, until it is other places which begin to have a disconcertingly unfamiliar smell, they have neither been accepted nor accepted their position. (Burns and Stalker, 1961, p. 258)

DEGREES OF EMPOWERMENT

Empowerment strategies can therefore be morally evaluated according to the degree to which they help to form and maintain the virtues of employees or whether they lead to the erosion of virtue and the active development of vices. On the whole this is not a matter that can be determined *a priori* but needs to be assessed empirically. Perhaps one method of identifying empowerment strategies that improve the moral virtues of their participants is to use MacIntyre's distinction between practices that have internal goods and work that produces only external goods (MacIntyre, 1981). A practice is a social and co-operative human activity realising goods that are internal but determined by human conceptions of excellence and value. Internal practices involve a set of standards or criteria which serve to identify what counts as a good or bad, exemplary or worthless, competent or incompetent instance of the activity concerned. Internal goods are judged by those inside the practice but their achievement is a good for the whole community. Work institutions are more likely to be concerned with the production of external goods in a competitive exchange which may add nothing to the common good. Although MacIntyre claims that all business organisations have no notion of internal goods which serve the common good, the empirical evidence suggests that many companies do indeed create internal goods and cultivate empowerment practices which make a contribution to the common good.

Reed and Anthony's review of studies of British management in practice notes:

> Accumulating evidence shows that managers (real managers...) depend upon their effectiveness upon the norms of reciprocity, upon trust, obligation and the maintenance of defensible social relationships... on leadership and community, and finally, upon authority, which is essentially moral. (Reed and Anthony, 1992, p. 608)

These internal goods are beneficial for both business and society. Salaman's study of the occupation of railwaymen, noted that its internal goods consisted of three virtues commonly shared by the railwaymen: the ability to accept responsibility as it was a potentially dangerous business; that being a railwayman was a vocation, needing a non-instrumental attitude to work; and that punctuality, reliability and steadiness were key virtues (Salaman, 1974). Salaman quotes a railwayman, 'The good railway man does not do his work just for the weekly wage; he does it because he takes pride in it, for the satisfaction of a job well done' (Salaman, 1974, p. 103). Salaman also describes the sense of fraternity between the railwaymen who even set up mutual improvement classes, which were organised and administered by older, more experienced railwaymen to help the younger ones get through the promotion examinations, and that those who ran the classes did not get paid.

The movement to identify managerial competencies that specify good and bad practices in empowerment is a sign that the internal goods developed in companies are now increasingly sought after and are now openly described and assessed. Watson's recent study of managers gives some interesting examples of these empowerment competencies:

> Good managers are sensitive to the attitudes and feelings of all those they work with; they treat others and their ideas with respect...
> Bad managers have little regard for the people they work with; they are insensitive to the feelings, views and interests of others...
> Good managers work with teams they lead to build up a positive climate...
> Bad managers work on their own and tend to maintain power by keeping information from others... (Watson, 1994, pp. 227–8).

These benchmarks of managerial behaviour gave the managers in his study indicators against which they could match their own behaviours. It helped them cultivate a sense of what kind of manager they wanted to be and provided a moral resource to identify rogues and heroes in the process of managing to manage. As Watson noted in his own conclusions,

> managers can be seen as appreciating that a high level of trust and reciprocity is vital to achieving what I call 'productive cooperation': people who do not trust each other and have a strictly calculative concept of exchange are unlikely to achieve together work tasks of any complexity, or to solve organisational problems of any difficulty. The achieving of a high level of trust between the members of any group or organisation requires commitment to a shared set of values relating to their shared activities. (Watson, 1994, pp. 210–11)

In the light of this evidence, which is substantial and long-standing, why has the generation of internal goods which help to serve the common good not been recognised more widely in the empowerment literature? The actual contribution to the moral climate of society of empowerment practices is often ignored or discredited by modern management commentators. Their talk of the limited, contractual nature of the relationship is often at odds with the deep and personal investments made by the members of a company. Perhaps the employment contract is an example of a shared symbol in a community culture which can mean different things to employers and employees, and yet still brings them together.

After all, if it were just a contract, why do so many people, most of the time, go beyond contract? Many employees make a deep investment and personal commitment to their firms which have not generated a reciprocal sense of obligation on the firm's behalf. Watson's study is full of examples of managers who wanted to give more commitment to their firm but felt that this would not be recognised and appreciated. A senior manager described his relationship with his company in the following terms:

> The people who are running things now. I'm not sure they really believe in all this team-working stuff and empowering talk that we've gone for in the last few years... I really wonder whether we are valued at all. The pension problem is only a symptom. Do the people running this company recognise what we put into all this? what about my empowerment? What about my personal development? (Watson, 1994, p. 119)

The present institutional framework of business in Britain does not recognise the variety of stakeholder interests in business nor does it appreciate the company's contribution to the common good. This is at odds with elsewhere and with much of the evidence on actual behaviour in business organisations. This is because the corporation is institutionalised as an instrument of the shareholder and other stakeholders interests go unrecognised and are given little credence beyond contractual liabilities.

Most advocates of empowerment consequently propose definitions of purpose and advocate changes which take little account of the wider moral dimension in business endeavour. It has been argued that this approach is both limited and misguided. Empowerment initiatives must be judged against ethical criteria and praised when they match up to these criteria, and condemned when they do not. It is therefore time to reappraise our approach to empowerment and the fundamental terms of corporate governance.

THE INSTITUTIONAL FRAMEWORK OF EMPOWERMENT

We need to start by recognising that business is a contributor to the moral order of society. Importantly, we should follow Mahoney's advice and not seek to over burden business with too many responsibilities (Mahoney, 1990). But the present system of legal incorporation perhaps needs to be changed to include principles of corporate governance similar to those advocated by White in the USA, which state that 'the business corporation should always endeavour to act as a responsible citizen in its economic and other activities' (White, 1985). This means that the company is incorporated as a form of collective citizen in society, and its function is not just to make money but also to do good.

However, we should acknowledge that there are different types of collective citizen, some are more active and contribute more than others to the common good. Some companies are active centres of virtue formation and development: beacons which radiate moral energy to other parts of society. Some companies have a very weak light and some are black holes. We need to create regulations which recognise that the purpose of business is to make life better for everyone, and that a multiplicity of motives are often present in business practice. We should be prepared to acknowledge and esteem the companies which make a real contribution to the common good because at their best they are the equivalent of one of Edmund Burke's 'little platoons' of society. Instead of rubbishing empowerment initiatives we should be trying to preserve and support those of the right type, those that involve employees in a deliberation about the nature of their common purpose, and those that develop the moral virtues of their participants. The company can be a virtuous community as well as a flourishing business; it can further the type of occupation one can be proud to be a member of, with a sense of calling which serves the common good. Even employees in the 'de-layered' firm can take pride in its sense of community and in the internal goods its members help to produce despite facing a limited career ladder and increased job rotation.

In the field of empowerment, we need to learn more from Europe, and move away from the traditional Anglo-American paradigm of business upon which we have relied so heavily in the past. Michel Albert has distinguished two types of capitalism: Rhenish and neo-American (Albert, 1993). The former depends upon a subtle blend of competition and cooperation, market based but not wholly market-driven; the latter is competitive, market-driven and focused upon short-term profitability. The firm in the former case is not driven by individual self-interest and the relentless exposure to market forces, but is constrained by a network of intersecting interests held together by collective values and cooperative behaviour. Consequently, the Rhenish firms trade off short-term efficiency losses against long-term investments in human capital and its attendant competitive advantage. What often holds the Anglo/American firms back even when they understand the difference is that they are constrained by the limited rhetoric of empowerment which does not provide the necessary concepts and paths towards a change of view.

Empowerment needs to be underpinned by the notion of virtuous character in a set of institutions in which cooperation and consensus can be forged, and in which market mechanisms are tempered by moral constraints. We need to institutionalise the conception of business as a community of purpose which will take its wider social and moral functions more seriously alongside those of its economic ones. Real empowerment is constitutive of the community of purpose. As Michel Walzer wrote in *Spheres of Justice*:

> At a certain point in the development of an enterprise, then, it must pass out of entrepreneurial control; it must be organised or reorganised in the same political way, according to the prevailing (democratic) conception of how power ought to be distributed. (Walzer, 1983, p. 303)

Note

The author would like to thank Basil Blackwell Publishers for permission to reproduce some material taken from his articles published in *Business Ethics: A European Review*.

References

Albert, M. (1993) *Capitalism against Capitalism* (London: Whurr).
Anthony, P. (1976) *The Foundation of Management* (London: Tavistock).
Bellah, R. et al. (1985) *Habits of the Heart* (New York: Doubleday).
Bellah, R. et al. (1991) *The Good Society* (New York: Alfred A. Knopf).
Blyton, P. and Turnbull, P. (1992) *Reassessing Human Resources Management* (London: Sage).
Burns, T. and Stalker, G. (1961) *The Management of Innovation* (Oxford: Oxford University Press).
Byham, W. and Cox, J. (1988) *Zapp! The Lightning of Empowerment* (London: Business Books).
Claydon, T. and Doyle, M. (1996) 'Trusting me, Trusting you? The Ethics of Employee Empowerment', *Personnel Review*, vol. 25(6), pp. 13–25.
Durkheim, E. (1933) *The Division of Labour* (London: Macmillan).
Durkheim, E. (1957) *Professional Ethics and Civic Morals* (London: Routledge).
Follet, M. (1941) *Dynamic Administration* (London: Pitman).
Fox, A. (1985) *Man Mismanagement* (London: Heinemann).
Friedman, A. (1977) *Industry and Labour* (London: Macmillan).
Fukuyama, F. (1995) *Trust: The Social Virtues and the Creation of Prosperity* (London: Hamish Hamilton).
Grenier, G. (1988) *Inhuman Relations* (Philadelphia: Temple University Press).
Hawkins, K. (1972) *Conflict and Change* (London: Holt Rinehart & Winston).
Jackson, J. (1996) *An Introduction to Business Ethics* (Oxford: Blackwell).
Lorenz, E. (1992) 'Trust and the Flexible Firm: International Comparisons', *Industrial Relations*, vol. 31(3).
MacIntyre, A. (1991) *After Virtue: A Study in Moral Theory* (London: Duckworth).
MacMurray, J. (1961) *Persons in Relation* (London: Faber).
Mahoney, J. (1990) 'Spheres and Limits of Ethical Responsibility in and of the Corporation', in G. Enderle et al., *People in Corporations* (London: Kluwer).
Mahoney, J. (1994) 'Stakeholder Responsibilities: Turning the Ethical Tables', *Business Ethics: a European Review*, vol. 3(4), pp. 212–8.
Millward, N. (1994) *The New Industrial Relations?* (London: Policy Studies Institute).
Popper, K. (1945) *The Open Society and its Enemies* (London: Routledge).
Rabinow, P. (1984) *The Foucault Reader* (London: Penguin).
Reed, M. and Anthony, P. (1992) 'Professionalising Management and Managing Professionalisation: British Management in the 1980s', *Journal of Management Studies*, vol. 29(5), pp. 591–613.
Sacks, J. (1995) *Faith in the Future* (London: Darton, Longman & Todd).
Salaman, G. (1974) *Community and Occupation* (Cambridge: Cambridge University Press).
Selbourne, D. (1994) *The Principle of Duty* (London: Sinclair Stevenson).
Selznick, P. (1992) *The Moral Commonwealth* (Berkeley: University of California Press).
Smith, A. (1976) *The Wealth of Nations* (Oxford: Clarendon Press).
Sternberg, E. (1994) *Just Business* (London: Warner Books).

Townley, B. (1994) *Reframing Human Resources Management: Power, Ethics and the Subject at Work* (London: Sage).

Walzer, M. (1983) *Spheres of Justice* (New York: Basic Books).

Watson, T.J. (1994) *In Search of Management* (London: Routledge).

Webb, B. (1938) *My Apprenticeship* (London: Penguin).

White, J. (1985) 'How Should we Talk about Corporations: The Languages of Economics and Citizenship', *Yale Law Journal*, vol. 94, p. 1424.

14 The Social Responsibility of Businesses: To Empower Employees by Listening and Responding

Paul Joyce and Adrian Woods

INTRODUCTION: A THEORY OF SOCIAL RESPONSIBILITY AS A PRACTICAL PLAN FOR EMPOWERMENT

Under present conditions the idea of empowerment can mean one of two things in practical terms. It either means delegated decision-making within a tight accountability framework, or it means creating a more inclusive and fraternally associated work community through managers listening and responding to employees' ideas, desires and needs. Both meanings might be attributed to an agenda for organisational reform based on ideas of innovative and entrepreneurial organisations. The latter we regard as a viable agenda for social responsibility.

Does it really make sense to see managers engaged in listening and responding to employees as not only socially responsible but also as empowering their employees? One argument is that we know that there are managers who affirm such a view of empowerment. For example, Zegans (1992) conducted research on senior public sector management using focus groups. The managers interviewed 'agreed that employees should have the maximum amount of discretion feasible... They also agreed that employees who brought forward proposals for specific innovations should be encouraged in their efforts' (1992, p. 150). These same managers were keen on fostering innovation. Zegans reports:

> They identifed their principal responsibilities in this regard as creating a climate in which employees felt comfortable coming forward with ideas... Participants identified three overlapping challenges in meeting these goals: overcoming civil service complacency, empowering employees, and opening lines of communication to permit good ideas to surface. (1992, p. 151)

The idea of listening to employees is endorsed by the gurus of innovation and excellence. Peters and Austin (1985) suggested that the secrets of business success were blindingly obvious. It was all about customers, innovation and people. In a little more detail, as far as the people bit was concerned, this meant giving 'everyone in the organization a little more space to innovate' and listening to employees and asking them for their ideas – 'Then acting on them' (1985, pp. 3–4).

Then again, developing arguments from the complexities of chaos theory, Stacey (1991) expounds the virtues of informal contributions to strategic control, rather than formal mechanisms for empowerment. Indeed, he rejects an ideological basis for democracy and empowering people. 'The chaos perspective suggests that prescriptions to distribute power through the organization and get everyone involved in everything could well reduce the organization's ability to cope with uncertainty, rather than increase it' (1991, p. 341). Stacey wants management to learn about open-ended changes, but he does not think it comes from dispersing power and encouraging widespread participation. Informal communication contributions are seen as the key. This emerges in his discussion of an express delivery company:

> This was not an organization in which power was dispersed. There was a clear hierarchy and there was no questioning the superior power of the most senior managers. There was no formal mechanism for widespread participation in decision making. It was the attitudes and behaviour of the most senior managers that in effect invited contributions from middle managers. (1991, p. 275)

We have taken the trouble to quote these arguments in detail in order to show that the new thinking on the role of employees – an essentially liberal programme for reforming the management of industry and commerce – amounts to both more discretion for employees and more efforts by management to listen to, and respond to, employees. In both cases, employees cease to be merely 'hired hands'. The making of management into a listening and responsive function is therefore not only socially responsible but also in an important sense linked to the empowering of employees as part of the process of self-command.

Social responsibility in business deserves to be treated as a phenomenon in its own right, and not merely as a deviation from profit maximisation. There is much to be discovered about social responsibility and empirical studies are needed to guide the building up of theories appropriate to specific situations. These theories may then be brought together to build more general theories which have a wider application.

A theory of social responsibility needs to recognise the differences and variations in business practices. It might be expected that some businesses do things on social responsibility which are big and dramatic.

Others may be socially responsible in quiet, everyday ways. And some businesses may do nothing at all, believing that charitable acts and other forms of social engagement are best kept a private and individual matter. Such variations may reflect differences of attitude, outlook and awareness of individual business owners and managers. Even if many of them feel that businesses have social or moral obligations, they may think quite differently about the nature of the obligations and how business decisions should be modifed in the light of them (Hussey, 1994). Likewise, there may be important variations in owners' and managers' awareness and understanding of social and moral issues which are of concern to policy-makers and local communities. Perhaps many business people are relatively uninformed on social and environmental matters, in line with the rest of the population?

This chapter is intended as a contribution to the development of the theory of social reponsibility in business. It makes use of data from the 1995 CENTEC and CILNTEC Employer Survey, which we will refer to as the 1995 London survey. (CENTEC and CILNTEC were two Training and Enterprise Councils set up to cover the central London area, which were merged to form a larger Training and Enterprise Council in 1997.) This survey covered a representative sample of 659 establishments in the centre of London. A majority of the respondents (who were owners, partners and managers in generally very small businesses) felt they were not able to answer knowledgeably about social and environmental impacts on central London businesses. However, some 249 respondents did feel themselves to be knowledgeable about such matters, and questions regarding social responsibility and related topics were addressed to them. Amongst the 249 respondents to the social responsibility section of the 1995 London survey, only a quarter felt that their businesses were very socially responsible, whilst another quarter reckoned their businesses were not at all socially responsible. Typically, therefore, businesses were moderately socially responsible. The data from their responses is used below to develop a conceptualisation of socially responsible business.

It will be seen that socially responsible businesses tend to have important social objectives about their workforces and their local communities. The existence of such objectives provides organisations with an internally generated means of judging the 'goodness' of their business practices. It will also be argued that the social objectives of a business are the foundation of business practices that are socially responsible. Finally, it will be suggested that such practices may be articulated with

SOCIAL OBJECTIVES

As Ansoff (1968) pointed out long ago, the responsibilities of the firm can originate as the personal objectives of owners and managers. He specifically refers to social responsibility as a sense of personal obligation by the individual to serve larger purposes. He suggested that the consequences could include economic benefit to the firm: 'Since the respective policies stimulate growth and stability, the firm thus contributes to its own long-term growth objectives' (p. 63).

However, he saw social responsibility obligations of the kind which are expressed as philanthropic objectives as having a siphoning effect on retained earnings, thereby reducing the resources for business growth and expansion. The Friedmanite view of social responsibility also takes a negative view, and presents it as the antithesis of sensible business practice (Friedman, 1995). Social responsibility is seen as a constraint on increased profit-making, as a managerial betrayal of the owners of the business, and ultimately as harmful for a national economy.

The implicit and explicit definitions of social responsibility used by protagonists in the debate over the beneficiaries of business can be a barrier to theoretical development in this area. If, for example, social responsibility is defined as any business practice which harms profitability then of course it is incompatible with attempts to increase profits. If it is defined, instead, as businesses using their resources to solve or ameliorate social problems, the impact on profit maximisation still appears, at face value, to be a negative one.

The possibility that socially responsible business practices damage business performance is not a central concern of the present study. Attempts to study this relationship empirically have proved inconclusive, and there are complaints that the concept of social responsibility has not been satisfactorily operationalised for research purposes (Aldag and Bartol, 1978; Aupperle, Carroll and Hatfield, 1985). Theoretical arguments about the relationship remain locked in disagreement. For instance, Friedmanites argue that expenditures by business on social responsibility reduces profit (or puts up prices or lowers wages), whilst it has also been suggested that the direct pursuit of profits is self-defeating and that profit is best seen as a result of achieving other corporate goals (Friedman, 1995; Bowie, 1995). It is even possible, however, to argue that profitability is helped by philanthropic initiatives which, if done strategically, give businesses a competitive edge (Smith, 1994).

If the relationship is difficult to investgate empirically, or specify theoretically, it may be because, as Solomon (1992) argues, profitability and ethics have to be brought together in and through business practice, and their unity is not automatic nor guaranteed. In this vein, Solomon refers to businesses as a grand experiment: 'whether or not the experiment works will depend on whether it does indeed encourage excellence and inspire virtue in its practitioners or only fosters a mad scramble for survival and quick profits' (p. 160). Thus, the challenge of social responsibility could be characterised as consisting of the need for determined and long-term effort to combine the interest of a business with the larger good of society, so that the business reconciles its need for profits with obligations to contribute to the solving of social problems.

As a result of bypassing the debate about the link between social responsibility and profitability, it is possible to proceed directly to the issue of what non-economic objectives are actually important. We will not be following Ansoff's (1968) assumption that responsibilities are constraints because they do not interact with a firm's choice of products or markets, nor his view that responsibilities represent limits within which the firm must operate and are not goals in their own right. Instead, we think it is worth assuming that firms may have economic and social objectives, and that each limits the pursuit of the other. The 1995 London survey data showed that businesses did have both economic and social objectives.

Economic objectives were very important. Most of the respondents said that providing an acceptable financial return to the owners was a very important objective of the business. Most said making a profit was very important. But many of these same respondents identified social objectives as very important. There was, for example, evidence of an obligation to the 'internal' community of the business; thus a majority of the respondents indicated that ensuring employee well-being was a very important business objective. About one in five said that providing jobs was a very important objective. Some objectives clearly reflected the existence of obligations to the wider community beyond the boundaries of the business. About one in five said that contributing to the well-being of the local community was a very important objective of their business. Over one in ten said that providing job opportunities for disadvantaged people was very important.

These social objectives were especially a feature of the businesses rated by respondents as being very socially responsible. This does not mean that the respondents defined socially responsible business as being business which formally espoused obligations to their employees or to the wider community. In fact, when asked to justify their rating and give examples of social responsibility, respondents cited a very wide range of behaviours. Many referred to acts of giving to charity, looking after the environment, caring for employee welfare, helping the local community, supporting schools, working with disadvantaged groups, giving good service to customers and the community, sourcing locally, ensuring equal opportunities, and so on. But beneath the complexity of all these diverse examples of being socially responsible, there was a greater tendency for businesses with important social objectives to be rated as very socially responsible, as against other businesses. For example, a half of the businesses that said employee well-being and contributing to the well-being of the local community were very important were rated as very socially responsible; this was three times the proportion of the businesses that saw neither of these as very important objectives.

Social business objectives did not appear to suppress or supplant economic objectives. Making an acceptable financial return to the owners and making a profit were very important for most of the businesses wanting to ensure employee well-being and to contribute to community well-being. They were no less likely than other businesses to say these economic objectives were very important. In summary, socially responsible businesses had very important social as well as economic business objectives. As Solomon (1992) has put it, business and ethics, profits and doing good, are false dichotomies: 'Social responsibility does not mean sacrificing profits to "do-gooding" or fleecing the stockholders' (p. 180).

What does it mean that businesses set social objectives, even whilst they are no less concerned than others to achieve profitability within the constraints of the competitive framework of the free enterprise system? This means only that businesses which are choosing to act ethically are actualising a moral purpose in the context of a necessity to make a profit. But how else can moral purposes be actualised other than in the context of objective necessities? It is as foolish to reduce ethics to the necessity of making profit as it is to define the pursuit of the ethical as the denial of the need for profit-making. Therefore, it looks as though Friedmanites are wrong to say that the only responsibility of business is to increase profits. But it is also wrong to dogmatically reject the possibility of an ethical practice within a competitive market system.

It can be argued that the achievement of economic objectives enables businesses to pursue social objectives. This was, in effect, argued by

Whyte (1985). In rethinking models for economic development, he challenged the concept of profit maximisation. His point was not that profits are unimportant, but that profits are a limiting condition: 'If a firm is to survive in the long run without government subsidy, then obviously it must earn enough income not only to cover its operating expenses but also to build reserves for investment so as to remain competitive' (p. 16). This means, therefore, that making a profit is something a business must do, but that making a profit is not necessarily the point of business for the owner.

It has been known for some time that 'lifestyle' businesses, defined as being ones where the owner seeks only a satisfactory financial return, are not uncommon amongst small businesses (Storey, 1994). The owners of such businesses may, for example, be seeking to maximise their independence and scope for autonomous decision-making, and have set up their own business as a vehicle for such aspirations. Other owners may have a powerful motivation to pit their energy and abilities against the market, and measure their success by the expansion of their business. We cannot, therefore, assume that we know the meaning of the business for the owner; there are a variety of meanings for different owners.

It has been argued that people who work seek not only pay and opportunities, but also enjoyable working relationships and meaning in their working lives. It is often claimed by those in the quality-of-working-life movement that this has been brought about by higher standards of living and higher levels of education. These trends, at least in the United States, are seen as critical to new types of employee motivation. 'For people in these new circumstances to be satisfied, it helps enormously if they can see the link between what they do and a higher purpose' (Pascale and Athos, 1981, p. 187). If this is so, why should it not apply to the owners of businesses as well? Why should it not help owners to see their business activity as linked to a higher purpose? Why, in other words, should they not have social objectives for their businesses?

As noted above, a number of the respondents in the 1995 London survey who rated their business as very socially responsible justified this in terms of their actions to provide high quality and good service to their customers and the community. Some of the respondents felt that they had a social obligation to provide the best service they could and they saw their social responsibility as being discharged by providing services to the highest possible standard. Also, the firms with the strongest concern for social objectives, as measured by the importance they placed on employee well-being and contribution to community well-being, were slightly more likely to say that providing high-quality products or services was a very important business objective. Since nine out of every ten businesses claimed to have quality as a very important business objective, this meant that the businesses without very important social objectives accounted for many of the businesses rating quality as less than very important.

A notion of business activity as linked to a social purpose is not a recent invention. In a paper presented in 1925, Follett was arguing that: 'Business is, and should be considered, truly a social agency' (Follett, 1941, p. 132). She had in mind the idea that businesses involve everybody in providing essential services to each other. This interchange of services involves all people in the give-and-take of community life. She especially appreciated the different connotations of the word 'service' in this context. 'If a man thinks of his business as a service, he will certainly not increase private profits at the expense of public good' (*ibid.*, p. 133). She thought that work performed as a business activity was itself a service to the community, and preferable to the idea of business people doing good works as an out of hours activity, or of business people simply donating money to charities.

This very same notion of business as a social service has been powerfully advocated by Solomon (1992). He argued that he was not intent on idealizing or attacking the free enterprise system. He set out to 'defend its values and virtues against its self-misunderstanding and self-abuse' (p. 21). He attacked metaphors such as those of business as a jungle, or as war, or as a game. In relation to the last metaphor, he suggested that business 'becomes a game when it loses its essential aim, not just to make money but to provide essential goods and services and bring about a general and not a selfish prosperity' (p. 32). According to this notion of the free-enterprise system, business is to be judged by its ability to supply people with employment and to ensure that they obtain good quality products and services that they can afford. A business person, wishing to be socially responsible according to this notion, should emphasise the production of good quality products and services that the community wants, produced efficiently, and through business practices stressing creative and humanised values. Charitable donations are quite peripheral to this conception of business ethics. This is an ethics which rejects the Friedmanite view that social responsibility in business is exhausted by profit-making:

> The much-touted 'challenge' of business is, outside of Wall Street, almost always a challenge of creativity, of hard work and perseverance, of organization and cooperation, of good ideas and keen sensitivity to public needs and moods. It is not the challenge of 'making money'. (Solomon, 1992, p. 36)

The Friedmanite theory of the free-enterprise, private-property system must dismiss social objectives as window-dressing, harmless self-delusions or dangerous mistakes (Friedman, 1995; Argenti, 1993). Obviously it can be argued that a genuine commitment by a business to social responsibility is a form of 'false consciousness' – that business has been ideologically subverted by false theories of business. But, this can be just a cloak for dogmatism. What if businesses have good reasons for being socially responsible and this social responsibility is actually viable?

CARING AND LISTENING TO EMPLOYEES

In the 1995 London survey there were many businesses that said that employee well-being was a very important business objective. This finding, if taken in isolation, seems to support Curran's (1991) view of small businesses being run in many cases as a benevolent autocracy. The owner or manager of a business cares about the well-being of employees. We might say that they value their employees. For, if they did not value them, they might not see that they had an obligation to take care of them. But, within a benevolent autocracy, employees are not to be valued to the extent that their views are respected and listened to. The obvious metaphor for these benevolent autocracies is that of the 'family', a metaphor which presents the owner in a parental role, and employees in the role of dependants. A culture of caring, therefore, must not be equated with a culture of employee influence.

This model of benevolent autocracy was not, however, really applicable to the businesses in the 1995 London survey. Most of the respondents said that employees' views had a big influence on business decisions. Indeed, it seems that employees tended to have a big influence on business decisions where employers had an organisational commitment to employee well-being.

Some organisations pride themselves on listening to employees' views. They may have an open door access policy for employees. Indeed, in some small businesses, with a culture of fraternalism, the owner may work along side employees or the whole organisation may operate on the basis of team-working. These firms, if they listen to their employees because they respect and value employees' views, might be said to have 'partnership oriented' cultures to distinguish them from the 'dictatorial cultures' of the businesses run by benevolent autocrats. If Bowie (1995) is correct about the trust relationships underpinning the application of enlightened management techniques, it seems likely that partnership cultures would be based on an employee perception that there is a genuine concern for the employees. It may be that some firms think of adopting less authoritarian styles of management because they think it confers a competitive advantage (Green, 1994, p. 186), but, in our view, partnership cultures would, logically speaking, be unstable where the employer motivation for partnership with employees was entirely instrumental.

Most of the healthy and growing businesses in the 1995 London survey were typically likely to say that employees' views had a big influence on business decisions. The poorer the performance of the business, the less likely were the employees' views to be influential. We would guess that the most likely cause of this finding was that successful firms feel they can afford to listen to their employees. Thus, if we are right, listening to employees was not simply an ethical phenomenon. But there was an ethical component to listening to employees. First, the influence of employees' views was more prevalent amongst businesses with a commitment to employee well-being, suggesting that listening to employees was also a choice for many companies. Second, amongst businesses that were stable rather than healthy and growing, only those businesses with a commitment to employee well-being typically listened to employees. In other words, the firms which were serious about employee well-being allowed employees influence over decisions even when the business was not expanding.

EMPLOYEE INFLUENCE AND COMPETITIVENESS

An analysis of the 1995 London survey showed that organisations which reported that employees had a big influence on their business decisions were slightly more likely than others to undertake regular market research and were more likely to say that they were influenced by listening to customers. Similarly, organisations which said that they took public concerns on ethical and environmental matters into consideration when making strategic decisions were also more likely to carry out market research regularly, and more likely to report that listening to customers was a big influence on their business decisions. Socially responsible behaviour by businesses is therefore associated with a stronger market and customer focus than that found in other businesses.

We suggest that allowing employees' an influence on business decisions was an important form of socially responsible behaviour (we will explore this claim below). It looks as though the data bears out, or at least is consistent with, the popular 1980s view that customer-oriented companies require motivated employees, and that employee motivation can be achieved by managers listening to employees and valuing their opinions. Indeed, Peters and Austin (1985) linked the treatment of people by management to customer-service and constant innovation, which they saw as the two critical sources of competitive advantage. 'Both are built... on a bedrock of listening, trust and respect for the dignity and creative potential of each person in the organization' (p. 5).

CONTRIBUTING AND DEFERRING

Many of the London businesses in the 1995 survey – almost one in three of them – claimed that public concerns about ethical and environmental matters were a very important consideration in their firm's strategic decisions. We see this practice of deferring to public opinion as a primary form of socially responsible behaviour (again, we explore this claim below). Most businesses, however, gave such public concerns little or no consideration when making strategic decisions. For this sample of businesses, therefore, sensitivity to public opinion was common but not universal. The firms that did take account of public concerns in their strategic decision-making varied enormously, but it was noticeable that businesses which expressed a commitment to making a contribution to the local community were unusually prone to take account of public concerns.

CO-OPERATING NOT COMPLYING

There has been much discussion in recent years of social and environmental laws which could affect UK industry, and there have been some legal changes too. Yet only a minority of businesses in the 1995 London survey envisaged strategic or entrepreneurial responses to any new legislation on social and environmental matters. Most were going to wait until the law was passed before making a response, or stated that they would do nothing until forced to change.

These answers suggest that firms do not recognise that: 'Often it is in the interests of business to keep ahead of legislation' (Hussey, 1994, p. 128). Keeping ahead of the legislation can be entrepreneurial in the sense that opportunities are identified and innovations in products or services planned. They can be strategic in the sense that there is anticipation of required changes and then the planning of incremental adaptations. However, the businesses seem to bear out the assessment made by Cannon (1994), that it is rare to find a positive environmental stance by British businesses, and that the immediate reaction of most businesses to claims that they are causing environmental harm is to counter-attack: 'A defensive approach to environmental concerns is widespread' (Cannon, 1994, p. 229).

Cannon's pessimistic assessment of the business response to environmental problems suggests that businesses do not feel obliged to act with a sense of voluntary responsibility, and will react at best only in terms of compliance to the law. As we have noted, this was not true of all businesses. Some were envisaging a planned adaptation or an entrepreneurial approach. These more positive responses might reflect different appraisals by companies of their economic interest. It was clear from the data that these positive responses correlated with socially responsible behaviour in terms of strategic decision-making. Thus, a slight majority of the firms which were strategically responsive to public concerns about ethical and environmental matters said they would respond to future legislation on social and environmental matters by anticipating changes and adapting incrementally, or by seeking opportunities and being innovative. Most of the other businesses claimed that they would respond intuitively when new legislation happened, or said they intended to do nothing until forced to change.

Thus, an organisation's willingness to plan and act in advance of the passing of new legislation partly reflects a judgement that public opinion has a moral force which businesses should respect. Without such a respect for public opinion, or perhaps with an unawareness of public opinion, then legal changes are perceived as merely a constraint, which requires nothing more than compliance.

ETHICAL PLURALISM

At this point in the analysis we want to justify and explore how listening to employees' views and deferring to public concerns about social and environmental matters may be understood as important forms of socially responsible business practice. The key concept here is that of 'ethical pluralism'.

This might be defined as a situation where there are different viewpoints on the ethical decisions and courses of action which a firm can take. In the absence of an absolute consensus, the various actors in the situation will diasagree about the ethical character required of individuals and the rules which should be applied to govern the situation. Since all real circumstances present a mixture of agreement and disagreement amongst the participants, processes are needed to confront and negotiate ethical pluralism. There may be a multitude of different processes which can be used to confront the problems of ethical pluralism, but they share in common the intention of increasing the number of voices heard, and listened to, in business decision-making.

Bowie (1995) has put forward several ideas for processes which allow the voices of stakeholder groups to be heard and to have an influence on business decisions. He suggests, for example, that the owners and managers of companies should not make unilateral decisions on charitable giving. They should give the money to groups that have broad public support, so that, in a sense, it is the community which is involved in deciding how the money is used. Or they should appoint community representatives to foundation boards and community affairs councils. Another example he provides is that of the policy of 'involving' employees in the decisions about how to dispose of charitable funds by allocating company funds on the principle of matching employee contributions. Such a policy gives up some company control over charitable giving; specifically it yields control over to what charities money is donated. Presumably such process solutions can be sought in all kinds of business decision-making, including key strategic decisions about products, markets, environmental standards, recruitment policies, training, and so on.

Philosophically, this set of examples seems to us to invite an attitude towards the development of business as an institutional experiment in cooperation. In particular, Bowie's examples challenge us to think of various experiments in cooperation which owners and managers of businesses can attempt. These experiments can involve, as his examples above illustrate, deferring to public opinion, involving community representatives, and listening to employees and endorsing their choices. The experiments may also involve attempts at co-operation with customers, suppliers, shareholders, government environmental agencies, government economic development agencies, and so on. Such experiments may be underpinned by a liberal tolerance of other viewpoints, and need not be justified by the promise that co-operation will end in ethical consensus (Rorty, 1991). If we take ethical pluralism as a starting point, then maybe we must have liberal tolerance if there is to be any prospect of successful co-operation.

In line with the argument above, we would like to suggest that listening to employees and deferring to public opinion are two important forms of ethical behaviour by socially responsible businesses. Both forms of behaviour can lead to decisions and actions by business which can be seen by others as cooperative. For example, employees may express a preference for being represented collectively by trade unions. If a business listens to this and responds by recognising a union and establishing procedures and facilities voluntarily, then a pattern of cooperative industrial relations may be forged. Likewise, if a business had become aware of increasing public concern about the environment and decided unilaterally to develop green policies on recycling and waste management, this could be seen as co-operating with societal views.

THE END OF FRIEDMANITE IDEOLOGY?

Friedman sets out a theory of the free-enterprise, private-property system of business under which top managers have a moral responsibility to decide and act in ways which increase profits (Friedman, 1995). This responsibility of top managers is labelled a moral one because there is a feeling that top managers *should* strive to increase profits, and because the integrity, dynamism and health of the system are seen as resting on an undeviating pursuit of increased profit. Therefore, morality in this sense is seen as a requirement of social solidarity. Acceptance of this Friedmanite position can lead to the conclusion that social or ethical business objectives should not be formulated by firms. It follows on from this that business performance is evaluated solely by the profit figure (Argenti, 1993). This theory of free-enterprise, and the reduction of the meaning of business life to the profit figure, leads to the idea that businesses are run by proprietors who make decisions on the basis of rational and individual economic interest (Whyte and Blasi, 1985).

This theory of free-enterprise suggests that a problem is posed by the idea of social responsibility, particularly where this idea is applied by businesses run by paid managers. In Friedman's opinion there is a danger that top managers might act against the interests of the employers as a result of pursuing social business objectives. So, for example, paid top managers should not, he argued, spend money on reducing pollution beyond the point required by the best interests of the business or beyond the point required by law. He did not see a problem, or a significant problem, where an individual proprietor was managing the business; he took the view that the individual proprietor was free to pursue social responsibility because it would be their own money they were using. Logically speaking, this theory implies that top managers should do anything which increases profit, providing it is legal. If it offended the individual paid manager's own sense of social responsibility, then as an individual, they could exercise their moral right to choose by resigning.

The obedience of businesses to the moral imperative of increasing profits and obeying the law is getting more complicated in the contemporary world. First, now that capitalism has more or less triumphed over alternative forms of social economy, there is an impetus to understand which forms of capitalism are the best. This can lead to an appreciation that the performance of capitalist systems depend on social capital as well as private property. Bowie (1995), for example, argues that enlightened management techniques which work very well in Japan and Sweden do not work so well in the US because trust – created by genuine concern for employees – is missing. Trust, then, is an asset which helps to mobilise human resources, and thus assists productivity growth and capital formation. Social capital is a key determinant of economic performance, but its effect is not limited to the application of management techniques within businesses.

Societies with a high level of social capital, that is, trust, do not need the state to regulate markets, or contracts, or individual behaviour, as much as do those with low social capital. Those with low social capital require far more state regulation and control. Is the low social capital of the USA part of the explanation for its huge prison population and the enormous scale of expenditure on private security firms to guard businesses and homes? A high trust society, one based on a high level of social capital, has to be built, it is not spontaneously created. All relationships in society are drawn in to helping to build social capital, including relationships inside business organisations. Trust inside a business can only be built on a durable base if there is a degree of genuine concern by owners and managers for others: concern for employees, customers, and others has to be an end for business as well as a means.

Second, the role of top managers may be getting more complicated as societies become more complex and dynamic, and governments turn to governance as a means of catalysing change and solving collective problems. Governance involves less reliance on laws and direct service provision; instead there is more cooperative problem-solving and more efforts to mobilise the resources of private businesses and the community:

> Suddenly there is less money for government – for 'doing' things, delivering services. But there is more demand for governance – for 'leading' society,

convincing its various interest groups to embrace common goals and strategies. (Osborne and Gaebler, 1992, p. 34)

There are increasing examples of governments choosing governance rather the reaching for new laws to regulate away problems. For example, van Vliet (1993) describes an attempt in the Netherlands to deal with emissions of volatile organic compounds. Between 1985 and 1988 representatives of business and government developed an emission reduction strategy for implementation over a 12-year period. It seems that the government hoped to achieve a more effective solution to the problem because the business sector would deal with practical implementation of the strategy on a voluntary basis, whilst business gained various advantages including influence over the measures to be taken by government, a more generous time-path, and a more predictable development of government policy over a period of time. Of course, such participation might also allow business to help government to find those solutions to environmental problems which are more in the interests of business.

So, new understandings of their moral responsibilities may have to be developed by business managers in the future, so that the drive to increase profits can be combined with concern for others, and concern for building and leveraging high-trust relationships with employees, customers, suppliers, and so on. At the same time, business managers will increasingly be expected not merely to comply with the law, but to co-operate with state agencies in developing strategies that can be used to solve economic, social and environmental problems. Signs of this changing relationship of businesses to the law can be seen in the advice to businesses to adopt integrity-based approaches to ethics management: at the heart of such approaches is the infusion of a sense of responsibility which goes beyond mere compliance with the law (Paine, 1994).

CONCLUSIONS

From the preceding analysis we are left with a number of indications of the outline of a model of social responsibility. It is obviously based on the conditions facing small London businesses in the mid-1990s, and is not generalisable beyond these conditions without replication of the study. This model does not involve a concept of a set of absolute standards by which social responsibility can be identifed and measured as such. It draws attention to the existence for individual businesses of an internal community (employees) and an external community. The discharge of social responsibility, moreover, takes place in response to both of these two groups of people. In respect of both employees and the wider community it has been suggested that social responsibility is a search by business owners for agreement, sought in one case by listening to employees and being influenced by employees' views, and in the other case by deferring to public concerns about social and environmental matters. In neither case is it assumed that total agreement is possible, since we accept the assumption of ethical pluralism. The act of social responsibility is, therefore, equated with the search by business for social solidarity based on agreement. In a sense, we would argue that social responsibility is moral as well as ethical, not just knowingly doing right, but constituting a form of social engagement too.

So, it is now concluded that social responsibility is where businesses act on their obligations to their employees and their obligations to their local community. These obligations involve listening to employees and seeking to involve them in a partnership in the provision of good quality services/products that are needed by their local communities. These obligations involve seeing public opinion as having a moral force that should be listened to, and calls for a proper response from businesses, for example in relation to concerns about ethical and environmental matters. Merely caring for employees and complying with the law is not enough for the socially responsible business. This definition of social responsibility can be understood in the context of emerging forms of business system in which business effectivity depends on social capital and the solution of social and environmental issues involves co-operative problem solving by governments and other groups (including business).

If we are right about this model of social responsibility, rooted as it is in an ethical pluralism, it is clear that the conditions for social responsibility might be more favourable where owners and managers are of good ethical character and we feel we can trust their integrity and values in applying business objectives to situations which will evolve and change. But this good ethical character must grow into a disposition and capability for solidarity with employees and the community if it is to amount to social responsibility. Likewise, we might be impressed by owners and managers who profess and abide by a set of demanding ethical rules that regulate their decisions and actions when implementing business objectives. This too would not be sufficient to attain a practice of social responsibility, which requires a social interaction and engagement rather than a personal identification by the individual with an ethical code.

Note

The authors and publishers are grateful to Focus Central London for permission to use data generated by the Central London Quarterly Employed Survey between 1994 and 1998.

References

Aldag, R.J. and Bartol, K.M. (1978) 'Empirical Studies of Corporate Social Performance and Policy: A Survey of Problems and Results', in L.E. Preston (ed.), *Research in Corporate Social Performance and Policy*, vol. 1 (Greenwich, Conn.: JAI Press).
Ansoff, H.I. (1968) *Corporate Strategy* (Harmondsworth: Penguin).
Argenti, J. (1993) *Your Organization: What is it for?* (London: McGraw-Hill).
Aupperle, K.E., Carroll, A.B. and Hatfield, J.D. (1985) 'An Empirical Examination of the Relationship between Corporate Social Responsibility and Profitability', *Academy of Management Journal*, vol. 28(2), pp. 446–63.
Bowie, N. (1995) 'New Directions in Corporate Social Responsibility', in W.M. Hoffman and R.E. Frederick (eds), *Business Ethics: Readings and Cases in Corporate Morality* (London: McGraw-Hill).
Cannon, T. (1994) *Corporate Responsibility* (London: Pitman).
Curran, J. (1991) 'Employment and Employment Relations', in J. Stanworth and C. Gray (eds), *Bolton 20 Years On: The Small Firm in the 1990s* (London: Paul Chapman Publishing).
Follett, M.P. (1941) *Dynamic Administration: The Collected Papers of Mary Parker Follett* (Bath: Management Publications Trust).
Friedman, M. (1995) 'The Social Responsibility of Business is to Increase its Profits', in W.M. Hoffman and R.E. Frederick (eds), *Business Ethics: Readings and Cases in Corporate Morality* (London: McGraw-Hill).
Green, R.M. (1994) *The Ethical Manager* (New York: Macmillan).
Hussey, D. (1994) *Strategic Management: Theory and Practice* (Oxford: Pergamon).
Osborne, D. and Gaebler, T. (1992) *Reinventing Government* (Mass.: Reading, Addison-Wesley).
Paine, L.S. (1994) 'Managing for Organization Integrity', *Harvard Business Review*, March–April, pp. 106–17.
Pascale, R.T. and Athos, A.G. (1981) *The Art of Japanese Management* (Harmondsworth: Penguin).
Peters, T.J. and Austin, N.K. (1985) *A Passion for Excellence* (New York: Random House).
Rorty, R. (1991) *Objectivity, Relativism, and Truth* (Cambridge: Cambridge University Press).
Smith, C. (1994) 'The New Corporate Philanthropy', *Harvard Business Review*, May–June, pp. 105–16.
Solomon, R.C. (1992) *Ethics and Excellence: Cooperation and Integrity in Business* (Oxford: Oxford University Press).
Stacey, R. (1991) *The Chaos Frontier* (Oxford: Butterworth Heinemann).

Storey, D.J. (1994) *Understanding the Small Business Sector* (London: Routledge).
van Vliet, M. (1993) 'Environmental Regulation of Business: Options and Constraints for Communicative Governance', in J. Kooiman (ed.) *Modern Governance* (London: Sage).
Whyte, W.F. (1985) 'New Approaches to Industrial Development and Community Development', in W. Woodworth, C. Meek and W.F. Whyte (eds), *Industrial Democracy: Strategies for Community Revitalization* (London: Sage).
Whyte, W.F. and Blasi, J. (1985) 'The Potential of Employee Ownership', in W. Woodworth, C. Meek and W.F. Whyte (eds), *Industrial Democracy: Strategies for Community Revitalization* (London: Sage).
Zegans, M. (1992) 'Innovation in the Well Functioning Public Agency', *Public Productivity and Management Review*, vol. XVI(2), Winter, pp. 141–56.

15 Ethical Guidelines for an Empowered Organisation
Peter Jones

INTRODUCTION

The change of government in 1997 has encouraged questions about both the effectiveness and appropriateness of the utilitarian and short-term emphasis on economic success, profits and shareholder benefits that were the hallmarks of its predecessor. How, and it is indeed how rather than why, should businesses balance short-term economic success indicators with their responsibility, in the long as well as the short term, to all their stakeholders; not just those who own shares but employees too. Additionally, there are questions about the leadership models that are presented by people in senior roles in private and public sectors. Do they reflect the kind of practices and behaviours that they want to encourage in their wider organisations? Are their behaviours the right ones for others to follow – and what should be the ethical approaches for them to display?

The issue for employing organisations is how best to meet their business objectives as well as contributing to society and creating fulfilling environments for their employees. There *can* be a virtuous circle where organisations recognise their responsibilities to create fulfilling and continuing roles for those they employ; and where those they employ recognise their own responsibilities, individually and collectively, to contribute to the success, financial and otherwise, and well-being of their employer. A new century is an appropriate time to recognise this need for contribution and fulfilment from the organisation and the individual – and thus challenge some of the old ideas seen in the UK during the last two decades of the twentieth century.

Many of the contributions made by individuals will be in the context of their own community, from local to regional to national. But it is at work that people have the greatest opportunity to develop – as individuals and as groups; and as stakeholders, to use a term which has some favour with the New Labour government. As employees, they are part of organisations that survive and thrive by adapting and developing through internal initiatives and external pressures. They may well be encouraged to develop their own roles beyond the confines of one limited job in order to increase their effectiveness. They are at the interface of all relationships with customers and are expected to cooperate with and support other employees. They may well be shareholders. They are very likely to be members of a pension scheme with its concerns about longer-term investment. They may be customers too. Unlike other shareholders, they have made a 100 per cent investment in the organisation for which they work; all their financial and skill eggs are in the one basket. And there is a reasonable basic assumption that each of us should contribute to the best of our abilities rather than just do the minimum necessary.

That basic assumption, in itself, raises significant issues about what individuals should expect of themselves not only at work but also in the wider community in which they and their families live. It opens up issues about what is right, and ethical, in terms of behaviour and approaches to work. And it asks those who lead organisations to consider what they have to do themselves to provide the appropriate kinds of environment where individuals can grow and flourish. The old phrase of 'job enrichment' can have a much more radical definition than just knowing about one's immediate job. That is where concepts of ethics, empowerment and stakeholding responsibility come to the fore in practical terms.

Is this an idealistic picture of the world of work and the relationship of business to society generally? Is this the kind of work environment which people would like? It is certainly very different from the kind of environment that most people are currently used to, but it is not incapable of achievement. Individuals can act, groups can act, organisations can make the changes involved. Nor is it an environment that is incompatible with a successful and profitable business. Indeed some of the existing financial measures will provide the marks of achievement of different ways of working. Success, and survival, may be the appropriate measures of progress with such different ways of working. A successful division of a US high-technology company had as its mission the objective of growing people; a key indicator, determined by the people themselves, of their success in moving towards their mission was to meet the owning company's profit and return-on-investment targets. That provided some very 'hard' measure of progress for apparently 'soft' visions. And the employees took full responsibility for achieving the targets.

It seems an entirely appropriate and realistic objective to achieve a working environment where people can be fulfilled and can grow themselves and their skills. Growing themselves is a fundamental requirement so that they develop not only appropriate business and technical job skills but also grow in terms of their awareness and commitment – and in the ways they work with, respect, trust and are honest with others and with each other. It already works to some extent for businesses with fast-growing markets and new technologies because they depend on flexible and committed staff rather than on stressed and over-worked employees who are expected to do what they are told, whether right or not. It works for individuals because they really function as fully-responsible adults, aware of what is expected of them and learning in a work community; their 'brains' are no longer left outside the factory or office gate. It also works for the external community, including suppliers and customers, because the stakeholder approaches are inclusive rather than exclusive. And that, brought together, develops an ethical approach to people at work who are empowered, and encouraged to be so, by the ways in which their work environment has developed.

EMPOWERMENT AND BUSINESS STAKEHOLDERS

The 'socio-technical' approach to work

There are significant positive developments in the very nature of the business environment and the way work is done too. That is where the idealistic picture of what people can contribute and receive from their working life coincides with the new demands of technology and business improvement. That is why concepts of enrichment, fulfilment and empowerment link together with technical and business developments.

Empowered people will make the difference to success for organisations faced by new technical challenges and wanting to take advantage of them to their benefit. New technologies and the simplification of organisational structures depend on the potential of people at all levels, not just those who are managers, to widen their perspectives of business needs and their contribution to them. The fundamental review of ways of organising business and doing work, for example through business process re-engineering, has recognised the necessity for the participation and involvement of people at all levels in the goals of their businesses. Indeed, there is ample evidence that problems and failures in major systems changes in organisations, especially where they are IT-led, fail largely because employees have not been fully engaged in the changes in processes and approaches that are required of them. The irony is that massive investment in new technologies fail because of minimal investment in helping people to understand and take ownership of the changes needed.

This re-thinking about business processes must also mean re-thinking fundamental behaviours both of those who do the work and those who manage them. Do people need close management if they understand the context of their business and are encouraged and trained to develop their contributions and performance and have much increased decision-making built into work processes? Fewer levels of management, increased flexibility and emphasis on teamwork encourage people to see their roles as being to contribute as widely as possible to the aims of the business – and to develop their own skills in doing so. In manufacturing, the application of just-in-time, total quality management and self-managed teams depend on people being able to exercise their judgement, make decisions and take full responsibility for major processes. These are a long way from operators just doing what they are told and being the human cogs in the wheel.

There is a significant challenge in achieving some of these fine principles. They require hard thinking on behalf of those who lead. After all, in an obvious example, it is easy to make jobs and people redundant; it is harder to think about how best to develop their skills so that they become more flexible and can move from role to role as their 'old work' ceases to provide value – to them and their employing organisation. And individuals too need to think in different ways. It is no longer 'this is my job' but a move towards 'what can I do next to help us move forward'.

The role of managers also changes to focus on tasks as leaders and coaches when everybody at work shows the capability of acting as a responsible adult (the transactional analysis model is used deliberately!). That capability was always there but it was convenient to ignore it whilst responding to short-term economic issues. It is much harder for managers to learn and use these skills, but they pay off. People can become willing to seek help and feedback; they want to know how they can develop their skills; they want to know how they are doing. Old assumptions suggested that this was not the case so managers used instruction, exhortation, bribery and threats – none were ethical (and no-one even thought of that word anyway) and none worked particularly well.

Some of these ideas have been incorporated into empowerment initiatives; some have succeeded, a number have failed. This does not mean that empowerment does not work. It just requires some further thinking about what worked and what did not. Telling people that they empowered and then expected major change is unlikely to work; it just seems like another annual initiative as managers search for new solutions. Setting empowerment within the right context is more likely to work. The context means that people need help to make fundamental change (after all, they have been expected to follow management directives before); they need to know the ground-rules and the guidelines – what I can do for myself? when do I need to talk to someone else about what I am doing? There is a context in which empowerment operates – so individuals understand that they cannot say, 'well, you told me that I was empowered, so why did I need to tell anyone what I was doing?' Full empowerment requires individuals to recognise where the limits are and to take responsibility for communication as well as action. That is even more significant when they are working in organisations which depend on technological development and that move fast.

The socio-technical approach recognises that old-style 'command and control' is no longer sustainable. Organisations are too complex for directors to be in control of everything – there have been too many cases of financial fraud in the City to support that approach. Instead, organisations need to find approaches which grow and encourage employee commitment and which find the right balance between technological developments and the ability of employees, alone or together, to keep the right balance between doing what they see needs to be done, an empowered approach, and involving others when appropriate.

Business stakeholders and the community

Businesses have a much wider role in society than just being providers of jobs and profits. That simplistic view ignores social and ethical dimensions. Companies are a key part of the society in which they exist and do business. They also depend on that community for their suppliers, their customers and their employees. Companies are members of society just like individuals and they too have rights and obligations. They do not operate in a vacuum just to achieve profits, nor can they claim to set their own specific objectives without recognising their roles in, and obligations to, maintaining and developing the society to which they belong. They exist to provide goods and services which society wishes to have, but equally are a part of that society. They, therefore, have obligations to their employees and also to the people whom they serve. It is not sufficient for organisations to have charity budgets and make public-relations gestures to show their commitment to parts of the community, to arts and to sports sponsorship. There is more to stakeholding than that, including the need for action within their organisations.

Business obligations include being successful and surviving as an employing organisation. They also include some duty to create and sustain employment so that society can remain stable and people can continue to consume the products of business. We have to reconcile the need of business to be profitable with the requirements of the wider community if we are to sustain a viable society that can resolve the social problems and achieve some measure of social equity. That viewpoint was regarded as having limited relevance to business when short-term demands took precedence. It now seems an essential component for the stakeholding society where collective organisations like businesses and their employees, directors and managers included, all have both rights and responsibilities.

Making profits and providing the products and services, including employment, that society needs are not incompatible. Downsizing and cutting jobs may be and have been the easier alternative to hard thinking about keeping people in employment and encouraging greater flexibility from them. It had become too easy to claim that it was one or the other, rather than both, and that all businesses were required to do is to make profits and serve their shareholders. There is more to it than that, otherwise businesses have very limited horizons and aspirations. Organisations exist within the wider society and it is in their business interests to adhere to the current standards of that society.

Business stakeholders need to consider how they can move forward from current standards – and these may be before and after employment as well as during employment. Responsibility should not stop and start with the contract of employment because of the consequences, for business and society, at each formal end of that relationship. Before employment, employers complain about the supply and standards of school-leavers and graduates joining them. What should they do to invest and support their future human capital as it progresses through education? They benefit ultimately from the supply and so should the individuals and society generally. It makes competitive sense in business terms and it seems the right thing for business to be involved with. After employment, should business responsibility cease with the payment of a redundancy cheque and maybe some outplacement support? Does business need to care about the social consequences of unemployment and the challenge of seeking alternative employment? The people involved are, after all, their customers, their suppliers and may be their future or former employees. The old National Coal Board and British Steel Corporation recognised that they had some responsibility to the redundant community when mines and steelworks closed down. Should businesses see some responsibility for those, even just one, whose jobs are lost for short-term business or longer-term technological reasons. Having gained the benefit of that individual's labour, does the employer merely pay the redundancy cheque and wash its hands and accept no responsibility for what happens afterwards? Initiatives to create jobs for long-term young unemployed seem to be making a start to encourage businesses to face society as well as their competitors.

Managers in organisations need to look in the mirror and reflect on their own working arrangements as well as those they create for others. Is it really acceptable and necessary that people *have to* accept, rather sadly, that there is more pressure, more stress and longer hours at work? That is not an environment to encourage employee commitment and responsibility. Nor is it an essential requirement to maintain competitiveness and keep people 'on their toes'. Given the opportunity, they will seek other less-stressful roles.

A leadership issue emerges here too. The leaders of businesses and public sector organisations are necessarily leaders in society. It follows that they should see themselves as having a duty to set appropriate models of behaviour and action. How do the directors of large corporations resolve the paradox of awarding themselves substantial salary increases whilst at the same time cutting job numbers in the claimed interest of greater efficiency? Or for dividends to be increased much faster than average pay levels? Or for City firms to feel impelled to follow each other like lemmings in granting large bonuses to some of their staff – and often guaranteeing both golden 'hellos' for new staff and golden 'hand-cuffs' for those they fear to lose? The argument that market forces must apply in determining pay levels has some value but seems to have become the sole arbiter of what must be paid, irrespective of job value. Market forces seem to rule rather than the directors who otherwise claim the 'right to manage'.

People stakeholders at work

The stakeholder concept aims to describe and emphasises the reciprocal set of rights and responsibilities which exists between individuals and society. We earn and deserve rights by recognising our personal responsibility to make appropriate contributions to society. The general concept holds good at work too.

Developments called 'empowerment' or increasing people's responsibilities, usually brought about by business or technical imperatives but none the worse for that, provide the opportunity for people to grow at work. Successful empowerment requires a set of supporting ground rules which give people scope to act on their own initiatives and which allow and encourage them to achieve major objectives and success within boundaries which are clear and which they understand. It also requires those in management roles to accept their obligation to communicate and explain the changes clearly and to support their employees with a continuing programme of training, coaching, general communication and specific feedback. Companies and managers need to develop a culture of trust in which mutual support flourishes. Trust can be an elusive concept but it is an essential component if people at work are to take on these new responsibilities as genuine stakeholders. Even companies in the financial sector are discovering that trust, responsibility and commitment, 'soft' words which are based on attitudes and behaviours, are more likely to ensure that they comply with external regulatory bodies and achieve success than old-style 'hard' measures of control.

Many organisations have recognised some aspects of this stakeholder involvement with the preparation and communication of mission and vision statements which describe the general aspirations of the business, what it wants to achieve and its relationships with its customers, its suppliers and indeed its employees. They may even have used the word 'stakeholders' to recognise each of the parties, including but not just limited to shareholders, which have roles to play in achieving the business's plans and who will benefit from it doing so. Visions seek to set the general map of why the organisation exists, what it does, how it plans to grow and develop. They lead, inevitably, to descriptions of the kinds of behaviours that individuals should aspire to and seek to develop, recognising (sometimes implicitly) that the organisation is a community which depends on positive behaviours to achieve its objectives, and which will not do so if the behaviour of individuals is inappropriate.

US companies have found it easier to address this issue of behaviour; British companies have often found it difficult to do so, almost as if asking for changes in behaviour involves undue interference with individual freedom, or is not the kind of thing which should be discussed openly. The American practice of openness seems more sensible. Behaviour, corporate or individual, does have a clear impact on performance and achievement. The 'old' British behaviour of strict job demarcation led to inflexibility; the 'new' behaviour of teamwork both contributes to business success and creates a more positive work environment. Open discussion of appropriate behaviours is more likely to lead to changes than pretending that such discussion is not necessary.

Rights and responsibilities

Developing a statement of the rights and responsibilities of stakeholders fits with the practice of individual organisations to have their own vision statement or charter. Some of the elements seem appropriate to all kinds of organisations, recognising that they fit with the assumption that corporate success is a fundamental requirement – but no more fundamental than acknowledging and respecting the rights and responsibilities of the people who work in that corporate community. To some extent, both the rights and responsibilities must be underpinned by legislation to reflect the development of views in society. Some, such as protection against unfair dismissal or discrimination on subjective grounds, are more amenable to legislative control than others, such as the right to be treated as an individual who has a positive contribution to make. However, in all cases, the law can at best only set minimum standards. For a charter of rights and responsibilities to succeed it requires the commitment of the employers and employees who are party to it.

Taking the model presented from its early days by the Blair Government, it is feasible to identify some key *Responsibilities* and some equally important *Rights*. This is not a simple balance-sheet approach where each responsibility buys a right. They can (but do not have to) be the subjects of formal agreement between the employing organisation and its employees. Perhaps more radically, individuals can choose for themselves to take on the responsibilities – and model the right behaviours for their colleagues and employer. It is clearly the case that people at work have responsibilities to their employers and to their colleagues as well as to themselves. In fundamental terms, the concept of dealing with and managing others in the ways in which we want to be dealt with and managed ourselves provides the model for these obligations.

Key areas to include within the *Responsibilities* might be:

- *Commitment* Where individuals accept a duty to contribute to the best of their abilities to the achievement of the organisation's goals through their own activities and also through their understanding of their organisations' aims and environment. It does not mean an unthinking commitment which demands long and unsocial hours and placing the organisation ahead of personal considerations.

- *Performance* Being prepared to work flexibly. Individuals accepting that they do what needs to be done without time being wasted discussing what others should be doing. Nor is this performance only in return for payment. There is an obligation to 'do one's best'.
- *Learning* Taking personal responsibility for developing skills and seeking opportunities to do so both individually and with the support of employers. Both parties, employees and employers, have an obligation (and also a basic necessity) to develop organisational and personal capability. And this responsibility for the individuals has the common-sense benefit of also widening their opportunities in the labour market when they choose to, or have to, look for other employment.
- *Respect* Working with and helping each other at work on the basis of positive cooperation and mutual respect, valuing the different approaches offered by diversity. The fact of difference does not mean that the other person is somehow wrong; it is just a difference. This is where teamwork, trust and respect become key values in real life rather than just aspirations.
- *Well-being* Protecting the health and safety of themselves and of others in physical, mental and emotional terms. This will mean a willingness to care for others and their well-being rather than merely ensuring that safety standards are maintained. Fear and stress are inappropriate features of any environment and have become too much accepted as an inevitable aspect of working life.
- *Coaching* Giving appropriate feedback to others, to help improve performance and relationships and seeking and welcoming such feedback about one's own performance and contribution. Recognising that feedback and supportive coaching are key skills that everyone can seek to develop for their own benefit and that of their colleagues. They require a willingness to listen too.
- *Leadership* For those in leadership roles, accepting that they provide a model for the behaviour of others and that this adds a special responsibility for the appropriateness of their personal behaviour and performance both in words and in deeds. And everyone can provide leadership and set the right examples too without needing to have formal organisational authority. For those who manage others, recognising their particular obligation to develop those who report to them, to communicate effectively with them and to explain and justify any actions which affect them.

And the *Rights* are about:

- *Employees being treated as individuals*   Treating people individually means responding to their particular needs and wishes rather than enforcing some conformity with common but inappropriate standards.
- *Performance feedback*   This needs to be given appropriately, together with the opportunity to improve their skills and overcome any shortcomings with the support of their employers.
- *Dismissal being a last resort*   With all practicable steps being taken to ensure that dismissal is used only as a final sanction of last resort. This requires willingness on the employer's part to forgive and to sometimes forego the apparent right to terminate employment.
- *Objective employment choices*   Between people regarding appointment, promotion, pay increases and all other employment matters, whether before or during employment, with objective and open criteria.
- *Consultation and combination*   Giving people the right to be consulted, and to combine together if they wish, in order to have an effective collective voice in representing their views to their employers. The individual's voice can always be drowned by the apparently urgent commercial imperatives of the business.
- *Fair pay*   By acknowledging the right of people to be paid at a fair and equitable level in relation to their skills and responsibilities and also to the external labour market, imperfect though that may be as a measure of 'fair pay'. The concept of 'felt fairness' is not capable of direct measurement but we know it when we see it – or do not.
- *Public involvement*   Encouraging employees in their rights as citizens to participate in public bodies and contribute to public debate – as part of the social responsibility of the individual and also the business.
- *Well-being*   Through taking all practicable steps to protect the health and safety of employees, including the positive avoidance of unreasonable or unnecessarily stressful work demands whether in terms of hours worked or workload.
- *Personal life*   A recognition and support of the right of employees to a reasonable personal life outside work and not to intrude upon the privacy of their home life, nor make excessive work demands which deprive them of time for it.

There is a business case for these rights, and in some cases it is very straightforward. For example, it is the most sensible business course to avoid unfair discrimination in selection because in that way the employer gets the best person available for the job. In other cases, it is more indirect. Society's disapproval may be less specific, so that certain actions damage the employer's reputation and its sales or its ability to recruit. This might apply, for example, to the manipulation of employment contracts to avoid providing employment rights (which had been a growing practice).

BUSINESS ETHICS AND GOVERNMENT – SETTING MINIMUM STANDARDS ONLY?

What role does government have in setting ethical standards? There are some basic rights which need to be set by legislation – from the content of an employment contract to protection of conditions in take-overs to ultimate protection against unfair and unreasonable dismissal. Social attitudes must influence the work environment and government best represents those standards through introducing legislation to both protect and enhance the rights of those at work. What holds good generally in a democratic society also applies at work. Government 'holds the ring' by setting minimum standards through legislation and sometimes moves those standards forward so that business follows.

There are some clear areas where legislation can set the 'right' standards at work in terms of:

- *The right to fair pay* – through the introduction of a minimum wage;
- *The right to protection from unfair dismissal* – from the first day of employment and irrespective of the length of the working week or the duration of contract;
- *The right to protection from discrimination* – on grounds of age, sexual orientation, marital status and religion; and
- *The right to reasonable hours of work*.

Obvious changes with good grounds for their introduction and likely to move the limit of what people regard as acceptable from an employer at work – and none placing significant burdens on those employers who already act reasonably and recognise that they must have a good relationship with their employee-stakeholders.

The concept of a national 'Vision' for people at work seems to fit with the aspirations of the Blair government and the hopes inspired by a new century. Democratic issues do not stop at the office/factory door nor can they be overcome by short-term business imperatives (if they did, we might still have children cleaning chimneys!). People have the right to expect fair dealings at work, whatever their jobs may be and irrespective of the form of their employment contracts, whether they are full or part-time or casual and short-term. All these rights are justified by the fact of employment. The basic proposition is that people have the right to be treated fairly and honestly by their employer. In return and alongside these rights, employees have responsibilities too – to contribute to their organisation's aims and to work to the best of their abilities. That is how they contribute to their organisation's and the wider society's well-being.

CONCLUSION

These rights, and the responsibilities, will seem very sensible to most people. They seem more likely to help businesses succeed than limit their competitiveness and adaptability. They will certainly encourage employees who, as a minimum, will feel more secure in their workplace. They certainly conform with creating a work environment which considers and applies appropriate ethical standards. Empowerment is a powerful concept at work but can be regarded with a degree of scepticism *if* it is not set within the context of this kind of 'Vision'. In this context, it can be seen as setting out the 'right' ways in which organisations can operate and be successful and in which individuals can contribute fully and achieve some fulfilment – a reasonable aspiration. It leaves open the wider issue of ownership (see Davies and Mills, chapter 6 of this volume).

Empowered people taking on a greater responsibility for decisions in their organisations will rightly begin to expect not just more involvement in the basic decisions (what do we produce, for which markets, at what prices); they will also begin to expect more fundamental rewards related to the financial returns that they bring. The nature of stakeholders, the different relationships that they have to each other, and the kinds of rewards they expect (in the medium and long term as well as the monthly pay cheque) will change again. Ethics develops and changes and this might be the area where new views will develop as employees see themselves being responsible for what their organisations achieve. That is where organisations and their leaders need to consider how their business objectives, ways of working and encouraging their people, and the messages provided by their reward systems must speak in the same language.

Name Index

Aceland, A., 362
Ackermann, R., 48
Ackoff, R.L., 41, 48, 50, 86, 116, 120
Adler, P.S., 264
Albert, M., 390
Aldag, R.J., 396, 397
Alexander, A.V., 361
Allen, J., 332
Angotti, T., 8, 157–9, 161–2, 165
Ansoff, H.I., 397
Anthony, P., 341, 384, 387
Anthony, T., 329
Argenti, J., 401, 406
Argyris, C., 4, 120, 334
Ariès, P., 158
Aristotle, 116, 179, 378
Armstrong, M., 272
Arthur, M., 112, 173
Ashforth, B.E., 131, 132
Athos, A.G., 399
Aupperle, K.E., 396
Austin, N.K., 393, 403

Bader, E., 188–91
Bader, G., 192
Badham, R., xi, 11–12, 235–70
Bandura, A., 130, 132–3, 198, 233
Banfield, E., 52
Banks, J.A., 366
Barthes, R., 147–8, 152, 164
Bartol, K.M., 396
Batstone, E., 276
Bell, D., 333
Bellah, R. *et al.*, 384, 386
Bennis, W., 124
Benson, J., 348
Bentham, J., 151–3
Berger, P.L., 137
Birchall, D., 338
Birchall, J., xi, 9, 16–17, 346–68
Bird, F.B., xi, 3, 4–5, 6, 10, 24, 34, 41–89, 112

Bittner, E., 137
Blasi, J.R., 44, 406
Block, P., 115, 130, 197
Blyton, P., 373
Boddy, D., 260, 267
Bok, S., 83
Bolger, A., 276
Bonner, A., 363
Boreham, P., 269
Bound, G., 90
Bowie, N., 396, 401, 405, 407
Bradford, D.L., 133
Bradshaw-Camball, P., 136, 137, 140
Brady, N., xi
Branton, P., 324
Braverman, H., 47, 119, 141
Britton, W., 112
Brown, M., 111, 112
Brown, R., 111, 112
Buchanan, D., xi, 236, 260, 267, 268, 276
Burawoy, M., 171
Burawoy, M., 31
Burke, E., 389
Burnett, J., 349–50, 353
Burns, T., 386
Burrell, G., 136, 137, 140, 141
Byham, W., 372

Cannon, T., 404
Cappelli, P., 31
Carbery, T., 348, 361, 362
Carr, C., 334
Carroll, A.B., 396
Carr-Saunders, A.M. *et al.*, 362, 363
Carson, T.L. *et al.*, 83
Child, J., 338
Christensen Hughes, J.M., xi, 3, 6–7, 10–11, 16, 30, 33, 44, 115–46, 197–234, 302, 303, 311
Chryssides, G.D., 111
Clarkson, 129

427

428 Name Index

Claydon, T., 275, 278, 334, 373
Cohen, A.R., 133
Cohen, S., 276
Cole, G.D.H., 350, 352,
Cole, R.E., 264
Coles, A., 367
Colgan, F., 326, 327
Conger, J.A., 127, 128, 129–32, 135, 136, 198, 233, 284, 298
Corbetta, G., 183
Cotton, J.L., 42, 44, 47, 50, 74, 75, 82
Couchman, P., xi, 11–12, 235–70
Cox, J., 372
Cressey, P., 334
Cropanzano, R., 84
Culbert, S.A., 41, 84
Curran, J., 338, 401
Currie, L., 162

Dahl, R.A., 49
Dansereau, F., 35
Davies, M.L., 363
Davies, P.W.F., x, xii, xiii, 1, 4, 7, 9–10, 16, 170–94, 424
Deakin, N., 347
Deci, E.L., 130, 198
Deleuze, G., 157, 158
Deming, W.E., 111
Descartes, R., 149
Dewey, J., 4, 35
Di Martino, V., 336
Dickson, W.J., 273
Dixon, B., 276
Donkin, R., 112, 272
Doyle, M., 275, 278, 334, 373
Dreyfus, H.L., 155
Du Gay, P., 174, 328, 329, 330, 331, 335
Durkheim, E., 18, 377, 383
Durrick, M., 81

Echiejile, I., 333
Elliott, S., 360
Estok, D., 123, 140
Ewing, D.W., 43, 48, 74, 85
Ezzamel, M. *et al.*, 333

Fauldner, C. *et al.*, 326
Fetterman, D.M., 200
Fielding, M., 328
Fletcher, B., 111, 112
Folger, R., 85
Follett, M.P., 3, 21, 23, 25–6, 370–1, 400
Ford, H., 119, 127
Foucault, M., 4, 8, 18, 35, 117, 126–7, 136, 141–2, 143, 148, 150–2, 154–6, 158, 160, 374–7
Fournier, R., 90, 111
Fox, A., 26, 371
Foy, N., 41, 78
Freedman, B., 85
French, J.R.P., 110, 111
Friedman, A., 117–20, 125, 137, 370
Friedman, M., 19, 26, 76, 177–8, 179, 378, 396, 401, 406
Fukuyama, F., 18, 371, 382

Gaebler, T., 408
Gaffin, J., 363
Gaitskell, H., 365
Galbraith, J.K., 52
Gandz, J., 43, 112, 133, 197
Garavan, T., 276
Garber, J., 131
Gardner, W.L., 132
Garrahan, P., 174, 277, 331
Gartman, D., 118, 119, 140
Geary, J., 273, 275, 276
Gillespie, A. *et al.*, 337
Glendon, M.A., 43
Glisson, C., 81
Goodwin, B., xii, 14–15, 17, 32, 44, 300–25
Goold, M.J., xiii, 14
Gore, G.M., 111
Goyder, G., 181, 183, 184, 192
Graham, J.W., 80
Graham, P., 25
Grant, C., 176
Green, R.M., 402
Greenberg, E.S., 42, 56
Greenberg, J., 43, 85
Greer, G., 327
Grenier, G., 373

Name Index

Gruber, J.M., 79
Gryna, F.M., 29
Guattari, F., 157, 158
Guba, E.G., 201
Gunn, C.E., 42, 56, 57, 74

Haddon, L., 337
Hadland, M., 111, 112
Halal, W.E., 48, 85
Hamilton, A., 384
Hampden-Turner, C., 177, 180, 186, 187
Hancock, K., 269
Handy, C., 162–3, 165, 328
Hansen, D., 112
Hardy, C., 49
Harvey, B., 180
Hatfield, J.D., 396
Hawken, P., 178
Hawkins, K., 370
Hayek, F., 378
Heery, E., 329, 332, 333
Heidegger, M., 149
Hellriegel, D., 197
Heron, C., 118
Herzberg, F., 120, 273
Hill, N., 123
Hill, S., 14, 30
Hirschmann, A.O., 51
Hobbes, T., 5, 46, 96–8
Holyoake, G.J., 357
Houlihan, M., 336, 338
Hughes, T., 357
Hussey, D., 395, 403
Huws, U., 336, 337

Jackson, J., 377
Jeffreys, J.B., 355, 364
Jenkins, D., 111
Johnson, N., 163
Jones, D.T., 27
Jones, M., 192
Jones, P., xii, 20–1, 412–25
Joyce, P., xii, xiv, 19–20, 328, 393–411
Judkins, P. et al., 336
Juran, J.M., 29, 111, 327
Jurgens, U., 265, 266

Kakabadse, A., 110
Kaler, J.H., xii, 5–6, 44, 90–114, 111, 324
Kamuta, Y., 164, 165, 169
Kant, I., 155, 178, 182, 185
Kanter, R.M., 41, 74, 77, 81, 124, 128, 136
Kanungo, R.N., 127, 129–32, 135, 136, 198, 233, 284, 298
Kay, J., 367
Keenoy, T., 329
Keller, T., 35
Kelly, J., 242
Kerfoot, D., 29, 111, 308
Ketchum, L.D., 120–3, 125
Kidder, D., 80
King, W., 350–1
Kingsley, C., 357
Kinlaw, D.C., 91, 111, 112, 275, 295
Kinsman, F., 336
Knapp, K., 235
Knights, D., 29, 111, 308
Konovsky, P., 85
Kouzes, J.M., 128, 129, 130, 132, 136, 203
Krishan, R., 123

Lakatos, I., 90
Lawler, E.E., 41, 44, 47, 74, 120, 124, 128, 136, 235
Leck, J.D., 48
Ledford, G.E., 128
Ledwith, S., 326, 327
Legge, K., 29, 170, 173–4, 192, 236, 264, 265, 266, 278, 297, 328, 329, 330, 331, 333, 340
Lessing, Doris, 158
Levy, Pierre, 163
Lewicki, R.J., 43, 84
Lewis, A., 337
Lewis, D., 303
Likert, R., 120, 334
Lincoln, Y.S., 201
Lind, E.A., 85
Lippke, R.L., 186
Locke, J., 183
Lorenz, E., 370, 382
Lorsch, J.W., 95

430 Name Index

Lowe, R., 347
Lozano, Eduardo, 162
Luckmann, T., 137
Ludlow, J.M., 357
Lukes, S., 45, 49
Lyons, L., 338

MacIntyre, A., 18, 386
Macmurray, J., 384
Mahoney, J., 389
Mansell, J., 120, 121, 140
Marglin, S.A., 116
Martinko, M.J., 131
Marx, K., 118
Massey, D., 147, 332
Mateijko, A., 78
Mathews, J., 240
Mausner, B., 120
Maxwell, R., 98
Mayo, E., 120, 273
McCalman, J., 276
McCamus, D., 124
McCardle, L. et al., 28, 111
McDonough, J.J., 41, 84
McGrath, P., 336, 338
McGregor, D., 120, 272
McHugh, D., 174–175
McHugh, P., 90
McKendrick, N. et al., 348
McLoughlin, I., xiii, 11–12, 235–70
Mears, R., 366
Merton, R.K., 120, 137
Mill, J.S., 356–7
Mills, A., xiii, 4, 7, 9–10, 16, 170–94, 424
Millward, N., 382
Minton, J.W., 43, 84
Mintzberg, H., 68, 69
Mitchell, J.T.W., 358, 359
Moats Kennedy, M., 340
Mohrman, S.A., 128
Moon, C., xiii, 15–16, 326–43
Morgaine, C.A., 128, 134–5, 140, 142, 199, 233
Morgan, C., 313
Morgan, G., 124, 136, 137, 140, 159–60
Morley, M., 276

Mowday, R. et al., 80
Mumford, E., 11–12, 235, 236, 237–9, 240, 259, 260, 265
Murgatroyd, S., 313
Murray, V., 136, 137, 140

Naschold, F., 240, 242
Neale, E.V., 357
Nightingale, D.V., 119–20, 121, 122, 124, 129, 133, 135, 137, 140, 141, 199, 233
Nixon, President Richard, 121
Nord, W.R., 118, 126, 133, 135, 140–1, 198, 233
Norman, E., 357
Nykodym, N., 332, 334

Oakland, J.S., 29
Oates, D., 111, 112
Ogbonna, E., 187
Ojeifo, E., xiii, 12–14, 271–99
Oliver, N., 27–8
Onstad, K., 126
Organ, D.W., 80
Orsburn, J., 235
Osborne, D., 408
Overmier, J.B., 132
Owen, R., 350–1, 353

Paine, L.S., 408
Parker, M., 28, 112, 331
Parks, J.M., 80
Parsloe, P., 111
Pascale, R.T, 275, 399
Pateman, C., 273
Percy, Senator C., 122
Peters, T.J., 172, 327, 328, 393, 403
Pettigrew, A., 240
Pfeffer, J., 45, 128, 137, 198
Pheby, K., xiii, 7–9, 147–69
Pickard, J., 112, 331
Plunkett, L.C., 90, 111
Polanyi, K., 348, 351, 353
Pollitt, C., xi, 309, 325
Popper, K., 379–380
Portis, B., 123

Name Index

Posner, B.Z., 128, 129, 130, 132, 136, 203
Potter, B., 349, 350, 358

Quinn. J.J., x, xiii, 2–4, 24, 21, 23–37

Rabinow, P., 155, 374
Rainbird, H., 295
Randolph, W.A., 90, 112
Rankin, T., 123
Rappaport, J., 128, 135, 142, 199, 233
Raven, P., 110, 111
Rawson, D., 269
Reed, M., 171, 192, 387
Rehm, M., 128, 135, 142
Remer, P., 111
Rinehart, J.W., 75
Ripley, P., 330, 332, 333, 335, 337
Ripley, R., 330, 332, 333, 335, 337
Rodriguez, C., 333
Roethlisberger, F.J., 273
Roos, D., 27
Rorty, R., 405
Rose, M., 240
Rothwell, S., 337
Rotter, J.B., 132
Rubenwitz, S., 78

Sacks, J., 383
Sako, M., 33
Salaman, G., 174, 328, 329, 330, 331, 335, 387
Salancik, G.R., 45
Saunders, D., 48
Sayer, A., 31
Scott, P., 334
Selbourne, D., 383
Seligman, M.E.P., 131, 132
Selznick, P., 43, 80, 82, 385
Sen, L.A., 153
Sewell, G., 174, 327, 331, 332
Shapiro, D.L., 84
Sheppard, B.H., 43, 84
Simon, B.L., 46
Singer, A., 335

Singer, M., 192
Sisson, K., 327
Slaughter, J., 28, 331
Slocum, J.W., 197
Smith, A., 378, 380
Smith, C., 397
Smith, T., 28
Snyderman, B., 120
Solomon, R.C., 179, 397, 398, 400
Sparrowe, R.T., 198
Spinoza, B de, 46
Stacey, R.D., 178, 394
Stalker, G., 386
Stanworth, C., xiii–xiv, 15–16, 326–43
Stanworth, J. *et al.*, 340
Stares, M., 338
Steedman, H., 295
Sternberg, E., 26, 378–80
Stevenson, O., 111
Stewart, M., 111
Stewart, P., 174, 277, 331
Storey, D.J., 399

Tawney, R.H., 181, 182
Taylor, F.W., 119
Taylor, M., 111
Terry, A., 111, 112
Thomas, K.W., 133, 198
Thompson, E.P., 353
Thompson, J.L., 110
Thompson, P., 174–5
Thoms, D., 363
Toffler, A., 336
Tomaney, J., 31
Townley, B., 341, 374–7
Trickett, E.J., 79
Trist, E., 120–3, 125
Trompenaars, F., 177, 180, 186, 187
Tuckman, A. 324
Turnbull, P., 373
Turnbull, S., 359
Tyler, T.R., 84, 85
Tyson, S., 172

Vaines, E., 127, 128, 134, 140, 199, 233
Van Beinum, H., 121, 122, 140

Van Dyne, L. *et al.*, 80
Van Einjatten, F.M., 240
Van Gerwen, J., 179, 182, 192
Van Vliet, M., 408
Velasquez, M., 86
Velthouse, B.A., 133, 198
Vincenti, V.B., 116, 127
Vroom, V.H., 288, 334

Walker, D., 276
Walzer, M., 390
Warren, R.C., xiv, 7, 17–19, 21, 369–92
Waterman, R.H., 172, 327
Waterson, A., 361
Watson, T.J., 34, 385, 387–8
Weaver, W.G., 35
Webb, B., 352, 358, 359, 381
Webb, S., 358
Weber, M., 45
Webley, S., 30
Weisbord, M., 140
Wellins, R., 235
Werhane, P., 43
Westley, F., 80
White, B., 123, 140
White, J., 389

Whyte, W.F., 399, 406
Wilkinson, A., 28, 111
Wilkinson, B., 27–8, 174, 187, 327, 331, 332
Williams, B., 153
Williams, R., 348
Willmott, H., 111, 278
Windsor, D., 99
Winstanley, D., xiv, 12–14, 271–99
Wirth, L., 336
Wobbe, W., 242
Wolfe, Alan, 169
Womack, J.P., 27
Woodall, J., xiv
Woodman, R., 197
Woodroffe, G., 347
Woods, A., xii, xiv, 19–20, 328, 393–411
Worell, J., 111
Wright, A., 347

Yeo, S., 359

Zegans, M., 393
Zuboff, S., 339
Zwerdling, D., 120

Subject Index

a priori judgements, 33, 91
accountability, 5, 6, 58, 73, 81–2,
  93, 99–103, 105, 182, 190,
  254, 274, 286, 301, 310, 318,
  320, 322, 327, 393
adjudicatory powers, 45, 49–86
agency-empowerment, 14, 23
agents: of change, 11, 12;
  of power, 54–5
alienation, 7, 8, 118–20, 177
Alliance & Leicester Building
  Society, 6, 105, 108
allocation of resources, 285–6
altruism, 290
apartheid, 17
Australia, 11, 235–68
audit(s), 210–1, 311
authoritarian management, 13, 135
  (*see also* command and control
  management)
authority, 304, 308
automation, 242–6, 264
autonomy, 2, 4, 8, 73, 82, 115, 117,
  159–62, 172, 174, 237, 266,
  276, 301, 317, 320, 333, 337,
  339, 399; doctrine, 263;
  -ous workgroups, 277
autopoiesis, 8, 159–65

bargaining power, 82
behaviour, 115–17, 135, 250, 419;
  -al change, 132, 152, 289,
  292–3; ethical systems
  of, 337
benchmarking, 280, 282
benevolent autocratic
  management, 20
best practice, 248, 256, 260
blame culture, 174 (*see also* company
  culture; organisational
  cultural system)
bonus scheme, 33
boundary, 148, 158; management,
  252, 292; personal, 147

British consumer co-operative
  movement, 16, 349–67
British Steel Corporation, 418
budgetary powers, 71, 86
bureaucratisation, 119–120
business: and community
  involvement, 393–409; as a
  community of purpose, 18,
  369–90; as a responsible
  collective citizen, 389–90;
  as an intermediate association,
  18, 384; environment, 20, 124,
  412–13; in society, 1, 413;
  purpose, 378–81, 396–401;
  purpose for ethical
  empowerment, 381–2
business ethics, 21, 380–1, 400;
  and government, 423–4
business process re-engineering, 11,
  77, 124, 414

Canada, 200–1
capitalism, 7, 347, 373, 406–7;
  European version of, 186–8;
  two types of, 390
capitalist, 7; control of labour, 31,
  118, 141, 174–5; framework, 3,
  180; -ic structures, 8, 340, 396;
  organisations, 31, 133, 266;
  -owned, 9
Cartesian thinking, 8, 149
catholic, 19; social
  philosophy, 382
catch-22, 219, 224–6, 227,
  231–2
CBI (Confederation of British
  Industry), 331
change: agent, 11–12, 236, 238–9,
  259–66 (*see also* agency);
  control agenda of, 260;
  programme, 260; time-scale
  of, 267
chaos (theory), 328, 335, 394
character formation, 385–6

charter of responsibilities
and rights, 21, 321–3, 330
(*see also* social charter)
Chartists, 353
christianity, 154, 177
Ciba UK, 331
citizenship, 19, 92, 161–5, 383, 389, 422
civic duties, 383
(*see also* duties; duty)
civil service departments, 14
co-determinate power, 52–53
(*see also* power)
code of ethics/conduct/practice, 30, 65, 189–90, 320
collective: bargaining, 43; responsibility, 56, 57, 318; voice, 347–8
collectivist ethic, 35
collegiality, 62–7
command and control management, 20, 94–5, 99–103, 106, 108, 210–16, 215–16, 227, 243, 275, 295, 305, 335, 337, 416
commitment, 3, 26, 30, 72, 129, 197, 200, 218, 307, 321, 330–1, 335, 375, 381, 414, 420
common: good, 18, 381, 387–8; ownership, 181–91; purpose, 370–90; responsibility, 189; values, 61
communication, 83–4, 106, 252, 268; levels, 294; skills, 59, 62, 64, 159, 163–4, 219, 273–6, 281, 307, 393, 416
communitarianism, 23, 142, 188, 351, 383
community: development, 161–3, 396–9; of purpose, 369–90
company: culture, 191–2, 201, 203, 226, 261, 337, 401; law, 183–4
competitiveness, 26, 275, 371, 373, 398, 424 (*see also* market)
conflict: of interest, 261; of values, 115; resolution, 20, 59, 63, 74; -ual relationships, 153–4
Conservative government, 14

constitutive rights, 43
consultative power, 52 (*see also* power)
consumer: co-operation, 17; empowerment, 17, 347–67; pressure groups, 16; protection, 16, 347; society, 348–9, 354 (*see also* co-operative movement)
consumerism, 23
Consumers Association, 16, 348
context of empowerment, 283–8
contracting-out, 7
contracts: breach of, 117; five types of, 237–9, 268; nexus of, 17 (*see also* employment contracts)
contradictions in empowerment programmes, 286–8, 298 (*see* also catch-22)
contractual: empowerment, 4; power(s), 47, 49–86; trust 33
control, 2–3, 4, 6–7, 9, 14, 51, 115, 165, 272, 277, 301; behaviour, 115; by employees, 179; by consumers, 354 (*see also* co-operative movement); by the customer, 329–30; degrees of, 170, 179; doctrine of, 265, 292; ethics of, 29–30; hierarchy, 171; lack of, 105, 310; of labour, 32, 117–20, 125, 170–1, 174–5, 211–12, 215–16, 335; of resources, 323; of self, 92; of teleworkers, 336–40; old measures of, 419; over budgets, 69; scale of, 151; span of, 201, 206; strategies, 117–18; systems, 127 (*see also* power and control); top-down, 297, 328; via technology, 338–40; 370, 375
controlled violence, 35
(*see also under* Foucault *in Name Index*)
conventional rights, 183 (*see also* rights)
Co-operative Bank, 17, 365

Subject Index 435

co-operative movement, 4, 16, 42, 347–367 (*see also* producer co-operatives; consumer)
Co-operative Party, 348, 359–62
Co-operative Women's Guild, 362–3
co-ownership, 9
COPE (Centre for Organisational and Professional Ethics), 1, 2
corporate: communication, 10; downsizing, 13; goals, 396; governance, 20, 381, 389; life, 8; veil, 381 (*see also* organisational)
corruption, 31
cost-cutting/control, 20, 213–4, 275, 278, 330
cost/productivity, 10, 11, 206, 277
CQI (Continuous Quality Improvement), 43, 67; programmes, 67
creativity, 242
craftsmanship, 73
culture of empowerment, 33, 281, 291, 307, 329–30 (*see also* empowerment)
customer: control by the, 329–30; empowerment, 29, 321–2; -focused empowerment, 202–6, 208–16; perceptions, 308; revolution, 202–6, 208, 393; satisfaction, 62, 124, 208, 280; service, 10, 174, 208–10, 281, 311, 318 (*see also* consumer)
customs, 80
CWS (Co-operative Wholesale Society), 348, 356, 359–61, 364–5

decentralising, 61, 129, 338
decision-making, 13, 25, 27, 44, 128, 161, 272, 293, 405; bodies, 182–3; delegation of, 393; discretion, 13–16, 19, 24, 26, 41, 46, 67–9, 73, 79, 93, 184, 243, 280, 296, 304–5, 313, 317, 339, 370–1, 382, 394; power, 30, 36, 298, 382, 399, 401; responsibilities, 33, 330; rights to, 182–3
Deck, 282
degradation of work, 47
degrees of power, 45, 49–54 (*see also* power)
dehumanisation of work, 116
delayering of organisations, 6, 106, 109, 124, 275–6, 333, 390 (*see also* downsizing)
democratic: deficit, 365–6; empowerment, 92–4, 103, 108, 137, 354; institutions, 164
democracy, 41–2, 92, 170, 366, 394
demoralising, 292
demotivation, 27, 285
deontology, 16, 156, 179–80
deskilling, 7, 47
development dialogue, 64
development of personal ethics, 21
dictators, 53
Digital, 197, 282
dignity, 115, 124, 130, 182, 188, 382, 403
directors' viewpoints, 221–4, 418
discipline, 28 (*see also* commitment)
discretion, *see* decision-making
discretionary powers, 71 (*see also* power)
discrimination, 43, 75
disempowerment 1, 9, 56, 78
distributive justice, 4, 35, 379 (*see also* justice)
downsizing, 7, 11, 20, 67, 77, 124, 126, 272, 275, 284–5, 333, 417
DSS (Department of Social Security), 303, 307, 313, 322
duties, 105, 172, 185, 314, 317, 320
duty, 69, 420

education, 8
effective power, 53, 279
efficiency contract, 12, 238, 252–5
electronic surveillance, 6 (*see also* surveillance)

Subject Index

employee(s): behaviour, 125; commitment, 30; development, 3, 29; -employer relationship, 25, 33, 119, 126; empowerment, 12, 16–17, 29, 30, 62, 94–5, 104, 109, 273, 280, 320; firing of, 216, 231; -focused empowerment, 226–7; influence, 402–3; -owned, 9; ownership, 274; participation, 103, 123, 273; rights, 326 (*see also* rights); self-development, 26; well-being, 19, 397–9, 401–3, 421, 424

employment, 15, 190, 351

employment contract: 19, 20, 374, 417, 423–4; implicit elements of, 12, 237–9, 388; severed by empowerment, 33

employment protection legislation, 31

empowered: consumer, 16; decision, 30; employees, 26, 30, 33, 198; feeling of being, 331; organisation, 93, 295, 372–3, 412–25; teams, 172 (*see also* team-based working); worker, 28

empowering agent, 26

empowerment: adjudicatory, 4, 10; agency, 14; and business purpose, 377–81; and decision-making, 34; and ethics, 334–5; and ethics in a rule-governed organisation, 314–16; and justice, 41–89; and labour process theory, 273–5; and rule-bound tasks, 15, 306–24; and targets, 308–14; and teams, 235–68; and the post-modern organisation, 328–9; and virtuality, 338–40; and virtue, 377–8; as a doctrine, 104; as a doctrine of convenience, 317; as a management tool, 30–2, 115, 128, 170, 198, 376; as a strategy, 142–3; as a term of managerial art, 90–2, 108; as an ethical endeavour, 25–6; as the management of meaning, 328–9; as voice, 137; barriers to, 208–10, 219, 231–3; classification of, 10–11, 136–43; critique of, 3–4, 326–35, 374–7; culture of, 33; cynicism concerning, 125, 143, 207, 213, 227, 301; debate, 370–4; definition of, 3, 6, 101–2, 127–35, 197–200, 226, 271–2, 275, 369–70; degrees of, 24, 386–9; demand for, 331–2; dimensions of, 271; ethical critique of, 27–3; ethics of, 31–4; evaluation of, 373–4; expectancy of, 13, 288–91; experience of, 291–7; external, 12; framework, 283; genuine, 9, 175–86; internally generated, 21; levels of, 135, 199, 382; limitations of, 322–4, 333–4; meaning of, 12–14, 90–110, 271–98, 300–24; moral evaluation of, 109–10; moral underpinnings of, 384; of the customer, 29; of the public, 321; paradox, 6; perceptions of, *see* experience of *and* expectancy of; perspectives of 1, 2–3, 271–9; programme(s), 1, 2, 4, 6, 10, 13, 16, 41–2, 54–72, 81–2, 85–6, 200, 274, 276–7, 279–97, 385; resistance to, 306–7; rhetoric, 10, 14, 24, 29, 31, 45, 170, 197–233; strategies, 10, 128, 197–233, 271–2, 278, 328–9, 373, 375, 381, 384, 390; themes, 12; theories of, 2; training for, 63–4; types of, 1, 6, 202–31, 301–2; typology, 197–233; uses of the term of, 326–35; utilitarian interpretation of, 18; *v.* rules, 315–16, 318–19, 323–4

Enlightenment (The), 149, 154

environmental issues, 295, 413–14, 407–9

equal opportunities, 315, 354, 398, 422

equal rights, 24 (*see also* discrimination; rights)

Subject Index 437

ethical: ambiguity, 268; business, 21; dilemma(s), 323; empowerment, 3–4, 18, 19, 79–80; empowered selves, 8; ethical empowerment, 2, 18, 25, 33; guidelines, 20–1, 412–25; justification for empowerment, 26; plurality, 20; problems, 14; role, 20; -self, 8; standards, 423–5; systems design, 159–65, 235; trading policy, 17; unethical forms of empowerment, 31–4, 109–110
ethically pluralist, 20, 404–6
ethico-power, 7, 8, 147–68
ethics: and socio-technical systems, 235–68; course on, 317; management, 408; of control, 30; of empowerment, 30; of human-centred change, 264–7; of the self, 148–9
Europe, 42, 52, 86, 327, 337, 390
excellence, 326, 340, 386, 393, 396
exercise of force, 45
expectancy of empowerment, 13, 288–91
experience of empowerment, 291–7 (*see also* empowerment programmes)
exploit: -ation, 18, 31, 119, 137–8, 235, 277; -ative, 26, 369, 373; -ative management, 3, 31 (*see also* command and control management)

factory system, 7, 116–18
fair: pay, 422; warnings, 43 (*see also* justice)
federalism, 162–3
feminism, 23
feminist: activists, 24; thinking, 375–6
firing employees, 216, 231, 422
firm as a social institution, 17–18
flexible attitudes, 277, 320, 414, 417, 421
free-will, 6, 115–16
Friedmanite ideology, 19, 118–20, 125, 137, 176, 178, 396–401, 406–8

Gas Consumers Council 16
German system of co-determination, 103
Germany, 42, 177, 186
give-and-take, 35
golden rule, 14
goodwill, 33
governance, 409–10; empowerment, 4, 24; power, 85–6; powers, 45, 48–86
government(s), 21, 75, 82, 187, 197, 352, 354, 360, 407, 412–13, 423–4
government agency, 14, 300–24, 405
granting power, 3, 23
Greek philosophy, 153–6

HarperCollins, 105
Harvester Chain, 105, 331
hierarchies, 121; flattening of, 59–62, 172, 300–1, 316–22; traditional, 71, 96, 99–103, 188, 266, 328
high trust, 20, 278, 337, 388; and low trust, 26, 371–2, 382; culture, 13, 33–4, 334, 419; organisations, 3; relationship(s), 20, 339–40 (*see also* trust)
historical perspectives, 6, 16–17, 115–43, 183–4, 275, 348–65
Holland, 187
honesty, 129, 239, 312, 414
human: -centred design, 240–1, 259–60 (*see also* socio-technical systems); nature, 377; potential, 135; rationality, 153; right(s), 170–1, 182; welfare, 199
human relations movement, 7, 120–1
HRD (Human Resource Development), 276
HRM (Human Resource Management), 24, 78, 170, 172, 201–2, 206, 213, 219–21, 231, 236, 263, 278, 327
HRM policies, 374

identity, 7, 148, 158
ideological dominance, 93, 120, 176

ideology(ies), 31, 140, 370, 376, 406–8
IIP (Investors In People), 321
implementation barriers, 6
imposition of power, 23, 31
 (*see also* power; decision-making)
increasing managerial control, 35
 (*see also* command and control management)
independent responsibility, 58–59
individual: autonomy, 2; discretion, 28; freedom, 419; -organisation dimension, 12; perspectives of the, 271; responsibility, 318
 (*see also* autonomy)
industrial: democracy, 7, 42–3, 67, 74, 177–8, 273; -isation, 370; power, 24; relations, 250, 266, 381; revolution, 116; system, 122, 350–1
influence in the workplace, 41
information, 13, 375; access to, 33
innovation, 393–4
instrumental powers, 5
integrated diversity, 7, 159–65
internal goods, 18
internal markets, 330
interpersonal skills, 73
 (*see also* communication skills)
intrinsic worth, 19
IPA (Involvement and Participation Association), 274
IPD (Institute of Personnel and Development), 274, 327
Ireland, 280
IT technology, 20, 33, 165, 272, 275, 287, 293, 319, 414

Japan, 7, 27, 148–68; -isation, 170, 188
Japanese: automobile industry, 27, 173–4, 282; management ideas, 184, 276, 332
job: design, 10, 130, 198, 242; enrichment (programmes), 44, 47, 73, 81, 103, 109, 413; provision of, 397; rotation schemes, 58, 81, 60–2, 390; satisfaction, 13, 26, 31, 109, 301; security, 110, 203, 242, 377; sharing, 188
John Lewis, 191
justice 4, 9, 41–86, 177–80, 192; and empowerment 41–89, 170, 181–3; distributive 35, 176, 184–5, 379; procedural 35
just-in-time (JIT) production 254, 331, 415

key questions in the ethics and empowerment debate, 1, 23–37, 41, 44, 54, 78, 79, 115, 143, 199, 246, 248, 251, 252–3, 255, 267, 323, 347, 365, 369, 377–8, 393, 396, 401, 412–13, 417
know-how, 45, 51
knowledge-based power, 28, 375
knowledge contract, 12, 237–8, 246–8
Kyoto, 7–8

labour: division of, 383; market, 15–16; process theory, 9, 117–19, 173–5; theory of value, 352, 358
labour–management negotiations, 75
leadership, 418, 421 (*see also* directors' viewpoints)
lean production, 3, 27, 29–32
legal standards, 21
legislative changes, 43, 184, 187, 403–4, 423
legitimacy of change, 260–1, 268
level of discretion, 26
 (*see also* decision-making)
liberation movements, 92
liberalising, 19
lifetime employment, 28
listening and responding, 19, 393–411
London, 1, 19, 313, 395, 408
loss of control, 30
loyalty, 3, 27, 118, 238, 312, 317, 332, 360, 367

Subject Index 439

majority power, 53
male–female integration, 249, 362–3
management: by stress, 17, 29, 33, 331; consultants, 24; control, 29, 215–6, 235; diktat, 34; fad, 34, 180; freedom, 305–6; of meaning, 329, 338; power, 190, 415–16; strategies, 44, 173; styles, 215–16, 293, 334–5, 401–2, 415–16; theorists, 93
manager–managed organisational model, 20
managerial: control, 18, 35, 117–27, 326, 381; discourse, 15, 326–41; hierarchy, 11; responsibilities, 6
marginal power, 51–52
market(s): competition, 373, 381, 396; forces, 184, 347, 371–2, 390, 418; -ing, 208–9, 217, 273, 317; regulation, 349; relationships, 330; research, 402; share, 290, 364–5; value, 352
Marxists, 17, 141
Maxwell Communications Corporation, 98
McDonald's, 324
meaning: at work, 6, 133–4; -ful goals, 7, 198–9; of empowerment, 12–14
measures of power, 45
military training, 28
minimum wages, 43, 75, 363
minorities, 24, 52, 61, 75, 92
Mirror Group Newspapers, 98
modern management, 24
Mondragon co-operative, 351, 359
monitoring work, 126, 274, 311, 334, 383 (*see also* surveillance)
monopoly power, 349–50, 361
moral, 387; code, 315; competence, 385; conduct, 379; communities, 341, 386; corruption, 312; decision-making, 153; development, 18; dilemmas, 14, 314–15; dimension of business, 389; energy, 389; framework, 19; imperative to increase profits, 407; judgement, 15; justification, 133, 198; obligations, 395; order of society, 383, 389; purpose of business, 380; relationships, 384; resources, 71; responsibility of top managers, 406–8; revolution, 357; significance, 385; test, 381; values, 124; worth, 239
morale, 128, 173, 340
motivation, 295, 297, 317, 336, 399, 403; -al construct, 128–30; empowerment strategies for, 7, 135; problems, 14
motives, 26, 385
multiple: meanings, 13, 115, 297; rationalities, 156
mutual self-interest, 373
mystery-shopper programme, 214–15, 232

National Coal Board (now British Coal), 417–18
national cultures, 186
natural: justice, 85; law(s), 118, 178; rights, 183
negotiated reality, 12, 271–98
negotiation, 83
neo-Marxists, 18
Netherlands, 408
New Labour (government), 192, 412
norms (*see under individual norms*, e.g. dignity, reciprocity, respect, trust, *etc.*)
North America, 52, 55, 86, 197 (*see also* USA)

obedience, 28, 129
objectivity, 380
OD (Organisational Development), 217–18, 221–4
OE (Organisational Effectiveness), 44, 6–63, 77, 275–7, 278
operations management, 24, 203, 207, 212–14, 225, 251
organisational: ability to cope with uncertainty, 394; authority, 48, 421; barriers to empowerment, 202; change, 4, 62, 64, 124; control, 6, 29, 202, 332;

organisational (*contd.*)
cultural system, 267–8, 386–7 (*see also* company culture); culture of empowerment, 3, 11, 291, 373–4; delayering, 31; democracy, 90; dynamics, 8; empowerment, 115–43, 277 (*see also* empowerment); focus, 200; ideologies, 4, 35; justice, 43; management, 42; policy, 4; politics, 66, 240–2, 267–8, 293, 375; power, 5, 34, 121, 375; rewards, 41; self-analysis, 64; structure, 257, 276, 280; systems, 34, 159–68

Owenism, 350–3
owner-worker, 55–57
ownership, 9, 48, 63, 104, 170–92, 256, 350, 362, 424; definition of, 179–80; of changes needed, 415; of organisations, 179–80, 424 (*see also* shared ownership; co-operative movement)

paradigmic perspectives on empowerment, 7, 128, 134, 136–43, 192, 198–200
participative management, 128, 135, 268, 272–9, 334, 371, 394, 401, 414
partnership-oriented culture, 20, 357–8
patronage, 31
pension, 43, 75
perception(s): of empowerment, 271–98 (*see also* expectancy, and experience of, empowerment); of ethical issues, 300–24
performance, 421; appraisal, 84, 286–7, 309–12, 332–3; targets, 308–14
personal: control for responsibility, 310; development, 34, 104, 188, 191, 297, 388, 413–14, 421; empowerment, 4, 24; ethics 21; feed-back, 422; growth, 15, 335–6; needs, 19; objectives, 396; power(s), 5, 45–6, 49, 54, 60, 67, 71, 73, 80–1, 97–101, 108 (*see also* empowerment; power); responsibility, 281, 300–24, 385, 418
personhood, 153
PINS (Planning Information Network System), 164–8
policing, 148
political striation of space, 148–59
positional power, 5–6, 97–101, 108
positivism, 116, 374
post-modern, 7, 141–3, 328, 340–1; -ist paradigm, 326, 336
power, 2–4, 116, 138; and control, 149–50; and empowerment, 91–2, 106–9, 306; and knowledge, 141–2, 150; and responsibility, 101–3; and resistance, 50; agents of, 54–5; asymmetry, 16, 178; conceptual framework of, 45; countervailing, 52; definition of, 45, 127, 370; degrees of, 45, 49–54; distribution of, 390; forms of, 96–8; Foucauldian understanding of, 374–8; imposition of, 23, 96; knowledge-based, 28; measures of, 45; mechanics of, 151–2; of command, 5; of language, 327–8; over, 25, 50, 134, 199; over, the market, 348; positional, 5–6, 97–101, 108; redistribution of 279, 306, 369; -relations, 7, 27, 143, 176; sharing, 6, 8, 125, 129, 136, 142, 212, 233; to, 50; taking of, 3, 23; types of, 45–8, 51; with, 134, 199
powerlessness, 6, 130, 135, 198
powers: adjudicatory, 47–8, 49–86; budgetary, 71; contractual, 45, 47, 49–86; discriminatory, 71; governance, 45, 48–9, 49–86; Hobbesian, 96–8; in organisations, 98–9; instrumental, 5; of decision-making and implementation, 30; personal, 45–6, 97; symbolic, 79; task, 45–7

Subject Index 441

pragmatic approach to
empowerment, 171–3, 266
pragmatism, 239, 265, 267
pre-empowered organisation, 34
Price Waterhouse Change
Integration Team, 273,
275, 295
privatisation, 301–3, 319, 347
problem-solving discretion, 24
(*see also* decision-making)
procedural: justice, 4, 35, 84–5;
rationality, 155
process empowerment, 15
producer co-operative, 42, 55–7, 72,
76, 86
product(s), 396: empowerment, 15;
quality, 213, 355; rationalisation,
249; simplification, 212
production line employees, 27
productivity, 57–8, 116–17, 128,
171, 284, 340, 370
professional(s), 94, 197, 316, 332;
associations, 76, 82; bureaucracy,
68–9; elimination of, 17;
employees, 15; services, 338;
staff, 69–72, 81
profit, 119, 335, 396; maximisation,
19, 341, 394, 396, 399; -oriented,
19; -sharing, 44, 273, 354, 359;
without prosperity, 380
programme management, 67–8,
70–1, 74, 86
promotion, 60; diminished
prospects, 109
pseudo-empowerment, 9, 171–81
psychological: contract, 12, 237–8,
248–51; development, 331;
testing, 59–61
public: concerns, 403; good, 379, 400;
opinion, 406; sector 14, 300–24,
393, 412, 418; sector ethic, 319

quality: and empowerment, 29, 103–4,
107, 133–4, 204–5, 224–6, 370;
assurance, 63, 309, 365; circles,
30, 44, 76, 128, 273; commitment
to, 276, 399–400; culture, 29;
improvement, 51, 77 128, 197;
Japanese-style production

methods, 105; management, 29,
61–7; management initiatives,
65–7, 247, 280; management
programmes, 55, 62–7,
77; movement, 6, 301;
of products 116, 173, 213, 399;
of workmanship, 62, 73, 355;
problems, 253–4; responsible
for 327; standardisation, 3, 212
quality-process focused
empowerment, 217–26
QWL (Quality of Working Life), 7, 43,
75, 103, 121–4, 213; movement,
141, 399; programmes, 75, 371

radical social change, 7
rationalism, 374
rationality, 134, 136, 154, 156, 199
reciprocity, 34, 129, 388, 418
redundancies, 190, 319, 415, 418
reformation of industry, 19
relationship(s): multidimensional, 80;
of business to society, 19
(*see also* business; team-based
working)
relative power, 68
relativistic ethics, 18
remuneration, *see* rewards
representation, 266
reputation, 232
research methodology, 200–2,
242–3, 271–2, 283, 296, 300,
302–4, 395–6
respect, 8, 21, 80, 124, 130, 164, 276,
387, 403, 414, 421
responsibilities, 393, 412; ability to
discharge, 72, 285; and rights, 5,
16, 21, 417–18, 420–3; for
governance, 85–6, 102–3, 110;
of business, 378–81; of command,
6, 102–3, 110; of quality, 6;
of subordination, 6, 102–3, 110;
review of, 62; supervisory, 207,
275–6; transfer of, 107–8;
without power, 330
responsibility, 5–6, 242, 257, 262, 291,
301, 327; acceptance of, 387, 414;
and power, 101–3, 272, 382; civic,
156; definition of, 8, 319;

responsibility (*contd.*)
fiscal, 209; increased by empowerment, 9, 310, 318; passing up the organisation 1, 4, 302; personal, 156, 310; pushed down the organisation, 14, 172, 206, 300–1, 307–8, 331; redefinition of, 8, 154, 316; (re)delegation of, 369, 372, 381; shared, 276; to serve society, 21
responsible autonomy, 117–20, 125, 320, 333
reward(s) 271, 280; in flat organisations, 59–60, 295–6; systems, 130, 198, 276, 282, 286–7, 425
rhetoric, 376; consistent with changes 14; of empowerment, 2, 10, 24, 29, 271–2, 278, 328; -reality gap, 297, 300–2, 322, 328, 340–1
right to a personal life, 422–3
rights, 82, 124, 150, 326; and duties, 185, 341; and responsibilities, 5, 16, 21, 417–18, 420–3; bill of, 175; conventional, 183; government protection of, 423; of employment, 423; of workers, 9, 182–3; natural, 183; to empowerment, 340; universal declaration of, human 177
risk, 282, 327
Rover Group, 105–6, 108, 110, 172–3, 282
rule-bound tasks, 15, 306–24

Sainsbury, 365–6
scant power, 51
scientific management, 7, 118–20, 141
Scott Bader, 9–10, 170, 188–92
self: -accountability, 5; -actualisation, 15, 264, 331, 336; -command, 394; -contempt 133; -control, 35, 332, 371; -development, 26, 81, 286; -determination, 130, 198, 335; -directed, 235, 332; -discipline, 8, 385; -efficacy, 7, 130, 135, 198, 284; -employed workers, 31, 126–7, 338, 340; -empowerment, 12, 24, 197; -esteem, 373, 383; -evaluation, 133; -expression, 35; -fulfilment, 334; -governance, 115, 191, 358; -interest, 143, 290, 312, 370, 373, 377; -management, 64, 235, 320; -managing teams, 6, 57, 62, 76, 105, 107, 246, 276, 282, 330–2, 415; -organising units, 71, 276; -referentiality, 8, 159–61; -regulation, 156, 243, 276; -respect, 118; -understanding, 8
secrecy, 288
semi: autonomous work-groups, 276; self-governing, 71; self-managing, 64
service: sector, 30; quality, 330, 396, 399
shared: commitment, 370; decision-making, 103, 108, 382; meaning, 161; ownership, 9, 44, 273; responsibility, 307
shareholder value, 18, 378–9, 412
shareholders, 16, 21, 42, 381, 405
short-term/long-term, 210, 219, 222, 338, 390, 418
short-term pressures, 128–9, 412, 417, 424
situational: ethics, 267–8; factors, 13
skill development, 46, 51, 60, 73, 109, 248, 276, 295, 333, 421
social: background, 239; body, 149–50; change, 128, 140, 142–3; cohesion, 8, 148, 164; construction, 7, 137; control, 375; encoding, 148; fragmentation, 8; good(s), 18, 182; justice, 179; objectives for business, 396–400; order, 134, 142; organisation, 159; reality(ies), 79, 164; structures, 13, 199; system(s), 148, 164; values 1, 18, 165
Social Chapter, 274
social charter, 185
social responsibility, 2, 19–20, 393–6; definition of, 396; of business, 393–409

socio-technical approach to work, 414–16
socio-technical systems, 11, 12, 235–68; and organisational politics, 240–2; change, 236–7; ethics of design of, 237–9
South Africa, 17
stakeholder, 5, 16, 21, 33, 381, 412; approach, 18, 266, 413–25; concept, 20; group(s), 257–8; -ism, 1; link between ethics and empowerment, 413–23; theory, 175
standardised grievance procedures, 48
status of workers, 31 (*see also* worker)
stewardship, 103, 191
strategic management, 24, 127, 236, 272, 278, 281, 286, 397, 403–4
stress, 132, 311, 418, 421 (*see also* management by stress)
structuralism, 157
subject–object distinction, 163
subordinate(s), 132, 135
subordination, 8, 103, 110, 376; of body to mind, 141
subservience, 35
subsidiarity, 86, 382
supervisors, 65–6, 78, 126, 257, 286, 296, 375
surveillance, 16, 80, 105, 117, 174, 239, 277, 331, 275
survey(s): Employee Motivation Satisfaction Survey, 13, 291–3, 296–7; 1995 CINTEC and CILNTEC surveys, 395, 397, 399, 401–2
survival, 265, 341, 373, 399, 413
Sweden, 177
symbolic power, 79
sympathetic (organisational) culture, 20
systems: industrial v. ecological, 178; role of designers, 259–64; theory, 159–65
Systems Age, 120–1

taking power, 3, 23, 373
targets and empowerment, 308–14
task: contract, 12; empowered, 10; empowerment, 4, 24; enlargement, 73; power(s), 45–7, 49–86; structure contract, 238, 251–2
Taylorism, 25, 174, 235, 237, 240–2, 243, 247, 337, 339 (*see also* scientific management)
TBCM (Team-Based Cellular Manufacturing), 236–7
team-based working, 11–2, 35, 235–68, 274–6, 280–97, 303, 307–8, 317, 320–1, 331–2, 401, 419–20
teleological concepts, 116, 120, 335, 341
teleworking, 15–6, 326–41; definition of, 336; management of, 336–7
Tesco, 365–6
theory X and theory Y, 30, 272, 291, 371
Third Wave, 163
tightly-coupled systems, 31
top–down, 27; management 66 (*see also* command and control management)
total power, 51, 53
totalitarian government, 54
TQM (Total Quality Management), 3, 27, 29, 43, 54, 173–4, 308, 327, 331, 371, 415
trade union(s), 376, 416; legislation of the, 118; movement, 42, 74, 351–3, 358; power, 49, 52; representation, 31, 54, 266–7, 273; suspicion, 75, 306; voice, 47–8, 255–6
trade-unionism: decline of, 24; rise of, 7 (*see also* co-operative movement)
training, 260; for empowerment, 60–4, 104, 107, 109, 203, 258, 294–5, 372; programmes, 81, 190, 201, 213, 219–21, 247, 282, 304, 314

transparency, 8, 164, 293
trust, 3, 105, 130, 164, 239–40, 267, 275–6, 282, 333, 385, 387, 401, 403, 407, 409, 414, 419, 421; atmosphere of, 290; building, 268, 419; degrees of, 26; in professionals, 81; kinds of, 33; levels of, 65; norms of, 34 (*see also* high trust)
trustees, 189–91
truth, 154–5, 240, 267, 273, 328, 376
types of power, 45–48

UDHR (Universal Declaration of Human Rights), 177 (*see also* rights)
unethical, 26, 31; behaviour, 14; deceit, 15
unjust, 179 (*see also* justice)
United Kingdom, 31, 175, 177, 179, 184, 186–8, 279, 282, 300, 309, 334, 381, 403, 412
United States, 31, 86, 119, 121, 128, 186–7, 200–1, 256, 300, 327, 328, 340, 389, 399, 407, 413, 419 (*see also* North America)
universalism, 267–8
urban planning, 23, 157
User Charters, 17
utilitarian: interpretation, of business, 412; interpretation of empowerment, 3, 8, 18, 25, 265–7, 370; theory, 156, 178–80, 373, 377

value: -added activities, 15, 352, 358, 372, 386; congruence, 61; -ing employees, 401–3; of empowerment, 14
values, 390, 400, 409; contract, 12, 220, 238, 255–8
virtual: -ity and empowerment, 338–40; organisation, 15, 338; society, 16; villages, 8
virtue(s), 8, 156, 387; ethics, 178–9, 377–8; theory perspective on ethics and empowerment, 369–90
virtuous: character traits, 385–6; circle, 412; community, 389–90; organisation, 19
vocation, 387
Volvo, 282

wealth, 18, 49, 51, 126, 181; access to, 45
welfare benefits, 14
well-being, *see* employee well-being
Western morality, 147
whistleblowing, 311
women's movement, 326–7
work: as a meaningful activity, 386, 399; design, 235; -load, 66, 272, 275, 285–7, 306; pacing, 10; patterns, 124
worker: antagonism, 17; control, 358–9; democracy, 28 (*see also* co-operative movement); empowerment, 17, 24, 43, 54, 71–8, 265; participation, 28, 44; -owner(s) 55–57, 76; rights, 42–3, 79–80, 277; status of, 54–5, 79, 117
workers' co-operatives, 4, 347–67 (*see also* co-operative movement)
working conditions, 43, 116–21
workplace, 3; control, 116–8, 127 (*see also* command and control management); democracy, 43–4, 78–9, 121–3, 140, 273; purpose of, 21; struggle for empowerment, 6, 128
wrongful dismissal, 43